POST-HOLOCAUST DIALOGUES
CRITICAL STUDIES IN
MODERN JEWISH THOUGHT

POST-HOLOCAUST DIALOGUES

CRITICAL STUDIES IN MODERN JEWISH THOUGHT

STEVEN T. KATZ

NEW YORK UNIVERSITY PRESS
NEW YORK & LONDON
1983

Library of Congress Cataloging in Publication Data

Katz, Steven T., 1944–
Post-holocaust dialogues.

Includes bibliographical references and index.
1. Judaism—20th century—Addresses, essays,
lectures.   2. Judaism—Doctrines—Addresses, essays,
lectures.   3. Holocaust (Jewish theology)—Addresses,
essays, lectures.   4. Philosophy, Jewish—Addresses,
essays, lectures.   I. Title.
BM565.K358 1983   296.3'09'04   82-22303
ISBN 0-8147-4583-0

To the memory of my father,
ABRAHAM KATZ,
my teacher, my friend and
the kindest man I have ever known.
"May his memory be for a blessing."

CONTENTS

ACKNOWLEDGMENTS

It is a pleasure to be able to publicly thank a number of friends who have read parts of this work. Professors Fred Berthold and Bernard Gert of Dartmouth College helped me to formulate my account of the Free Will Defense with more precision. Professor Reuven Kimelman of Brandeis University kindly read the chapter on Emil Fackenheim and offered some valued reactions. I have carried on a close, very cordial conversation with Professors Emil Fackenheim and Richard Rubenstein over the last decade and though my disagreements with them will be self-evident, I have learned much from their seminal efforts. I have benefited from conversations with Professor Joseph Dan of the Hebrew University regarding Hasidism and with the late Professor Gershom Scholem regarding Buber's Hasidic writings. Professor Yitzchak Twersky of Harvard University has also helped me to clarify certain elements of my understanding of Hasidism and its relation to Kabbalah. On a different front, Colin Jones and Despina Papazoglou of New York University Press have been wonderful to work with and have helped improve the quality of the book in many ways. Finally, on a more personal level, my debt to my wife Rebecca is, as always, greater than I can adequately express.

The time needed to write the new essays for this volume, as well as to revise the older ones, was provided by a grant from the *National Endowment for the Humanities.* Additional help of various kinds came from the Dartmouth College Research Committee, the Center for Jewish Studies at Harvard University and the staffs of the Widener Library, Harvard University and Baker Library, Dartmouth College. In the latter case I would especially like to thank Mrs. Patricia A. Carter who looks after the Inter-Library Loan operation at Baker.

I would like to thank the Editor of the *International Philosophical Quarterly* for permission to reprint the article on "Martin Buber's Epistemology" (June, 1981); the Editor of the *Journal of the American Academy of Religion* for permission to reprint the chapter on "Richard Rubenstein, the God of Israel and the Logic of History" (September, 1979); the Editor of *Tradition* for permission to reprint the material on "Eliezer Berkovits and Modern Jewish Philosophy' (Winter, 1978); to Keter Publishing Company for permission to republish "Jewish Faith After the Holocaust" (*Encyclopedia Judaica Yearbook*, 1976) and to Johns Hopkins University Press for permission to reprint "The Unique Intentionality of the Holocaust" which originally appeared in *Modern Judaism* (September, 1981). Thanks are also extended to Basic Books for permission to reprint several passages from Emil Fackenheim, *The Jewish Return to History* and *idem, Encounters Between Judaism and Philosophy;* to the University of Indiana Press for permission to reprint several tales from Dan Ben Amos and Jerome Mintz, *In Praise of the Baal Shem Tov;* to Schocken Books for permission to use material from Martin Buber, *Tales of the Hasidim,* volume I; to Alvin Plantinga for permission to reproduce an argument from his *God, Freedom and Evil;* to Macmillan and Company for permission to use material from Martin Buber, *Between Man and Man;* and to Athenaeum-Polak & Van Gennep for permission to reprint material from Ignaz Maybaum, *The Face of God After Auschwitz.*

INTRODUCTION

I

Philosphical truth develops through criticism. Since Socrates interrogated the Sophists and Pre-Socratics, and Aristotle, in turn, reinterpreted Plato's theory of forms, philosophy has continually grown through the dialectic of creative proposal and deconstructive analysis. Of course, the conceptually original mapping of human experience and of the constitutive features of the world in which it occurs often makes itself manifest in unexpected and unpredictable ways. But even in the midst of such luminous inventiveness, the particular directions in which one strikes out have almost always been, even if only by way of negation and reaction, influenced by one's forerunners. Thus Kant was "awoken from his dogmatic slumbers" by Hume and, in turn, Kierkegaard and Nietzsche in their way and Moore and Russell in theirs, reacted against a transcendental Idealism rooted in Kant in general and Hegel in particular. Likewise, in the Jewish sphere, Maimonides was engaged in a process of careful sifting of earlier Kalamist, neo-Platonic and Aristotelian traditions as part of his cognitional self-maturation. Thus, for example, his estimation of Kalam is, in many ways, the most lucid presentation we have of its central tenets, even though Maimonides portrays it only to reject it on the way to his own novel solutions to such problems as Creation,[1] God's existence and nature, and religious language. But his, too, was not the last word and in later generations one finds Ḥasdai Crescas, Joseph Albo and hosts of others including Spinoza, reacting, in turn, to Maimonidean rationalism. In our own time Martin Buber and Franz Rosenzweig were rebelling not only against Hegel but also against Hermann Cohen and the older inheritance of Jewish rationalism stretching from Saadiah to Mendelssohn.

This defining dimension of the history of thought needs to be recalled for recent Jewish philosophy has either forgotten or at least not fully understood this primal hermeneutical demand. While historical studies continue to be spawned, authentic, imaginative, technically competent philosophical criticism is nearly absent from the current Jewish intellectual landscape. Of unexciting exposition there is too much, but of sophisticated, probing, reconceptualization and inquiry there is almost nothing. What the difference is, and what difference it makes will, I hope, become clear in working through the essays presented in this collection. In them a sustained attempt has been made to disclose, through the actual exemplification of such reasoned decoding, what the yield of such analytic decipherment and discrimination is. Descriptively translated, this means that the studies in this volume are not essentially expository or historical. They are not primarily interested in questions of historical causality and influence or mere textual clarification, though this is done as required. Rather their pre-eminent concern is whether, and in what sense, certain well worked claims in the corpus of modern Jewish thought can be said to be true.

Thinking of philosophy in this way, my purpose in presenting these studies is not to criticize for the sake of criticism. Rather, my intent is to challenge accepted views, so that through their examination and, where required, their revision a more comprehensive, defensible set of methodological, logical and metaphysical judgments can come into being. Put differently, I am certain many of the most widely circulated and deeply held opinions found in the body of modern Jewish philosophy are inadequate, if not false. Hence the task is twofold: first, to expose the lacunae in and weaknesses of prevailing schemata and secondly, to attempt then to fashion a more compelling, more tightly composed, more phenomenologically inclusive account. I am continually at work on this constructive program and hope to make it public in due course. But one need not wait on the latter to share one's views on aspects of the former: hence this collection.

II

Of the nine essays in this collection five have been published before in various scholarly journals. The four chapters published here for the first time are "Martin Buber's Misuse of Hasidic Sources," "Emil Fackenheim's Response to the Holocaust," "The Crucifixion of the Jews: Ignaz Maybaum's Theology of the Holocaust" and "Eliezer Berkovits's Post-Holocaust Jewish Theodicy." The previously published articles have all been quite extensively revised.

I am aware that the subject matter of these essays is not in the usual sequence for volumes concerned with contemporary Jewish thought, for example, there is no separate treatment of Hermann Cohen or Rosenzweig or Mordecai Kaplan.[2] However, the justification for the present arrangement is simple: though I have worked through all the modern thinkers[3] one would expect to be treated in a volume of studies such as this, I have found that the figures and the specific issues chosen for analysis here—e.g., the extraordinarily influential work of Martin Buber, responses to the Holocaust, or the meaning of Hasidism for a Jew today—seem particularly meaningful in the current circumstances. Thus, I have organized the assembled material in the present order; as the book, even now, is long enough, I withhold the other, additional studies for another time and place. Yet readers should not be mistaken by this arrangement. These studies are not random but rather are parts of a larger mosaic: an intellectual wrestling with the entire body of modern Jewish thought, its meaning and truth. The unifying link between these compositions is their common concern with the spiritual condition of contemporary Jewry, of which philosophical and theological ruminations are a reflection.

NOTES

1. See, for example, Maimonides' discussion in the *Moreh Nevuchim* (Guide of the Perplexed) I, 74–76. For analysis of these issues see Harry Wolfson, *The Philosophy of the Kalam* (Cambridge, 1976), and idem, *The Repercussions of Kalam in Jewish Philosophy* (Cambridge, 1979).

2. A brief glimpse of my reading of these thinkers will be found in the analysis provided in the essay "Eliezer Berkovits and Modern Jewish Philosophy." Some further, though still brief, critical comments on Kaplan will be found in my note "Mordecai Kaplan: A Philosophical Demurrer" in Sh'ma (Nov. 1, 1974), pp. 156–7.

3. For some indication of my analysis readers are referred to my exegetical review of the major modern Jewish philosophers in my edited volume on Jewish Philosophers (New York, 1975). Other efforts of mine will also be referred to in various footnotes appended to the separate chapters of this work.

MARTIN BUBER'S EPISTEMOLOGY: A CRITICAL APPRAISAL

Martin Buber has been one of the most influential thinkers of this century. His seminal contribution to many areas of intellectual concern are well known and need not be rehearsed here. Rather, given Buber's significance within the contemporary debate, it seems an appropriate time to ask whether his essential philosophical outlook is sound, and if not, why not. In undertaking such a fundamental review no aspect of Buber's thought is of more consequence than his epistemology; it is with this subject that the remainder of this essay will deal.

I

Before embarking on a detailed analysis of Buber's *oeuvre*, however, one preliminary methodological exploration is required. Many scholars with whom I have discussed Buber, either orally or in print, have replied to my various criticisms of him that he is not a "philosopher," that he did not count himself a philosopher, and that to fault him, as I do, from a rigorous logical perspective is inappropriate because I judge Buber harshly by standards foreign to his work. Indeed, the frequency with which this defense has been offered has prompted the present opening excursus. For though this line of refutation, on the face of it, appears plausible, the more I have pondered it the more inapposite it reveals itself to be. To begin with, Buber himself, all his life, carried on a close dialogue with the great philosophers of past and present. In *Between Man and Man,* for example, he feels free to exegete and judge on *philosophical grounds* such predecessors and contemporaries as Kant and Hegel, Feuerbach, Marx, Stirner and Heidegger. In *Eclipse of God* he engages in a philosophical polemic against Spinoza, Sartre, Hermann Cohen and Kierkegaard, among others, and this critique is in no way atypical of his work. Despite the constant refrain that Buber is something other than a philosopher, the fact is that he was intensely concerned with the technical philosophical criticism of other noted philosophers, and saw his own creative labors as efforts of genuine philosophical inception.

As an example of this profound engagement consider Buber's critical comments on Kant in *What is Man:*

It is remarkable, that Kant's own anthropology, both what he himself published and his copious lectures on man, which only appeared long after his death, absolutely fails to achieve what he demands of a philosophical anthropology. In its express purpose as well as in its entire content it offers something different—an abundance of valuable observations for the knowledge of man, for example, on egoism, on honesty and lies, on fancy, on fortune-telling, on dreams, on mental diseases, on wit, and so on. But the question, what man is, is simply not raised, and not one of the problems which are implicitly set us at the same time by this question—such as man's special place in the cosmos, his connexion with destiny, his relation to the world of things, his understanding of his fellowmen, his existence as a being that knows it must die, his attitude in all the ordinary and extraordinary encounters with the mystery with which his life is shot through, and so on—not one of these problems is seriously touched upon. The *wholeness* of man does not enter into this anthropology. It is as if Kant in his actual philosophizing had had qualms about setting the question which he formulated as the fundamental one.[1]

Then in answer to Kant's question Buber writes:

A legitimate philosophical anthropology must know that there is not merely a human species but also peoples, not merely a human soul but also types and characters, not merely a human life but also stages in life; only from the systematic comprehension of these and of all other differences, from the recognition of the dynamic that exerts power within every particular reality and between them, and from the constantly new proof of the one in the many, can it come to see the wholeness of man. For that very reason it cannot grasp man in that absoluteness which, though it does not speak out from Kant's fourth question, yet very easily presents itself when an answer is attempted—the answer which Kant, as I have said, avoided giving. Even as it must again and again distinguish within the human race in order to arrive at a solid comprehension, so it must put man in all seriousness into nature, it must compare him with other things, other living creatures, other bearers of consciousness, in order to define his special place reliably for him. Only by this double way of distinction and comparison does it reach the whole, real man who, whatever his people or type or age, knows, what no being on earth but he can know, that he goes the narrow way from birth towards death, tests out what none but he can, a wrestling with destiny, rebellion and reconciliation, and at times even experiences in his own blood, when he is joined by choice to another human being, what goes on secretly in others.

Buber continues, in order to drive home the philosophical intent of his remarks:

Philosophical anthropology is not intent on reducing philosophical problems to human existence and establishing the philosophical disciplines so to speak from below instead of from above. It is solely intent on knowing man himself. This sets it a task that is absolutely different from all other tasks of thought. For in philosophical anthropology man himself is given to man in the most precise sense as a subject. Here, where the subject is man in his wholeness, the investigator cannot content himself, as in anthropology as an individual science, with considering man as another part of nature and with ignoring the fact that he, the investigator, is himself a man and experiences his humanity in his inner experience in a way that he simply cannot experience any part of nature—not only in a quite different perspective but also in a quite different dimension in which he experiences only this one part of all the parts of nature. Philosophical knowledge of man is essentially man's self-reflection (*Selbstbesinnung*), and man can reflect about himself only when the cognizing person, that is, the philosopher pursuing anthropology, first of all reflects about himself as a person. The principle of individuation, the fundamental fact of the infinite variety of human persons, of whom this one is only one person, of this constitution and no other, does not relativize anthropological knowledge; on the contrary, it gives it its kernel and its skeleton. In order to become a genuine philosophical anthropology, everything that is discovered about historical and modern man, about men and women, Indians and Chinese, tramps and emperors, the weak-minded and the genius, must be built up and crystallized round what the philosopher discovers by reflecting about himself. This is a quite different matter from what, say, the psychologist undertakes when he completes and clarifies by reference to his own self in self-observation, self-analysis and experiment, what he knows from lit-erature and observation. For with him it is a matter of individual, objectiv-ized processes and phenomena, of something that is separated from con-nexion with the whole real person. But the philosophical anthropologist must stake nothing less than his real wholeness, his concrete self. And more; it is not enough for him to stake his self as an *object* of knowledge. He can know the *wholeness* of a person and through it the wholeness of *man* only when he does not leave his *subjectivity* out and does not remain an untouched observer. He must enter, completely and in reality, into the act of self-reflection, in order to become aware of human wholeness. In other words, he must carry out this act of entry into that unique dimen-sion as an act of his *life*, without any prepared philosophical security; that is, he must expose himself to all that can meet you when you are really living. Here you do not attain the knowledge by remaining on the shore and watching the foaming waves, you must make the venture and cast yourself in, you must swim, alert and with all your force, even if a mo-ment comes when you think you are losing consciousness: in this way, and in no other, do you reach anthropological insight. So long as you "have" yourself, have yourself as an object, your experience of man is only as of a thing among things, the wholeness which is to be grasped is not yet "there"; only when you *are*, and nothing else but that, is the wholeness there, and able to be grasped. You perceive only as much as the reality of the "being there" incidentally yields to you; but you do perceive that, and the nu-cleus of the crystallization develops itself.[2]

Now is this Buberian statement of his most central concern, philosophical anthropology, not philosophy? Is not Buber engaged in philosophical criticism and construction of a very high order? And if Buber is free, indeed feels it necessary, to enter into such decisive logical and metaphysical argumentation against others, e.g., Kant, why is it inappropriate for others to engage in such critical scrutiny of his work?

I push this criticism still more directly. *Beiträge zu einer philo-sophischen Anthropologie* is one of Buber's late studies (translated by M. Friedman into English under the vague title *The Knowledge of Man*, 1965). The original title *explicitly* states the main focus of the work, philosophical anthropology. Still more, the discussion is as technically philosophical as any in the contemporary literature. In fact, it is most accurately described as an essay in neo-Kantain metaphysics, for as Buber has forthrightly noted: "I have not fully liberated myself from Kant." Thus, Buber can write in this context, for example:

It is only man who replaces this unsteady conglomeration, whose constitution is suited to the lifetime of the individual organism, by a unity which can be imagined or thought by him as existing for itself. With soaring power he reaches out beyond what is given him, flies beyond the horizon and the familiar stars, and grasps a totality. With him, with his human life, a world exists. The meeting of natural being with the living creature produces those more or less changing masses of usable sense data which constitute the animal's realm of life. But only from the meeting of natural being with man does the new and enduring arise, that which comprehends and infinitely transcends the realm. An animal in the realm of its perceptions is like a fruit in its skin; man is, or can be, in the world as a dweller in an enormous building which is always being added to, and to whose limits he can never penetrate, but which he can nevertheless know as one does know a house in which one lives—for he is capable of grasping the wholeness of the building as such. Man is like this because he is the creature (*Wesen*) through whose being (*Sein*) "what is" (*das Seiende*) becomes detached from him, and recognized for itself. It is only the realm which is removed, lifted out from sheer presence, withdrawn from the operation of needs and wants, set at a distance and thereby given over to itself, which is more and other than a realm. Only when a structure of being is independently over against a living being (*Seiende*), an independent opposite, does a world exist.[3]

How are we to react to this tightly woven epistomological description? Can it be catalogued as anything but philosophy in its most elemental and traditional sense? Then again are we being seriously asked by the Buberians not to pose the very sorts of questions Buber himself feels it legitimate to ask here, and still more, to which he offers these thoughts as solutions?

The "poetic" defenders of Buber, moreover, mistake style for substance. That is, they hold, for example, that an assertion in favor of paradox and other logical oddities makes one a poet. It doesn't. What it does make one, certainly in Buber's case, is a philosophical advocate of paradox, i.e., an advocate of a certain sort of philosophical approach, a proponent of an *argument* in favor of paradoxical arguments. In turn, then, this contention, even if not presented in the form of an argument (which in fact it sometimes is), is legitmately evaluated as one. Either it is true or false, sound or unsound, informative, dull, full of explanatory force, or incoherent. The statement of the position in a nontechnical form does not shield it from being judged as an argument because, whatever the form of its presentation, it is, in fact, being employed in order to convince others of the correctness of certain significant claims and positions that Buber worked to advance.

This same sort of analytic recognition also needs to be insisted upon regarding the interrelationship of the technical metaphysical character of Buber's reflections and the form in which these ideas are presented. Thus, for example, when Buber states "The Eternal Thou can never become an *It*," this is a metaphysical thesis whether it looks like one or not in the context of *I and Thou*. The style of *I and Thou*, of course, however, works to confuse the issue in two ways. First, and more generally, most "defenders" of Buber seem to have read little more than *I and Thou* and take its oracular, purposely unphilosophical, style as paradigmatic of Buber's work, which it is not. Reviewing the Buberian corpus as a whole, one recognizes that, in contradistinction to the impression gained from *I and Thou*, the sibylline, prophetic style of that composition is idiosyncratic. His writings on the Bible, on Hasidism, on art and education, on current events, on Zionism and, above all, on matters philosophical, are largely straightforward, if artistically impressive, prose compositions. Secondly, even *I and Thou*, or rather particularly *I and Thou*, is a philosophical book through and through despite its style. It takes up, evaluates, accepts, rejects, or revises, standard and well-worked philosophical arguments and opinions throughout. One has to be philosophically learned, as Buber was, to recognize the internal debate in which *I and Thou* is engaged, but this does not mean that it is poetry. Indeed, to read *I and Thou* as poetry is to profoundly misunderstand it altogether. Those ignorant of the metaphysical problems which Buber has inherited and the contemporary philosophical problematic with which he is wrestling might mistakenly liken his text to, for example, the works of Kahlil Gibran or Kafka. But in reality it should be likened to, and belongs together with such philosophical classics (at least in its concerns if not its importance), as Aristotle's *Metaphysics*, Kant's first *Critique* and Hegel's *Phenomenology*. It is *not* an accident that *Ich und Du* is reprinted in Buber's *Werke* in the volume titled *Schriften zur Philosophie* (Heidelberg, 1962).[4]

All this is not to say that Buber's work is only to be considered as philosophy. His Hasidic and Biblical work, for example, at least in large part, belongs to other realms of the human spirit, but insofar as he does produce philosophical works such as those cited above, these works are not to be bypassed—or defended—as less or other than philosophy. Maurice Friedman, Buber's leading American disciple, for example, felt it appropriate to write an essay titled "Martin Buber's Theory of Knowledge" and to publish it, not in a literary journal, but in the *Review of Metaphysics* [Dec., 1954]. In his now standard secondary study *The Life of Dialogue*, Friedman has a chapter on Buber's "Theory of Knowledge" in which he claims that Buber has, in effect, made the most important contribution to epistemology in our [any?] century through his dialogical epistemology, which solves the major conundrums left by the older, classic epistemological theorists. Friedman approvingly quotes Karl Heim's well-known praise of Buber, which states that Buber's I–Thou/I–It distinction ". . . is one of the decisive discoveries of our time—'The Copernican revolution' of modern thought."[5] Is such a claim to be ignored or conveniently forgotten when one finds *philosophical* weaknesses in this claimed epistemological triumph? Is it fair when faced with real structural or ontological difficulties to move the discussion from the logical and metaphysical to the aesthetic and affective and to attempt to hide behind the poet's fig leaf against philosophical critics? And how much cover does the poet's fig leaf provide?

Much additional evidence could be mustered here, but the case is clear enough: Buber is a philosopher and as such is to be judged by appropriate standards. I leave Buber the last word. In response to a question by F. Heinemann about whether his "dialogical principle could be the basis of a philosophy," Buber replied: ". . . to join a basic experience [the dialogical], which became evident to me as a basic experience of man, with its proper sphere of thought *I had to go the only way suitable to that purpose, the philosophical*."[6]

I now believe myself justified in devoting the remainder of this essay to a discussion of the philosophical substance of Buber's epistemology.[7]

II. EXEGESIS OF SOME BASIC THEMES

Before embarking on a critical analysis of Buber's position it is important that there be no confusion about our understanding of the basic components of his epistemology. In this section a brief, though I hope adequate, exegesis of the three basic elements of Buber's outlook will be sketched, namely his Kantianism; his formulation of the *I–Thou/I–It* distinction; and his account of revelation.

BUBER'S KANTIANISM

A close reading of Buber's work, especially if informed by a reasonable acquaintance with Kantian and post-Kantian German Idealism, will reveal a significant dependence of Buber on the Kantian tradition which is of primal significance for understanding Buber's dialogical epistemology. Not only did the great master of Konigsberg save Buber from madness at the age of 15, but he remained *the* philosopher, *the* philosophical influence on Buber's thought for the remainder of his life, as evidenced to in *I and Thou* and other works. This abiding influence is clearly seen even in such late essays as "Distance and Relation." Indeed, Buber's entire mature world view is structurally and fundamentally built on the back of Kantianism.[8] Buber assumes for his own work that Kant is, in some fundamental way, right. We see this initially and most clearly in his dichotomous account of reality, described through the realms of *I–Thou/I–It*, which parallels Kant's noumenal/phenomenal distinction in striking ways. We can begin fully to understand this dialogical dependency by noting, at the outset, three structural elements. First, like Kant, Buber sees the world as essentially "twofold;" second, Kant's understanding of "noumenal" reality is the *basis*, though, of course, not the sum total, of Buber's understanding of the *I–Thou* reality; third, Kant's account of "phenomenal" reality provides the foundation, if not the whole, of Buber's understanding of *I–It* reality. These three structural characteristics can be further fleshed out through a consideration of the following:

1. For both Kant and Buber "what we know" is determined by "how we know." The "knower" is central to all epistemic activity even to the point of determining the "what" that is known as well as the conditions under which it is known. In Kant's system the categorical conditions of mind determine the "phenomenal" nature of things; likewise, in Buber's account, the knower, the *I*, determines through his "knowing" activity whether he "encounters" reality in all its manifoldness as *Thou* or as *It*. One must remember that for Buber there is no "fixed" being of the "other" that determines its character for us. Rather the nature of that which we encounter is determined by our relation to it. Phrased less esoterically, this means that we can have either *I–Thou* or *I–It* relations with the same "thing." Similarly, Kant's "phenomena" is not a "something" different from "noumena" but rather the same one reality "known" differently; "phenomena" is reality as apprehended through the formal structure imposed by the categories of mind while "noumena" is an intuitive, immediate, non-categorical grasp of things as they are.

2. The general specifications provided by Kant of what constitutes phenomenal knowledge is nearly exactly duplicated by Buber in his description of the *It*. Both the "phenomenal" and the *It* are defined by the presence of the following objectivity conditions: (a) They are determined by and subject to the coordinates of spatial location and temporal succession; (b) they are determined by and subject to the laws of causality; (c) they are available, because of their orderliness, to us as objective knowledge (indeed it is only "phenomenal"/*It* reality that we can claim to *know* in the objective sense); (d) as a consequence of the conditions (a, b, c) already described these categories can be described in language; (e) finally, as a consequence of these conditions (a, b, c, d) such knowledge is subject to the rules of logic.

3. Kant's understanding of the "noumena" provides the basis for Buber's characterization of the *Thou*, but only its basis, and then primarily in its formal aspects. In respect of the *Thou*, Buber's re-

lation to Kant stands at the end of a century of post-Kantian thought that had already well begun the reconstruction of the concept of "noumena" which it had inherited. That is to say, in structural if not in all substantive ways Buber's *Thou* is close to Kant's "noumena." In order to gain some clearer insight into this relationship note that both "noumena" and *Thou* are defined, at least in large part, by the fact that the objectivity conditions listed above in describing "phenomena" and *It* respectively do not apply to them. (For a more detailed description of what sorts of things do apply to the category of the *Thou* see below.) Thus as a general observation on this structural dependence it is, I think, permissable to summarize a complex situation by suggesting that Kant bequeathed to Buber, as he bequeathed to the nineteenth century, the doctrine both of fixed limits to "knowledge," as well as the grounds for holding that the sum of the real extended beyond these parameters. In this sense his remark in the "Introduction" of *The Critique of Pure Reason* is to be taken with the utmost seriousness: "I have destroyed reason in order to make room for faith."

Moreover, though Kant essentially limited our contact with the noumenal to morality he did postulate the general nature of the noumenal, which Buber among many others adopted. That is, the noumenal is a realm of freedom, i.e., it operates independently of the limiting conditions that govern the phenomenal, and one relates to it by means of an "intuitive" apprehension. Kant's own term for this sort of apprehension was "practical reason" as compared to the "pure reason" that provides one objective knowledge gained in the phenomenal realm. Likewise, Buber's epistemology is built around the asserted "intuitive" apprehension possible of others as *Thou*. The term "intuitive" is used advisedly and in recognition of his demands that awareness of an "other" as *Thou* is *not* subject to any of the predicative and classificatory epistemic conditions that rule in the domain of objective knowledge. *I–Thou* relationship *necessarily excludes* all the limiting conditions itemized in paragraph 2 above. As a consequence, Buber, following Kant, argues that the "knowledge" gained in such epistemic situations is not only different from that gained in *It/phenomenal* matrices but that it is also subject to altogether different rules of meaning and criteria of verification, if indeed one can legitimately speak of verification in these altered circumstances at all.

This brief sketch of the basic skeletal parallelism and dependence should suffice to support my contention of Buber's indebtedness to Kant's transcendental, idealist, reorganization of how we come to know the world. Moreover, further phenomenological description of Buber's philosophical anthropology, as well as of his ontology, epistemology, and ethical doctrine, would disclose that all have their roots here. Of course, all these themes become deepened, in some cases even transmogrified, after Kierkegaard and Nietzsche, but their basic explanatory force remains Kantian: Buber's dialogical thinking is a variety of the neo-Kantian metaphysic.

Buber's relationship to Kantianism interests us not because we are in search of answers to questions of historical primacy or so that we might revise downwards Buber's contribution. Rather it is done to highlight a fact that seems almost always underplayed if not ignored altogether by Buber scholars, namely, that the ultimate success of Buber's epistemology, as of his philosophy as a whole, depends on the correctness of some form of Kantian Idealism. We shall return to consider the implications of this element in Part III of this essay.

I–THOU/I–IT

As the basic epistemological skeleton of Buber's dialogical philosophy is constructed around his famous *I–Thou/I–It* dichotomy, let me spell out briefly my understanding of the essential characteristics of this typology.[9] This exegetical exercise is all the more salient as it is on the basis of this understanding that I shall later predicate certain significant reservations. I begin by stating the general rule that for Buber *I–Thou* are "personal" relations and *I–It* are "impersonal" relations, while remembering that according to Buber's basic metaphysical schema one can have "personal," *I–Thou*, relations with non-persons, e.g., objects of nature, and "impersonal," *I–It*, relations with persons.

The term *I–It* is the counterpart, though not the exact parallel, of what is referred to in more usual philosophical language as the subject–object relation. In such a relation the self, the subject, treats all objects of experience, including other people, and all possible content of human knowledge as things which can be ordered and itemized but which, though adding to the information and experience of the knower, in no way touch the deeper level of his personal existence and the meaning of his own life. The *I–It* relation is primarily a utilitarian relation. The *I* observes, indexes, calculates, uses, and manipulates the *It* (even if another person) for his advantage without concern or regard for the Other. The prominent feature of such a relation is the detachment that governs the intercourse between the active, knowing consciousness and the object to which this consciousness is directed. This does not signify that in such a relation the knower and known are unrelated, as this would contradict Buber's relational premise that everything is in some relation; rather it suggests that in such relationships the parties do not "affect" each other. "The object may be 'present,' but we are not in the 'presence' of the object." [10]

The most general characteristics of *I–It* relations, strongly reflecting that profound indebtedness of Kantian metaphysics already sketched, are: (a) they operate under and reflect the law of causality ("causality has an unlimited reign in the world of *It*"); [11] and (b) they are located in and regulated by space and time ("The world of *It* is set in the context of space and time"). [12] That is to say, *I–It* relations are subject to and exhibit the rule-governed activity of causal determination and necessity, the central observation being that what belongs to the manifold of "experience" is, in orthodox Kantian fashion, regulated by causal law. Likewise, in order for there to exist an externally structured and coherently intelligible world, objective succession and determinate spatio-temporal location must be a constitutive feature of that world.

The rule of causal and spatio-temporal law under which *I–It* operates inhibits freedom, encouraging instead a behavioristic and mechanistic model of relation. As a consequence Buber argues the important proposition that all objective knowledge is by definition *I–It* because such knowledge is inextricably linked to and requires the causal and spatio-temporal nexus. In addition, objective knowledge requires syntactical and semantical correctness, logical coherence, rules of criteria, falsifiability, verification, and evidence. All these objectivity concepts are, according to Buber, opposite to the dialogical immediacy of *I–Thou*. Moreover, Buber argues, all knowledge gained through the *I–It* relation is necessarily indirect and mediate. That is, it is mediated through the categories listed above and these necessarily interpose themselves between "what is" and "our knowledge of what is." Thus objective knowledge is necessarily subject to distortion and is reduced thereby to approximation.

To understand what Buber means by an *I–Thou* relation it is helpful to begin by simply inverting the description already given of *I–It*. Thus, where *I–It* is a "subject–object" relation, *I–Thou* is not; where *I–It* is determined by its subjugation to indexical procedures, to categorization, to refined and precise measurement, *I–Thou* is not. If in *I–It* the knowing self is unaffected in an essential way by the relation, in *I–Thou* the opposite is true. Whereas causality and the spatio-temporal order reign supreme in the world of *I–It*, in *I–Thou* other conditions are operative. Just as *I–It* knowledge is mediate and indirect, *I–Thou* is immediate and direct. Significantly, insofar as *I–It* is neutral on matters of moral concern, *I–Thou* is not.

We gain a good deal of information from this not very rigorous inversion. However, what one learns from such an oblique method is, in the end, limited; positive statement of the doctrine is required. But here a serious difficulty arises, because Buber claims that language does not make a true "fit" with *I–Thou*: *I–Thou* can only be pointed to; it cannot be described. Accordingly, description itself is a characteristic of *I–It* and is out of place in *I–Thou*. We can only break this logical log-jam by being bold; recognizing that despite Buber's insistence to the contrary, descriptive statements regarding *I–Thou* can be properly suggested for at least two reasons. Firstly, and in anticipation of my critical view on the issue of the relation of *I–Thou* to language, because I maintain that Buber's position here needs to be rethought, and secondly, because despite Buber's own cautionary proviso, he actually does provide a considerable amount of descriptive information on all aspects of *I–Thou*.

Buber fills out the skeleton of the *I–Thou* relation as follows:

A. In *I–Thou* relation, both partners to the dialogue retain their own subjectivity in the encounter while becoming aware of the "other" as a "subject." "The *I* of the primary world *I–Thou* makes its appearance as a person and becomes conscious of itself as subjectivity."[13]

B. Learning that the "other" is a subject means learning that the "other" is essentially a free being like the knowing self: an echo of Kant's noumenal self. Man is unique in creation in that he alone possesses possibility and potentiality. This awareness brings with it the recognition that the constitutive properties of the *Thou* cannot be measured, quantified, or translated into propositions.

C. The freedom of *I–Thou* entails the total autonomy of both dialogical partners. To act in accordance with external rules is heteronomy, and this violates the premised freedom of the "other" as *Thou* as well as of the self as *I*.

D. As the *I–Thou* encounter is an intersubjective relation between equals, at least in terms of their relation to each other for the duration of the encounter, this relation is characterized by mutuality. This is an especially important feature of *I–Thou* meeting. The symmetry of the relation is a basic premise of the whole dialogical life.

E. What emerges from *I–Thou* relation, and only from such relation, is not objective knowledge but rather an ontological certainty about the foundations of one's life and a surety about the unbreakable umbilical cord that runs from man's spiritual navel to the center of Being itself. This ontic connectedness, however, Buber tells us, "does not help to sustain you in life, it only helps you to glimpse eternity."[14]

The myriad profound implications of this dialogical structure will be critically examined below.

REVELATION

For two reasons, separate note must now be taken of a central component of Buber's dialogical outlook—his account of revelation and the role it plays in his thought. First, in Buber's epistemology the kind of knowing that is labeled *I–Thou* is made synonymous in character with what passes under another name as "revelation." The *I–Eternal Thou* relation is formally parallel to human *I–Thou* dialogue; indeed it is modeled in this dialogical epistemology on it. Second, Buber's is an epistemology wedded to a theistic metaphysics. As such Buber knows in advance which elements of reality, including revelation, he intends to be available in his ontology, and so constructs his epistemology accordingly.[15]

In what follows I now offer a detailed outline of the constitutive elements of the dialogical account of "revelation." I do so because of its importance for understanding Buber's thought as a whole; and because, despite its significance, little solid exegetical or critical analysis exists in the literature.

We can summarize the essential features of Buber's account, either stated or implied, in the following seven propositions:

1. Revelation is an act of meeting between God and man.

2. In this meeting, God does *not* reveal propositions; He reveals only His "Presence."[16]

3. Revelation is *not* about God, but about God acting on man.

4. Because of (2) and (3), revelation, when translated into human life, must take on human meaning.

5. Despite (4), and Buber would agree it is paradoxical, we still have in that which issues from revelation an authentic pointer to the original dialogical situation.

6. The goal and the result of revelation is the improvement of man's own understanding of himself and his place in the world. Anthropological, rather than cosmological or metaphysical, insights result from revelation.

7. Due to its anthropological character, revelation must have the following characteristics:

a. It can never be perfect; all human, or admixture of Divine–human, truth is always partial, limited and liable to error.

b. It can never be tested by any criteria, except the knowledge that one acts with the personal certainty that what one does is grounded in the revelatory moment.

c. It can never be definitive: a "once and for all" truth.

d. Man himself decides what calls to him as revelation and only those things which he feels are addressed to him have obligatory force.

e. Responsibility to act in accordance with revelation means one thing only: to act "authentically."

f. Revelation must always remain personal, spoken to and acted upon only by the one addressed in dialogue.

g. It can never be the basis of universal prescriptions.

h. As the content of revelation cannot be universalized, one can never know the meaning of revelation for a specific act in advance of the event.

i. There is always the possibility of new revelation, whatever "revelation" may be.[17]

In *I and Thou* Buber sums up much of what is creative in his thinking about revelation in the following description:

Man receives, and he receives not a specific "content" but a Presence, a Presence as power . . . Man can give no account at all of how the binding in relation is brought about, nor does it in any way lighten his life—it makes life heavier, but heavy with meaning. Secondly, there is the inexpressible confirmation of meaning. Meaning is assured. Nothing can any longer be meaningless. . . . But just as the meaning itself does not permit itself to be transmitted and made into knowledge generally current and admissible, so confirmation of it cannot be transmitted as a valid Ought.[18]

As a corollary of this re-assessment he states anew the conditions for entering into a living relationship with God. God is the "Thou who can, by its nature, never become an It;"[19] that is, He is a being who escapes all attempts at objectification and transcends all description. The Eternal *Thou* can never be treated as one particular among many particulars, one thing among many things. Nor can God be known through "experience" because "experience" yields only It, not *Thou*. God cannot be "known" outside the committed existential act of relation. All attempted philosophical theologies based on any and all forms of theological empiricism or deductive metaphysics that attempt to "prove" His existence must always fail because He can only be addressed, not defined. "A conceptual apprehension of the Divine," Buber argues, "necessarily impairs the concrete religious relationship."[20]

Review of each of the items outlined above is presently impossible, and for our limited purposes, unnecessary. Instead, I wish only to call attention to the most fundamental and most striking feature of Buber's reflections on revelation, i.e., the grounds for his continual concern with this category/experience, namely, his insistence that man cannot understand himself in isolation from God nor can our human world find its direction except in and through this relationship. Revelation informs us, and this is its essential epistemic—as well as metaphysical—purpose, that God alone justifies human existence by guaranteeing its essential integrity; without God and without knowledge of God, human life would be engulfed by nihilism. The revelation of "Presence," the core of authentic revelation, while unhelpful to those seeking the security of a finished way, provides, according to the dialogical modality, a profound existential and ontological certainty. Though revelation forces man to return to the world and to "realize creation" such revelation at one and the same time discloses the transcendent capacity, the ontic depth, of the immanent, which we now know not to be immanent alone. It is this analysis of not only the intricacies of the revelatory mode, but even more basically of the depth of the human predicament, in the midst of which the moment of revelation is the redemptive factor, that provides the dynamic for Buber's entire *Weltanschauung.*

III. CRITICAL REFLECTIONS

With these introductory exegetical remarks in place I trust I have laid the groundwork for a reflective probing of the most prominent features of Buber's epistemology.

BUBER'S KANTIANISM: A CRITICISM

"Kantianism" is certainly the most suggestive and highly influential of all modern philosophical systems, yet more and more it seems clear to me that for all its suggestiveness and explanatory force ultimately Kantianism is unacceptable.[21] Hence any essentially post-Kantian system that takes over the fundamental epistemological and metaphysical skeleton of Kant's Critical Philosophy, as, for example, does Buber's, is also flawed. To state the most essential objections as simply as possible, first consider that Kantianism is unable to protect itself against subjectivism, even be it a transcendental subjectivism of the sort evident in Buber's dialogical view. Modern conceptual relativism is the logical outcome of the Kantian "Copernican" revolution. Given the conditions of knowledge and the role of the "knower" in Kant's speculations it is impossible for the final results of a Kantian-like mapping to avoid being construed as knowing only the "appearances" of "appearances," or, again, as being unable to provide any conditions for determining the objective character of one's knowledge. This "subjectivity" is abundantly in evidence in Buber's epistemology too, despite all his attempts to guard himself against it.

Second, the various derivative transcendental metaphysical accounts, among which I include the basic form of Buber's *I–Thou* perspective, modeled after the metaphysical schema sketched in the *Critique of Pure Reason*, seem to me confused and finally incapable of justifying any coherent metaphysical schema and *ipso facto* Buber's metaphysical schema. The reason for this inevitable failure is that "transcendental deductions" in the Kantian sense, which are constitutive and essential for the Kantian program, cannot be performed.[22] The consequence of the impossibility of their performance undermines the metaphysics of the Critical Philosophy as well as any subsequent philosophy which builds upon it, e.g., Buber's dialogical metaphysics. Though Buber does *not* provide anything like the elaborate architectonic arguments of the first *Critique* it is evident that he assumes their essential validity. This implicit assumption, in fact, provides the *a priori* theoretical constellation of the dialogical structure.

As a specific example of the difficulties inherent in being a Kantian, consider Buber's employment of the inherited Kantian formulation of the nature and employment of space-time. Kant's dicta about the source of space-time being grounded in the "self," the employment of space-time as the regulator of phenomenal reality, i.e., "appearances," and the inapplicability of the categories of space-time to the noumenal, are all accepted by Buber and reappear in his own formulation of the nature of the realms of *I–Thou/I–It*.

This dependence and parallelism, however, has unacceptable consequences for a truly existential dialogical philosophy for many compelling reasons, only the most important of which can be discussed here. In the first place, Buber's employment of these notions creates philosophical confusions because it stretches beyond any legitimate employment (if indeed there is any legitimate employment) the very character of the space-time-causality continuum. Thus, for example, to assert that the *I–Thou* relation is a way of meeting that occurs in space-time seems an intelligible proposition, while to argue, as Buber does, that space-time is only a capacity of selves, and *I–It* selves at that, makes the claim of and for *I–Thou* meeting difficult to maintain, for it is hard to know what we can possibly mean by "I," "Thou," and "meeting" in such circumstances.

Here it is instructive to add a historical note. Kant, though maintaining his problematic theory of the subjectivity of space-time, coupled moreover as it is with his opaque theories of "appearance," "affecting," and "selves," was nonetheless aware that difficulties did lie here. Thus, he wisely argued *against* what in his terminology was a knowledge of things or other selves "as they are in themselves," calling this a form of "non-sensible" intuition that can belong only "to the primordial being" (*Critique of Pure Reason* B. 72). Yet it is precisely this sort of non-sensible "intuition" that seems present, though in somewhat transmuted form, in Buber's claims to *I–Thou* knowledge. Buber, as an heir of the nineteenth-century post-Kantian tradition, here seems to go well beyond Kant's own principles of intelligibility. It is a case of wanting to be a Kantian and more than a Kantian at the same time, but the proposed dialogical synthesis by which this is to be accomplished is inadequate to the task in the same manner, if for different reasons, as were previous ninteenth- and early twentieth-century attempts to do essentially the same thing.

To probe one step further, let me introduce one additional consideration. It may well be that space-time regulates only *I–It*, but wherein does this spatio-temporal regularity fall? That is to say, imagine that X and Y have an *I–It* encounter that operates under the Kantian norms, but, in turn, under what regulative conditions do these Kantian norms operate? Put another way, what is the on-tic status of the separate particulars that enter into this relation-ship, as well as of the relational unit as a whole? A simpler way of articulating the logic of this argument is to note that even if space-time and *I–It* are "appearances," surely these "appearances" are real. If one is not prepared at some point to admit this, then metaphysical confusion ensues. But admitting this breaks the Kantian-Buberian schemata. In other words, denying reality to space-time leads to self-contradiction as well as to the impossibil-ity of establishing objective knowledge, a truth Kant himself seems to have begun to be aware of in his own version of the "Refutation of Idealism" in the second edition of the *Critique of Pure Reason*, while not denying this negation means abdicating the basic Kan-tian metaphysical position. Buber, however, does not consider this and similar difficulties, and continues to treat the spatio-temporal conditions of *I–It* in the strict subjectivist manner, with the result that he is unable to account adequately for the reality that goes by that designation. In short, Buber's maintenance in his formulation of *I–It* of the Kantian principle that we impose the space-time or-der on an otherwise non–spatio-temporal reality is paralyzing. As a consequence, Buber's estimation and description of the world he labels *I–It* is inadequate to its being and totality. To reverse this line of argument and state the conclusion more directly, a larger dose of metaphysical realism than Buber's dialogical idealism per-mits of is necessary to account for the world of "things" and "his-torical events."

My ontological recommendation for more "realism" encourages two corollary remarks. The first is that Kant's description of the phenomenal was built on a now outmoded model of Newtonian physics and Euclidean geometry. After Einstein, Planck, and Hei-senberg this physical model is dead. Hans Reichenbach,[23] among others, has, I believe, demonstrably shown the difficulties of being a Kantian after the revolution created by the theory of relativity. The significance of this fact for Buber is that he *cannot* describe the realm of *It* in the inherited Kantian fashion with any philo-sophical security. Then again, the realm of *It* and our encounters in the *I–It* relation are far richer, more pliable, more variegated, than the dialogical philosophy allows. Franz Rosenzweig[24] already saw and communicated this objection to Buber on his first reading of the then unpublished manuscript of *Ich und Du*. To this reservation, which is all the more serious in an ontology that counsels a pansacramental "hallowing of the everyday," Buber replied that indeed Rosenzweig was correct, but that *Ich und Du* was only the first volume in a larger work and this failure would subsequently be remedied, with the *It* receiving its proper due. Those later volumes never appeared; Buber never gave the *It* and *I–It* relation their proper explication. The resultant distortion is significant not only because it fails to adequately represent the dimension of *It*, a realm Buber and his heirs largely pass over, but also because it thus distorts the character of the dimension of the *Thou*, for *It* and *Thou* are two complementary halves of one whole. Moreover, given the inadequacy of the dialogical account of *I–It*, what grounds are there for confidence in the dialogical explication of *I–Thou?* It seems certain that we will require a more adequate, more contemporary, more technically sophisticated account of *I–It*, which in turn will necessitate transformations in the explication of *I–Thou*, if we are to get a proper equation regarding the relation and complementarity of *It* and *Thou*.

In place of a Kantian prescriptive epistemology, with its accompanying dualistic ontology, a more sober philosophical "realism" is required to account for our world and our place in it. Only some such form of "realism," accepted as a working hypothesis, seems able to account for all we have come to know about history and nature, and how we have come to know it. In his way, even Kant saw this point when he insisted that his position is one of empirical realism wedded to transcendental idealism. Unfortunately, the transcendental idealism undermines the empirical realism, finally reducing both to "appearances only." In summation, the same may be said of Buber's dialogical epistemology which, as a species or mutant of idealism, is also unable to serve, because of its lack of sufficient metaphysical "realism," as the model for a contemporarily informed, philosophically rigorous theory of knowledge.

THE "I" OF RELATION: A RECONSIDERATION

The I of man is two-fold.
For the I of the primary world I–Thou is a different
I from that of the primary world I–It.

So Buber tells us in the opening paragraph of *I and Thou*. The relational quality of the *I* is here primary, its self-isolated character denied. But can this account, for all its real epistemic and metaphysical suggestiveness, be held? Or do we not need a different account of the *I*, even of the *I* of the *I–Thou* relation? Three critical difficulties (at least) arise at this point.

The first is that the concern to define the *I* in terms of and through its relationships does not adequately handle, nor does it exhaust, the reality we usually know by the term "self-consciousness." For there is a form of "self-consciousness" that is to be classed neither as *I–It* nor as *I–Thou*, and any such arbitrary classification of this primitive *I* would be doctrinaire and hollow.

Secondly and related is that the dialogical dictum loses sight of the requirement that there *must* be, and this is a logical as well as ontological *must*, a necessary unifying center of consciousness that is *not* touched by talk of *I's*, *Thou's*, and *It's* as this talk is presently performed in the dialogical context. Here two clarifying remarks are required. The first is descriptive: Buber, again relying on Kant, does actually employ at least late in his life, a doctrine of *self* that is close to the master's "transcendental unity of apperception." For example, in *Distance and Relation* he writes: "It is only man who replaces this unsteady conglomeration [sense data], . . . by a unity which can be imagined or thought by him as existing for itself" (cf. here Kant's *Critique* B 130ff, A 117 and throughout). And again, Buber's entire view of man as free and transcendental echoes Kant's noumenal "self," who is an autonomous moral being not subject to the constraints of the phenomenal environment, as Kant says: "But though I cannot know, I can yet 'think' freedom" (*Critique* B. XXVIII). Secondly, an evaluative observation: Buber needs to explicate the nature and implications of this self-consciousness, the character of this act of self-awareness which he notes "replaces this unsteady conglomeration . . . by a unity," through a philosophical description of the mechanics of this extraordinary yet necessary behavior in a manner consistent with his other dialogical requirements, especially in that its employment seems to violate the essential relational thesis of *I and Thou* quoted above. Buber himself seems to have become increasingly aware of this conceptual demand after World War II and his most sustained, yet still fragmentary and unsatisfactory steps in this direction, are to be found in his late essay *Distance and Relation.* Though still incomplete, Buber's efforts are significant, for they reflect Buber's continual rethinking of his position and its implications, and also indicate that he became aware, as I would argue, that the employment of a doctrine something like Kant's unity of self-consciousness, though shorn of its full-blown transcendental Kantian superstructure, is a *necessity of thought* in general; it is, perhaps, *the* basic necessity of human self-consciousness. Thus, Buber came to recognize that he *must* employ it even at the risk of self-contradiction, though trying, without too much success, to accommodate it within his pre-existent dialogical thinking.

Thirdly, in light of the preceding two remarks, we are in a position to enquire after the nature of this "self" whose being makes possible the conditions of all knowing. That is, we need to know something of the structure of that "self" that creates the mechanisms for the ordering of all series of happenings into an assimilable form of reality which can be coherently understood as a world, be it the world of *It's* or of *Thou's*, of which *It's* and *Thou's* are part and are known to be a part. Further, as an element of this enquiry, we need to remember, as noted, that there *must* be a self that sustains itself through time, which is marked out especially by a common memory, if not by a common body.[25] In other words, here we must entertain the investigation of the conditions and criteria of the use of the term "I" in its empirical and trans-empirical contexts.

Buber did not participate in this sort of enquiry in the philosophy of mind in any fundamental way. For whatever reason, he felt it incompatible with his main dialogical objectives to enter into such a conversation. Yet this neglect is not a plus. For all philosophizing, including dialogical philosophizing, must at some point offer a thorough justification of its philosophical anthropology and re-lated theory of consciousness. It has to argue—not just assert—a view on such issues as the mind-body problem; the correctness or otherwise of philosophical behaviorism; the dilemma of "personal" ascriptions without reference to a body; the nature of first-person ascriptions, their particularities and conditions of predication, as compared to third-person ascriptions, and the like. In other words, we need a defensible theory of personal identity. Buber's account of the "I" that alternates according to its relational modality is *not* such a theory. It neither accounts for the enduring character of the "self" who enters into the chain of relational encounters as the subject, nor the nature of the identity of the "self" that is molded by each encounter in succession so that throughout the sequence one can say either "it is all happening to me" or "it is all happen-ing to 'X'." It is the case that Buber relies generally on Kant's model, but this is not a justification, even were Kant's paradigm adequate. It is not, because the thoroughly dialogical model that must be provided for the relational "I" of *I–Thou* is *not* that provided, and providable, for the isolated "I" of classical idealism. Indeed, this is one of the major attractions of *I–Thou*, but to sustain its attrac-tiveness it must be able to supply a new intersubjective theory of the self for which there is philosophical support. I take this to be one of the major items which Buber has left on the agenda of his heirs to accomplish.

I–IT/I–THOU: EPISTEMOLOGICAL DILEMMAS

As we have noted, there are difficulties with Buber's rendering of what is involved in knowing something in an *I–It* manner, but I will pass over them without any further comment. Instead I turn directly to interrogate Buber's version of the epistemological char-acteristics of *I–Thou* knowing.

As Buber's account of *I–Thou* relies on his analysis of the sort of dialogical cognition found paradigmatically exemplified in inter-personal relations, it is best to begin our analysis with these. The initial question to be raised in response to his description of *I–Thou* relation must be whether in knowing other persons as *Thou's* we are ever, or could ever be, completely free from objectivity concepts, as Buber argues, or whether in contradistinction to Buber, these delimiting and identifying concepts are necessary and integral to the knowing of others as *Thou* such that the absence of these concepts would preclude *all* knowledge of the other, including knowledge of the other as *Thou*. The most direct answer to this epistemological question is that in all interpersonal relations, no matter how intimate, we cannot do without objectivity concepts if the reality, and our knowledge of that reality, of the other with whom we are in relation is to be maintained. That is, we must take full cognizance of the substantial and particular nature of the *Other* in order to relate to him or her as a *Thou*. The concept of *"Thou-ness"* is a conceptual abstraction however it is employed and to whomever it is applied.

Here it is instructive to consider the logic of pronouns, something which is as philosophically difficult as it is necessary, especially in light of the essential pronominal character of Buber's epistemology. To do this, consider these two examples: Buber and I say "Hanover is cold in January." Here we are both making the same assertion, i.e., ascribing the same predicate to the same object. But, if Buber and I say "I like Hanover," we are saying two different things although we are uttering the same words, because of the logic of the pronoun "I"; namely, every "I" context is different because every "I" is different. Of course the same is generally true of second- and third-person pronouns, i.e., *Thou* or *You* can have many references. But here a proviso is required, noting that the logic of *Thou* and *He* is not exactly the same as that of *I*, for several *I's* can refer to a *You* (or *Thou*) and mean the same thing, for example, Buber and I can both say "You" and be referring to Kierkegaard or to God.

These brief remarks are significant because I believe that Buber caught sight of this important linguistic fact: he chose to work with pronouns because he thought their inherent ambiguity would protect his concern for real people as over against philosophical abstractions; this concern for "existing individuals" and their situation was itself seen as a reflection of what he took to be fundamental ontological realities. Thus, his employment of a pronominal schema is integrally tied to his most fundamental anthropological-cum-ontological commitments. Yet, despite Buber's essentially correct intuition with regard to the suggestive possibilities opened up by a pronominal rather than a nominal ontology, his own employment of this insight is problematic, ultimately producing consequences that are antithetical to his basic intention to protect the "lived concreteness" of particular, individuated beings. Intentions to the contrary, the conditions Buber set for the use of pronouns actually leads away from the concrete rather than towards it. Why this is so I shall now try to explain.

To speak of *I's* and *Thou's*, etc., as Buber does, fails to recognize the implications of the necessary ambiguity of pronouns; an ambiguity only clarified by providing more concrete contextual information about the *I's* and *Thou's* in question. Unfortunately, however, Buber's epistemology precludes the possibility of providing the needed concrete referential information because of the overly strict rules governing the employment of pronouns in Buber's dialogical grammar. As a consequence, the primacy of pronouns produces, in spite of the existentialist intent, an abstract essentialist and reductionist quality, i.e., abstracting and reducing "existing individuals," to ghostlike *I's* and *Thou's*, which is the antithesis of the effect desired. It even begins to appear that every time that one writes *I*, in accord with Buber's dialogical notation, one means the same thing, some general class-indicator, rather than a particular existing being. This occurs because Buber's phenomenology, with its ban on objectivity categories and substantive spatio-temporal content, does not allow reference back to the speaker of the *I*, or the addressee of the *You* or *Thou*, for such reference would require the abandonment of the strictly schizophrenic Buberian reading of the relation of *It* and *Thou*.

To individuate the speaker of every *I* utterance as well as every *Thou* addressed means conditions of identity, but such conditions have been defined in advance by Buber as being only illegitimately applicable in the *I–Thou* context. Note as well that this individuation of the referent of pronouns would begin to involve us more directly not only in personal categories but also in ontological ones, for the items we count as filling out the notions of *I* etc. will be part of some ontological schema. That is to say, to describe the nature of being an *I* will involve a more determinate and concrete procedure relative to the detailed investigation and description of what sort of understanding one has of reality and its constitutive elements. Thus, for example, one will have to consider questions regarding such items as the relation of being an *I* to bodily and material conditions, or alternatively, the possibility of disembodied existence, or again the conditions of being an *I* relative to the larger spatio-temporal manifold and the identifying conditions of all other individuals in one's ontology. Still further, one needs to enquire into issues such as the nature of memory in the criteria of establishing the identity of an *I*, the role of names and naming, the difference between self-consciousness and our consciousness of others as well as of the relation that obtains between physical and nonphysical behavior and identity. One can therefore begin to see that the fleshing out of the already employed dialogical pronouns will begin to introduce, as well as to considerably deepen, some of the truly interesting aspects of the present metaphysical situation.

These remarks concerning the relation of objectivity categories to dialogical language, coupled with the character of pronominal speech, suggest as a consequence that as a minimal condition for employing dialogical language meaningfully some identifying skeleton of the notion of *Thou* must be given. This will dictate understanding the indissoluble tie between *what* the other is and *who* the other is. Such a requirement, in turn, is necessary to avoid transposing the notion of *Thou* into a form which violates any acceptable standard of intelligibility. This means that when I know another as *Thou*, say in the case of husband and wife, I know my wife as *Thou* only in and through her being "objectively" and determinately who and what she is. Of course there is more than her behavior and the related objectivity concepts in her being a *Thou* for me, but her behavior and aptitudes, and the corollary conditioning concepts, e.g., her bodily form, her spatio-temporal locus, her memory, her intelligence, her education, as well as all the manifest and introspective characteristics that constitute what can, for a shorthand, be called her personality and character, must also be fully present if she is to be the real *Thou* of my life. Thus, for example, our relation is affected by my recollection of past shared (as well as private) events, by my knowledge that we are building a life together and all the public and private elements this entails, and even by the simple yet easily overlooked facts that I know that she is a woman, that she is my wife, that she is the mother of my children. I do not just have a spontaneous, contentless *Thou* relation to her in some space-time vacuum. Nor do I have a *Thou* relation with other women of the sort that I have with my wife. The meeting with my wife as *Thou,* her being a *Thou* for me and my knowing her existentially as a true dialogical partner, is grounded firmly in space and in time and is the product of events, experiences, feelings and conditions that Buber would relegate exclusively to *I–It.* There is, in effect, an indissoluble connection between the "who" and the "what" of another that Buber's strictures would necessarily, if perhaps unwillingly, tear asunder.

Then too, in any *I–Thou* relation with my wife, or any other *Thou* of my life, the relation is affected by the assumption, which we would call in the world of the everyday "knowledge," that this Other who now stands over against me is the same One who stood there yesterday and will do so tomorrow. This easy, unquestioned assumption (questioned only by philosophers!) rests on metaphysical, ontological, philosophical, psychological, physical, and social criteria that are integral to the other being a *Thou* for me; without them there is no other and there is no *Thou.* Likewise, in the case of "knowing," i.e., relating to God, the *Eternal Thou,* parallel assumptions about continuity and the like (all the metaphysical theses tied up in using the term "God" or *Eternal Thou*) and all that such assumptions imply is surely involved.

Let us pursue this line of argument further. Buber places great emphasis on "responding" to the address of the *Thou* and to the two-sidedness of dialogical encounter. But he has misconceived the essential character of "address" and "response" so that his stress on the "sincerity" or "authenticity" of this existential act becomes a caricature. "Address" and "Response" are not simply intelligible given data of experience, even dialogical experience. There are no direct uninterpreted dialogical "facts" that are totally unrelated to the categorical range of our objective conceptual understanding. The claim to the contrary rests on a mistake—and, it should be noted, is itself a confused and concealed metaphysical claim. What we call "facts" are to some necessary extent always a function of our conceptual and linguistic schema. There must be forms and rules, at least internal dialogical forms and rules, according to which Buber's utterances make sense. The very notions "address" and "response," even the address of an *I* to a *Thou,* are intelligible only within the particular universe of discourse Buber employs. Thus "Sound" has to be organized and shaped to be "Speech," and "Speech" has to be channelled through complex and highly structured interpretive schemata to be understood as "Address,"[26] even if these terms function only as metaphors for Buber. Metaphors also require structure to obtain meaning. Likewise "Response" calls for ordering principles and conceptual norms in regard to both that which we claim to experience as "Address" and in expressing and giving shape to our reply. The Buberian emphasis on and assertion of dialogical immediacy, stressed so forcefully by Buber as the means of short-circuiting such conceptual, cognitive and interpretive activities and all their attendent logical and philosophical difficulties, only obfuscates the issue because it reduces a complex situation to a shadow of its true self. Buber's position loses sight of the fact that when one wants to talk meaningfully of "Address" or "Response" one has to recognize the objectivity requirements involved in these sorts of activities, i.e., one has to know to and with whom one is in relation and again who one is "Addressing" and to whom one is "Responding" in order to know what to say or how to act. I address my wife and respond to her quite differently from the way in which I address or respond to other women with whom I do not live and with whom I have not chosen to link my future. Likewise in respect of the *Eternal Thou,* I address God in prayer because I believe Godlike things about Him and respond to His address in unique ways for the same reason. I do not pray to my Dean or respond to the address of the President in the way that I do to the *Eternal Thou.* If I thought of God differently or "interpreted" my encounter with Him differently I would pray to Him differently or perhaps not at all. We have no clearer example of the significance of such understandings than in the differing interpretations given by Buber and traditional Judaism to their respective

God-Idea. For example, Buber does not place much store in prayer or ritual while traditional Judaism does, and again, the Biblical God is understood by the tradition primarily as a law-giver, while for Buber this is something He cannot be.

Furthermore, with reference to the *Eternal Thou* it should be noted that the oft-used Buberian term "Presence," i.e., that what is "revealed" in the dialogical moment is God's Presence and nothing more, only starts the epistemological discussion; it does not end it. The meaning of the "Presence" of the *Eternal Thou* is dependent on the meaning of *Eternal Thou*, which in turn is a notion that is given its intelligibility only within a larger linguistic-cum-metaphysical framework. For example, the *Eternal Thou* is meaningless to a Buddhist for his ontology has no place for such a personal God—nor even for permanent selves, *I's* and *Thou's*. Again, it is not enough to assert that revelation understood as "Presence" means "event" and not content and thus that all talk of logic and criteria is out of place, for an "event" is also something that has to be made sense of and it too is clearly grounded in the necessary conditions of our experiential life. Even the revelatory "event" Buber treats as paradigmatic, the theophany at the Burning Bush[27] is a historical phenomenon temporally and historically bound—God calls "Moses, Moses!" not "Thou, Thou!"—i.e., Moses is a concrete and definite *Thou* with a unique place and history. The same is true of every *I–Thou* relation. In actual relations we encounter the historically individuated and temporally bounded Moses, Aarons, Abrahams and Sarahs of our world, not disembodied *Thou's*. And the historical and other conditions that mold the actual shape of these encounters are not incidental to their "essence." Even more, what God has to say to Moses is not "contentless" despite Buber's sometimes illuminating rendition of *Ehyeh Asher Ehyeh*, but contains the all-important act of God's self-identification—"I am the God of thy fathers, the God of Abraham, the God of Isaac, the God of Jacob." This is no Buberian "moment God" who is not identifiable or re-identifiable. Quite the contrary. Furthermore, God then makes the all-important promise to Moses on behalf of the nation: "I have surely seen the affliction of my people who are in Egypt, and have heard their cry . . . and I am come down to deliver . . ."

The concreteness of the whole episode makes the theophany *Eh-yeh Asher Ehyeh*, pregnant with meaning. Devoid of its context, historical milieu, and "content," it is not revelation or theophany but an "event" shorn of all significance.[28]

Likewise, any valid account of what it is to be a person will involve bodily, psychological and metaphysical criteria; any satisfactory account of the *Eternal Thou* will involve similarly identifying predicates that are appropriate to His ontological status. These considerations force themselves upon even a dialogical outlook for they are of the essence of such unavoidable philosophical issues as the problem of identification and re-identification; continuity and discontinuity; permanence and impermanence; the ability to specify with whom one is having a relation. In other words, they are integral to any discussion of "selves" or persons, even be they dialogical "selves" or persons. They certainly are consequential for a theological vocabulary that talks of God as *Eternal Thou.*

Here the role of context must also be considered afresh. Buber's signal philosophical contribution is his insistence on the "social" interhuman nature of man's being: "There is no *I* taken by itself." The direct consequence of this emphasis was the theory of dialogical relation with its demand that pre-eminence be given to relation over substance, a requirement that has had the effect of radically altering the entire form and focus of the epistemological dimension. The insight contained in this Buberian reorientation of the direction of thought is considerable, possessing the seeds of powerful illumination in many areas of philosophical concern. Yet one is uneasy with the account as it stands, for Buber's fundamental intuition(s) about dialogical relation, the ontology of "the between" (to use his technical designation of the correlative metaphysical issues), is underdeveloped. Though there are many pressing considerations with regard to it, I mention in line with our present concerns only one of them. Despite his intentions, can Buber maintain his existential claim that dialogue is true meeting with an Other when he insists that this encounter is aspatial, atemporal, wholly nonsensual, and nonexperiential in all the ordinary senses? Can there be any residue of substantial meaning left in the notions of "meeting," "encounter," "Other," and "Thou" when all experiential and empirical content is denied them? Can there be any ontology of "the between" in such a situation? Likewise, can Buber's original intuition that we must understand our basic and most important relations to nature, other men, and God in *personal* terms be championed when the terms "person," "personal," "personality" are divorced from all behavioral or material predicates? Thus, to say "I encounter a Thou" when none of the ordinary limiting conditions and experiential concepts apply is to over-stretch the limits of language, for we do not have a clear sense as to what is being asserted with regard to the terms "encounter" and "Thou."

What seems to be the case is that Buber's employment of "encounter," "between," "meeting," "Thou," etc. is at best metaphorical and analogical, dependent on the nonmetaphorical use of these concepts in ordinary discourse, and that Buber's usages retain a descriptive appearance because of the covert retention of attachments that have been overtly rejected in the formulation of his dialogical presuppositions. However, even this route may be closed to the philosophy of dialogue, for we must consider whether we can properly understand an encounter to which no predicates apply even as a metaphor or analogue of ordinary encounters, or whether Buber has gone so far with his negative stipulations that even the notion of a metaphor or analogue is saying more than it is permissible to say. In any case, this metaphorical "justification" seems closed to Buber who explicitly tells us that "*Thou* is no metaphor."

This sort of difficulty is seen to be particularly acute in assigning *Thou* predicates to God, the *Eternal Thou*, as all such terms ascribed to things in this world are tied to experiential conditions obtaining as a minimum yet constitutive feature of such attributions. Yet in God's case, none of the ordinary experiential modalities obtain. In fact, God is defined, so it seems, by the very absence of these regulative structures. A necessary regressive logic appears to be operative in which every predicate is required to point beyond itself. In what sense then is God a "person," even the *Eternal Person,* and in what sense is it legitimate to speak of "personality" in the case of the Divine? This is a crucial question and in Buber's work the way the problem presents itself is only a new way of putting a classical problem about God-language. To say, as Buber does, that ascribing certain personal predicates to God is "more appropriate" than employing impersonal notions like "Creator" is no answer in itself for this preference, this "appropriateness," has itself to be justified. Why is God more correctly spoken of as *Thou*, or *Eternal Thou* to be precise, rather than as *Creator?* In what way is God a "Person?" In what way the *Eternal Thou?* What are the criteria of "appropriateness?"

This diagnosis is related to another hermeneutical concern: the need for a more rigorous, more substantive, personalist, dialogical metaphysics. This is required, first, to disentangle the difficulties inherent in the *I–Thou* philosophy. Second, it is needed to support, or rather to deepen, the structural foundation of the positive accomplishments of the *I–Thou* position. Buber, like many if not most of his existentialist colleagues, erred in thinking that a considered disregard, one might even say disrespect, for metaphysics is a satisfactory substitute for it. This is not the case; when dealing with such issues as man, nature, and God it is doubly not so. If nothing else, it needs to be acknowledged that a statement critical of metaphysics is at least partly a metaphysical statement. Again, every philosophically interesting proposition in, for example, *I and Thou* or *Between Man and Man*, is wedded, if only implicitly, to an entire spider's web of metaphysical assumptions from which it is spawned, toward which it appeals for intelligibility and support, and whose structural contour or dynamic principle(s) it is trying to point to or explicate. Not to grasp this, not to see the profound implications of this, is not to be fully self-reflective. It is a *dis*service to the novel sensibility and often striking originality of Buber's intuitions to leave them as fragments of thought.

At this juncture, unrepentant and by way of self-defense, Buber turns to the asserted necessarily "paradoxical" quality of religious propositions. In all these difficult circumstances, however, talk of paradox or in paradoxes will not salvage the situation. First, "paradox" is almost always just an honorific title for contradictions that we utter, while the same statements are recognized as nonsensical and plain contradictions when uttered by someone else. Second, before invoking the escape potential of "paradoxes" Buber has to give us a rule for distinguishing contradictions from paradoxes. This he does not and of course cannot do within his own frames of reference. Failing this, however, Buber's position is burdened with a host of logical difficulties in the face of which the embrace of paradoxical non-sequitors provides no real comfort. Foremost among these difficulties is that if no predicate or category applies to *I–Thou* or to *Thou* and so on, then *I–Thou*, *Thou* and the *Eternal Thou*, etc., effectively drop out of the language. Of course, Buber continues to talk about these realities at the risk of self-contradiction, and this discourse gains power and plausibility by suggesting the referential connotations ordinarily associated with concepts on which *I–Thou* and *Thou* normally draw. However, one cannot have it both ways. Either (a) the meaning of *I–Thou* and *Eternal Thou*, etc., is not available in language and so one cannot draw on the ordinary associations usually invoked, or (b) the meaning of the dialogical concepts are at least partly known and it is on the basis of this knowledge that the ordinary associations, i.e., "personal," "free," and so on are made, in which case the basic claims of Buber's epistemology vis à vis *I–Thou* and the *Eternal Thou*, etc., have been contradicted.

These antinomies force Buber to confront foundational issues concerning the minimal conditions of linguistic and conceptual adequacy. In the light of these and like considerations no amount of dialogical "intuition" or reference to the special status of paradoxical claims or appeals to subjective truth will be adequate rejoinders. If all statements about God are unwarranted, then Buber's statements about God are unwarranted. The situation is not materially altered by the intensity with which Buber holds his beliefs. "I *believe* that X is true" does not make "X is true," true!

This last observation encourages another word about the logical distinction between "Belief in" and "Belief that" which Buber so much abuses in framing his phenomenological and epistemological mapping of interpersonal relationship. Buber argues that:

It is not necessary to know something about God in order really to believe in Him; many true believers know how to talk *to* God but not *about* Him. If one dares to turn toward the unknown God, to go to meet Him, to call to Him, Reality is present.[29]

Buber here makes a complete separation between "Belief in" and "Belief that" which is erroneous and entails disastrous consequences. Consider Buber's suggestion that in relation to God all that is required is "to go to meet Him, to call to Him." How does one begin to set about going "to meet Him" if nothing is known about this "Him?" Does one pray? If so, why? Given that we lack all information about the "unknown God," why pray? Perhaps one offers charity and "loves one's neighbor," but again, why should this be a step in the direction of the unknown God. Perhaps the "unknown God" is Descartes' "Deceiver" or Marcion's "Devil." Reflect also upon Buber's final phrase, "Reality is present." This statement, while suitably seductive, is completely fuzzy. What are we to understand by the term "Reality" in this context? As any student of philosophy knows, the term "Reality" is notoriously promiscuous in its liaisons. While Buber constantly appears to be making factual assertions about "Reality" and thus indirectly about the *Eternal Thou*, his remarks are, given the limitations under which they operate, actually pseudo-factual assertions with no definite sense or reference.

Buber, and many others who urge a similar subjective posture upon the unwary, fails to confront an inescapable critical issue: if I claim to believe *in* (or *that*) "P," the question "What does 'P' mean?" must make sense. It must at least be possible that this question can be posed for otherwise "P" would not *in fact* be believable at all. One cannot believe in something that is unintelligible. Finally, it should not go unobserved that Buber's statement about the "unknowable Thou" which has been quoted assumes, at the very least, the following four "belief that," i.e. objective metaphysical propositions: (a) God exists (otherwise it would be absurd to recommend that one believe in Him); (b) God is the sort of being who is capable of being addressed; (c) God is the sort of being whom one ought to address; (d) not only does God exist and not only is He the sort of being capable and worthy of being addressed by human beings, He also enters into relation with human kind.

To take Buber's thought seriously means to wrestle with these and like problems arising from his work. To ignore them is to indicate respect for Buber as an oracle, not a philosopher.

REVELATION: A CRITICISM

We need now to rethink the epistemological implications of Buber's account of revelation. Its importance and complexity have already been noted; here we will consider its viability and power to illuminate the world we live in and the phenomenological character of the human situation.

Our line of criticism will center on the last item, item 7 (7a–7i) of our exegesis of Buber's position given above. We begin with a general consideration, namely, "What does the concept of 'revelation' mean?" On the negative side we know, from the combination of the various theses in our outline, that it does *not* mean a set of perfect, eternal, and universal propositions. Further, it does not involve information about God in Himself, or about God's will. Switching to the positive, we must go more slowly. We know it is supposed to entail God's "Presence;" that it means human form and human meaning, and that it guarantees that life is authentic and salvaged from the absurdity of sheer radical contingency. But we must ask, with utmost seriousness, do we know what it really means to talk in this way?

Let us, however, bracket this large question for the moment and consider instead the implications for dialogical existence of items 7c through 7h of our outline. Buber has told us that

The key to truth is the next deed, and this key opens the door if one does what one has to do in such a way that the meaning of the action here finds its fulfillment.[30]

That is, when the "Presence" encountered in the revelatory moment is translated into human life, no specific program of prescribed actions is necessarily entailed by the "revelatory" event. The "how" rather than the "what" is all-important. This negation of revelatory "content" is predicated on the coalescence of four major trends in Buber's thought: (a) his pansacramentalism; (b) his antinomianism; (c) his adaptation of the thesis that "truth is subjectivity" in the light of his understanding of Hasidic *Kavanah* and the influence of Kierkegaard and his heirs; and (d) his Kantian insistence on the ultimacy of human autonomy wherein we have an open-ended, i.e., nondeterministic, nonheteronomous, noncoercive, field, not subject to any prescribed norms, in which *any* action can be the translation of revelation if man so chooses.

As a consequence of these various influences Buber propounded a view of revelation that in effect is equivalent to the thesis that the nature of that which is revealed is that which out of the manifold of our experience, including our experience of the *Eternal Thou*, man chooses to treat as revealed. The criteria of something being "revealed" is no longer related to the idea of something spoken by God in propositions; rather it has been turned around, and the source of its content, if not of its being (which Buber locates in "the between"), is transported from the Divine to the human will. Autonomous activity is now holy activity because human autonomy is vouchsafed by God's act of self-limitation in the revealing of "Presence" alone. It is not that God, as *Eternal Thou*, is a *Deus Absconditus*, for He meets us in dialogue and reveals His presence, becoming in this dialogical intercourse a *Deus Revelatus*. But the *Eternal Thou*, in the very act of being a *Deus Revelatus*, respects the *Thou-ness* of His human partner, and turns him back upon himself with the assurance that no Divine coercion will interfere with man's freedom, which is exercised in the face of the Divine Reality. Ontological truth and anthropological truth here merge in the existential situation of the existing individual.

What are the implications of Buber's position, which attempts to harmonize the reality of God as *Deus Revelatus* and also to protect human autonomy? Does it really do both these things without injury to either? Though there are many difficulties with this view, both with regard to its significance for the human situation as well as for its implications in respect of the *Eternal Thou*, the present format limits us to three critical considerations.

First, what is the relation between those human processes which Buber claims are free while yet guaranteed by the *Eternal Thou*, and the *Eternal Thou*? Another, simpler, way of putting the question is: In what sense are man's free actions guaranteed by the *Eternal Thou*? If revelation is to maintain any meaning whatsoever, there must be a *necessary* tie between the occasion of revelation and that which flows from it—in Buber's case, uncoerced human conduct. Yet at this point in Buber's reasoning a paradox arises, for if human behavior is causally determined by revelation, then of course it is heteronomous and dialogically illegitimate. On the other hand, if human action is severed from any revelational ground, then revelation seems, at best, a purely formal rather than a material notion. Therefore, to repeat, what relation does exist between revelation and human deeds? Even if we take with the utmost seriousness Buber's idea of revelation as "Presence," this notion seems unable to provide the necessary clarification of the above dilemma, for, if knowledge of God's "Presence" *causes* man to do X rather than Y, the situation is still a heteronomous one. Although the motivating ground is now God's Being rather than His Will, the human agent has acted out of respect for an external consideration, i.e., God's Being. If, however, a sense of God's "Presence" in no way determines the choice of a human agent, then this "Presence" is without existential import, as it makes no material difference to human behavior. In sum, the entire discussion of what the significance of the revelation of "Presence" is for human action is ambiguous. Conversely, if it is legitimate for God's "Presence" to influence human conduct why is it illegitimate for God's Will to do so?

Our second difficulty, which is related to the first, has to do with the religious and ethical consequences of Buber's account. Buber certainly wanted to eschew religious and ethical relativism and took offense when criticized in these terms. Yet his position seems un-avoidably mired in just that relativism to which he objects. For example, in *I and Thou* Buber wrote regarding revelation that "man receives . . . not a specific 'content' but a Presence, a Presence as power."[31] This means, according to Buber, that "The meaning that has been received can be proved true by each man only in the sin-gleness of his being and the singleness of his life."[32] But, we must ask in all seriousness, can such a theological (and moral) position lead to anything but religious and ethical relativism?

Buber's emphasis on personal decision rather than objective and public norms misleads him. "Only one thing matters," he tells us, "that as the situation is presented to me I expose myself to the word's manifestation to me . . . and that I perceive what is to be perceived and answer it . . . there is not the slightest assurance that our decision is right in any but a personal way. . . ."[33] That is, the criterion relevant here is not objective but rather that "I give the word of my answer by accomplishing among the actions possible that which seems to my devoted insight to be the right one."[34] In this arena no public criteria enter, nor is there any appeal to nonsubjective norms or evidence or results. Instead the notion of "right" has been interiorized completely, with the result that one can neither legislate a course of action for another nor object to the behavior actually manifested by another. For in any situation a person can say: "This seems to my devoted insight to be the right action," at which point one must stand mute, without judgment, without censure.

Of perhaps still more consequence is the fact that, given this idiom, not only does subjectivity completely replace public ethical norms but the Buberian recomposition of the ethical totally empties the notion of ethical obligation of all content. "I beg you to notice that I do not demand," Buber replies to a critic. "There is no ordering of dialogue. It is not that you are to answer, but that you are able" (BMM, p. 35). But being invited to do X or being able to do X is not being obligated to do X. The logic of ethical obligation is contradistinctive to the logic of ethical possibility.

Buber and his disciples do not seem to realize the force of these objections. In fact Buber went so far as to write:

It is not the "finger of God," to be sure: we are not permitted to expect that, and therefore there is not the slightest assurance that our action is right in any but a personal way.[35]

However, if this is the case, has the word "right" retained a use? Have we here a recipe for anything but spiritual and ethical anarchy? I pose this challenge in a sharp form because of its many reverberations not the least of which is that given Buber's vehement denial of objective ethical content, all possibility of moral judgment is obviated. No moral determination can be defended over against either individual or collective behavior. Of course, Buber does not eschew specific moral decisions, nor does he shy away from attributing moral blame, activities that appear to support the credibility and functionality of his dialogical ethic. However, these particular acts as well as the more universal ethical prescriptions Buber does, in fact, offer are deceiving. This is because they are made in spite of rather than because of his dialogical ontology and *I–Thou* morality. His ability to make moral judgments lies in his retention of the content and tonalities of traditional morality, even while advocating its overcoming. Thus while the constraining convictions of the classical ethical sphere are evacuated, their particular substance, as required in "given situations" (*BMM*, p. 107), is held dear, even if at the price of adopting an inauthentic posture rooted in logical self-contradiction.

One might object that I misrepresent Buber, for he has written that in response to a call to "suspend the ethical"

It can happen, however, that a sinful man is uncertain whether he does not have to sacrifice his . . . son to God for his sins (Micah 6:7). For Micah mutates the voice of God. In contrast to this, God himself demands of this as of every man (not of Abraham, His chosen one, but of you and me) nothing more than justice and love, and that he "walk humbly" with Him, with God. (Micah 6:8)—in other words, not much more than the fundamental ethical.[36]

But given Buber's view of religious law and his rejection of the objective existence of that very "fundamental ethic" to which he here appeals, it is logically impossible for him to maintain this line of defense. Micah can refer to the "fundamental ethical" because he accepts the Torah as literally true and its ethical precepts as objective standards that are binding on all without question. Buber, in contrast, knows neither Torah as revealed content nor ethical norms as objective prescriptions commanded by the Divine. "Certainly," we are told, "man ` receives from all things and events a divine claim on his person, but in general no indication is thereby given him as to what he should do for God in this hour, in this situation."[37]

In light of this description what becomes of the "fundamental ethical" in the existential moral circumstance? What becomes of the notion of "right" religious or moral behavior when we are instructed that "What he [man] now grasps, concludes, decides *from out of himself, this he draws out of his conscience.*"[38] Has not the relative here been enshrined, the ethical suspended?

Our third critical consideration turns on the extremely problematic Buberian idea of a "moment God." In *Between Man and Man,* Buber asks the question "Who Speaks?" He gives the following suggestive answer:

It would not avail us to give for reply the word "God," if we do not give it out of that decisive hour of personal existence when we had to forget everything we imagined we knew of God, when we dared to keep nothing handed down or learned or self-contrived, no shred of knowledge, and were plunged into the night.

When we rise out of it into the new life and there begin to receive the signs, what can we know of that which—of him who gives them to us? Only what we experience from time to time from the signs themselves. If we name the speaker of this speech "God," then it is always the "God" of a moment, a moment God . . .

In such a way, out of the givers of the signs, the speakers of the words in lived life, out of the moment Gods there arises for us with a single identity the Lord of the voice, the One. [Pp. 14 f.]

Given that this "moment God" leaves nothing behind but an awareness of His "Presence," if we can even claim this, we need to enquire "What are the considerations for identification and re-identification of this 'Presence' as God?", i.e., how do we know that the "Presence" revealed is the *Eternal Thou,* The "Lord of the Voice, the One?" And again, how can we ascertain that the *Eternal Thou* revealed in situation A is the same *Eternal Thou* as revealed in situation B, and so on? Moreover, and perhaps still *more* pressing is the critical question: How does Buber get to the notion of *Eternal Thou* from a series of encounters with "moment Gods?" In other words, how do "moment Gods" become God?

The present context forbids a lengthy review of these matters and requires instead a direct reply: despite the centrality of the *Eternal Thou* for his epistemology Buber is unable to handle such difficulties regarding the identification and re-identification of the

Eternal Thou. Indeed, his *a priori* claims as to the structure of the *I–Thou* relation makes it impossible for him to give any convincing answer to the question as to how the "moment Gods" become "God." Buber himself, in the continuation of the passage quoted above, suggests that the only grounds for this identification is that which we experience when "plunged into the night."[39] That is, this connection between the "moment Gods" and "God" is established only by dint of a direct religious experience. While this at first seems a justification, it is not. For Buber cannot just *posit* this fact; he needs to establish it. But this is more difficult than it first appears, for even granting the reality of religious experience, which is a large, much-debated concession, it is not at all obvious how such experience can give us the sort of knowledge required to identify the "moment Gods" with "God," given Buber's embargo on "content" in such encounters.[40] Moreover, the nature of the mystical or religious experience to which Buber here makes appeal is a far more contextual and mediated experience than he allows and, as such, appeal to it, even if real, will not provide the cosmic justification he is in search of here.[41] Then again, there is a deep internal problematic to be attended to between what Buber writes of the encounter with "moment Gods" and his claim that these are united by some unifying experience, i.e., he needs to show us the link between the "One" and the "many." Consequently, Buber's "defense" itself needs supporting, yet keeping in mind the entire structural matrix of his thought it is hard to imagine how such a defense could be mounted.[42]

The significance of this inherent inability to provide more orderly and substantive rules for the description of elements and relations necessary for Buber's entire dialogical stand, as well as rules for identification and re-identification and the like, can be clearly seen when we reflect on the following example. Consider as a paradigm of the problematic element in Buber's hermeneutic, his essential contention that "The *Eternal Thou* can never become an *It*." The ramifications within the dialogical structure of this claim for the *Eternal Thou* are many. For the readers of this volume, I need not spell them out in detail. Instead, I would only call attention to the fact that this statement is a universal proposition of the sort it would seem the dialogical system cannot offer—and even probably, if not certainly, requires that we explicitly rule out. How could we know as a result of a dialogical relation with a "moment God" that this "moment God" could *never* (note the universality), become an *It?* Given the conditions set out for *I–Thou* relation with a "moment God" one is justified solely, if at all, in speaking of the fact that, *for the moment,* He is not an *It.* Here we again run into the need for—and the absence of—metaphysical deliberations that are essential. Here again we recognize that our language, even or perhaps especially, our dialogical language, is not ontologically neutral. Its ontology may only be implied for the most part, but the need for its necessary clarification is no less pressing for that.

A corollary of these difficulties with the Buberian concept of "moment God" is that it rules out references, for example, to "God the Creator," or more familiarly, to the "God of Israel." For the claims necessarily entailed by the proposition "God the Creator," which Buber does not like to talk of, or "God of Israel," which is one of Buber's main preoccupations, transcend those permitted by the dialogical account and require an enduringness through time and a metaphysical substantiality a "moment God" cannot possess. The nub of the difficulty is that saying that "moment God" A encountered at time T is either the same or different from "moment God" A1 at time T1, while seeming a simple exercise in identification, similar to identifying the Talmudic tract in the study, or the dog's biscuits in the kitchen is, in fact, far more difficult, because what criteria of re-identification is Buber able to employ? Anything to do with time and space is ruled out and all psychological states are subject to the now familiar embargo on content. Thus, what is Buber going to use to decide that A1 at T1 is the same as A at T, (or that the God of Abraham is the God of Isaac), and what criteria is he going to employ to check whether he has decided correctly or not? It would seem that to conclude correctly whether A at T is the same as A1 at T1, A would have to have some constancy and internal coherence that could make it available to the faculty of human judgment. But it is precisely this quality that the very name "moment God" is intended to deny.

Translating the import of this technical idiom into its more pragmatic implications means arguing that the dialogical model makes it difficult to construct an epistemology that is capable of dealing adequately with history, a philosophy of history, or a God of history. Again it runs counter to a coherent epistemological analysis of social interaction, which is public and endures through time and space, and social history past and present. And these are just two of its more serious limits.

Let me back up a moment and fill out my comment about history just a bit. Buber's "history" is not the real history in which man lives. Rather it is a meta-history, a trans-historicity that fastens on those heightened and rare moments of human life as paradigmatic, and discards or merely ignores the everyday world-historical situation in which most men are not prophets or in direct encounter with God and have to live out their lives accordingly. The need is to make God's presence understood as manifest in the everyday, and not to transpose the ordinary worldly matrix into some supra-historical mythos of *I–Thou* relations. In the end Buber presents not God in history but a devaluation of history itself: "What we are accustomed to call history is from the biblical standpoint only the facade of reality."[43] While Buber is searching for the really *real*, the inner meaning, the holy of holies, and devaluing history in favor of "inner history,"[44] we must insist that the dialectic of "encounter," of *I–Thou* relation, is no substitute for the embodied facticity of, for example, the Exodus-Sinai event.

Such reductionism not only destroys the meaningfulness of authentic temporality, it necessarily eliminates the valence of historic tradition. Thus no value can be attached to communal and religious memories. If *I–Thou* is always a revelation of "Presence" that must speak to the here and now, historic tradition, even if true, can have no value for the present moment and cannot make any demands on the man of today in the present hour. All history and all tradition are *I–It*.

What possible connection can there be between me sitting in my study in Cambridge in 1982 and enjoying an *I–Thou* relation and the fact that, some time during the reign of the Pharaohs, a man named Moses led a small, scruffy band of Semites out of Egypt and across the barren wastes of Sinai, etc. What necessity, what nexus, links my meeting with the *Eternal Thou* and Moses' encounter, even if both of us have met God? On Buber's ahistorical, content-less grounds, there is certainly no actual historical connection; yet without such connection no significant Jewish theological linkage is possible either. Buber is forced, by his own canons of meaning, to reduce the concretized realities of the Exodus-Sinai event to their supposed essence: the *I–Eternal Thou* dialogue. He would also have to do the same with my contemporary experience, but when he does this he destroys rather than protects the integrity of each event as the unique historical moment each is and severs the bond which ties the two together.

This move from history to meta-history, from concrete reality to theological hypostasizing, shows itself again in Buber's rendering of the stages of Jewish spirituality. Beginning with the Patriarchs and the events of the Exodus and Sinai,[45] moving through the Prophets,[46] the spirituality of Jesus (as compared to Paul and the Church),[47] the subterranean religiosity of Kabbalah come to light in Hasidism,[48] and culminating in his own "re-discovery" of the dialogical principle,[49] Buber interprets all true Jewish piety as being, in essence, the renewal and repetition of *I–Thou* relationship. Despite evidence to the contrary, all history, all particularity and uniqueness, all individuating detail and context, is subordinated to this over-arching and superimposed explanatory model. With a bold rhetorical daring all textual analysis or source exegesis is carried on so as to produce this result. What is wrong with all this is that it passes as historical analysis, or rather as the excavation of historical texts and movements. But such it is assuredly not, being instead a sophisticated variant of metaphysical eisegesis, dialogical misreading and concealed theology. While posing as close textual deconstruction and careful scholarly determinations, the historical record is effectively used to present a particular Buberian version of the *philosophia perennis*, otherwise called *I–Thou*. And this is rendered conceivable because of the ahistorical, essentialist form that Buber gives to all that he holds religiously authentic. The historically discrete gives way before the ontologically universal, the historical gives way before the atemporal and theological.[50]

These reflections, whether having to do with the substance of ethical judgment, the logic of speaking of "moment Gods," or co-nundrums in the philosophy of history and especially a Jewish philosophy of history, should have by now made it evident and indisputable that one of the pressing needs for the ongoing development of the Buberian schema is another, more penetrating look at revelation.

CONCLUSION

Such is the yield of a rigorous examination of Buber's epistemology. While his work is suggestive in many ways, in particular as a consequence of the original conceptual and hermeneutical paradigms if offers, it is not yet the final word on any subject, not least because it does not possess the transcendental immunity from interrogation and logic it claims for itself. To overcome this present impasse, to reconstitute itself more persuasively, the philosophy of dialogue must be rethought particularly in terms of its epistemological categories. Whether this can be done is the challenge before us.

NOTES

1. M. Buber, *Between Man and Man,* (New York, 1971), pp. 119–120 (hereafter abbreviated as *BMM*).

2. Ibid., p. 123–125.

3. *Knowledge of Man* (New York, 1965), p. 61.

4. M. Buber, *Werke,* 3 vols., plus a fourth of his Jewish writings. The philosophical writings are in the volume entitled *Schriften zur Philosophie* (Heidelberg, 1962). On the philosophic issues and background to the writing of *I and Thou* see Rivka Horwitz, *Buber's Way to* I and Thou (Heidelberg, 1978). However, care must be taken in using this work. On this see P. Vermes in *The Journal of Jewish Studies,* Vol. 30, No. 3 (Summer, 1981), pp. 363–368; and my review in the *Association of Jewish Studies Newsletter* (October, 1981). On this early period in Buber's life see also Paul Flohr, "From *Kulturmystik* to Dialogue," (Ph.D. diss., Brandeis University, 1974). In addition, the first volume of M. Friedman's biography of Buber, *Martin Buber's Life and Work, 1878–1923* (New York, 1981), has now appeared.

5. M. Friedman, *The Life of Dialogue* (New York, 1960), p. 164, quoting K. Heim, *Glaube und Denken*, 1st ed., pp. 450 ff.

6. B. and S. Rome, eds., *Philosophical Interrogations* (New York, 1964), p. 22.

7. For further consideration of these issues see Prof. Robert E. Wood's interesting article "Buber's Conception of Philosophy," in *Thought*, Vol. 53, No. 210 (Spring, 1978), pp. 309–319. I gladly acknowledge debt to Wood's argument. For the "Buberian" view, see, for example, Haim Gordon, "A Method of Clarifying Buber's I–Thou Relationship," *Journal of Jewish Studies*, Vol. 27, No. 1 (1976), pp. 71–83, and George W. Morgan, "Martin Buber and Some of His Critics," *Judaism*, Vol. 18, (Spring, 1969), pp. 232–241.

8. The complex nature of Buber's use of and relationship to the Kantian tradition cannot be dealt with adequately in this paper. Some readers, if not most, may be surprised by the importance I attribute to this relationship. My position here is fully discussed as part of my larger study of Buber's philosophical position, which will appear as the second volume of my comprehensive study of Buber's work. (The first volume, dealing with Buber's Hasidic writing and tentatively entitled *Hasidism and Martin Buber: A Critical Analysis*, is to go to press next year.)

9. A more detailed exegesis of Buber's views is given in my "Dialogue and Revelation in the Thought of Martin Buber" in *Religious Studies*, Vol. 14 (March, 1978), pp. 57–68.

10. James Brown, *Subject and Object in Modern Theology* (London, 1955), p. 115.

11. *I and Thou* (New York, 1937), p. 51.

12. Ibid., p. 33.

13. Ibid., p. 62.

14. Ibid., p. 33. See also pp. 32 ff. for Buber's entire discussion of this theme.

15. Buber does not even attempt to prove God's existence. Indeed, he explicitly rejects the very idea of such proof and repudiates all such attempts. See, for example, *I and Thou* pt. I; the various essays in *Eclipse of God*, and *BMM* pp. 12f. Rather, Buber's position rests on his unshakeable belief in God's existence and flows from this presupposition. There is nothing inductive about Buber's procedure here, nor was there any chance that he would arrive at the end of his philosophical interrogations and conclude there was no God.

16. This is a *very* sensitive point in Buber's work, fraught as it is with moral, philosophical, and theological implications of tremendous import. First, to substantiate the exegesis I have offered, I quote Buber's own description as given in *I and Thou* of what does and does not occur as a consequence of revelation.

It [Revelation] does not wish to be sealed within me, but it wishes to be born by me into the world. But just as the meaning itself does not permit itself to be transmitted and made into knowledge generally current and admissible, so confirmation of it cannot be transmitted as a valid Ought; it is not specified on any tablet, to be raised above all men's heads. The meaning that has been received can be proved true by each man only in the singleness of his being and the singleness of his life. As no prescription can lead us to the meeting, so none leads from it. As only acceptance of the Presence is necessary for the approach to the meeting, so in a new sense is it so when we emerge from it. As we reach the meeting with the simple *Thou* on our lips, so with the *Thou* on our lips we leave it and return to the world.

For a second essential source of Buber's views see his discussion of the issues of Revelation, Law, Torah, and Mitzvot in his letters to Franz Rosenzweig, reprinted in *On Jewish Education*, ed. N. Glatzer (New York, 1954). For the debate generated by Buber's view see: A.A. Cohen, "Revelation and Law: Reflections on Martin Buber's Views on Halakah" in *Judaism*, Vol. I, No. 3 (July, 1952), pp. 250–256; M. Fox, "Some Problems in Buber's Moral Philosophy" in *The Philosophy of Martin Buber*, eds. A.S. Schilpp and M. Friedman (La Salle, Illinois, 1967); and M. Diamond, *Martin Buber, Jewish Existentialist* (New York, 1960). M. Friedman's defense of Buber appears in *Judaism*, Vol. 3, No. 1 (Winter, 1954). See also George Morgan's article cited above in note 7 which also attempts, unsuccessfully in my opinion, to defend Buber against his philosophical critics. M. Friedman has also tried, without much success, to defend Buber's ethical theory in his contribution to the *Philosophy of Martin Buber* volume he co-edited.

17. Items 2–6 are distilled primarily from Buber's remarks in *Eclipse of God* (New York, 1952) (hereafter *Eclipse*), pp. 129–130, and pp. 135 ff; *I and Thou*, pp. 109–120; and *Between Man and Man* (hereafter *BMM*), pp. 67–70. Item 7 and items 7a to 7i are also derived from these sources but, in addition, are based on the following texts: (7a) *Israel and the World* (New York, 1963) (hereafter *Israel*), p. 87 ff, p. 114, p. 142; *Hasidism and Modern Man* (New York, 1958) (hereafter *HMM*), pp. 227 ff., 232; *The Prophetic Faith* (New York, 1960), p. 164; (7b) *Israel*, p. 114, pp. 87 ff.; *HMM* pp. 227 ff., p. 232; (7c) *HMM*, pp. 229 ff; (7d) *BMM*, p. 16, p. 35; *Eclipse* pp. 95, 129; (7e) *Eclipse* pp. 125 ff.; *The Knowledge of Man* (New York, 1965), pp. 85 ff; (7f) *On Jewish Learning* p. 115; *HMM* pp. 12, 14; *Eclipse* p. 129, p. 173; (7g) *On Jewish Learning* p. 115; *Good and Evil* (New York, 1963) p. 43; *BMM* pp. 114, 182; *Eclipse* p. 129; *Moses* p. 188; (7h) *HMM* p. 135; *Israel* pp. 163; (7i) All of the above.

18. *I and Thou*, pp. 110 ff.

19. Ibid., p. 112.

20. *Eclipse*, p. 14.

21. I realize my remarks on Kantianism in this critical discussion may be obscure to readers unfamiliar with the fine details of Kantianism. I refer such readers to note 8 above.

22. On this question see P. Strawson, *Bounds of Sense* (London, 1966);

M. Gram, "Transcendental Arguments" in *NOUS*, Vol. 5 (1971), pp. 5–26; and Gram again in "Hintikka and Spurious Transcendentalism" in *NOUS*, Vol. 8 (1974); J. Hintikka, "Transcendental Arguments" in *NOUS*, Vol. 7 (1972), pp. 274–81.

23. Hans Reichenbach, *Kant and The Theory of Relativity* (California, 1954).

24. Interestingly, Franz Rosenzweig saw this on reading the galleys of *I and Thou*. On his response to Buber, see the discussion in G. Schaeder, ed., *M. Buber: Briefwechsel* (Heidelberg, 1972–75), Vol. II, pp. 109–42.

25. The enormous literature produced on these sorts of issues since World War II, particularly among analytic philosophers, indicates both how important and how difficult it is to do this philosophical job. See among many other works L. Wittgenstein's *Philosophical Investigations* (Oxford, 1958); S. Shoemaker, *Self-Knowledge and Self Identity* (Ithaca, 1963); A. Rorty, ed., *The Identity of Persons* (Berkeley, 1976); S. Kripke, "Persons and their Pasts," *American Philosophical Quarterly*, Vol. 7 (1970); P.F. Strawson, *Individuals* (London, 1959); S. Hampshire, *Thought and Action* (New York, 1960); B. Williams, *Problems of the Self* (Cambridge, 1973); G. Ryle, *The Concept of Mind* (London, 1949). The most recent investigation of novelty and substance is R. Nozick, *Philosophical Explanations* (Cambridge, 1981), pp. 27–114.

26. Of course there are many kinds of "Address;" speech provides only one of them. In recognizing this Buber's position is more sophisticated than that found in certain of the other "speech" thinkers, e.g., F. Ebner, F. Rosenzweig, E. Rosenstock-Huessy. On these philosophers see Harold Stahmer, *Speak That I May See Thee* (New York, 1968).

27. See Buber's discussion of the episode of the Burning Bush and the events surrounding this revelation in his book *Moses* (New York, 1959).

28. For more on the philosophical issues being considered here, especially as they touch upon the question of religious experience see my "Language, Epistemology and Mystical Pluralism" in S. Katz, ed., *Mysticism and Philosophical Analysis* (New York, 1978), pp. 22–74.

29. *Eclipse of God*, p. 28.

30. *Origin and Meaning of Hasidism* (New York, 1960), pp. 228 ff.

31. *I and Thou*, p. 111.

32. Ibid., p. 111.

33. *BMM*, p. 69.

34. *BMM*, p. 68.

35. *BMM*, p. 68.

36. *Eclipse*, p. 118.

37. *Hasidism and Modern Man*, p. 228.

38. Ibid., p. 228. Emphasis added.

39. *BMM*, p. 15.

40. Buber's appeal to "religious experience" raises many interesting, if

difficult, philosophical issues. Internal to Buber's own thinking is what the appeal means given his own criticism of certain forms of appeal to mystical experience. See, for example, Buber's discussion in Part II of *I and Thou*. For a relatively sympathetic exegesis of Buber's position, in particular with regard to this appeal to mystical experience, see Johannan Bloch's discussion of "Die Symbolfrage" in his *Die Aporie des Du* (Heidelberg, 1976). Space prevents discussing here all the philosophical issues relevant to this issue. Instead, I refer readers to my paper "The Logic and Language of Mystery," in *Christ, Faith and History*, S. Sykes and J. Clayton, eds. (Cambridge, 1972), pp. 239–262. Readers should also consult the newer study by Roger Moser, *Gotteserfahrung bei Martin Buber* (Heidelberg, 1978). Moser's study, however, is weak in its handling of certain important aspects dealing with just this question of Buber's mysticism. It also lacks a highly developed critical sense.

41. For more on this mediated aspect of mystical and religious experience see my essay referred to in note 28 above and my essay on "The Conservative Character of Mystical Experience" in S. Katz, ed., *Mysticism and Religious Traditions* (New York, 1983). See the other essays in this volume as well. For additional aspects of Buber's treatment of mysticism see James Walters, "Martin Buber's Philosophy of Relationality and Mysticism," in *Encounter: Creative Theological Scholarship*, Vol. 39 (Spring, 1978), pp. 189–201; William Kaufman, "The Mysticism of Martin Buber," in *Judaism*, Vol. 27 (Spring, 1978), pp. 175–183; and Hugo Bergman, "Martin Buber and Mysticism," in *The Philosophy of Martin Buber*, pp. 297–308.

42. Buber attempts to clarify his meaning here by drawing an analogy, which he recognizes is weak, between the mystical experience that establishes the unity of God and the unity of the poet known to us through his many poems. He writes: "I will now use a *gauche* comparison, since I know no right one.

"When we really understand a poem, all we know of the poet is what we learn of him in the Poem—no biographical wisdom is of value for the pure understanding of what is to be understood: the *I* which approaches us is the subject of this single poem. But when we read other poems by the poet in the same true way their subjects combine in all their multiplicity, completing and confirming one another to form the one polyphony of the person's existence" (*BMM*, p. 15). This comparison, however, is not only weak but in fact helps make one of the essential points of my approach to the problems under consideration, namely, that, in contradistinction to Buber's claim, *embodied* existence seems essential to the knowing of an Other when this Other is a person. That is to say, we know the *I* of the poet because the poet is embodied, has a memory, and is locatable in space-time, etc., as well. It is easy to overlook, or forget, these "trivial" facts about the poet when we seek some "higher" poetic truth, but they cannot really be forgotten if we are to arrive at a full coherent, defensible account of the unity of the being of the poet. Now in the case of God, by analogy, we of course do not require *embodied* existence or material predication, but we do require some intelligible form of linguistic usage, some reasonable form of non-material predication, if the term "God," and related terms such as *Eternal Thou* and the like, are to find significant employment in our—and Buber's—dialogical vocabulary.

43. *Israel and the World*, p. 133.

44. This is Buber's own term, used on page 133 of *Israel and the World.*

45. Buber's interpretation of the Exodus-Sinai event is given in his *Moses* (New York, 1958).

46. For Buber's analysis of the Prophets see his *The Prophetic Faith* (New York, 1949) and several of his essays in *Pointing the Way* (New York, 1957) and *Israel and the World*. For criticism see the articles by Nahum Glatzer, James Muilenberg and Jacob Taubes in *The Philosophy of Martin Buber* volume.

47. Buber's understanding of the relation between Judaism and Christianity and more particularly of the difference between the religion of Jesus and the religion of Paul and the Church is set out in his *Two Types of Faith* (London, 1951). His typology has been subjected to penetrating critiques by Emil Brunner and more particularly by Hans Urs von Balthasar in *The Philosophy of Martin Buber* volume.

48. Buber's presentation of Hasidism is found in a series of studies and translations. For details and a thorough analysis see my essay "Martin Buber's Misuse of Hasidic Sources" in this volume.

49. Buber's own understanding of the "History of the Dialogical Principle" is found in his "Afterward" to the new edition of *Between Man and Man* (New York, 1955).

50. Jacob Taubes closes his discussion of "Buber and Philosophy of History" with this salient observation: "The ecstatic moments of human life have to be judged whether they are closed in themselves or whether they carry consequences creating social time and social space, dividing the periods of history into a before and after." *The Philosophy of Martin Buber* volume, p. 468. For some additional valuable observations on these aspects of Buber's outlook see Nahum Glatzer's "Aspects of Martin Buber's Thought," *Modern Judaism*, Vol. 1, No. 1 (May, 1981), pp. 1–16. By comparison, the recent exegesis of Buber's view of historical movements presented by Alexander Kohanski, *Martin Buber's Philosophy of Interhuman Relation* (Rutherford, New Jersey, 1982), pp. 166–198, lacks all critical distance.

MARTIN BUBER'S MISUSE OF HASIDIC SOURCES

I. INTRODUCTION

Martin Buber is, without doubt, the world's best known interpreter of Hasidism, the mass Jewish religious folk-movement of Eastern Europe. It was he who almost single-handedly took this parochial Jewish possession and made it part of the more general religious consciousness of the Jewish and non-Jewish world alike. Over a span of more than 60 years Buber labored, through a series of translations and original studies, to discover and to transmit Hasidism's inner meaning and significance to the modern world. Yet for all of his efforts and devotion his interpretation of this phenomenon is not without its serious difficulties, difficulties which arise in large part because of Buber's method of analyzing the original Hasidic sources. Because of the importance of this essential hermeneutical issue I would like to explore its implications in more detail in this essay.

To help organize the discussion I propose that we consider four critical theses in the analysis that follows.

1. Buber's fundamental decision to choose the corpus of Hasidic tales as the primary data for his Hasidic investigations is based on his own *dialogical* philosophical concerns rather than on the nature of Hasidism or the character of the available Hasidic evidence. This exegetical element colors every aspect of his study of Hasidism.

2. Buber's reliance on the Hasidic tales to the complete exclusion of Hasidic theoretical texts does not reflect the actual historic-theological situation operative in the Hasidic community and results in a serious distortion in the presentation of Hasidism.

3. In addition to his basic decision to work primarily from the Hasidic tales, Buber's method(s) (and goal) of interpretation of this material is highly idiosyncratic and provides both much of the appeal of his work as well as much of its abiding confusion. A set of sophisticated interpretive principles and methodological presuppositions underlie Buber's analytic essays and his retelling of the Hasidic tales, though it is not always easy to discern what these are. We shall attempt to make these methodological guidelines explicit, showing why they tend to obfuscate rather than illuminate the nature of Hasidism.

4. Having decided, for poor reasons, to concentrate on the tales as his primary source of data for his reconstruction of Hasidism, Buber then uses the legendary material in arbitrary and questionable ways, resulting in a still further distortion of what the tales themselves reflect of the Hasidic *Weltanschauung*.

The reason for this severe critique of Buber's work on Hasidism and Hasidic sources is to establish Buber's unreliability as a guide to this movement and to clear the stage for a new investigation, some outlines of which I shall suggest,[1] of these materials and hence of the origin and meaning of Hasidism.[2]

II. THE PRIORITY OF LEGENDS

The clue that furnishes our methodological review with its starting point is the well-known fact that Buber's most important contribution to the study of Hasidism lies in his retelling of the Hasidic tales that have been passed on from one generation to another. These tell of the simple piety as well as the great and miraculous deeds of the Hasidic Zaddikim (leaders), and of the social interaction of the Hasidic communities which revolved around them. Both in practice and in theory Buber was committed to the Hasidic legends as the most genuine source of Hasidic truth and also as the most satisfying and authentic way of bringing this truth to the larger non-Hasidic world. In the second earliest of his collections of Hasidic material, *Die Legende des Baalschem*[3] (the earliest being *Die Geschichten des Rabbi Nachman* (1906)),[4] Buber wrote: "The Hasidic legend is the body of the teaching, its messenger, its mark along the way of the world."[5] He then went on to talk about the content of this legendary material and his own approach to it:

The life about which we shall learn here is not what one ordinarily calls the real life. I do not report the development and decline of the sect; nor do I describe its customs. I only desire to communicate the relation to God and the world that these men intended, willed, and sought to live. I also do not enumerate the dates and facts which make up the biography of the Baal Shem. I build up his life out of his legends which contain the dream and the longing of a people.[6]

Buber had not the disinterested manner of the academic; he was not preoccupied with what we would call "facts," nor was he concerned with all the minute addenda of scholarship—sources, dates, footnotes and the like. He was intent on one thing only and that was to refashion and retell the legendary material in such a way that it exposed its claimed inner power to a non-Hasidic world. It must be remarked in passing that it is undoubtedly true that Buber identified what constituted the essential force of Hasidism differently throughout his life, and that at each stage in his own philosophical development Hasidism underwent a parallel alternation. Nevertheless, although the content of Buber's message, and with it the content of Buber's Hasidism, underwent a variety of evolutionary changes, the object of Buber's labors never varied; according to his lights, Buber was intent on spreading the "essence" of Hasidism in the world at large.

In 1940 Buber wrote an essay entitled "The Beginnings of Hasidism"[7] in which he began the enterprise of trying to construct a more systematic account of what Hasidism was, where it fitted into the totality of contemporary life, and what its importance was for contemporary man. In this essay, as in his earliest work, he reaffirmed as his methodological starting point the priority of the legendary material in trying to come to an understanding of Hasidism.

Hasidism in the first instance is not a category of teaching but one of life, our chief source of knowledge of Hasidism is its legends, and only after them comes its theoretical literature. The latter is the commentary, the former the text, even though a text that has been handed down in a state of extreme corruption, one that is incapable of being restored in its purity. It is foolish to protest that the legend does not convey to us the reality of Hasidic life. Naturally, the legend is no chronicle, but it is truer than the chronicle for those who know how to read it. One cannot reconstruct from it, certainly, the factual course of events. But despite its corruption, one can perceive in it the life-element in which the events were consummated, the element that received them and with naive enthusiasm told them and told them again until they became legend.[8]

The primacy given the legendary sources is far and away Buber's most essential procedural decision and it is not at all surprising that everything else in Buber's rendering of the Hasidic message flows from it. In a complex internal dialectic everything in Buber's presentation of Hasidism leads to this judgment and everything leads away from it. And yet, interestingly, as will emerge from our study, the absolute pre-eminence of the legendary material over other available information is itself the product of yet undiscussed factors in Buber's conception of how things in the world are, or at least ought to be. In order to elicit these Buberian presuppositions, however, we must pay close attention to what Buber's commitment to legend entails.

III. MYTH AND LEGEND

To appreciate Buber's reasons for according pride of place to the legendary material in his reconstruction of the Hasidic *Weltanschauung* we must enter into Buber's complex analysis of the relation that he contends obtains between myth and positive religion. From the very beginning of his philosophical career Buber considered myth the most valuable source in ascertaining the energizing impulses that create and maintain a specific religious community. He argued for this proposition in the Introduction to his early book on the Baal Shem Tov.

All positive religion rests on an enormous simplification of the manifold and wildly engulfing forces that invade us: it is the subduing of the fullness of existence. All myth, in contrast, is the expression of the fullness of existence, its image, its sign; it drinks incessantly from the gushing fountains of life. Hence religion fights myth where it cannot absorb and incorporate it. The history of the Jewish religion is in great part the history of its fight against myth.

> It is strange and wonderful to observe how in this battle religion ever again wins the apparent victory, myth ever again wins the real one.[9]

Fifty years later, in *Hasidism and Modern Man*, he repeated the same theme, though in a less romantic idiom.

> I cannot concur with the postulate of the hour—to demythologize religion. For myth is not the subsequent clothing of a truth of faith; it is the unarbitrary testimony of the image-making vision and the image-making memory, and the conceptual cannot be refined out of it. No sermonic teaching can replace the myth.[10]

Myth is the elemental and essential data for those who would fathom and reveal the essence of religious phenomena, and in particular, for those who would make Hasidism their own. This is the one constant in Buber's shifting and evolving interpretation of religion in general and of Hasidism in particular, and the reason the tales always remain hermeneutically primary.

To grasp fully the significance of this doctrine for Buber's rendering of Hasidism we must follow his exegesis of the argument a little further. In his early work on the Baal Shem he tells us that myth undergoes a transformational process out of which "legend" is generated. "Myth," in its pristine character, has an "undifferentiated ontic character." I confess to both my unease with such phrases as "undifferentiated ontic character" and to my inability to deconstruct completely Buber's discussion of the mechanics whereby "myth" generates "legend." I shall not, therefore, try to reproduce it in inadequate and obscure paraphrase, but quote Buber's own account:

> The legend is the myth of the calling. In it the original personality of myth is divided. In pure myth there is no division of essential being. It knows multiplicity but not duality. Even the hero only stands on another rung than that of the god, not over against him: they are not the I and the Thou. The hero has a mission but not a call. He ascends but he does not become transformed. The god of pure myth does not call, he begets; he sends forth

the one whom he begets, the hero. The god of one legend calls forth the son of man—the prophet, the holy man.

The legend is the myth of I and Thou, of one caller and the called, the finite which enters into the infinite and the infinite which has need of the finite.[11]

Apparently, Buber was himself dissatisfied with the imprecision of what he had written in *Die Legende des Baalschem* about myth and legend, and in the foreword to *Der Grosse Maggid und seine Nachfolge* (1921) he tried to clarify his position by introducing a still further process into the stages of the operation, so that now there were three elements: (a) "myth," (b) "saga," (c) "legend." In the discussion surrounding this new analysis Buber does seem to have made a genuine advance and, if the view presented is still not free of ambiguity, it is at least intelligible. "Myth" is now construed as an image of reality which places man and God on the same ontic level. "Saga" is the first step in the growth of man's awareness that God and man are not alike categorically, but have differing ontological status. "Legend," in the new script, is read as the final and finished form of the evolution of man's apprehension of his distinctiveness and distance from God. According to this analysis, in "legendary" material man has become cognizant of the relative status of God and man, and the gulf which separates them; yet "legend" also informs that communication and dialogue between God and man is possible. "Legend" is now (1921) reconstituted and discussed in near-dialogical terms.[12] Describing Jewish "legend" in the Preface to *Der Grosse Maggid*, Buber went so far as to say that it was: "wholly based on the two-directional relation of human I and divine Thou, on reciprocity, on the meeting."[13] In other words, "legend" is now seen as the embodied residual remembrance of the meeting of God and man.

Using this proto-dialogical paradigm of "legend" as his basis, Buber progressively increased the dialogical nature of "legend" as his own thought moved increasingly towards *I and Thou*. Whether "legend" is in actual fact the residue of Buberian-style encounter between an *I* and a *Thou* need not concern us at this point; what matters here is that Buber thought it was.

Insofar as Buber "found" a remarkable confluence between his "independent" analysis of "legend," his maturing dialogical philosophy, and his explanatory reconstructions of Hasidism, he held fast to his initial intuition to accord "legends" priority in his Hasidic work. He now had what he considered an analytic exposition of "legend" that was suitably dialogical, and which, because of the undeniable presence of legendary material in Hasidism, he viewed as supporting his thesis that Hasidism was an embodiment of an *I–Thou* relation.

IV. THEORETICAL HASIDIC LITERATURE

Buber translated his theoretical endorsement of "myth" and "legend" into practice in his Hasidic exegesis. So dominant is the legendary material in his account of Hasidism, and so unquestioned is his pre-eminence as the prophet of Hasidism to the non-Hasidic world, that most people are not even aware that there exists another fundamental source of information about the Hasidic movement: their theoretical (mystical-kabbalistic-halachic) works.[14] Buber tries to ignore this material altogether, and where he does very occasionally mention it it is only to disparage its importance. Yet this approach cannot be allowed to go unchallenged, because this theoretical corpus is of the most fundamental significance in trying to excavate the true nature of Hasidism both as a teaching and as a form of life.

The first theoretical Hasidic writings had already begun to appear in manuscript form during the lifetime of the Maggid of Mezritsch (c. 1700–1772) and the first theoretical book appeared in printed form in 1780, twenty years after the death of the Baal Shem Tov (1700–1760) and eight years after the death of his successor, the Maggid of Mezritsch. This first printed Hasidic volume, the *Toledoth Yaacov Yosef*, was the work of Hasidism's greatest intellectual and most ardent polemicist, R. Yaacov Yosef of Polnoye. Yaacov Yosef was the Baal Shem Tov's confidential secretary and lieutenant during his lifetime, and this text is the greatest single collection of the actual teachings of the Baal Shem Tov. Soon after, four volumes of the "theoretical" teachings of the Maggid were printed by his disciples, including the most important record of his thought, *Maggid Devarav La'ya'akov*, followed by three more "theoretical" works by Yaacov Yosef himself. These first efforts were soon followed by literally hundreds of additional theoretical writings. During the first half century of Hasidism's existence, 1760–1810 (dated from the death of the Baal Shem Tov), that period during which it rose from obscurity to become the dominant force among Eastern European Jewry, the entire printed corpus of Hasidic literature consisted only of theoretical works. It is true that a body of Hasidic legends existed in oral form in the 1780s and 1790s, e.g., those in the works *Degel Machne Ephraim* and *Keter Shem Tov*, but it is a historical, as well as a methodological-philosophical, error to think that the legendary compositions and compilations were, or are, either the most voluminous or the most important Hasidic sources. The record shows that the first printed collection of tales only began to circulate as late as 1814–1815, more than 50 years after the death of the Baal Shem Tov and after Hasidism had established its ascendancy in the Jewish community. This first collection, the *Shivche Ha-Besht*, dealt with traditions concerning the Baal Shem Tov and it was followed later in the same year (1815) by a collection of tales about the Maggid of Mezritsch and by the first edition of R. Nahman of Bratzslav's *Sippurei ha-Ma'asiyyot*. From there the literature continued to expand, the greatest body of Hasidic stories being published between 1880 and 1910.[15]

Given the details of the relative ancestry of the theoretical and legendary material one must ask why Buber felt it necessary to denigrate and disregard the former so completely. In addition to his presuppositions regarding myth and legend already reviewed, Buber's answer is given in terms of a basic discontinuity he claims exists between Hasidism and the earlier forms of Jewish mysticism. Whereas Lurianism[16] and Sabbatianism[17] were both essentially gnostic teachings, Hasidism, according to Buber, is not. In his view Hasidism rejects gnosis in favor of a dialogical pansacramentalism whose character is captured only in the legendary material, whereas, by comparison, the theoretical literature remained tied to the gnostic form and content of the earlier speculative theology. According to Buber Hasidism "breaks with the basic principles of Kabbala."[18] As compared to Kabbala "what Hasidism has to tell of its central men . . . is . . . almost entirely of a wholly other existence then that of kabbalism;"[19] and again: "The protest against the Kabbala, unexpressed yet strong in its factuality, announces itself in twofold fashion in Hasidism. The one protest is directed against the schematization of the mystery . . . The other Hasidic protest against the Kabbala turns against the magicizing of the mystery . . . in its teaching Hasidism at its periphery preserves but at its center neglects the Kabbalistic-gnostic schemata."[20] As a consequence of this claimed disjunction Buber contends that the theoretical literature, still Kabbalistic as it is, fails to capture the revolutionary substance of the Besht's[21] teachings and gives the erroneous impression that the radical discontinuity Buber is arguing for does not actually exist. Buber can thus be seen to place especially strong emphasis on the contended conservatism[22] of the theoretical literature in justifying his exclusive preference for the legendary sources.

There is much that needs to be said about this argument and we shall come back to it in a moment. But first, I should like to introduce a general comment about the comparative nature of the theoretical and legendary material, which I think goes further towards explaining Buber's preference for the legendary sources than does his own discontinuity thesis. In its original state (that is, prior to Buber's editorship and allowing for some skillful editorial activity on the part of the original editor-compilers of the legendary collections) the meaning of many if not most tales as well as the meaning of the whole body of legendary material is obscure and ambiguous. A particular tale can "mean" many things and can be used to "prove" many alternative, even completely opposing views. Thus one can, as Buber did, impress one's own set of interpretive canons and one's own specific message on the material seemingly without fear of being contradicted.

The fact is that the tales *need* unpacking; they are not self-revealing, and a dialogical explanation can be made to fit, given suitable modifications, as well as most others. On the other hand, the theoretical material is relatively clear both in terms of style and content. Of course, like all mystical literatures, it exhibits a specific kind of opaqueness and esotericism, but this is an expected feature of mystical writings and is quite different from the sort of ambiguity that one finds in the legendary material. The plain and systematically self-explanatory meaning of the theoretical texts in terms of its own highly developed system of kabbalistic theory, language, and symbols leaves comparatively little latitude for the interpreter. The systematic direction of the texts is visible, within the limits of kabbalistic clarity, and one has to work within the parameters of the expressed technical system, restrained by the nature of the material from too free an exegesis. Buber's imagination was thus regulated and constrained by the theoretical data; a dialogical analysis could not easily be read into and out of the material. This aspect of the issue comes decisively to the fore at certain points, especially when Buber tries to establish the discontinuity between Hasidism and Lurianism. We defer further comment until examining the ramifications of the matter further.

Let us now scrutinize the actual argument that Buber advances regarding the separation of Hasidic and Lurianic mysticism and the corresponding polarity of Hasidic myth and theory which is claimed to mirror it. We begin by noting that this thesis held with ever-increasing passion by Buber after 1920, is significantly at odds with Buber's own view as presented in his earlier Hasidic products. When he was a younger man and still a self-avowed mystic, his explanation of the relationship between Hasidism and Kabbalism not only did not insist on a radical bifurcation between two forms of Jewish mystical life but actually located the essence of Hasidism in its having taken the mythic elements of the Kabbalah and made them "the possession of the people."[23] It is also significant that in his early efforts Buber does not argue that there is any difference in outlook and meaning between the theoretical literature and the legends. Instead he stresses their unity: "The Hasidic *writings* have given us their teachings and their legends."[24] Rather than disunity we are told "The Hasidic legend is the body of the teaching theory, its messenger, its mark along the world."[25] Of equal interest is Buber's explanation in his *Tales of Rabbi Nachman* (1906) of the outlook of Nachman of Bratzlav towards his death and the purpose it would serve. Buber explains it not by reference to the abundant legendary material surrounding this event, but as follows:

It was Rabbi Nachman's belief, *a result of the doctrine of souls that he took over from Luria and further developed*, that . . . a great band of souls were bound to the place of their death and could not ascend until a soul came to them with the power to lift them. He [Nachman] felt in himself the summons to redeem the waiting ones.[26]

The importance of this reflection lies in its clear recognition that the actions of the Zaddikim are intelligible only through recourse to the theoretical literature of Hasidism and its spiritual predecessors. Buber would never have allowed for such dependence in his later works. Rather, in his post-World War I writings, as his own position became more and more dialogical and he became increasingly suspicious of "gnosticism" and "mysticism," he continually widened the breach between what he saw as creative in Hasidism from what he saw as basic in earlier Jewish mystical movements.

On the still broader critical plane Buber's carefully drawn bifurcation and the resultant rejection of the theoretical literature which follows from it is inaccurate. Buber's own early ventures, before *I and Thou*, Hasidism's self-understanding (which we shall examine shortly), and the best modern scholarship[27] all suggest that this judgment cannot be sustained. All three sources indicate that Buber's distinction between the "gnosis" of Kabbalah and the "devotio" of Hasidism is a consequence neither of the study of the theoretical nor of the legendary material but only of Buber's highly irregular use of both. The legendary output "supports" Buber's views only after he has "edited" it. It is of the utmost importance to appreciate that Buber offers no detailed historical or philosophical rebuttal of the theoretical material, dismissing it solely on the undefended premise that it is gnostic and Hasidism is not. Such cavalier treatment, however, is not enough to establish Buber's conclusion regarding the disjunction between Kabbalah and the Besht and between the theoretical and legendary material, as I shall show.

There is a second, related argument that Buber employs to support his revisionism that needs to be introduced at this point.

Whereas Kabbalah is a gnostic teaching, Buber asserts that Hasidism is not a teaching at all:

What constitutes the uniqueness and the greatness of Hasidism is not a teaching, but a mode of life, a mode of life that shapes a community and that is consonant with community by its very nature.[28]

This view of Hasidism rests essentially on Buber's vision of the Baal Shem Tov, whom he describes as follows:

The Baal Shem did not have new theological concepts to impart . . . the Baal Shem belongs to those central figures of the history of religion whose effect on others has arisen through the fact that they *lived* in a certain way. These men did not proceed *from* a teaching, but moved *to* a teaching, in such a way that their life worked as a teaching, as a teaching not yet grasped in words.[29]

Most significantly, Buber adds:

Of the words of the Baal Shem that are known to us, in so far as we may regard them as faithfully handed down to us, it is not the objective content that may be detached from them that is significant, but their character of pointing to a life.[30]

Buber thus insists that the Baal Shem had no doctrine and that, when among his disciples, Hasidic teaching did emerge and was not a distortion of the original voice (I am unsure how one judges this), it represented only the formal organizing of that "living truth" which the Baal Shem Tov's life manifested and is not to be confused with the creation of yet another gnostic system.

This presentation unfortunately is not convincing. We must seriously question Buber's portrayal of the Baal Shem Tov and consequently of Hasidism "as a mode of life, not a teaching." The Baal Shem Tov was undoubtedly a remarkable individual, but it is disengenuous for Buber to represent him as a figure without a "message." That his "personality" was indissolubly intertwined with his "message" to those who knew him is obviously true, but it is erroneous to think that one can understand either the Baal Shem

Tov or the Hasidic movement while denying that the Baal Shem Tov had a teaching that he propounded and left to his disciples. Buber is here making another basic distinction, in this case a division between the Besht's "life" and "teaching," that is indefensible.[31] The Besht influenced those around him by the unity of his life and teaching. To separate the two is artificially to segment the living reality the Besht presented; a reality whose essence was in the lived concreteness of what he taught. We can no more re-present the Besht by subordinating his "teaching" than we can by subordinating his "life." The term "life," as Buber uses it, is as much an abstraction, and a commentary, when trying to understand the Besht as is "teaching" or "theory."

Here we need to engage a larger interpretive issue in the study of the history of religions that Buber's comments on the separation of the Besht's "life" and "teachings" raise. This claim for the Besht is not unique in the world's religious literature. It has been made for great religious figures ranging from Abraham and Moses, through Jesus and Mohammed, up to and including the Besht and Ramakrishna. As such it requires a closer examination, a dismantling that illuminates the subject in its totality as well as the particular claims being made for the Founder of Hasidism.

To begin in unraveling the "life" of the Besht, as with other religious giants, one needs to consider not only, or even primarily, psychological or personal-subjective factors, but also, and still more fundamentally, the ontological character of the "problematic" presented by such singular human beings. All such individuals reflect ontic concerns, and this in many ways, and come with a "solution" to a quite specific ontological-metaphysical diagnosis of reality.

First, one must recognize the peculiar historical-temporal dimension(s) of such figures. Such personalities become important not as individuals *per se* but rather as the medium of some more universal teaching: the instrument for the revelation of more general truths. Thus the particulars of their life become the tokens of a larger truth. Then again, such personages as the Besht, though rooted in a given temporal frame, speak atemporally; that is, they reveal truths that have no chronological limits and are regulative for all time. Thus, their "pastness" is never at issue. The historic modality is inappropriate. The Besht points to a "new heaven, new earth" that is always both present and absent, until its final messianic completion. Yet, at the same time he *shows* the reality of this nontemporal norm in history, hence making its reality present for all who would follow—while guaranteeing its presence for all future followers. Precisely this quality of liberating us from our particular temporal parameters is an essential aspect of a life such as that of the Besht. That is, it suggests original, existentially and metaphysically energizing concerns that overreach our own day-to-day context with its narrow drudgeries; it forces us to consider ourselves in a wider field, our existence in larger terms. The more significant the life of the religious founder or "hero," the more we are challenged; the more luminous the "life" the more profound the agenda of the community of believers. A "life" such as the Besht's thus can be seen as metaphysically and existentially fecund.

Secondly, an individual such as the Besht provides a cosmological-metaphysical mapping of the order of things. He shows us how things are; where we are in the scheme of things; what is before and what after; what is expected of us; how we can get from where we are to where we want to go; why we should want to get to where he wants us to go; what is above and what is below. That is, such teachers carry and convey "content" of a very high order. They explain, in a special though nonetheless meaningful way, how and why our experience, our life's journey, is the way it is. Still more, they provide an organizing principle for shaping our experience and ordering it into a cohesive whole—a partly epistemological role—to parallel the metaphysical and moral roles they occupy. In other words, the paradigmatic individual, the Besht, gives us one way, among many (hence the many, different, and differing paradigmatic individuals and traditions), to make sense of our lives and our world, and this on many levels. He provides what we can call conceptual coherence; a quite particular mapping of the nature of the interrelationship existing among entities in space and nature and beyond. Where the "message" of the teacher fails to provide an adequately fertile schemata it soon loses its coherence and hence its power of influence. If the world, and the problematics of living, no longer find adequate "explanation" and account through a given model the model passes away or becomes, at best, anachronistic, an archaic remnant. It is precisely this which Buber claims has *not* happened to the "message" of the Besht.

This ontological-cosmological-moral content needs to be emphasized because of Buber's sharp denial of just this side of the Besht's "life." In this respect Buber's treatment is analogous, and perhaps derivative, from Max Weber's[32] analysis of charismatic leadership. Weber's reflections on religion, while suggestive in their generality, are, unfortunately, particularly unsound on just this much-praised, much-used notion of charisma. Persons such as the Besht are not influential merely by force of personality, by gifts of self that transcend context and content. Though much could and needs to be said on this point, i.e., on the entire essential rubric of charisma and charismatic leadership in religious communities, I will make only one fundamental objection, and that by way of an example: the Baal Shem Tov would not have been found charismatic by Apaches, nor Geronimo by Eastern European Jews. The Buddha would have been unintelligible to Jews—and hardly "charismatic," while Moses would hardly carry the day in a Zen community. There are many topics here that need careful sorting out, but this must wait for another occasion. Rather I draw out the point of these examples, of the argument that lies behind them, explicitly: charismatic leaders are made charismatic by context and content, doctrine and insight, as much as, or more so, than by their "style"[33] or their "life," in Buber's sense. Another way of putting this conclusion is to recognize that the paradigmatic individual intends to be understood[34] by the audience addressed. Thus, there must exist a common linguistic and nonlinguistic backdrop to which both appeal, usually implicitly taking it for granted, which provides the grounds for the intelligibility of the model's utterances and behavior. For example, the Besht and his audience assume or presuppose the shared traditional world of the rabbinic heritage as well as of at least a "common man's" understanding of Lurianic Kabbalah as it has become a common possession of Eastern European Jewry as a consequence of the work of numerous scholars and more popular preachers and teachers. To attempt either to extract the paradigmatic individual, in this case the Besht, from this setting or to ignore it in one way or another makes the transaction between the master and the faithful unintelligible. Insofar as he intended, as he undoubtedly did, to teach, explain, reveal, enlighten, his "life" cannot be analyzed in subjective, or in Buber's phrase, "living" ways. One could, I venture, go so far as to argue that without the ontological theory, the context, the inherited "language game," and the like, the biographical events of the archetypal journey would be irrelevant beyond themselves.

Of course the Besht's concrete reality has a different quality than that of a text, a quality that provides existential confirmation of what would otherwise be mere abstractions. That is to say, he brings together in a lived, and hence livable, way the theory and practice, the ideal and the real. He closes the gap between normative "ought" and practical "is." He displays the possibility of instantiating the norm and making present the transcendent. He provides new or renewed *authentic possibilities* for the community of the faithful. His evocative power lies precisely in his "living in two worlds," his channeling of insights from one realm to another, usually from the "higher" to the "lower" worlds. In addition, in the case of the Besht the belief in his magical powers, another sign of Divine Grace, is of *major* importance.[35] But all this and more is not a matter of personality or of a life vaguely described as having been "lived in a certain way," but of action that instantiates specific moral and metaphysical imperatives, and without which it makes no sense at all. We need to put back together the two, actually inseparable, sides of the Besht's wholeness that Buber has torn asunder.[36]

With this hermeneutical schema in place we can assert with confidence, and in contradistinction to Buber, that it should be clearly appreciated that in the reality of the Besht's circle, when the Besht told a parable or a tale, it was understood *only* because of the general mystical pattern of thought and language which he and his disciples shared. Without this theoretical framework the tales Buber so highly prized would lose their point. Furthermore, and this cannot be emphasized too strongly, the Besht's disciples came to join him *not* because he was an effective storyteller or even a Jewish Aesop. They came to him and stayed with him, as their testimonies show, because he possessed enormous magical and mystical knowledge through which he could influence the cosmic process. As the greatest of his disciples, the Maggid of Mezritsch, testified, the Besht showed him "great unifications,"[37] i.e., great acts of *Tikkun* (mystical-kabbalistic unifications). Of course, this knowledge worked itself out in the Besht's life—as Buber said, "he lived in a certain way"—but it would be extraordinary if he did not. What sort of schizophrenia would be required for such profound kabbalistic sympathies not to manifest themselves in one's life? But it is only the teaching that allows us to understand the basis of this new way of living.

Furthermore, all the available records, both theoretical and legendary, depict the Baal Shem Tov as a kabbalist. An important tradition to remember about the Baal Shem is that he is said to have possessed and treasured various kabbalistic manuscripts, especially those of one Rabbi Adam Baal Shem.[38] Every early biography of the Baal Shem, including and especially the *Shivchei ha-Besht*, which Buber would acknowledge as legendary material, and which he draws on very heavily in his own edited version, yields a portrayal of the Baal Shem Tov as one who, through his knowledge of "secret things," i.e., the gnostic kabbalistic practices Buber so abhors, brought about various miraculous deeds and healings, as well as heavenly ascensions and powers in the world above. Consider, as one example of a very large set of parallel material, the following tale which tells of the Besht's miraculous powers:

The Besht said to [Rabbi Jehiel Mikhel]: "Return home in peace. You will find your wife in difficult labor surrounded by many women. Send them out of your home. Whisper in her ear what I taught you, and you will have a baby boy. Mazel Tov." And so it was. He arrived home two hours before nightfall. He did as the Besht had ordered him and she gave birth to a baby boy. This boy was Rabbi Joseph of Yampol.[39]

As an instance of his mystical ascensions and his power in the worlds above, consider this interesting tale:

There was a man, one of the Besht's followers, who lived in a village. The rabbi had favored him in various ways, and he used to stay with the Besht during the Days of Awe. Once when he came to the rabbi, the rabbi turned his face away. It surprised him, and he assumed that perhaps he was either preoccupied thinking about great matters or that he was angry with him. After an hour he entered the Besht's room once more, and again the Besht turned his face away from his. He did this three times, and the man became very depressed. Certainly it was not an empty matter. It was unusual because before the Besht had always favored him in various ways.

The man went to the rabbi, our teacher, Gershon of Kuty, and told him the whole story. The rabbi, our teacher and rabbi, Gershon, went to his brother-in-law, the Besht, and talked with him: "Why do you reject him when he has not committed any evil and all his actions are proper?"

He answered him: "Why do you want me to become involved with the people and befriend them and talk with them? I do not want it."

When this man realized that there was no solution, he went to the rabbi, our teacher and rabbi, Gershon, and cried from his bitter and broken heart: "I know that this is not an empty matter. I have no life. I will not be able to bear it much longer."

The rabbi, our rabbi and teacher, Gershon, went to the rabbi a second time, and he said that it was actually a matter of life and death. He should reveal to him what it was all about.

Then the Besht answered that the sin of adultery was written on his forehead.

The man argued that it was not true, and that he had been continent with his wife for more than sixteen years. How was it possible?

The rabbi, our teacher and rabbi, Gershon, told the Besht that it was up to him to look into the matter. "I cannot perceive it. Since you are the only one who knows it, the sin is not a physical one but is rather an intangible matter."

The Besht said to him that on Friday, Sabbath Eve, in the Minhah prayer, which is the time for the ascension of the soul to the upper palaces, he would look into it. When the Besht's soul ascended to the palace of the *tosaphists,* he did not find any impression of the sin that the man had committed. Then he ascended up to the *Rambam's* palace, and there he found the man's sin impressed. The matter was that he had imposed upon himself abstinence from sexual relations with his wife, and according to the opinion of the *Rambam* it was as if he said: "You are like my mother to me." The person who takes the vow of abstinence towards his wife is forbidden to touch her jewelry. When he had needed money for a wedding, he had taken his wife's jewelry and pawned it. Thus he had enjoyed her and he had broken his vow. According to the opinion of the *Rambam* it was as if he had committed adultery with a married woman. The rabbi argued with the *Rambam* (and I heard that he called to the *Rif* and the *Rosh* who argued with him also). Then the *Rambam* conceded to them and the sin was erased. Since then there is not any hint of the matter in the *Rambam's* book.[40]

This material is *typical*, it must be emphasized, in the corpus of early Hasidic tales about the Besht. They are of the essence of the matter.[41]

There is also a strong connection between the Baal Shem Tov and messianism. In one of the few authentic letters of the Besht, written to his brother-in-law in Jerusalem, he narrates the following episode. Once, on the first day of Rosh Hashanah, the Besht had a mystical experience (he referred to it as a "lifting of the soul"), and his soul entered the palace of the Messiah. There he asked the Messiah, "Master, when wilt thou appear on earth?" and the Messiah answered: "This shall be a sign unto thee: when thy wisdom shall become known throughout the world, and the fountains of thy wisdom shall be poured forth, [imparting to others] what I taught you to apprehend, when all other men shall have the power to perform contemplative unifications and ascents [of the soul] like you, then shall all the shells of impurity disappear, and the time of great favor and salvation shall arrive."[42]

However one evaluates this letter it most certainly felt the residue of the Sabbatian and Frankist theology as well as classical Kabbalah.[43] We should not fail to appreciate the technical kabbalistic ideas central to the substance of the letter, and said to be required for the eventual spread of Hasidism and its concommitant, the coming of the Messiah, e.g., the doctrines of "contemplative unifications" (*yihudim*), which is a formal kabbalistic meditation based on the proper use of certain divine names, and again of "ascents of the soul" (*aliyot neshamah*), and the doctrine of the "shells of impurity" (*kelipot*), which is one of the cardinal dogmas of the kabbalistic school.[44] In addition, as in kabbalism, there is a very highly developed magical tradition in Hasidism that traces itself directly to the Besht.[45] Still further support of the importance of the theoretical tradition in Hasidism is found in that both the prayerbook and the form of Hasidic prayer followed the practices established by Isaac Luria. Nor should we forget the telling but little-known detail that the author of Besht's own prayerbook, which the Besht treated with a mystical reverence, was a known Sabbatian. These elements are all the more salient in properly evaluating Hasidism in that prayer is *the* pre-eminent "purely" religious activity in the

Hasidic community; the recognition that it followed earlier and well-established kabbalistic patterns is richly suggestive.[46]

Finally, we should not forget that Baal Shem Tov is not a name but a title meaning "Master of the Good Name," i.e., one who knows how to use God's name in practical magic. There was an entire class[47] of such men of whom Israel ben Eliezer (the Besht) was only one, although he is the most famous. He was expected to perform deeds of practical magic, indeed this was his main source of livelihood, and his disciples placed much emphasis on his abilities in this sphere. Buber's description of this "title" begins on a sound historical understanding which recognizes this magical background. He writes:

Israel ben Eliezer of Mezbizh (Miedzyboz), called the Baal Shem Tov (1700–1760), the founder of Hasidism, was such a man. He first appears merely as one in a series of Baale Shem, of "Masters of the Name," who knew a Name of God that had magic force, were able to invoke it, and with this art of theirs helped and healed the men who came to them—manifestations of a form of magic which was absorbed by religion. The actual basis for their work was their ability to perceive intrinsic connections between things, connections which lay beyond the bounds of time and space (apparent only to what we usually call intuition) and their peculiar strengthening and consolidating influence on the soul-center of their fellowmen, which enabled this center to regenerate the body and the whole of life—an influence of which the so-called "suggestive powers" are nothing but a distortion. Certain aspects of Israel ben Eliezer's work constitute a continuation of the work of the Baale Shem.[48]

But, unable to acknowledge this magical tradition in its full historical potency he feels compelled to go on, in keeping with a certain romanticization found already in Dubnow[49] and certain Hasidic sources, to add:

[in the case of the Baal Shem Tov there is] one marked difference which even expresses itself in the change of the epithet "Baal Shem" to "Baal Shem Tov." This difference and what it signifies is unambiguously stressed in the legendary tradition.

In various versions we are told how either Rabbi Gershon, the Baal Shem's brother-in-law, who first despised him as an ignorant man but later became his faithful disciple, or one of the descendants of the Baal Shem, went to a great rabbi who lived far away—in Palestine or in Germany—and he told him about Rabbi Israel Baal Shem. "Baal Shem?" said the rabbi questioningly. "I don't know any such person." And in the case of the Baal Shem's brother-in-law, the rejection is more pronounced, for when Rabbi Gershon speaks of the Baal Shem as his teacher, he receives the reply: "Baal Shem? No, there is no teacher by that name." But when Rabbi Gershon quickly rights his first words by giving the full name "Baal Shem Tov," the rabbi he is visiting assumes an entirely different attitude. "Oh!" he exclaims. "The Baal Shem Tov! He, to be sure, is a very great teacher. Every morning I see him in the temple of paradise." The sage refuses to have anything to do with common miracle men, but the Baal Shem Tov—that is quite another matter, that is something new. The addition of one word altered the meaning and the character of the epithet. "Shem Tov" is the "Good Name." The Baal Shem Tov, the possessor of the Good Name, is a man who, because he is as he is, gains the confidence of his fellowmen. "Baal Shem Tov" as a general designation, refers to a man in whom the people have confidence, the confidant of the people. With this, the term ceases to designate a rather doubtful vocation and comes to apply to a reliable person and, at the same time, transforms what was, after all, a category of magic, into one religious in the truest sense of the word. For the term "Baal Shem Tov" signifies a man who lives with and for his fellowmen on the foundation of his relation to the divine.[50]

That the Baal Shem Tov was more than a simple magician is certainly true, but his magical powers were not marginal to his career and fame, nor to his "Name." For his disciples and contemporaries his magical skills were elemental aspects of his special theurgic powers and hence of his unique claims. Over and over the sources, written both by Hasidim and other contemporaries, refer to his magical and healing skills. For example, the *Shivchei ha-Besht* gave much evidence of the importance of amulets composed by the Besht.[51] Moreover, even the historical record itself needs to be put right. Gershom Scholem's correction of Buber's historiography is here apposite: "There is no distinction in the kabbalistic literature between the two terms *Baal Shem* and *Baal Shem Tov*. The title *Baal Shem* is to be found in the literature of practical kabbala before the appearance of the Baal Shem Tov, and actually so with regard to *Baalei Shem* of the 'despised' type, like R. Yoel Baal Shem and R. Benjamin Beinish HaCohen of Krotoszyn. In fact we have no trustworthy evidence of increasing spiritual development or, say, a new spiritual direction in the founder of Hasidism since his appearance as an unknown *Baal Shem*."[52]

When we compare Buber's anti-kabbalistic, anti-halachic, anti-magical and highly dialogical Besht to the image of the Besht that emerges from the original sources, including very definitely the legendary sources, there is little doubt that Buber's presentation is eccentric, forwarding a characterization of the Besht that is original primarily in its artificiality. This raises two parallel points. The first is that Buber's dichotomy between "theory" and "legend" in Hasidism perverts the unity of these two forms of Hasidic literature. The second is that the class of theoretical material should receive priority, though in a dialectical manner, over the legendary sources in trying to arrive at an accurate image of Hasidism. The position of pre-eminence the legends achieve in Buber's work is possible only as a consequence of his own arbitrary principles. What strikes one force fully on reading the source material relevant to the rise of Hasidism is how thoroughly it is infused with and committed, *both* in theory and in practice, or as Buber called it, "in life," to the theoretical kabbalistic-Hasidic material. To drive a wedge between "theoretical" and "legendary" Hasidism increasingly appears to be only an unwarranted Buberian prejudice.

The alternative approaches to Hasidism represented by according priority either to the theoretical or legendary sources hardly merit equal consideration. It is highly unsatisfactory to prefer legendary material of no definite shape or meaning, found in many different forms and often only in fragments, originating in most cases fifty or more years after the events of which they tell, to the texts which the personalities involved actually studied, wrote, referred to, and cherished, and which in turn had a decisive influence on their disciples and their disciples' disciples. That any serious scholar would adopt the first alternative seems ludicrous and yet, for a variety of complex reasons, not only has one scholar done so but almost the whole of contemporary scholarship has uncritically followed his direction.[53] This situation is the cause of an enormous amount of confusion about Hasidism and it can only be altered by going back to fundamentals and reordering priorities.

V. BUBER'S EXPLOITATION OF THE LEGENDARY MATERIALS

Having reached his problematic decision to work almost completely from the tales, Buber then exploits even these. To reveal the nature of this exploitation let us begin our examination of Buber's treatment of this material with a simple, concrete example. We call attention to one of the episodes concerning Yaacov Yoseph which Buber recounts, entitled by him "When the Sabbath was Over." In Buber's retelling this event (as others) is made to conform to his preconceptions of what Hasidism is, and so all the original gnostic and kabbalistic elements are denied and the existentialist, pansacramentalist philosophy of dialogue is introduced. The tale is given by Buber as follows:

Once Rabbi Pinhas of Koretz and I spent the Sabbath with the rav of Polnoye. At the close of the Sabbath, a messenger arrived to ask Rabbi Pinhas to go home at once, because of some urgent matter. The rav had retired to a room he always went to when he wished to give himself up to meditation. But Rabbi Pinhas could not bear to go away without taking leave of him. So he begged me to tell the rav of the message which had come, but I too hesitated. In the end both of us went to the door and listened. Inadvertently I touched the broken knob and the door flew open. Rabbi Pinhas fled in fright, but I stayed, stood still, and did not turn my eyes away.[54]

Now compare this expurgated revision of the tale with its more authentic, unedited version:

After the Sabbath a messenger came to Rabbi Pinhas telling him that he must return home at once, because pressing affairs awaited him. Now it so happened that at that hour the holy rabbi of Polnoy was in "seclusion" (*hitboddut*) in his private room. Rabbi Pinhas was troubled and did not know what to do. To delay returning home until after the "seclusion" of the rabbi of Polnoy was not possible, since such periods of concealment usually lasted twenty-four hours or more. To depart without the knowledge of the rabbi was likewise not possible. Thus the holy Rabbi Pinhas asked me to go to the rav, to the room of his "seclusion," and request him to give Rabbi Pinhas permission to return home on urgent business. When Rabbi Pinhas asked this of me, I found myself in a dilemma: if I went to the room of the rav, I was afraid I might disturb him; if I did not go, I would disobey Rabbi Pinhas. . . . Therefore I suggested to him that both of us go to his room together.

And so it was that the two of us came to his door. It was old and warped. When my hand touched the knob, it fell to the floor and the door opened of itself. We entered the room—and behold, a heavenly *maggid* was studying with him! Such fear fell upon Rabbi Rinhas, that he was afraid to stay there. But I remained standing in the room. *And it is because of this that I know what an angel is!* [55]

Buber's rendition may have greater aesthetic and literary appeal—and to most Buberians [56] this is justification enough for preferring Buber's narration—but one can quite easily see how far removed it is from the intention of the original. The object of this recital of events as told by the Hasidim was to indicate Yaacov Yoseph's greatness and to show his kabbalistic enthusiasms and to reveal his intimate intercourse with the higher rungs of spiritual and angelic beings: notice, for example, the technical kabbalistic term *hitboddut*. This, of course, is gnosis pure and simple, but Buber abhors gnosis, so the gnosis, and with it the point of the anecdote, is dropped without so much as an indication of what was involved in the original. The difference between the two versions may seem very small, but in fact it represents nothing less than the difference of radically alternative metaphysical schemata.

We are here introduced by way of a simple comparison to the issue that must concern us for the remainder of this paper, and beyond it to a more adequate study of Hasidism, namely, the need for a careful, detailed examination of the original Hasidic sources in order to see what they have to tell us independently of Buber's editing of them.

In defense of his questionable editorial procedures, Buber often claimed to have been "commissioned" to carry out his labors. For example, he has described his enterprise as follows: "I have not been concerned merely to narrate but to narrate something specific, something that seemed to me of the utmost import, *so that it cried out for narration,* something which had not yet been properly narrated *and to which to give its right form seemed my duty.*" [57] Buber suggests that duty is the cause of his retelling of the Hasidic tales. But "duty" to whom and to what? To the Hasidim and their form of life or to Buber's own philosophy of dialogue? Insofar as Buber denies all external norms and categorically rejects the ordinary rules by which one assesses the nature of duty in favor of a subjective account of responsibility, we find it difficult to understand what restraining effect the invocation of the notion of duty has here. If it allows Buber to disregard all questions of the dating of the sources, their authorship, and their authenticity, and also to omit parts of texts when it suits him and, on other occasions, to quite arbitrarily combine texts and materials that come from different sources, etc., without answering to any independent criteria or procedures of authentication, then the meaning and value of the term "duty" becomes uncertain.

In order to give some substance to the notions of duty and getting at the "right" form of the original narrative in its *sitz em leben* Buber, and all those who would use the tales as a source of many kinds of information, need to consider and respect the following methodological issues (a tentative and only partial list of requirements):

1. When was the tale first recorded in written form and when does it claim to have been first told? Does the date affect the reliability of the information? Buber's use of material, and his collections of Hasidic tales, use material from different periods quite indiscriminately.

2. Who tells the story: an eye witness? Second- or third-hand?, etc. It needs to be recognized that almost all early tales, e.g., about the Besht, are second-hand. For example, the tales in *Shivchei ha-Besht*, the first printed collection of material regarding the Besht, are derived from traditions in the possession of R. Shneur Zalman of Liady on the one hand and R. Dov Baer ben Shmuel the son in law of R. Alexander the Shochet, the Besht's scribe, on the other.

3. Why does the storyteller recount the episode, i.e., to whose benefit is it that the tale be told and what purpose does it serve? For example, is the content anti-*mitnaggid*? Antinomian? Pro-*halachah*? Pro-Kabbalah? Pro-magic? Told to emphasize the Besht's magical powers or great learning? Or, as Buber would have it, is the message: anti-gnostic, anti-kabbalistic, anti-magical, etc., etc. In answer to what critics was it being directed?

4. What sort of anecdote is it: a story? A miracle tale? A magical tale? Is its main motif messianic? Is it a first-person saying? A third-person saying? A teaching? A parable? A homily? etc., etc. Is it a *sihah*, a wise saying of a Zaddik, or a *ma 'aseh*, a more developed tale in which, usually, the Zaddik is portrayed as doing something miraculous or wonderful.

5. What is the relation of the tale to other forms of Eastern European religious and "folk" literature, and to earlier Jewish forms of literature such as the *Shivchei ha-Ari*?[58]

6. What historical and social situation is reflected in the tale and how does it serve as a vehicle back into this social history?

7. How does one decide, i.e., by what *public criteria* does one distinguish between authentic happenings and later figments of the Hasidic imagination? And does such a distinction matter? If so, how and when does it matter?

8. Buber emends the tales, as we have seen. What are the criteria for these emendations and when should they apply? Buber applies anti-magical, anti-halachic, anti-gnostic, anti-kabbalistic and pro-pansacramentalist, existentialist, dialogical, subjective, and antinomian criteria in arriving at his alterations, but the criteria for all this needs to be spelled out in detail and defended with arguments based on evidence, not metaphysical doctrines or apologetic musings.

9. An important question is what is the exact *role* of the retelling of *sichot* and *ma'asiyot* in Hasidic life? What is their relation to the theoretical texts according to the Hasidim? Did this relationship evolve or undergo any change from period to period? Did the anecdotal form become more or less central over time? Also, which Hasidism is one talking of: Lubavitch, Satmer, Belzer, etc.? Is the role of the tales the same in each tradition?[59]

10. How does one treat discrepancies between tales? How does one evaluate the *value* of each tale as evidence?

11. Do technical terms mean the same thing in every tale, whether early or late, whether told by Satmer or Belzer, etc.? When used by Buber they almost never mean what they did in their authentic Hasidic context.

12. There is a need for internal literary analysis of the tales to

discern if they are composed of different units of tradition, i.e., separate sources collected together and presented as one recollection. It is interesting to observe that Buber's own version of a given event is often made up of what were originally several tales.

13. As part of this internal analysis one has also to enter into questions of source criticism, i.e., comparing the contents of different versions of the same and differing episodes: the names, dates, attributions, contents, order of events discussed, etc., need to be studied and evaluated according to agreed canons of criticism to decide which is the *best* version of a tale.

14. What is the role of the editor (both of Buber's work as editor and of earlier editors) in collecting and presenting Hasidic tales? What are his principles of organization? Why does he leave certain material out? Are there editorial patterns reflected in the tales we have inherited and if so, who imposed them? Buber claims to edit the text in such a way as to discover the Ur-Tale but on what grounds is he sure there ever really existed an Ur-Tale, rather than just the later narrative we have?

15. Care must be taken *not* to draw more from the events recounted than the data permits—and the only way to guarantee this is to check the interpretation against the details of the originals.

16. Tales must be evaluated against the meaning structures and other aspects of the theoretical texts, and also against external evidences, e.g., of *mitnagdim* (the opponents of Hasidism) and of such sources as Solomon Maimon's *Autobiography.*

With these methodological strictures in mind let us take a further look at a few instances of Buber's editing of Hasidic tales and at the results. Let us see what sort of editor Buber was and how he did his "duty."

In fairness to Buber, I will not choose any samples from his *Tales of Rabbi Nachman* and will pass over without any further comment his retelling of these and the related early Baal Shem Tov stories, which were an early effort and require an extended treatment in their own right. In addition, Buber recognized their weakness, though he still permitted their English translation, with only slight modification and a half-hearted "apology," as late as the 1950s.[60] Instead, my examples will be drawn from his most mature effort in this area, his two-volume *Tales of the Hasidim*, published originally in Hebrew as *Or ha-Ganuz*.[61]

The first text I would like to introduce, which deletes a small technical detail regarding the Besht's mystical practices, actually, through this omission, points us to a complex theological issue. The original form of the tale runs as follows:

The Besht fasted *hafsakah*[62] for long periods. When he wanted to eat he dug a small pit and put in flour and water, which was then baked by the heat of the sun. This was his only food after fasting. All these days he was in solitude.[63]

Buber's version reads like this: "When Israel was hungry, he put water and flour into a little pit, kneaded the dough and baked it in the sun."[64]

Buber excised the references to "fasting," which he disapproves of as being anti-pansacramentalist. The original, on the other hand, gives the image of the Besht as one who, in his attempt to reach *devekuth* (cleaving to God), which was the goal of personal mystical devotions, performed the traditional fasting rite of *hafsakah* as a regular practice. We have earlier remarked on the magical and thoroughly kabbalistic program which the Besht practiced; here is a case in point. However, Buber treats the material to suit his own interpretive requirements and disregards, without any warrant from the sources, counterevidence to his remarkably "modern" image of the Besht. This tendency is neither uncommon nor unimportant. Small details, if systematically deleted or altered over the course of the retelling of several hundred tales, make a big difference.

This brings into sharp focus the awareness that in evaluating the content and veracity of Buber's work what is of the utmost importance is not only the accuracy of what Buber includes in his *Tales* but also what he purposely seeks to exclude. Especially telling is his pruning, almost to complete extinction, of the magical practices and theurgic kabbalistic rites that the Besht favored. Consider as paradigmatic here Buber's selection of material regarding the early career of the Besht as recounted in the *Shivchei ha-Besht*. He chooses to retell in quite a direct and uncolored way a number of tales from this most important early source, interspersing them with tales from other, later, works. Indeed, one is struck by how reliably these units have been reproduced. However, the matter is not as desirably handled as this state of affairs seems to indicate because in this case Buber achieves his affect not by editing out portions of individual segments but by deleting tales in their totality. Hence, for example, between the two reproduced episodes entitled "With Robbers," and "The Call," both of which are authentic, the *Shivchei ha-Besht* includes three additional stories. Despite their length I would like to quote them and comment upon them, for the exercise will prove considerably instructive in coming to a full appreciation of Buber's editorial technique and the ideology which governs it.

The three deleted tales are these:

I. THE BESHT AND THE FROG

There are people who say that once the Rabbi entered into deep meditation. He was absorbed in his thoughts for three days and three nights, and he was not aware that he was walking. Then he realized that he was in a vast desert, and he thought that his wandering was probably not without meaning. While engrossed in his thoughts, there appeared before him a frog that was so large he could not tell what kind of creature it was. He asked the frog, "Who are you?" And the frog replied that he was a scholar who had been reincarnated as a frog. (The Besht said: "You are indeed a scholar!" and with this pronouncement he greatly elevated his soul.)

The frog told him that it had been five hundred years since he had been transformed into a frog, and although Rabbi ha-Ari, God bless his memory, had redeemed all the souls, because of the severity of his crimes he had been expelled to a place without people so that no one could redeem him.

The Besht asked him: "What was your crime?" He said that once he neglected to wash his hands properly and that Satan accused him before God of his transgression. Satan had been told that it was impossible to indict him for a single sin; however, "since one transgression draws in its train another transgression," if Satan could trap him into committing another transgression, then the first would also be considered. But if he would remember God and not commit a second transgression then the first sin would be cleared. Satan had tested him again and had caused him to stumble, and so he had failed the trial. This had happened a second, and then a third time, until he had broken almost all the commandments of the Torah. Sentence had been passed to reject his repentance. Despite all this, if he would have knocked at all at the gates of repentance, he would have been accepted, since we know that in the case of the Other One a heavenly voice said, *"Return O backsliding children* except the Other One." This was the punishment for his sin: to reject him. But if he had persisted and repented they would have accepted him since there is nothing which can stand in the way of repentance. Satan led him astray, and he became so great a drunkard that he did not have time to meditate and to repent. He committed all the sins that there are in the world. Since the cause of the sins was the first one, his neglect to wash his hands, when he died he was transformed into a frog, a creature which lives in the water. He was consigned to a place where human beings do not live, because whenever a Jew might pass by or make some kind of blessing, or think some good thought, he could by that means *bring forth the precious out of the vile.*

The Besht redeemed his soul and elevated it, and the body of the frog lay dead.

2. THE BESHT SERVES AS RABBI GERSHON'S COACHMAN

After the Besht had spent seven years in solitude in the mountains, the time approached when he was to reveal himself. He went with his wife to the holy community of Brody to his brother-in-law, our master and rabbi, Rabbi Gershon. When they came to him he greeted them, and asked: "Where have you been?"

His sister return(ed) answer to him: "We wandered from village to village and were beset with many troubles."

He was filled with pity for her, so he settled them near his house and took the Besht as his personal servant.

Once he went on a journey and he took the Besht along as his coachman. In the course of the journey our master and rabbi, Rabbi Gershon, fell asleep, and the Besht drove the horses into a marsh filled with mud and mire from which it was impossible to pull them free. Just then his brother-in-law, Rabbi Gershon, woke up. He realized that they were in serious trouble. He thought that the Besht was a simpleton, and he feared that if he sent him to the village to find some gentiles to haul out the horses, he would wander wherever he pleased. He preferred to go and find help himself. He was forced to climb from the wagon into the mire and he walked to a certain village. He was returning with several people to pull the horses from the mud when he looked up and saw the Besht coming towards him. He asked: "Who pulled you out?"

He answered: "I struck the horses just once and they simply walked out."

Our rabbi the master, Rabbi Gershon, said: "It is impossible to obtain even this service from him. He is good for nothing."

3. THE BESHT REVEALS HIMSELF

After that our master and rabbi, Rabbi Gershon, rented a place for the Besht in a certain village where he would be able to earn a living. And there he achieved perfection. He built a house of seclusion in the forest. He prayed and studied there all day and all night every day of every week, and he returned home only on the Sabbath. He also kept there white garments for the Sabbath. He also had a bathhouse and a mikveh. His wife was occupied with earning a living, and God blessed the deeds of her hand and she was successful. They were hospitable to guests: they gave them food and drink with great respect. When a guest came she sent for the Besht and he returned and served him. The guest never knew about the Besht.

It was the Besht's custom when he came to the city for Rosh Hashanah to remain there for the entire month. Once during the intermediate days of Sukkoth, our master and rabbi, Rabbi Gershon, noticed that he was not putting on tefillin. It was his custom to pray by the eastern wall of the synagogue. And he asked him: "Why don't you put on tefillin today?"

He answered: "I saw in the *Taich* books that he who puts on tefillin during the intermediate days is sentenced to death."

The rabbi became very angry that the Besht followed the customs that are written in the books from Germany. There was no telling what the result would be. He went with him to the rabbi of the community so that the rabbi would admonish him. They considered the Besht to be a pious man, but as the saying goes, "an uncultured person is not sin-fearing."

The rabbi was a very righteous man. When they came to the rabbi's house, Rabbi Gershon kissed the mezuzah, but the Besht put his hand on the mezuzah without kissing it, and our master and rabbi, Rabbi Gershon, became angry with him over this as well.

When they entered the rabbi's house the Besht put aside his mask and the rabbi saw a great light. He rose up before the Besht. Then the Besht resumed the mask and the rabbi sat down. And this happened several times. The rabbi was very frightened since he did not know who he was. Sometimes he seemed to be a holy person and at other times he seemed to be a common man. But when our master the rabbi, Rabbi Gershon, complained to him about the teffillin and the mezuzah, the rabbi took the Besht aside privately and said to him: "I command you to reveal the truth to me." And the Besht was forced to reveal himself to him. But the Besht commanded him in turn not to reveal anything that had transpired.

When they came out the rabbi said to our master and rabbi, Rabbi Gershon: "I taught him a lesson, but I think he would not knowingly commit a fault against our customs. He has acted in innocence." Then the rabbi examined the mezuzah and they discovered that it had a defect.[65]

As a first hermeneutical comment on these compositions, it should be said that Buber may well have deleted them because of their length. He preferred shorter sayings,[66] thinking them more genuine. But this "form-critical" assumption is neither universally true nor methodologically foolproof. A large unit may well be "original," especially when is is found side by side with other tales, as is the case with this material from the *Shivchei ha-Besht*. Moreover, even in this instance, he does reproduce segments of equal length from this collection. Hence the principles of selection by which one anecdote is included and one rejected needs further examination and explanation. The *Besht and the Frog* is, I believe, rejected, because it was an amalgam of values Buber wanted to read out of Hasidism, the magic, the mysticism, e.g., the doctrine of *Gilgul* (reincarnation), references to the Ari (the great sixteenth-century Kabbalist), the elevation of souls, etc., and also the pervasive presence of *halachah* as seen in both the Frog's sin and its final overcoming by a "Jew who might pass and make some kind of blessing. . . ." The story entitled *The Besht Serves as Rabbi Gershon's Coachman* is deleted because it turns on the Besht's magical powers: "I struck the horses just once and they simply walked out." The tale entitled *The Besht Reveals Himself* is full of themes Buber prefers to sublimate. For example, the initial paragraph refers to the Besht's mystical devotions in a "house of seclusion," a common mystical practice; the reference to Sabbath, the special white garments for the Sabbath, the activity of *mikveh* (ritual bathing) before the holy day, all these are too *halachic*, too structured, too normative, too traditional, a far cry from the antinomian image of the Besht Buber would like to draw.[67] Again the *halachic* elements in the following paragraph regarding *Rosh Hashanah* and *Sukkoth* and the details of when one dons tefillin on the "intermediate days" of a festival, all these do not fit easily either with Buber's description of the Baal Shem Tov or of Hasidism. Lastly, the tale's relevance for those who told it was related, not least, to the Besht's mysterious power to detect a faulty *mezuzah*. A more un-Buberian detail is hard to imagine! Hence Buber dropped these three tales and with them eliminated the Jewish, *halachic*, kabbalistic, magical, and Eastern European "shtetl" context that they convey. Thus, and only thus, does he get the data to yield his Besht, so distant in tone and vision from the original. While attending to the significance of what Buber leaves out, it is worth remembering that in the *Shivchei ha-Besht*, which contains 251 tales, well over half would be classified under such motifs as "magic" or "working of wonders," e.g., exorcisms, amulets, and medicinal preparations, guaranteeing children to the infertile, etc. All these are factors in the life of the Besht that Buber attempts to submerge. Note should be taken of the fact that Buber offers only 86 tales *in toto* regarding the Besht in his *Tales of the Hasidim*, and these are chosen from many sources, not only the *Shivchei ha-Besht*, out of the literally thousands available.

This critique can be made still more explicit by examining Buber's expressive omissions in his retelling of the episode in which the Besht received the secret kabbalistic manuscripts of Rabbi Adam Baal Shem[68] through the Rabbi's son. Though in his *Tales of the Hasidim* Buber no longer gives this episode the strongly psychoanalytic turn he introduced in his earlier revision of the same event in the *Tales of the Baal Shem* (1908), and though he avoids extreme tampering with the form of the story so that it retains the two-fold attempt to conjure the "Prince of Torah" which was dropped in the earlier version, he now, much more subtly than before, leaves out much of the authentic tale, especially its kabbalistic and magical elements. Compare the narrative in the *Shivchei ha-Besht* and then as it appears, or does not appear, in Buber's compilation.

Buber's version:

Once Rabbi Adam's son asked the boy to conjure up the Prince of Torah with the aid of the directions given in the writings, so that they might ask him to solve certain difficult teachings. For a long time, Israel refused to undertake so great a venture but in the end he let himself be persuaded.[69]

Version in *Shivchei ha-Besht:*

When they went to their house of solitude, they studied the Gemara, the commentary of *Rashi*, the tosaphoth,[70] the writings of the legal codifiers, and all the Holy Scriptures. In the above mentioned manuscripts there was both Divine Kabbalah and Practical Kabbalah. Once, Rabbi Adam's son asked the Besht to bring down the Prince of the Torah[71] to explain something to them and the Besht refused him and said, "If we err, God forbid, in our kavvanah it can be dangerous. We lack the ashes of a red heifer."[72,73]

Buber's version:

They fasted from Sabbath to Sabbath, immersed themselves in the bath of purification, and—at the close of the Sabbath—fulfilled the rites prescribed. But, probably because Adam's son did not fix his soul utterly on the teachings themselves, an error crept in. Instead of the Prince of the Torah, the Prince of Fire appeared and wanted to burn up the entire town. It was only by a great effort that it was saved.[74]

Version in *Shivchei ha-Besht:*

But Rabbi Adam's son urged him every day until he could not refuse him. They fasted *hafsakah* from one Sabbath to the other, and they properly immersed themselves in the ritual bath; and at the end of the holy Sabbath, they concentrated on some particular kavvanoth. Immediately, the Besht shouted, "Oh! We made a mistake. The Prince of Fire[75] will descend and will probably burn the whole town. Now, since you are regarded by everyone as a pious man, go immediately to your father-in-law and to the others in the city and tell them to save themselves, because the town will soon be in flames." And so it happened. Then all the people thought of Rabbi Adam's son very highly and considered him a holy man and a miracle worker.[76]

Buber's version:

After a long time, Adam's son urged the boy to make another attempt. Israel steadfastly refused to do again what was obviously displeasing to

Heaven. But when his companion called on him in the name of his father, who had bequeathed the miraculous writings to the boy, he consented. Again they fasted from one Sabbath to the next. Again they immersed themselves in the bath of purification and, at the close of the Sabbath, fulfilled the rites prescribed. Suddenly the boy cried out that they were condemned and would die unless they watched through the night with unflagging spiritual intentness. All night they remained standing. But when day was just dawning, Rabbi Adam's son could not fight his drowsiness any longer and fell asleep on his feet. In vain Israel tried to wake him. They buried him with great honors.[77]

Version in *Shivchei ha-Besht:*

After a long time he again urged the Besht to bring down the Prince of Torah, but the Besht refused. But he urged him for several days until the Besht felt compelled to do his will. They kept *hafsakah* fasts as they did before. On the night of the holy Sabbath, when they concentrated on certain kavvanoth, the Besht cried: "Oh! Both of us are condemned to death tonight because of what we have done. There is one way we can escape. If we can gather strength to stand and concentrate on the kavvanoth the entire night without sleeping a wink, then the verdict will be postponed. Sleep is of the nature of death, and if we but doze, God forbid, the Evil One will overcome us and control us completely." They remained awake the whole night. Before the morning light, Rabbi Adam's son could not restrain himself and he dozed a little. When the Besht saw this he ran to him quickly and made a loud noise, but Rabbi Adam's son suddenly fainted. They tried to awaken him but it was no use. They buried him with great honor.[78]

Witness how Buber has carefully edited out as best he could the practical magical and kabbalistic dimensions. The reference to the "Divine Kabbalah and Practical Kabbalah" has disappeared and so have the references to *Kavvanah* which in this context are clearly gnostic acts of the kind emphasized by Luria and the classical kabbalah (the text refers to "particular kavvanoth" and "certain kavvanoth"). In comparison, Buber's nonspecific and modern interpretation of *kavvanah* equates it with "subjective intensity" or, as he specifically translates it here, "spiritual intentness," recalling Kierkegaard rather than the Besht. Moreover, the prominent reference to the purification rite of the "red heifer" is left out, as is the indication that the "fasting" was not just an arbitrarily selected method but followed a prescribed regimen, as is indicated by the reference to "fasting *hafsakah*." Buber has not mutilated the original as he did in his 1908 volume on the Baal Shem,[79] but he has systematically altered its detail so that the mood and impression created by his version is different from that of the original.

Let these examples suffice to indicate the directions in which Buber's "duty" to the Hasidic material led him. It is pellucid that, for all his love for this movement, and despite the real service he rendered in making it known throughout the world, his specific version of its nature and teaching cannot be left unchallenged.

CONCLUSION

Faced with such reservations it is usually suggested by Buber and more zealous Buberians that the admitted aesthetic-literary merit of Buber's *Tales* make them immune from philosophical, theological or historical criticism of the sort in which we have been engaged. This reply, however, embodies a non-sequitor. Objections of a philosophical, technical, or historical sort cannot be met and countered with arguments about literary standards or aesthetic "perfection." Literary-aesthetic ideals count only when discussing questions of aesthetic or literary merit. If, for example, a man were to write that Napoleon was an American Indian whose mistress was Cleopatra of Egypt, or that Leibniz was a Phoenecian, no defense on grounds of stylistic virtuosity would fend off severe and rightfully directed historical and philosophical criticism. The same is true in the case of Buber's *Tales*. Whatever their sublime quality, the questions "Are they accurate reflections of Hasidic life?" or "Are they authentic Hasidic tales?" are queries of an altogether different kind and require an altogether different—i.e., a historic-philosophic—kind of reply. The only literature for which the criteria of style and aesthetic appeal are sufficient is fiction. If Buberians are willing to admit that Buber's *Tales* are parallel, say, to historical fiction, then we can admit the validity of their suggestion. Otherwise we must stand firm against this change of emphasis from the historic-theological to the aesthetic-literary, secure in the knowledge that such a shift is just another instance of the confusion that reins in the world of Buberian dialogue.[80]

NOTES

1. The present paper is a longer, more detailed version of a paper delivered at the XIIIth Congress of *The International Association of the History of Religions*, held in Lancaster, England in August 1975. It was prepared with a somewhat polemical character in order to generate discussion and debate in that forum. I have decided to leave this polemical element unaltered for publication in order to convey some sense of what the actual meeting was like. Moreover, it is hoped that the publication of the paper will continue to generate the desired scholarly debate and rethinking of the issues raised. It should also be noted that the present paper is a brief summary of certain aspects of a monograph on *Buber and Hasidism* which will be published next year.

2. This is the title of one of Buber's own well-known studies on Hasidism, *The Origin and Meaning of Hasidism* (New York, 1966). Before my actual discussion I should like to note that this paper deals primarily with methodological issues. These, obviously, have the greatest importance for the image of Hasidism and an understanding of its "meaning." Unfortunately, the further implications dealing with substantive matters and the meaning of specific Hasidic doctrines cannot be drawn out and discussed here. Readers are again referred to my forthcoming volume on *Buber and Hasidism*.

3. This work was finished in Ravenna in 1907 and published in Frankfurt am Main in 1908; the English translation, *The Legend of the Baal-Shem* (New York, 1955), is hereafter referred to as *Baal-Shem*.

4. Frankfurt am Main (1906). The English translation, *The Tales of Rabbi Nachman* (New York, 1956), is hereafter referred to as *Nachman*.

5. *Baal-Shem*, Introduction, p. xiii.

6. *Baal-Shem*, Introduction, p. ix f.

7. This essay is reprinted in *Origin*.

8. *Origin*, p. 27.

9. *Baal-Shem*, Introduction, p. xi.

10. *Between Man and Man* (New York, 1965), p. 41.

11. *Baal-Shem*, Introduction, p. xiii.

12. It is important to remember that the first draft of *I and Thou* was completed in 1919 and that by 1921 the final version was well on its way to completion, appearing in print in 1923. On this phase in Buber's career see the sources cited in note 4 of the opening essay in this volume.

13. *Der Grosse Maggid und seine Nachfolge* (Franfurt A.M., 1922), Vorwort, p. vi. The date 1921 here cited in the text is the date of composition while 1922 is the date of publication.

14. G. Scholem has already raised this objection to Buber's work in "Martin Buber's Interpretation of Hasidism," in *The Messianic Idea in Judaism* (New York, 1971). The present section of this essay provides a more detailed discussion of the relevant issues in terms of both Buber's corpus and the Hasidic originals.

15. As a result of a government ban there was an almost complete absence of such publications in the middle third of the nineteenth century.

16. Lurianism is the mystical teaching associated with the great sixteenth-century Jewish kabbalist Isaac Luria. For details see G. Scholem's, *Major Trends in Jewish Mysticism* (New York, 1941) and his more recent study *Kabbalah* (New York, 1974).

17. Sabbatianism is the name of the mass seventeenth-century Jewish pseudo-messianic movement centered around the false messiah Sabbatai Zvi. For details see the two works by Scholem mentioned in note 16 above, and also his brilliant study of the Sabbatian movement, *Sabbatai Sevi* (English trans., Princeton, N.J., 1973).

18. M. Buber, *Origin and Meaning of Hasidism*, p. 173.

19. Ibid., p. 174.

20. Ibid., pp. 178–180.

21. "Besht" is an abbreviated form of the words Baal Shem Tov. It is formed, as is common in Judaism, by combining the first letters of each word.

22. On the essential issue of the dialectic between the conservative and radical elements in mysticism generally see my "The Conservative Character of Mystical Experience," in S. Katz (ed.), *Mysticism and Religious Traditions* (New York, 1983).

23. *Baal-Shem*, Introduction, p. xii; see also Buber's view in his later essay "The Myth in Judaism" in *On Judaism* (ed. by N. Glatzer, New York, 1967).

24. *Baal-Shem*, Introduction, p. xii.

25. Ibid., p. xiii.

26. *Nachman*, p. 32. Emphasis added.

27. This modern scholarship is primarily the work of three investigators of the subject, G. Scholem and his two students J.G. Weiss and R. Shatz-Uffenheimer. To this list must now be added the name of M. Pierkarz.

28. *Origin*, p. 24.

29. *Origin*, p. 25.

30. *Origin*, p. 25.

31. Here I amplify a point made by G. Scholem in his "Martin Buber's Interpretation of Hasidism," in *The Messianic Idea in Judaism* (New York, 1971) pp. 234–5.

32. There has been a good deal of important, more recent, work on this theme and second- and third-generation Weberians have begun to recognize the weakness of Weber's account of charisma and have begun the task of "reconstructing" it in a more satisfactory way. See, for example, the work of Edward Shils, "Charisma, Order, and Status," in *American Sociological Review*, Vol. 30, No. 2 (April, 1965); Rober Nisbet, *The Sociological Tradition* (New York, 1966) pp. 251–57; J. Bensman and M. Givant, "Charisma and Modernity" in *Social Research*, Vol. 42, No. 4 (Winter, 1975); J.H. Schutz, "Charisma and Social Reality in Primitive Christianity," in *Journal of Religion*, Vol. 54, No. 4 (January, 1974); Peter Berger, "Charisma and Religious Innovation," in *American Sociological Review*, Vol. 28, No. 6 (December, 1963). See also the discussion of these newer works by D. Wrong, *Max Weber* (New Jersey, 1970) pp. 44ff. Weber's own views are provided, for example, in his *Economy and Society* G. Roth and C. Wittich, eds. (Berkeley, 1978), pp. 246–254; and again pp. 1111–1144, and elsewhere. It should be noted that G. Scholem's discussion of the Besht as a charismatic leader in his essay on "The Historical Image of Rabbi Israel Baal Shem Tov," *Molad*, Vol. 18 (1960), pp. 335–56 (in Hebrew) is surprisingly brief and underdeveloped, concerning itself primarily with psychological rather than ontological factors. However, the citation he brings from Rudolph Otto's analysis of Jesus as a charismatic leader points in the direction of such public, active, categories, the correct categories to be employed in this type of analysis.

33. Anthony Cua has used this term to advance an argument regarding paradigmatic individuals not dissimilar from Buber's on this issue of personality and charisma. His argument, like Buber's, cannot be sustained. See Anthony Cua, *Dimensions of Moral Creativity*, (Pennsylvania, 1978), particularly his remarks on p. 40.

34. For a similar position vis à vis scientific models, see M. Hesse, *Models and Analogies in Science* (Indiana, 1966), pp. 164 ff.

35. More on this below.

36. I have developed these ideas much more fully, and in a comparative religious context, in my essay on the "Conservative Character of Mystical Experience," op. cit., and "Models, Modeling and Mystical Training" in *Religion*, Vol. 12 (July, 1982), pp. 247–75.

37. Buber's attempt to explain this away in Buberian terms is totally lacking in evidence and hence plausibility. See his analysis of this issue on p. 14 of vol. I of *The Tales of the Hasidim*, 2 vols. (New York, 1947–48).

38. See G. Scholem, *Major Trends in Jewish Mysticism*, pp. 331 ff. for the whole curious story regarding Adam Baal Shem Tov and his relation to the Besht. See below for additional material on Rabbi Adam Baal Shem's mystical manuscripts.

39. *Shivchei ha-Besht* had been accurately translated into English by Dan Ben Amos and Jerome R. Mintz under the title *In Praise of the Baal Shem Tov* (Bloomington, 1970). English translations from the *Shivchei* are from this translation. The present tale is told on pp. 205–206 of this edition.

40. *In Praise of the Baal Shem Tov*, pp. 231–233. The *tosaphists* were the line of medieval biblical exegetes descending from Rashi, the greatest of medieval commentators. *Rambam* is the acronym for Maimonides; *Rif* is the acronym for R. Isaac Alfasi; *Rosh* is the acronym for R. Asher Yehiel.

41. For additional evidence of the Besht's interest in and practice of kabbala see G. Scholem's Hebrew article in *Molad* cited above.

42. Yaacov Yosef of Polnoye, *Ben Porat Yosef* (Koretz, 1781). For more on this letter and the messianic element in Hasidism, about which there is much debate, see G. Scholem, "The Neutralization of the Messianic Element in Early Hasidism" in his *The Messianic Idea in Judaism* (New York, 1971), pp. 176–203; S. Dubnow, *Geschichte des Chassidismus Vol. I*, (Berlin, 1931); M. Buber, *The Origin and Meaning of Hasidism*; Ben Zion Dinur, *Bemifne ha-Dorot* (Jerusalem, 1955), pp. 181–227; I. Tishby, in *Zion*, Vol. 32 (1967); Abraham Rubinstein, in *Sinai*, Vol. 67 (1970), pp. 120–139; N. Lamm, in *Tradition*, Vol. 14 (1974), pp. 110–126. Lamm has carefully translated the entire letter into English.

43. For details of these kabbalistic movements and their doctrines see G. Scholem's *Major Trends*, and his more recent work, *Kabbalah* (New York, 1974).

44. For details of these technical kabbalistic doctrines see G. Scholem's *Major Trends*, and his more recent work, *Kabbalah*.

45. See the entire corpus of tales collected in the *Shivchei ha-Besht* (1814–15), the earliest and most famous collection of tales about the Besht. See also the *Midrash Rivash Tov*, and the works of Yaacov Yosef of Polnoye; also S. A. Horodezky's *Ha' Hassidut ve' ha-Hassidim* (1953) and the early Hasidic source *Maggid Devarav La'Ya'acov* (1781). In addition, *Degel Machne Ephraim* (1815) and *Keter Shem Tov* (1794–95), two early sources, contain material of interest. The literature of non-Hasidim about the Besht also reflects this factor.

46. For more on the importance of prayer in Hasidism see Louis Jacobs' study *Hasidic Prayer* (London, 1973).

47. For more on this see S. Dubnow, *Geschichte des Chassidismus*, Vol. I, (Berlin, 1931), pp. 84–91; G. Scholem, "Baal Shem" in *Encyclopedia Judaica* (Jerusalem, 1972), Vol. 4, pp. 6–7.

48. M. Buber, *Tales of the Hasidim*, Vol. I, pp. 11–12.

49. S. Dubnow, op. cit., pp. 84 ff. Dubnow, on the whole, however, though writing an important monograph on the history of Hasidism, was an unsympathetic observer of the movement.

50. M. Buber, *Tales of the Hasidim*, Vol. I, pp. 12–13.

51. See, for example, *Tales*. See also G. Scholem's discussion of this aspect of the Besht's career in his Hebrew article in *Molad* cited above.

52. G. Scholem, op. cit., pp. 337 ff. My translation from the Hebrew.

53. With the significant exception of the greatest student of the subject of Jewish mysticism, G. Scholem and his school. See his "Martin Buber's Hasidism" op. cit.

54. *Tales of the Hasidim*, Vol. I, p. 169.

55. This tale is found in *Botzina Nehora Hashalem* (1889).

56. See Malcolm Diamond's discussion in his *Martin Buber: Jewish Existentialist* (New York, 1960).

57. Foreword to the new edition of *For the Sake of Heaven*, (English translation, Philadelphia, 1945) p. viii.

58. The "form" of Hasidic tales is just now beginning to receive the attention it deserves in the work of scholars such as Arnold Band and Yosef Dan. See, for example, Yosef Dan's *Ha Novellah ha Hasidut* (Jerusalem, 1966) and again in his essay "Research Techniques for Hasidic Tales" in *The Proceedings of the Fourth World Congress of Jewish Studies* (Jerusalem, 1968), Vol. II, pp. 53–57, (in Hebrew). See also Arnold Band, "The Function of the Enigmatic in Two Hasidic Tales," in J. Dan and F. Talmage (eds.), *Studies in Jewish Mysticism* (New York, 1982), pp. 185–209; Y. Dan, *Ha-Sippur ha-Hasidi* (Jerusalem, 1975); C. Shmeruk, *Sifrut Yiddish: peraqim be-toledoteha* (Tel Aviv, 1978). On the relation of Hasidism to earlier forms of Jewish spirituality see M. Pierkarz, *Bi-Yeme tsemihat ha-Hasidut* (Jerusalem, 1978).

59. For those not too familiar with Hasidism it should be noted that from the third generation of Hasidic masters onwards the movement was divided into a large number of camps, each of which had its own dynasty of *Zaddikim* (leaders) and each of which claimed to be the authentic and authoritative heir of the Baal Shem Tov. There were significant differences of emphasis in style and teachings between the different groups and traditions. For the historical details of the growth of these Hasidic dynasties see my article on "The History of Hasidic Dynasties" in the *Encyclopedia of Hasidism* (forthcoming).

60. See the English translation of *The Tales of Rabbi Nachman*.

61. *Or ha-Ganuz* (Jerusalem, 1946).

62. This is a specific type of fast which is not broken at night.

63. *In Praise of the Baal Shem Tov*, p. 47.

64. *Tales of the Hasidim*, Vol. I, p. 41.

65. *In Praise of the Baal Shem Tov*, pp. 24–28.

66. See his methodological remarks on the form of Hasidic tales, pp. vii and viii of the Introduction to Vol. I of *Tales of the Hasidim*.

67. This substantive issue, i.e., of the role of *halachah* in Hasidism and

Buber's treatment of this theme, is beyond the scope of this essay. I address it in detail in my larger, forthcoming study.

68. See *Tales of the Hasidim,* Vol. I, pp. 37–39 and compare this to the original tale in *In Praise,* pp. 43 f.

69. *Tales of the Hasidim,* Vol. I, p. 38.

70. Commentaries on the Talmud and Bible.

71. The angel who can grant all explanations of the Torah.

72. The rite prescribed for purification in Numbers 19:1–14, 19:17–21.

73. *In Praise,* p. 43.

74. *Tales of the Hasidim,* Vol. I, p. 38.

75. Gabriel.

76. *In Praise,* pp. 43 f.

77. *Tales of the Hasidim,* Vol. I, pp. 38 f.

78. *In Praise,* pp. 43 f.

79. M. Buber, *Die Legende des Baalschem.* English translation, *The Legend of the Baal Shem.*

80. The focus of this essay has been on Buber's methodology. I have not tackled the issue of the accuracy of the substance of his presentation of Hasidism, i.e., its claimed dialogical, pansacramental, this-worldly, antignostic, "trans"-halachic character. These central theological concerns are analyzed in detail in my forthcoming monographic study of Buber's relation to Hasidism.

ELIEZER BERKOVITS AND MODERN JEWISH PHILOSOPHY

INTRODUCTION

Modern Jewish philosophy has, on the whole, been a relatively neglected area of investigation.[1] What interest has been shown in it has been directed primarily to historical studies that chronicle or exposit the lives and thought of the major thinkers of the modern age, while eschewing rigorous, reflective, analysis of ideas.[2] The result of this historical emphasis is that philosophically interesting contributions of creative and substantive criticism are almost totally absent from the contemporary Jewish intellectual landscape.[3] This critical neglect of modern Jewish philosophy is, at least in one sense, the legitimate consequence of the nature of much that passes for "modern Jewish philosophy"—whole regions of which manifest maximum pretension and minimum philosophical ingenuity. Yet the view that all modern Jewish thought is a confused philosophical aberration is unfounded. There is a substantial positive reservoir of genuinely interesting ideas in the corpus of modern Jewish philosophy that is instructive. But there is a pressing need to separate the ingenuity from the pretension. However, this sorting process is only one aspect of the larger investigation of the cognitive conditions necessary for the execution of a positive program aimed at constructing a satisfactory account of the nature of Jewish man in the midst of a coherent "Jewish *Weltanschauung*." It is to these critical, as well as constructive, philosophical areas that Jewish thinkers must turn with increasing skill and, it is hoped, in increasing numbers.

It is against this background that one must appreciate the labors of Eliezer Berkovits. For Berkovits is one of the few who has seen that the discussion of modern Jewish philosophy must be more than the history of ideas, that it must become at one and the same time more penetrating, more critical, more vital. This recognition has brought him to prominence and has made his book *Modern Philosophies of Judaism* something out of the ordinary and deserving of detailed study. Though this essay largely deals with the serious weaknesses in Berkovits's presentation the importance of his attempt to engage in serious, relevant rigorous debate with the leading modern Jewish thinkers should not be obscured. This last point needs to be emphasized because what follows is a considerably sharp, mostly negative, evaluation of the details of Berkovits's procedure, which might leave the reader with the impression that there is nothing of value in his work. This would certainly be an erroneous conclusion. However, Berkovits's study has been praised enough in other quarters to establish its importance, e.g., he was awarded the Jewish Book Award for philosophy in 1975. Moreover, most of the essays reprinted in *Modern Philosophies* are well known from their original publication as is the debate they aroused and the praise received. These are adequate grounds for assuming that this essay's severely critical stance is justified at the present juncture. Based on this premise I have dismissed an introductory exegetical review of Berkovits's exposition, except where necessary to the discussion, in favor of detailed critical engagement with Berkovits's conclusions, and especially the arguments and methods used to reach these conclusions. In addition, in order to clarify the essential nature of the issues under debate, I have also tried to show how modern Jewish philosophy needs to be done and how modern thinkers have to be approached.

In the volume under discussion, Berkovits selectively and vigorously reviews the five most influential Jewish thinkers of this century: Hermann Cohen, Franz Rosenzweig, Martin Buber, Mordecai Kaplan and Abraham Joshua Heschel. Before examining in detail the specifics of Berkovits's account, four general features must be noted. The first is that Berkovits, much to his abiding credit, attempts to be critical, i.e., to pay the thinkers surveyed the compliment of taking their thought seriously enough to ask whether it is true or false. That Berkovits's judgments regarding his subjects are almost universally negative and not always as well argued as they ought to be need not detract from the importance of his attempt to engage his interlocutors in serious, philosophically consequential debate. Second is Berkovits's constant tendency to use sources and arguments in philosophically unacceptable ways. As to texts, he commits several errors: he often seems to cite a text out of context, or one that is marginal, or one that serves his purpose while being out of character for the thinker concerned. As to method and analysis, again, he lapses into several difficulties with unfortunate regularity: he does not seem to know fully the difference between (and the force of the difference between) comments and arguments—and what he gives us are not always even clear and precise comments at that; he occasionally misrepresents the thought of his subjects on specific issues either in whole or in part; he does not always completely understand the position he is criticizing, thus providing unsupportable accusation where tightly reasoned theses are demanded; he does not always (perhaps never?) master the totality of the thought of his subjects and so his exegesis and criticism always give the impression of being slightly off center and somewhat beside the point; he makes simple errors of fact; he is often self-contradictory, and guilty of a variety of logical confusions. Third, Berkovits speaks from a normative-rabbinic stance—a viewpoint for which he is, on the whole, a most articulate spokesman. This rootedness, however, has both virtues and vices. On the positive side Berkovits's perspective is in close touch with Jewish tradition and classical Hebraic sources, and *halachah* is his standard of "Jewishness," which helps him overcome the excesses of subjectivism prevalent in many, especially existentialist, quarters. The negative side of this approach is that it lacks the sense of uncertainty and ambiguity that has been a cornerstone of modernity and the Jewish post-emancipation experience. As a corollary of this, it lacks the modern, questioning perspective on the classical authorities that is at the very heart of the crisis of "authority" that plays such a central role in the contemporary debate. Again, in its concern to be Orthodoxly correct, no less than in its desire to be "critical," it sometimes doesn't *listen* closely enough to the voices of the non-Orthodox, thereby turning their positions into something approaching caricature. All five figures studied here belong in various ways under the non-Orthodox rubric. Fourth, by way of prolegomena, it must also be asked quite independently of Berkovits, but obviously relevant to his success, whether what can broadly be called a normative-rabbinic point of view can ever fully engage philosophy with the degree of intellectual autonomy necessary for the encounter to be more than negative or at best apologetic. I am not as certain as many about the answer to this primary methodological question—either *pro* or *contra*—though I am certain that its resolution has not yet been decided definitely either way. Moreover, I suspect that attempted resolutions of this difficulty cannot proceed in an *a priori* fashion wherein it becomes only stipulative and a matter of merely drawing the implications of one's presupposed analytic premises.

II

The opening chapter in Berkovits's volume deals with the thought of Hermann Cohen, the great German neo-Kantian philosopher. This study clearly reflects the virtues and vices just sketched, and reveals many of Berkovits's failings. After paying Cohen the customary philosophical plaudits, Berkovits succinctly states what he takes to be the major themes in Cohen's work. One is immediately (on the first page) put on guard as to Berkovits's reliability, for his exposition presents erroneous facts as to Cohen's relationship to Judaism. He states that "after a life of estrangement from Judaism, the grand old man of German idealism [Cohen] . . . returned to the faith of his fathers, the faith of his youth."[4] He then goes on to add that in these late years spent at the Hochschule in Berlin (1912–18), Cohen wrote the numerous and well-known essays collected in his *Jüdische Schriften*.[5] This historical picture of Cohen's relation to Judaism—on which Berkovits will place much weight in formulating his criticism of Cohen—is false.

Cohen did keep Judaism out of his technical philosophical works[6] written between 1866, when he published his first substantial article, "Die Platonische Ideenlehre" in the *Zeitschrift für Völkerp-sychologie*, and through the publication of such works on Kant as *Kant's Theorie der Erfahrung* (1871) and *Kant's Begrundung der Ethik* (1877), which established his reputation. However, the absence of a discussion of Judaism in these efforts must not be misinterpreted as it is by Berkovits, because from 1879 onwards Cohen was in the forefront of discussions of Jewish issues. Thus in 1879–80 when a vicious anti-Semitic attack on the loyalty of Germany's Jews was made by the historian Treitschke in his *Ein Wort über unser Judentum* (1879), Cohen replied with an article entitled "Ein Bekenntnis zur Judenfrage" (1880). Later he testified publicly at the slander trial of an anti-Semitic school teacher, spoke out on the infamous Dreyfus trial, and in 1902 he attacked German university anti-Semitism. All these essays, which are included in the *Jüdische Schriften*, Berkovits seems to attribute to the post-1912 period. Moreover, a simple perusal of the chronological Table of Contents provided on p. ix of the *Jüdische Schriften* quickly shows that Cohen's very first reflections on a Jewish theme is found as early as 1867 in a lengthy article, "Heine und das Judentum," and continues thereafter uninterruptedly totalling 33 pieces (as republished in this collection) during his Marburg period (up to and including 1911). Franz Rosenzweig, in his Introduction to the collected Jewish essays, retells the now famous tale that in 1914, at a banquet in his honor, Cohen was referred to, no doubt well meaningly, as a "recent *Baal Teshuvah*." Cohen indignantly replied: *"Ich bin ja ein Baal t'schuwoh schon vierunddreissig Jahr"* ("I have been a *Baal Teshuvah* for 34 years") i.e., from 1880, the year of his reply to Treitschke.[7] The Judaism that Cohen defended in this period (or even in the Hochschule period) may not be acceptable to everyone, but it points out that any study of Cohen's thought will have to be more careful—both about the primary data and its interpretation—than Berkovits's promises to be. This historical element is stressed because it illustrates in a straightforward way the lack of precision that characterizes too much of Berkovits's attack and because much of Berkovits's thinking about Cohen seems to be related in a variety of ways to issues flowing from this historical misunderstanding.

This casual use of texts becomes still more troublesome when Berkovits begins his substantive exegesis and critique. He notes[8] that his attention will focus on Cohen's two most mature works, *Der Begriff der Religion im System der Philosophie* (1915) and his last, classic, and most extended statement on Judaism, *Die Religion der Vernunft aus den Quellen des Judentums*, published posthumously in 1919.[9] Berkovits then makes the gratuitous assumption, which rests on no grounds other than its assertion, that in working with these two texts it must be appreciated that "the latter [*Die Religion*] is contained in the former [*Der Begriff*],"[10] the reason for this duplication being that the former is intended "for the philosophically schooled gentile reader" while the latter is "for believing Jewish intellectuals."[11] This unfounded and undefended hermeneutical presupposition colors Berkovits's entire picture of Cohen and his mature relation to and reflections on Judaism, and, of course, distorts the careful distinctions that have to be made in philosophical exegesis. Though the two works have profound similarities—indeed, it would be strange if they did not given Cohen's lifelong preoccupation with systematic philosophy—they are very different from each other (and certainly very different from his earlier Marburg neo-Kantian works, namely the prominence given the term "Religion" in both titles, which underscores the new Cohenian emphasis). One cannot legitimately coalesce the two works and then treat them quite randomly, picking and choosing from both at will (as well as from earlier texts) for one's own eisegetical purposes, and reach a serious and sustainable understanding of Cohen's mature position on things Jewish. These methodological procedures do not encourage confidence in Berkovits's handling of the relevant sources.

Berkovits's actual exegesis of Cohen's thought is divided into and treated under the following two categories: (1) Ethics and Religion; and (2) The Religion of Reason; (2) is broken down into the following subtopics: Being and Becoming; Creation and Revelation; and "Ethics and Messianism."

The thrust of Berkovits's review is, to summarize it drastically, to present Cohen's mature thought as a form of Jewish neo-Kantianism which never moves beyond the limits of Kantian thought. In the penultimate paragraph of the essay, in discussing Cohen's concept of prayer, Berkovits, in what may serve as a summary of his overall judgment of Cohen's work, writes:

. . . prayer for Cohen could only be a monologue. And yet, Cohen could not give up the idea of the dialogue completely. It is the sign of the inner struggle between the intellect of the Neo-Kantian sage and the heart of the *baal t'shubah*, the old Jew returning to the house of his fathers. Thus, he conceives of prayer as the dialogical monologue. He is still not facing God in a dialogical situation. His Neo-Kantian past does not let him. Man is alone and God is only the "goal." Yet, he does not give up the dialogical meeting with the God of his fathers completely. God is really so near. This soul of mine is not completely mine, it is God's too. Thus it can bring together the two *persons* of the dialogue. It can not only search God; it can also speak to him. Finally he dared say—God, a person, but said it as if by a slip of the pen.

As to the details of Berkovits's exegesis, several items need to be commented upon. First, rather than doing what he stated he would do, i.e., concentrating on Cohen's last two works, Berkovits introduces into his review of Cohen's position, especially regarding his concept of God and his understanding of the systematic relation of ethics and religion, a great deal of material drawn neither from *Der Begriff* nor from *Die Religion* but from the earlier much different and universally acknowledged thoroughly Kantian study, *Die Ethiks des reinen Willens* (1904). Six of the first ten citations are from this earlier monograph. Thus from the outset, with the illegitimate aid of these quotations from Cohen's earlier labors, Berkovits tries unfairly to create a mood and conjure an image (largely Kantian in character) of Cohen's mature outlook which is not faithful to it. A coherent, fair estimation of the late material must be based on a reasoned reading of the late works. The procedure adopted by Berkovits makes this impossible. Of necessity it obfuscates the distinctiveness and the change in outlook in certain basic concerns which these last two monographs of Cohen represent. Of course, Berkovits follows this procedure precisely to obscure this change.

In addition, Berkovits's basic exposition of the main aspects of Cohen's "Religion of Reason" is not without its difficulties. His attempt (pp. 13–16), for example, to clarify the meaning of the foundational concept "Idea" as used by Cohen, does not seem to capture Cohen's meaning fully. Perhaps the simplest way to suggest the failure is to note Berkovits's phrase regarding the possibility that Cohen's God in *Die Religion* "is a *mere* idea" (p. 14, emphasis added). For Cohen there is no such thing as a *mere* idea. Even if Rosenzweig's interpretation of Cohen's position regarding God in *Die Religion* were wrong (which it at least partly is), there would still remain intact his instructive warning "That for Cohen an Idea is not a mere idea."[12] Steeped as he was in both Platonic and Idealist thought, Cohen's definition of an *idea* was different from and more significant than what the ordinary English term "idea" suggests. To appreciate Cohen's discussion, one has to take full cognizance of the Idealist milieu that generated it. That is to say, one has to recognize that Idea here means something both necessary to human reason as such and also something that possesses the power to motivate and regulate the behavior of human beings.

Again, Berkovits's particular paraphrase of specific Cohenian doctrines is suspect. Consider, for example,[13] the doctrine of "correlation," together with its related doctrine of God as Being, which, as Berkovits correctly notes, is the most seminal concept in both (late) texts. His treatment of this notion is problematic because Cohen's discussion of correlation, creation, and especially the relation of God to nature[14] and of God to ethics, in both *Der Begriff* and *Die Religion,* cannot be reduced to a replay of the God-Idea of the earlier Cohenian system. For whatever the final judgment on the meaning and validity of the theology of "correlation" and the "reality of God" in Cohen's late ontology one has to wrestle with the following factors correlative with it:

A. The radical departure from the Kantian system as to the relation of morality and religion which it represents, and Cohen's new recognition that religion is *sui Generis* and not merely an extension of ethics.[15]

B. The notable variety of original elements in *Die Religion* relating to the discussion of creation, revelation and messianism, which move it beyond anything presented in Cohen's earlier reflections.

C. The major significance of Cohen's introduction of the notion that God is both the only true Being, the only reality that truly is, as well as being a God that redeems men from sin.

This last point is essential to any full understanding of the significance of Cohen's late outlook. In Chapter I of *Die Religion* entitled *"Die Einzigkeit Gottes"* ("The Uniqueness of God") Cohen identifies the defining characteristic of monotheism in terms of God's "uniqueness" rather than unity.[16] Explicating the positive meaning of this conceptualization later in the same chapter he boldly asserts: *"Nur Gott hat Sein. Nur Gott ist Sein."* ("Only God has being. Only God is being").[17] Later in the same paragraph: *"Nur Gott ist Sein. Es gibt nur eine Art von Sein, nur ein einziges Sein: Gott ist dieses einzige Sein. Got ist der Einzige."* ("Only God is being. There is only one kind of being, only one unique being: God is this unique being. God is the unique one.")[18] Berkovits knows this text[19] yet explicates it in such a way so as to reduce the ontological character of Cohen's God to a matter of logic, i.e., God is, as in the earlier Cohenian system, only a necessity of thought analogous to Kant's theory of substance.[20] In support Berkovits argues[21] that this idea of God as Being is only a logical necessity, entailing no ontological status. Furthermore, it is not, he asserts, a new thesis in Cohen's position, having been stated in the *Ethik des reinen Willens*, published in 1904. However, after all Berkovits's arguments are offered and all his "evidence" is marshalled, it is clear that he has not wrestled deeply enough with the issue of God in Cohen's thought and that the case is neither as obvious nor as settled as Berkovits's overly reductive analysis suggests.

What does Cohen mean when he talks of God as "true being," when he says: *"Nur Gott hat Sein. Nur Gott ist Sein."* Admittedly the discussion of these and related topics in both *Der Begriff* and *Die Religion* are obscure and difficult to exposit with complete clarity. Yet, despite Berkovits's assertions to the contrary, it seems that Cohen intends to strike a new chord, particularly with regard to God's reality, that was absent from his neo-Kantian Marburg ontology. In defending his interpretation Berkovits quotes several brief texts, but they are quoted out of context or are misinterpreted. Especially regarding the earlier neo-Kantian notion of God as *Urbild* and the new concept of God as *Sein*, Berkovits's view shows a misunderstanding of the relation which obtains between Cohen's neo-Marburg epistemology and the new ontology argued for late in life. Whereas in the earlier period God is only the fundamental idea that logically guarantees the successful completion of the work of nature and ethics, in *Die Religion* God is the ontic—not only epistemic—and logical foundation of all this is, including both nature and ethics. Cohen now tries to work out a position, not with complete satisfaction, in which God is both the *Urbild* of moral action as well as the ontic ground of reality. Before the success of Cohen's attempt in this new direction can be satisfactorily evaluated, what he is attempting must be understood. Berkovits, unfortunately, distorts this reconstruction and misses the fundamental change from logic to ontology in *Die Religion.*

This central misunderstanding is brought to the surface with especial clarity by Berkovits's exegesis of the relation of Being and Becoming in Cohen's late philosophy. Berkovits reads *Die Religion* as arguing that:

Becoming demands for its explanation the logical ground of Being, which is identified as God . . . Being can only be used insofar as Becoming requires an origin in rest. It can, however, add nothing to the nature and character of Becoming. *It is from Becoming that Being is concluded* and it is not from Being that Becoming derives.[22]

Whereas this account might make an uneasy fit with certain aspects of Cohen's thought in the Marburg period, though, of course, in Marburg Cohen did not talk much of Being, it inverts the meaning Cohen intended in *Die Religion,* changing drastically the entire character of the later discussions. It is clear from everything that Cohen writes in this late book that God as Being is *not* logically derived from Becoming. That is, God as Being is *not* just the *answer* to "the origin" of Becoming. Quite the reverse. Now Being is not inductively arrived at as a result of the need to provide an explanation, reason or justification of things; rather it is the ground from which all else flows.[23] Note that Cohen makes the case for this view of God in the very first chapter of *Die Religion,* i.e., at the beginning of his systematic structure. God as Being (*Sein*) is the only truly real entity; Becoming (*dasein*) is inferior and of only secondary importance.

In arguing for God as *Being,* Cohen intends that God should *not* be reduced to a concept as He had been in the earlier system when He was seen only in terms of and in relation to "Becoming." Again, God as Being is intended, in contradistinction to the Kantian-Marburg thesis that everything has its source in human consciousness, to assert the autonomous origin and character of God's reality independently of human consciousness, i.e., to transcend the theoretical demand that God is only an Idea. Moreover, Berkovits misconstrues Cohen's related remarks about Being as a problem for logic, religion, and ethics, taking them to mean that Being serves in logic, religion, and ethics in the same way, i.e., is the *same* problem and requires the same solution: God as archetype. This is not Cohen's intent. Cohen means that Being is the problem for all three categories, but religion is seen to solve it by means of an ontological claim whereas logic and ethics solve it axiomatically and epistemically. In logic Being is arrived at as a conclusion; in religion it is the foundational reality from which all else proceeds and which makes everything else possible.[24]

What is the ultimate validity of Cohen's account? It is difficult here to be as enthusiastic about Cohen's success as were Rosenzweig and Shmuel Hugo Bergman,[25] but they caught a fundamental insight into Cohen's late work that Berkovits misses. Even if Cohen's late schema does remain within the circle of Idealism, as Professors Guttmann and Altmann have argued[26] on more subtle and persuasive grounds than Berkovits, it still marks a new stage in the development of modern Jewish philosophical thought about God and about God and man together. It struggles to resolve the demands of the impersonal God of ethics and the personal God of religion, recognizing the uniqueness of the latter and its incommensurability with the former. In so doing, Cohen's thought breaks the apologetic circle in which Jewish thought had been largely imprisoned since the time of Kant.[27] Moreover, not only does the late Cohen know in *Die Religion* that God must Be, but he knows also that God must be a Redeemer God who forgives sins. Here one has to feel the full weight of the Talmudic quotation with which *Die*

Religion begins: "Happy are ye Israelites! Who is it who purifies you?—Your Father in Heaven." Though Cohen is not able to provide an error-free demonstration of this theological claim, his failure is not the failure of intention that Berkovits attributes to him, that is, of never out-growing God as an Idea. Rather it is a failure of philosophical method.

Perhaps the clearest, as well as the most moving, testimony to this new awareness in Cohen's late treatises is the centrality that the Psalms assume over against the Prophets, who had held pride of place before. Now it is the Psalmist searching after personal intimacy with God who is seen as the paradigmatic expression of Israel's religious genius, as compared to the ethical monotheism of the Prophets which so appealed to the more youthful Cohen. The corollary of this, too, is telling: the mature Cohen rediscovers prayer, for after all, what are the Psalms but prayers?

Space forbids an extended investigation of Berkovits's remaining critique of Cohen's view of the relation of "The Religion of Reason and Judaism" and of "Philosophy and Religion." It must be said, however, that in these sections Berkovits's position cannot stand as presented because it is predicated on the oversimplistic and mistaken account of Cohen's late understanding of God and the related "concept of correlation" that has already been reviewed. As such, the whole discussion lacks the textured fineness that recognizes the alternating and competing strands in Cohen's late thinking, resulting in a situation in which the valuable and nonvaluable in Cohen's formulations are both disregarded. On the other hand, in these sections Berkovits often does come close to the mark with regard to individual issues, especially when he discusses the inadequacies in Cohen's attempts to reinterpret specific traditional Jewish concepts in his own ethical idealist language. Berkovits is especially right when he points out in several different arguments (e.g., with regard to such *topoi* as Torah, *mitsvah*, Messianism, Zion, etc.) the general ahistoricity of Cohen's *Weltanschauung* and all that this entails for an adequate interpretation of Judaism. The shortcomings of Cohen's thought with respect to history are a serious limitation when trying to come to grips with a religion such as Judaism.[28] Curiously, even here where he is on secure ground,

Berkovits weakens his case by making factual errors. For example, he makes the false statement that: "Cohen never makes mention of the Exodus,"[29] then states: "A religion of reason that disregards its [the Exodus] importance in the self-understanding of Judaism and in its world view is just not drawn from the sources of Judaism." Alas for Berkovits, Cohen *does* mention the Exodus—several times. In his discussion of justice Cohen writes: "All the commandments and all festive celebrations are a sign of 'remembrance of the Exodus from Egypt.' Hence, the entire Torah is a remembrance of the liberation from Egyptian slavery, which, as the cradle of the Jewish people, is not deplored, let alone condemned, but celebrated in gratitude."[30] Again, in his treatment of "Faithfulness" (*Die Treue*) Cohen, in keeping with the best of Jewish teaching, states:

Remembering is therefore the psychological function of faithfulness. Thus, God remembers the covenant with the fathers, and Israel has to remember the benefits God bestowed on it. However, while it should remember the liberation from Egypt, this remembering is an active duty: Thou shalt remember that thou hast been a slave in the land of Egypt. Through this the memory changes into the social virtue of loving the stranger . . .[31]

There are also references to the Exodus in Cohen's investigation of the revelation at the Burning Bush, the issue of love of the stranger, and the nature of the messianic future,[32] to name three further sources.

Finally, it should be recognized that Berkovits is correct when he urges that Cohen's late system, as found especially in *Die Religion*, introduces personal and religious categories into the discussion that run counter to elemental features of his earlier neo-Kantian systematic structure. Cohen does inject doctrines that are required without adequate justification according to the Kantian modality. However, in contradistinction to Berkovits's criticism, their very introduction is the interesting feature of the entire presentation: that the great neo-Kantian Cohen should find that he needs such notions as messianism, revelation, Redeemer God, etc., in order to give a comprehensive account of human life is the revolutionary aspect of his late writings, and it is this aspect of his rethinking that Rosenzweig, for example, was able to perceive. All Berkovits can see, however, is that Cohen failed to justify these moves adequately in a fully consistent systematic fashion, thus missing the forest for the trees.

Recognizing this subtle alternation between competing elements in Cohen's mature analysis requires that one's final judgment strike a balance between the enthusiastic Cohen supporters and the Berkovits-like critics. A sober conclusion seems to be that Cohen wanted to break with Kantianism, *did* break with Kantianism in essential respects, and yet his deep rooted attachment to Idealism did not allow him to move completely beyond its limiting parameters. Here, yet again, one is forcefully struck by Cohen's major contribution and perhaps the decisive achievement of *Die Religion*, namely, the recognition that in determining the fundamental general structure of human experience we *must* recognize individual, existential categories, which for Cohen are equivalent to the *religious* category, which had heretofore been excluded *a priori* from the Idealist phenomenology. Whether or not we agree with Cohen's methodological procedure or with his overall metaphysical approach to dealing with these categories, it is to his credit that he insisted on their recognition and established their distinctive character, as well as having gone a considerable distance in explaining this character.

Unfortunately, Berkovits catches very little of this originality, seeing Cohen's reformulations primarily in crude black and white tones. What little Berkovits does catch he portrays in pathetic terms as a struggle between Cohen's neo-Kantian intellect versus his Jewish *Baal-t'shuvah* heart.[33] This, however, misses the center of the *cognitive* thrust of Cohen's dialectical ruminations. Cohen insists that man's *reason* requires God, not only man's heart. To misunderstand this is to misunderstand the entire nature of Cohen's last efforts and their importance. Thus, while I, too, hold that Cohen was unsuccessful in establishing the reconciliation of Idealism and religion that he sought, it is clear that Berkovits has not done justice to what Cohen did accomplish and to the significance for Jewish thought which his *Die Religion* represents. Berkovits thereby vitiates the value as well as the validity of much of his critique—

whatever ultimate independent conclusions one holds regarding Cohen's reflections.

III

Berkovits's second study considers the religious existentialism of Franz Rosenzweig. After acknowledging the nobility of Rosenzweig's[34] life Berkovits gives a brief (seven pages) exposition of his thought under three headings: (1) Eternity, Holiness and Redemption; (2) Survival; and (3) Judaism and Christianity. This exegesis is perhaps the weakest of any of the exegetical reviews that Berkovits offers. Rosenzweig is notoriously hard to summarize and Berkovits's attempt reconfirms this fact.

Moving from exposition to criticism, Berkovits asserts directly:

With all due respect to the saintly genius of Franz Rosenzweig, it would seem to us that it is impossible to accept any of his categories as fitting either the essence of Judaism, the nature of the Jew, or the history of the Jewish people.[35]

Though far too sweeping, this charge is at least partially accurate. The critical issues that Berkovits presents in support of his contention, though for the most part well known and, unoriginal, are significant and identify many of the unsettling obscurities and confusions in Rosenzweig's thought. These issues center around Rosenzweig's atemporal, ahistorical image of the Jew and Judaism which colors everything else in his systematic analysis of the place and meaning of Judaism in time and reality.

Berkovits is also right to see at least some of Rosenzweig's ideas as "Judaized" versions of Christian stereotypes of the Jew, which forced themselves on Rosenzweig as a result of his personal encounter with Rosenstock-Huessey and Christianity. Again, as in his reflections on Cohen, Berkovits correctly stresses, in opposition to both Cohen and Rosenzweig, the significance of the actual, particular, national community of Israel and the historic centrality of the notion of Zion as a real historic possibility, related to the actuality of Jewish homelessness and exile. Yet there are, despite all that is pertinent in Berkovits's criticism, serious weaknesses in his review. Perhaps the most consequential of these is methodological, relating to his decision to explore Rosenzweig's thought almost exclusively on the basis of *Der Stern der Erlosung* (*The Star of Redemption*).[36] As Rosenzweig's later writings indicate, his thought continued to mature in a variety of directions after publication of *Der Stern.* To gain a full picture of his vision therefore means casting a wider net. As it is, Berkovits ought more accurately to have entitled his essay, "Some Remarks on Some Aspects of *Der Stern,*" rather than "Franz Rosenzweig."

Moving to specific issues, we begin by noting that Berkovits's use of traditional Jewish materials to counter Rosenzweig's portrayal of Judaism is often as one-sided as Rosenzweig's and again raises the question of Berkovits's use and misuse of sources. Consider, for example, Berkovits's discussion of the role of the Torah in history. Rosenzweig, it is argued, sees the function of Torah "as taking hold of the this-worldly and transforming it into the contents of the future world, the world beyond." Berkovits replies:

We know nothing of that . . . Not even the Torah is eternal according to Jewish tradition. As one of the great teachers of the Talmud said: "The commandments of God were given in order to purify man." Once the goal is achieved, the Law will no longer be necessary. Only in the imperfection of the temporal world does the Law serve a purpose.[37]

Berkovits's position oversimplifies the views found in "Jewish tradition." There are Talmudic and post-Talmudic sources that refer to the pre-existence of the Torah and its role in creation[38] and see the Torah as related to more than the "imperfection of the temporal world." And then there are perhaps the more telling texts that present considerable evidence that the Torah is binding and relevant far beyond the this-worldly parameters of the present age.

R. Hezekiah said in the name of R. Simon b. Zahdi: All the Torah which you learn in this world is "vanity" in comparison with Torah which you shall learn in the world to come.[39]

Again, in contradistinction to Berkovits, the eternity of the Torah in the future life was argued for by both Saadiah[40] and Maimonides.[41] Maimonides also believed that the Torah will not be changed even in the Messianic Era. Likewise, Crescas and Albo, while disagreeing with Maimonides that the "immutability of the Torah" is a necessary principle belief of Judaism, did hold that it is nonetheless a true belief.[42]

The Kabbalists, as one would expect, go still further regarding the cosmic significance of the Torah. Though a complex subject, one quotation from the kabbalistic material gives us a flavor of their view, which shows it far removed from what Berkovits claims "the Tradition" teaches (or he implies strongly permits):

In regard to the new interpretations of the Torah that God will reveal in the Messianic Age, we may say that the Torah remains eternally the same, but that in the beginning it assumed the form of material combinations of letters which were adapted to the material world. But some day men will cast off this material body; they will be transfigured and recover the mystical body that was Adam's before the fall. Then they will understand the mystery of the Torah, its hidden aspects will be made manifest. And later, when at the end of the sixth millennium (that is, after the true Messianic redemption and the beginning of the new aeon) man becomes a still higher spiritual being, he will penetrate still deeper into the hidden mystery of the Torah. Then everyone will be able to understand the miraculous content of the Torah and the secret combinations and will thereby learn much concerning the secret essence of the world . . .[43]

Independent discussion of Rosenzweig's view of Torah is important in itself, being central to the task of trying to unpack the theology of *Der Stern*. Valid criticism of Rosenzweig is indeed required, as the account advanced has many lacunae. But instead of doing what is needed, Berkovits confuses the issue by taking the easy but self-destructive course of misrepresenting the traditional Jewish sources to help achieve his goal. This lapse, which is not an isolated instance, calls into question Berkovits's investigative procedures.

This discussion of the Jewish view of Torah furnishes an opportunity to make a more general observation. Berkovitz is fond of labeling the positions of those he disagrees with "Christian," believing this rules their views out without further discussion. With regard to the understanding of Torah it would be a simple matter, given Berkovits's position *vis-à-vis* the Torah as here expounded by him, to class his analysis as "Christian," as it is shared by much, if not most, Christian opinion. However, I am not troubled by the fact that Berkovits's outlook is too "Christian"[44] and therefore not to be trusted. Rather, I mention this line of thought solely to indicate that this maneuver of attaching the label "Christian" to a certain schema and believing that this disposes of it is a hollow rhetorical gesture. Though this is one of Berkovits's favored polemical ploys, it is ultimately of little conceptual consequence. "Argument by label" is not philosophical argument.

Beyond these specific matters there is also a major philosophical issue at stake in Rosenzweig's analysis of the Jewish situation and Berkovits's passionate rejection of this account. Rosenzweig's positive affirmation of Judaism after his "return" was based on his evaluation of Judaism as an "eternal" religion which was removed from the everyday flow of the historical world. Berkovits summarizes Rosenzweig's view in the following way:

God withdrew the Jewish people from the dimension of history in which the nations live by giving Israel His law, which like a bridge arches over the flow of time "that rushes underneath in all eternity."[45]

Berkovits's further exegesis of *The Star* gives a distinctly negative and unappealing color to Rosenzweig's position that the original discussion does not convey, achieved especially by the introduction and constant repetition of the negative term "lifeless,"[46] which Rosenzweig does not use. Berkovits is correct to call attention to the well-known fact that Rosenzweig's understanding is problematic.[47] Indeed, in an early writing, Rosenzweig speaks of "the curse of historicity" which Judaism escapes, and this transhistorical claim remains a constant (problematic) feature of Rosenzweig's conception of Judaism.

Against Rosenzweig's ahistoricity Berkovits is right, especially after the Holocaust and the remarkable creation of the state of Israel, to stress the importance of Zionism and the dimension of history for both Jews and Judaism. Yet in correctly calling attention to history one must first be fair to Rosenzweig, who was writing in the first third of this century when the Holocaust was "unthinkable" and the establishment of a Jewish state an impossible dream. Being fair to Rosenzweig means understanding the Hegelian nature of his outlook and the implications of the Hegellian system *vis à vis* Judaism, against which he was directly philosophizing. Rosenzweig argued for the ahistoricity of Judaism in order to justify the eternal validity of Judaism in the face of the Hegelian thesis that Judaism had been overcome by the ongoing dialectic of history and thus made obsolete. Hegel's position denied Judaism any living spirituality or authenticity. Berkovits, despite his polemic, reveals no recognition of this fundamental feature of all of Rosenzweig's thinking. Indeed, he does not mention Hegel at all in deciphering Rosenzweig. (Hegel is not cited in the index.) Yet without the Hegelian milieu in which and against which Rosenzweig was always working, all reading of Rosenzweig is "out of context." Moreover, Rosenzweig's "motives," are irretrievably lost and the door for incorrect attributions is thereby opened.

Being fair to Rosenzweig does not make his position either more accurate or more acceptable in the post-Hegelian, post-Holocaust world of today. It does, however, remove any stigma that might attach itself to him as a result of views he held for idealistic motives. Thus, for example, Rosenzweig was not totally opposed to Zionism,[48] as was Cohen, and was known to support the idea of the establishment of religious kibbutzim in Israel.[49] Rosenzweig's main aversion was to secular Zionism, which he saw as a historical and theological betrayal of Judaism's deepest beliefs. Writing to a friend who was a Reform Rabbi, he stated "Among the Zionists I find, whatever the theory may be, better Jews than among us."[50] This recognition, however, pushes us to yet another level of reflection brought to light by Berkovits's critique of Rosenzweig: haven't the last 35 years of Jewish history, encompassing Auschwitz and the rebirth of the state of Israel, made *all* pre-Holocaust theology obsolete? Is there *any* pre-1940 theology, or post-1945 theology for that matter,[51] that can *adequately* deal with these overwhelming events in the life of the Jewish people? (Zionism per se is not a theology nor is the *halachah*.)

Ironically, Rosenzweig draws our attention to the really seminal subject: history. Rosenzweig called himself a "radical empiricist."

Though it is often hard to take this designation seriously while reading *Der Stern,* Rosenzweig did think his system reflected an authentic phenomenological account of Jewish identity and the place of the Jew and Judaism in the world, including what he perceived as Israel's "ahistoricity." In certain respects Rosenzweig is not wrong. Certainly from the first century c.e. to the rise of the state of Israel, Jews as a national group have not been *prime* movers in history, though they have made more of a contribution than Rosenzweig recognized. This fact may hurt our pride, but it is a fact nonetheless. Moreover, Rosenzweig is right to emphasize that Western history has, in large part, been the product of Christianity—though he had a blind spot *vis à vis* Islam. But his basic assertion was—is—right. The reality of *galut,* Jewish historical marginality and the imperialism of Christianity (and Islam) are *major* theological conundrums for a Jewish philosophy of history, especially when one understands that for Rosenzweig (as for any Jewish philosopher of history) they are facts that relate to actual temporal as well as suprahistorical metaphysical modalities. Rosenzweig recognized these phenomena, and forced them to the center of Jewish theological debate, even if he deals with them in ways that are inadequate. These limitations of his reckoning, however, do not obviate the fecundity of his grasp of past events, and one can suggest in good conscience that no major modern theologian has caught the problematic element in these categories as has Rosenzweig, something Berkovits is altogether obtuse to. Furthermore, Berkovits's own attempt to sketch a Jewish philosophy of history, which stresses the distinction between "power history" (the real history of nations) and "faith history" (the history of Israel),[52] is hardly as profound as Rosenzweig's. It is little more than an apologetic account of events, which tries to transform historical realities into cosmic values after the event.

As deep as one's philosophical disagreements may go with Rosenzweig, and they run very deep with me, as they obviously do with Berkovits, his work represents a pioneering attempt at a Jewish philosophical account that gives proper emphasis to the historic exilic conditions of the Jew. Still more, it must be acknowledged that he was attuned to something most modern Jewish thinkers, including Berkovits, miss. The idea of "history" does not mean the same thing in a Jewish context as in a secular one, and essential moments of Jewish life *are* transhistorical, e.g. creation, Torah, Redemption, messianism. "History" is a troublesome category for Jewish thinkers, despite the lack of this recognition by most of them.[53] It is also important to allow that Rosenzweig's reflections could well serve as an ideology that would be acceptable to both secularists and many a-Zionistic liberal and Orthodox Jews, for example, and *Naturei Karta* in Jerusalem. That is to say, it is not "unbelievable."

All this passes Berkovits by, at least in part because he seems deaf to what Rosenzweig means by the terms "life" and "eternity" and the dialectic between them in his discussion of history and history's relation to the meta-historical. Berkovits presents the two terms "life" and "eternity" as if they were not linked to each other, being encased in some isolated and static form which allowed of no dialectical interaction or flexibility. His gloss gives no sense of the fluidity, the open-endedness, the interpenetration of the two separate yet inseparable ideas as they actually take place in Rosenzweig's dynamic reflections. The sharp dichotomy between "life" (i.e., history) and "eternity" that Berkovits sees is based on an inadequate grasp of the immanent structure of Rosenzweig's position, which is pre-eminently dialectical, as one would expect from someone schooled on Hegel.

For Rosenzweig, history and eternity, i.e., Jew and Christian, do *not* exist divorced from one another but rather the former is the ground as well as the *telos* of the latter. Moreover, the dynamic of history is provided by the incursion of the eternal, and this in three ways—the three points of the Star—Creation, Revelation, and Redemption.[54] History begins in Creation, (one must recognize Rosenzweig's unique idealistic account of Creation, which is deeply indebted to Cohen's bold reinterpretations of this subject), is transformed by Revelation towards its true goal, and achieves its end in Redemption. As a consequence of this necessary intrusion and disclosure of transcendence in the historical, the historical becomes at one and the same time inseparable from the transcendental and the transcendental becomes inseparable from the historical:

"Eternity is a future which, without ceasing to be future is none-theless present."[55] This dialectic is symbolized for Rosenzweig in the relations of synagogue and church, Jew and Christian. The church, the Christian, history, all involve an eschatological dimension, a *final* cause, which defines both their present and their future. Thus, Rosenzweig argues "The world(s) future perfection is created, as future, simultaneously with the world."[56] Any schizophrenic rendering of these relations, Berkovits's included, is too Marcionite, and a heresy on Rosenzweigian grounds, as it has been on orthodox Christian ones. Certainly the preponderant activity of history belongs to Christianity and is, for Rosenzweig, Christian history, but having recognized this one must not go on to commit the metaphysical as well as the logical error of *reducing* history to a completely noneschatalogical, i.e., non-Jewish and noneternal dimension of reality.

Moreover, history, i.e., Christianity, is *not* the essential phenomenon for Rosenzweig, and here again we see his transvaluation of Hegelianism. Rather, history represents a preliminary stage whose purpose and end is defined and guaranteed by eternity, i.e., by Judaism. Just as God guaranteed the victory of morality in Kantian systematics, so Judaism, as the manifestation of eternity, guarantees the victory of the Spirit in Rosenzweig's transmutation of Hegel's dialectic. Now it is not Judaism that is taken up and transcended by Christianity, especially in its Protestant form, but rather the reverse. Christianity's fulfillment is to be experienced through its being taken back up into the womb from which it sprang, Judaism. For Rosenzweig this realization represents the *Eschaton.* Here we have a metaphysical version almost approximating the messianic vision of the prophets with regard to the eschatological centrality of Israel. And, as we have just argued, this eschatological dimension also necessarily involves itself in the historical[57] (though not being *of* history and in a special Rosenzweigian sense of "historical"). Eternity, as represented by the Jew, constantly reminds the temporal community of Christianity that the "end is not yet," that redemption still belongs to the future and that the imperative of Revelation are still to be completed in a future messianic consummation. Hence Judaism, though standing over against history, nonetheless enters into it as a commanding presence that gives history its meaning: "Life becomes immortal in redemption's eternal hymn of praise."[58]

The entire Rosenzweigian system is intelligible only when these dialectical exchanges are taken fully into account. As we have noted, Creation, Revelation (especially Revelation), and Redemption are all involved in these movements between above and below, history and eternity, Jew and Christian. To fail to understand them, that is, to try to interpret them in nondialectical terms, as Berkovits does, is to caricaturize them and miss their essential nature. Such a caricature cannot adequately realize the significance of Rosenzweig's final exhortation in *Der Stern:* "Into Life" (and thus also the whole intent of Rosenzweig's concern). Nahum Glatzer recalls the following incident:

> The liberal critics of Zionism who stressed "the essence of Judaism" and the idea of eternity, were told by Rosenzweig that eternity as understood by Judaism lies not in the metaphysical clouds of timelessness but in its realization in our days. There is no "essence of Judaism" Rosenzweig taught, there is only: "Hear, O Israel!"[59]

IV

The third and longest essay in Berkovits's collection[60] deals with the thought of Martin Buber and is divided into four sections: (1) The Teaching of Buber; (2) Buber's Testimony; (3) The Biblical Encounters; and (4) Buber's Metaphysics. As is his custom, Berkovits first exposits the major themes in Buber's dialogical position and then analyzes them.

Fundamental examination of Buber is long overdue; but, unfortunately, Berkovits's critique falls short for at least six reasons.

1. Berkovits's interpretation indicates that he does not have complete mastery of Buber's voluminous writings, nor a full appreciation of how each element in the structure supports each other and receives its meaning in terms of the whole. In certain cases this leads to either oversimplified paraphrase or to distortion. Moreover, his exegesis is stolid and stiff, and employs linguistic

forms that are so un-Buberian that it is hard to recognize the authentic Buber in Berkovits's paraphrase. Then again, the reconstruction is not altogether accurate because it tries to analyze Buber's position through concerns that are not always those of the philosophy of dialogue. In this respect, it is also apparent that Berkovits is not careful enough in working with the distinction between epistemological and ontological categories, often translating the former into the latter. This has especially negative consequences for his account of Buber's fundamental thesis of *I–Thou/I–It*. This is described primarily in ontological terms and presuppositions without recognizing the importance of the Kantian element in Buber's work, which must be understood epistemologically as well as ontologically: *how* I know is inseparable from *what* I know.

In addition, instead of analyzing the meaning of basic Buberian terms, Berkovits merely repeats or paraphrases them. For example, he writes "As the *I* of *I–Thou*, he [man] participates. The nonparticipating *I* [of I–It] is unreal."[61] However, one is never clear what "participation" entails. This failure of clarity, of course, is also found in the original Buberian sources, which owe much of their appeal to their obscurity. However, this lack of precision leads to simple logical errors. Compare the statement just quoted regarding "participation" and Berkovits's statement written a few lines earlier: "The *I* of *I–It* is *much less real* than *I* in *I–Thou*."[62] Notice the confusion regarding the meaning of the term "real" as applied to the *I* of *I–It* in these two statements. In the statement just quoted it is said to be "much less real," while in the former quotation the *I* is said to be "unreal." It cannot be both "much less real" and "unreal." Furthermore, which is the correct reading of Buber? To decide, we would first have to be clear about the use of the terms "real," "reality," etc., which are never defined, as well as many other features of Buber's epistemology and ontology which are ignored altogether. It certainly is of no help for Berkovits to add "To be real means to participate."[63] As we have no certain sense of what "participation" means, little, if anything, is gained by this additional, circular, exegetical detail. These serious logical and conceptual weaknesses can be multiplied with regularity throughout Berkovits's exegesis.

2. Let us now turn to Berkovits's evaluative review. Berkovits's major criticism of Buber is that Buber's appeal is subjective and "unprovable." Though correct, and though this criticism is obviously significant, Berkovits does not seem to realize that (a) most, if not all, philosophical arguments are "unprovable" in the sense in which he requires proof here; and (b) Buber's "subjective" claim is based on *philosophical* grounds, i.e., the Kierkegaardian-like thesis that "Truth is subjectivity." Buber takes the position he does for *philosophical* reasons—most of which have been stated by Kierkegaard in his *Concluding Unscientific Postscript* and echoed by all the existentialists ever since. To challenge Buber's teachings, one has not only to state that they are subjective—Buber, after all, is perfectly aware of this, but thinks it a major virtue—but has to show why the existentialist credo that "Truth is subjectivity" is a philosophical blunder. This Berkovits never takes up. Though this doctrine does lead to serious difficulties, as I have argued elsewhere, Berkovits does not locate these lacunae nor does he show signs of understanding the logic of Buber's methodology, of which these subjective and subjectivist claims are an integral part.[64] This is part of Berkovits's larger failure to grasp not only the explicit elements in Buber's thought, but also the implicit ones that are not stated in the process of Buber's argument. This in turn is related to the issue of "modernity," which has already been mentioned, for Buber is pre-eminently a modern man and a symbol of "modernity" and its concerns. His position, whether it be his "subjectivity," his "existentialism," his "situation morality" (Buber would not like this term applied to his work), or the like, is part of a movement of ideas, as well as a mood which largely dominated European thought since World War I. To do justice to Buber's conceptual schema, even if critically, one must be aware of the implicit elements (especially related to Kant and Kierkegaard) in his thinking, and the issues, problems, and historical circumstances to which he was replying.

3. Berkovits's critique of the moral anarchy implicit in Buber's position is correct,[65] though heavy-handed, as is his deep concern with the antinomianism of Buber's understanding of Judaism and *halachah*. However, in this latter case, Buber will not be persuaded

merely by the charge that he is an antinomian, because the *hala-chah* has no validity for him, being only a human response to *I–Thou* (at best) which then becomes an *It* that stands in the way of new *I–Thou* relations, rather than promoting them. Thus, citing the *halachah* against Buber is to miss the point and to argue in a circle. The only time halachic evidence is persuasive is when both parties to a debate accept the validity or at least the value of the *halachah*. This is not the case with Buber. As a consequence, one must be hermeneutically sophisticated in order to know just how to expose the weakness of Buber's stance. Unfortunately, Berkovits, while doing a good deal of solid criticism here, nonetheless is not fully sensitive to the logical and methodological difficulties Buber's position presents, and his remarks are therefore often wide of the mark.

4. The primary intention of Berkovits's critique is to show that Buber's philosophy does not meet the traditional standards of Jewish Orthodoxy, the essay's original title in fact being "A Jewish [i.e., Orthodox] Critique of the Philosophy of Martin Buber." However, as with so much else in Berkovits's approach, this comes as no surprise to anyone, least of all Buber, who was not at all concerned to square his thinking with traditional teaching. Quite the contrary. The very power and appeal of Buber's thought is predicated on a historic situation in which the traditional views, analyses, and answers are no longer seen to be viable and responsive to modern concerns. Buber's importance lies in the very fact of this recognition and his attempt, nonetheless, to affirm God's existence and presence in history while avoiding elements which seem "unbelievable" to him and many of his contemporaries. What Buber is calling into question is the whole of the rabbinic tradition. For him the rabbis had "misunderstood" the "essence of Judaism." If one realizes this, much of Berkovits's probing looks like intellectual shadowboxing. There is certainly much (everything?) that needs re-examination in Buber's approach to Judaism and Jewish tradition and his misunderstanding bordering on blindness of *halachah*. But all such deconstructive analysis has to be offered in a way that indicates it senses what it is in Buber that has made him the most influential Jewish philosopher since Maimonides (excluding Spi-

noza as a specifically "Jewish philosopher," and not forgetting Mendelssohn). Thus, even citing Biblical proof texts (with regard to which there are many problems in Berkovits's treatment) against Buber is to miss the point, for the literal validity of the Biblical text is perhaps the most serious issue of all that Buber and modern men have come to question. In other words, the entire philosophical and theological ground rules for engaging Buber are different from those used in more traditional debate. Buber can certainly be effectively criticized, but the care and sophistication of the critic are of paramount importance.

5. Berkovits's major charge against Buber's metaphysics is that it is pantheistic.[66] There is an element of truth in this and Berkovits is to be commended for catching it. Most expositors have missed it. But it is one thing to talk of an element of pantheism in Buber and another to set out his system as a thoroughgoing pantheism, which it is not. Berkovits's "proof" to this end is achieved only by doing violent injustice to the sources he cites. What is present here is not pantheism in the technical sense but an expression of the very Jewish urge to give value to man and creation. Though Buber's enthusiasm for creation does at times overwhelm him and lead him into some extremely injudicious assertions, he is *not a* pantheist, i.e., he does not equate the world with God or God with the world without remainder. What appears to be pantheistic in Buber has its source in an admixture of Hegelian and Buberianly understood (or misunderstood) Kabbalistic–Hasidic[67] elements, and these elements do run through much of Buber's metaphysical musings. But in no case was Buber a "pantheist" *per se.* In every instance where he had occasion to discuss the subject he vigorously criticized it as inimical to true, i.e., dialogical, religion. Moreover, Berkovits's specific attempts to support this charge do not hold up on closer inspection. For example, Berkovits's "pantheistic" exposition of what is represented to be Buber's view of the relation of freedom and causality[68] is really to be read as a Buberian admixture of Kantian and Kierkegaardian themes. There is no need at all to introduce pantheistic doctrines to account for Buber's position, unless one purposely wants to misconstrue what is at issue. What is wrong with Buber's ontology is not its "pantheism" but its logical incon-

sistency, metaphysical impossibility, and philosophical obscurity. Berkovits seems to see all "improper" Jewish philosophy as the result of either pantheistic or "Christian" tendencies—and he accuses Buber of both; but evidence shows that there are many errors Jewish thinkers can and do make that are not instances of these categories. It appears that Berkovits needs more philosophical imagination.

6. Berkovits's description and critique of many of Buber's basic concepts (dialogue, philosophical anthropology, encounter, revelation, etc.) are forced and inadequate. For example, consider Berkovits's treatment of encounter/dialogue as a paradigm. Berkovits asserts that Buber's version of these concepts is faulty because (among other things) in the encounter with God: (a) There is no dialogical equality; (b) There is no freedom; and (c) God is not always present to man. His reasons for so arguing are based primarily on his understanding of the Biblical accounts. But the analysis and "authority" of Biblical material are themselves subject to debate. Even more important, however, is that his representation of what the Biblical picture reveals of the God–man relation is not free of difficulty. For example, it is not clear that there is no dialogical equality or freedom in at least *some* Biblical God–man encounters. If it is true that Buber incorrectly reduces all Biblical meetings to his own dialogical model, it is equally true that Berkovits does the same in the direction of his nondialogical model. Meanwhile the truth seems to be that no single model of Biblical encounter can be adequate. The evidence is too varied, requiring a more complex, polymorphous phenomenology to handle it adequately. Furthermore, if there were no freedom in the relationship, as Berkovits argues, the majesty accorded man, and stressed so strongly in the traditional Jewish understanding of Israel's willingness to participate freely in the covenant and keep the Torah, would be without foundation. The structure of Torah/*mitsvah* requires an unfolding of Divine–human encounter that includes freedom. Finally, Berkovits's strictures against what he takes to be Buber's optimism regarding the eternal presence of God and the ever-present possibility of encounter is deficient on at least two counts: (1) Buber is not significantly at odds here with most of the Jewish tradition, Berkovits notwith-

standing; and (2) Buber, especially after the Holocaust, recognized this problem and tried to respond to it, coining in the process his suggestive phrase (and the title of his late book) *The Eclipse of God.* That this phrase is a metaphor that itself needs to be fleshed out is unarguable, but it seems that Buber at least recognized the problem which Berkovits wants to deny, and that his attempt was serious, if still problematic. In short, therefore, we can conclude this section by noting that we still await a substantive interrogation of Buber's views.

V

Berkovits now moves on to Mordecai Kaplan. Here we are provided with a reprint of Berkovits's well known critique of Kaplan, which first appeared in *TRADITION* (Fall 1959). Some of the faults common to Berkovits's approach are again in evidence: the misunderstandings, the forced renderings of passages, the unfairness of certain emphases and expositions. Yet it must be said that Berkovits's onslaught does strike home, especially his attack on the pseudo-scientific nature of Reconstructionism. This charge is on target, for Kaplan's program is marred by a mistaken estimation of modern science and what philosophical implications can be correctly drawn from contemporary naturalism and social science.[69] Though put too polemically, Berkovits's conclusion is accurate:

Since the Reconstructionist view of naturalism is so extremely naive and outdated, nothing but failure was to be expected from its "wedding of religion to naturalism."

And he is also moving in the right direction when he goes on to argue that "Anyone who undertakes the task will have to attempt to harmonize a mature naturalism with a mature supernaturalism."[70] This theme, which was also taken up and well made by Emil Fackenheim in his study[71] of Kaplan, is to the point. However, it should be recognized that it is not clear what a "mature naturalism" and a "mature supernaturalism" would be. Again, on the positive side, Berkovits's emphases on Kaplan's inability to deal with moral value and evil within his system is instructive and raises an issue of fundamental importance.

Berkovits treats Kaplan primarily as a metaphysician or theologian whose main concern is to propound an alternative metaphysics to that of traditional Judaism. The very title of Berkovits's essay unambiguously reflects this perspective: "Reconstructionist-Theology; A Central Evaluation." But, here is the rub, Kaplan does not want to be seen as a theologian. He has very little sympathy with theology, and is a poor theologian who does theology out of necessity in order to support his primary aim: the survival of the Jewish people. Kaplan is another paradigm of the modern Jew who is deeply committed to the Jewish people, while finding it impossible to believe in *Torah mi Sinai*. In order to make a rationale for Israel's continued existence he gives, as the English philosopher Bradley said, "bad reasons for what he believes on instinct." The primary lines of Kaplan's defense of the Jewish people proceed along the sociological avenues suggested by Emile Durkheim and his sociological and anthropological heirs. Kaplan's work is more a Jewish sociology than a Jewish theology in the formal sense; or, more precisely, it is theology generated by and done in support of sociological concerns and built upon sociological, psychological, and anthropological presuppositions. "My conception of God," he told Arthur Cohen, "is entirely derived from social psychology."[72]

Berkovits does not see this sociological dimension or its ramifications. He treats Kaplan's work in ways that are often inappropriate, forcing it into forms and patterns, especially metaphysical patterns, that it does not have, and which are of little or no concern to it. Berkovits treats Kaplan as a systematic theologian, which he is not and has no intention of being. While it is true that Kaplan's image of "supernaturalism" is a straw man, and out of touch with the best modern theology, Berkovits makes Kaplan into something of a straw man by not realizing that the center of his thinking is social reality—the *group*, in this case the Jewish people. Everything radiates from this center and all value is mediated and adjudicated in relation to it. Moreover, Kaplan's sociological emphasis reflects an aspect of modern rationality, with its inversion of transcendence and immanence, as well as with its anthropological and psychological emphases, which cannot be ignored or dismissed out of hand—even if Kaplan's particular presentation of these concerns is weak.

Moving to more specific items, one also finds certain aspects of the detailed charges Berkovits lays against Kaplan unsatisfactorily handled. For example, Berkovits argues that Kaplan's errors lie not only in his employment of various forms of pseudo-science and in his confusion over the difference between facts and values, but also in his pantheism. As with Buber, perhaps even more so, there are elements in Kaplan's thought that can be viewed as pantheistic in a broad sense, but to charge Kaplan with a technical pantheistic doctrine is an error. It would ascribe to Kaplan metaphysical doctrines about God and ultimate reality that Kaplan carefully eschews as part of his inherited Kantian reticence to do metaphysics at all. Then again, Berkovits's further attempt to elicit the claimed Spinozistic character of Kaplan's ethic is extremely forced.[73]

Whatever the failings of Reconstructionist ethics, it is not a deterministic pantheistic position akin to that propounded in Spinoza's *Ethics,* nor is its concern with the group at all akin to Spinoza's ontological concern for the unity of all things in the One Divine substance. Berkovits recognizes that Kaplan says contradictory things, yet presents Kaplan's view as essentially pantheistic. At the same time he also notes that Kaplan's thought includes doctrines that are in contradiction to his supposed systematic pantheism, and these contradictions are, of course, presented as further evidence of Kaplan's confusion. However, it makes as much sense, and is nearer in spirit to Kaplan's authentic concerns, to reason that Kaplan is not a pantheist although he holds certain unclear doctrines that lean in that direction. It is true that Kaplan is confused when it comes to systematic metaphysical doctrines, but confusion is not pantheism.[74] Moreover, Berkovits seems to mistake naturalism and pantheism and fails to make the important metaphysical distinctions that individuate the two concepts. This lack of precision leads Berkovits to misconstrue many of Kaplan's basic doctrines as ontological statements, whereas Kaplan seems to intend them primarily as socially pragmatic or ethical propositions. Of course, one cannot have a religious morality without a

religious ontology, but which is which needs to be carefully delin-
eated and the failure to do so à la Berkovits can only lead to incom-
prehensibility.

Finally, Berkovits is quick to pounce on those, like Cohen and
Rosenzweig, who do not seem to give enough weight to history in
their attempts to frame a philosophy of Judaism, but he fails to
come to grips with the technical issue of how one investigates the
past and how one evaluates the historical record. It is not simply a
case of reading "meaning" off the surface of events, for the "meaning" of history is obscure. In Kaplan's thought this methodological
problem forces itself to the fore, for he reads a different "meaning"
from history than does Berkovits. Indeed, he charges those like Berkovits who would defend an Orthodox position with not taking
history seriously enough, as well as with reading into history metaphysical and theological doctrines that are illusory and unjustifiable. Here the real issues appertaining to the formulation of a
systematic and methodological skeleton of a philosophy of Judaism
begin to be engaged, but precisely at this juncture Berkovits seems
unwilling to become party to the discussion.

VI

The final thinker considered by Berkovits is Abraham Joshua Heschel. His remarks, however, constitute neither an extended treatment of Heschel's work, nor of Heschel's treatment of "major
themes in modern philosophies of Judaism," but a review-essay of
Heschel's book *The Prophets*. [75]

Berkovits focuses on Heschel's analysis of prophetic religion in
terms of Divine pathos and sympathy. He sums up Heschel's depiction as follows:

God is passible; He is affected by what man does and He reacts according
to His affection. He is a God of pathos. He is "emotionally affected" by
the conduct of man. [76]

In support of this rendering he quotes this essential sentence from
Heschel:

This notion that God can be intimately affected, that He possesses not merely intelligence and will, but also pathos, basically defines the prophetic consciousness of God.[77]

Moreover, according to Heschel, this objective, prophetic consciousness has a subjective counterpart that can be defined as prophetic sympathy: the prophet aligning himself sympathetically with God's pathos so that he can fully represent God's desires to the people. For Berkovits this means that:

He [the prophet] feels God's feeling. The prophets react to the Divine pathos with sympathy for God . . . Sympathy is a feeling which feels the feeling to which it reacts . . . Because of this sympathy, the prophet is guided, not by what he feels, but rather by What God feels. In moments of intense sympathy for God, the prophet is moved by the pathos of God.[78]

On the basis of this interpretation of Heschel Berkovits moves to the attack. The target is obvious, the age-old problem of anthropomorphism and more precisely anthropopathism. Yet the target is more elusive than Berkovits realizes. Heschel knows as well as Berkovits that religious language is full of enigmas and confusions. He knows about anthropopathism and its attendant difficulties; yet as a man of profound faith he wants to sustain the intelligibility in some form of religious language, and hence of Biblical revelation. Berkovits even cites Heschel's constant disclaimers that the language of the prophets is not literal, that it constantly points beyond itself, that it is, when all is said and done, mysterious, paradoxical, evocative but not descriptive.[79] And yet Berkovits treats Heschel as if he were a simple-minded fundamentalist with no theological sophistication, as if what he were doing were ridiculous. He fails to understand that Heschel's attempt, even if it is unsuccessful, is profound. It is profound—and very Jewish, despite Berkovits's remarks to the contrary—because it is trying to explicate the depth of the Biblical imagery pertaining to the meaning of man's existential relation to God, while recognizing the wisdom inherent in the traditional dictum that the Bible "is written in the language of man." In no sense is Heschel seeking to write a metaphysical treatise about God's being; rather he is making one of the most sustained contemporary attempts to explain what the relation of God and man entails, and why God needs man as much as man needs God, themes he develops in his other works.[80]

To defend his literalistic reading of Heschel, Berkovits calls up the venerable ghost of Maimonides and the medievals, who were no strangers to the problem of anthropomorphism. Their introduction, however, does not really settle anything: the argument from authority is not a philosophical argument. Moreover, on reflecting on the medieval material, four responses suggest themselves.

1. Despite the universal veneration of Maimonides, his theory of negative attributes does *not* appear to be philosophically viable. Indeed, it is probably (a) more inimical to maintaining meaningful religious discourse than Heschel's attempt—fully recognizing all the obvious criticisms that can be raised against Heschel as well as the defenses made for Maimonides, especially regarding God's ethical attributes; (b) even Maimonides' own medieval contemporaries were not universally ecstatic over his solution, and this can be seen in both Jewish quarters and in the alternative theories, like the significant theory of analogy in Aquinas which specifically cites, evaluates, and rejects Maimonides' lead.

2. There is a curious blindness attached to Berkovits's appeal to the medievals. He notes that Maimonides rejected the attribution of emotional predicates to God on the philosophical grounds of God's immutability. To make such attributions would challenge God's immutability and hence His perfection according to the inherited Aristotelian notion of perfection. What Berkovits fails to appreciate is that the Maimonidean notion of perfection here involved is perhaps inappropriate and in need of rethinking. Heschel makes this precise point and Berkovits refers to it,[81] but he misses its force, thinking it only a historical allusion as to the origin of the Eleatic idea of perfection, which it is not. Some classical thinkers recognized the need to rework the meaning of God's perfection, and more recently it has been the subject of major theological reassessments by A.N. Whitehead and Charles Hartshorne.[82] It is this sort of theological reconsideration that Heschel intended in this connection.

As part of his analysis of Divine Perfection Berkovits asserts with considerable boldness that: "The truth is that even though the Bible calls perfect only His work and it never refers to God as Absolute, absoluteness is implied in the Biblical concept of God as well as perfection." And a little farther on he again writes: "The God of Abraham, Isaac and Jacob is not the God of Aristotle, but certainly [sic] includes the philosopher's concept of absoluteness."[83]

But is this so? One would have thought that the absence of certain attributions in the Bible would be cause to pause and proceed slowly with dogmatic assertions about the "God concept" of the Torah. It would also appear that it is by no means clear what these terms—absolute and perfect—mean when applied to God. Moreover, it would seem to involve certain logical convolutions to hold that though the God of the Bible is not the God of the philosophers "He certainly includes the philosophers' concept of absoluteness." If this is so what individuates the one from the other? Can the former include all the predicates of the latter and yet be the former? It is precisely the different entailments of the two concepts of God that was at the heart of the medieval debate: the absoluteness of Aristotle's Prime Mover was not—could not logically be— the absoluteness of the God of Genesis (who had a will, which was an imperfection for the Greeks); though the medievals did not always realize this either.

3. There is one irony here which must be noted. It was precisely the thesis of perfection entailing immutability that served as Spinoza's absolute presupposition which led him to his pantheism and determinism. Of all those who took the Eleatic idea of perfection seriously, it was primarily Spinoza who was willing to follow out the logical implications of this doctrine. If Berkovits finds the Eleatic metaphysic of immutability so plausible, it is he who may be a pantheist!

4. Lastly, one should appreciate that despite Berkovits's remarks, Heschel was fully aware of the medieval debate over anthropomorphism. It should be recalled that he wrote a number of learned papers on Maimonides[84] including a biography.[85] He was also the author of scholarly essays on Saadiah[86] and Ibn Gabirol[87] among others. In contradistinction to Berkovits, I would suggest that Heschel was consciously philosophizing against the medie-

vals, aware of their position and trying to do something quite different. It would prove, I think, a fruitful exercise to compare Heschel's analysis of Biblical language and Maimonides' analysis as offered in the *Guide*; I would suggest that Heschel may have had this exact counterpart in his mind's eye while working on the *Prophets*.

Berkovits's treatment of Heschel also reintroduces the question of sources, their use and interpretation. Not satisfied with calling up the medieval philosophers Berkovits calls in the other classics of Judaism: Biblical, Talmudic, and even kabbalistic. He even quotes from Ḥayim Vital's defense against the charge of anthropomorphism at the end of Chapter I of some editions of his *Eits Ḥayyim* and from Moshe Ḥayim Luzzato's remarks in his *Ḥoker u' Mekubbal*, charging that even these kabbalists would never go as far in attributing possibility to God as Heschel does in his theology of pathos. But I suspect it is just these kabbalistic texts that are at the root of Heschel's thinking, imbibed deeply in the rich Hasidic[88] world of his youth. There is certainly as much Divine possibility in classical kabbalah as there is in Heschel; and at the same time what the kabbalists try to protect through their postulation of the ineffable *Ein Sof* is precisely what Heschel wants to protect when he eschews talk of God's essence; indeed he could well have written the very phrases (and comes close in places) that Berkovits cites from the kabbalistic classics. The same may also be said about the Biblical and rabbinic compositions.

When all is concluded, one is faced with the inescapable fact that there are Biblical and rabbinic materials that are sound evidences for a theory of Divine possibility as they stand. One can explain them away in a number of fashions, but this is quite a different matter. This is not to say all the texts Heschel cites are what he suggests, but then again it is clearly not the case that none of them are, for after all the sorting and analyzing of the sources is done there is evidence for some real element of Divine passibility in the traditional materials. Berkovits indeed is forced to make the telling admission that there are "innumerable anthropopathic passages in the Aggadah and Midrash"[89] and that to deal with them one must recognize that "Theology demands meaningful interpretation"[90] and again that his judgment is dictated by "The theological climate [that] is determined by a long tradition of affirmation of Divine impassibility *in face of numerous Biblical texts to the contrary.*"[91] At this point, and only at this point, do the complex hermeneutical and theological issues begin to be engaged, and arguments, not assertions and oversimplifications, are required. Perhaps the "tradition" has to be rethought in these areas, perhaps "the theological climate" needs altering. And if not, why not? Moreover, it is in this context that Berkovits should show how religious language can work without analogical use of language or the like. It behooves him to indicate how the Biblical and rabbinic discussions can retain their theological meaning and value without committing some of the moves made by Heschel: and where one wants to dissociate oneself from Heschel, how one still protects the intelligibility of one's God-language.

Thus, for example, one has to push Berkovits on his agreement with Heschel that God is a personal God. Berkovits summarizes Heschel's view in the following manner:

The reality of God is experienced by the prophet as God's *care* and *concern* for His creation. "Man stands under God's 'concern' is the basic message of all prophecy."[92]

And then acknowledges his concurrence with these propositions by adding "These are, of course, familiar thoughts, well understood by all who have some knowledge of Biblical theology or religious philosophy."[93] But what does Berkovits mean when he agrees to speak of "God's care and concern?" Can he make out a philosophical case in which these terms retain their intelligibility while avoiding the anthropopathetic errors he attributes to Heschel? Berkovits does not seem aware that the position he advances is logically self-contradictory, for he does not attempt any resolution of the self-referential inconsistency. This is not surprising, however, as it is an easy thing this late in the history of philosophy to recognize that religious language presents large, perhaps even insuperable problems, foremost among them being a workable theory of analogy or something else that will do a similar job so as to avoid the error of anthropomorphism and anthropopathism, while it is quite another matter to advance any suggestion that will assist in the resolution of this issue. Moreover, returning to Berkovits's remarks about Heschel, it is not the case that Heschel simply "takes the metaphorical language of the Midrash and calls [it] a theology of pathos."[94] Rather Heschel is trying to show what this particular language is about, why the Bible and Midrash use it and not some other language, and how we are to do justice to the claims made for the sanctity and revelatory quality of the text without being literalists on the one hand or willy-nilly liberals on the other. Berkovits reminds us of the rabbinic use of the term *"keveyakhol,"* "as it were," to qualify anthropopathic and anthropomorphic expressions[95] and this is a reminder well worth heeding. But at the same time we must also realize that the text does use specific anthropomorphic and anthropopathic expressions even if it uses them as it were *"keveyakhol."*

Furthermore, Berkovits, after agreeing with Heschel that the Biblical God does know individuals, and does "realize them as a concrete fact,"[96] still feels compelled to disagree with Heschel's conclusion that this individual relation between God and man entails Divine passibility. To support this declaration, however, Berkovits does not resort to argument or evidence, but to an article of faith: "God's realizing man as a concrete fact and not an abstraction is enveloped in mystery."[97] He then concludes, as if he had really settled the issue, with the logical barbarism that "surely, [sic] our mystery is much more logical than Dr. Heschel's." How one mystery can be "more logical" than another is the greatest mystery of all.[98]

There remains one major component of Berkovits's critique of Heschel to note, and it stems from what is by now an expected charge: Heschel's theology of pathos/sympathy is too close to a Christian-like theology.[99] Berkovits attempts to document this accusation by some random citations from Christian literature, and a brief disquisition on Christian theology. This charge against Heschel is unworthy. Heschel's theology is deeply rooted in Jewish tradition, especially the Hasidic milieu of his youth. If he is guilty of perhaps overemphasizing the personal and subjective elements in these sources it is certainly not because he is in some sense a crypto-Christian or doing crypto-Christian theology. A perusal of the classics of rabbinic Judaism reveals adequate data to construct a Heschelian theology "out of the sources of Judaism." Berkovits's citations from Hermann Lotze's *Microcosmus* and A.M. Fairbairn's obscure work *The Place of Christ in Modern Theology* to substantiate this line of attack are so tendentious as to border on the ridiculous. There is a great deal amiss in Heschel's theology and it can be brought into the open without the absurdity of following Berkovits's passion for finding Christians under every modern Jewish theologian's bed, "conclusively" demonstrated by quoting thinkers like A.M. Fairbairn and showing that Heschel is a fellow traveller of Christian Patripassian theology.

In a letter to *Judaism*,[100] in reply to an article by Sol Tanenzapf, Berkovits, obviously stung by Tanenzapf's observations about his treatment of Heschel and Christianity, tried to back away from the topic by writing:

As if I had criticized Heschel for being "too" Christian. The truth is that I was showing that what makes sense within the frame of reference of Christianity is utterly meaningless in the context of Judaism.

If this straightforward point were all that Berkovits intended in the original article why didn't he just say that? I leave it to readers to decide this issue. Therefore, I merely reproduce, without further comment, the opening paragraph of Berkovits's discussion, as well as three of his later statements on this theme.

There is little doubt that in the context of Jewish thought and religious sensitivity, Dr. Heschel's position is most original. And yet, when he speaks of man's participating in "the inner life" of God and God's sharing in the life of man, there is a somewhat familiar ring about it. When he elaborates in innumerable variations on the prophet's feeling "His heart" and experiencing "the pain in the heart of God" as his own, or when he reveals the secret of sympathy as a situation in which "man experiences God as his own being," it does not take much perspicuity to realize that one has encountered these concepts in one's readings—in Christian theology.[101]

In Christianity, God does have pathos in exactly the same sense as Dr. Heschel understands the term.[102]

Already in the second and third century c.e., a theology of pathos was formulated in the Christian church which comes very close to that of Dr. Heschel.[103]

Heschel's view corresponds, as we have noted, to the position of the Patripassians in Christian theology.[104]

CONCLUSION

This essay has indicated serious weaknesses in Berkovits's endeavor. It has objected to the terminology, methodology, logic, and tone of much of his exposition and criticism with respect to major modern Jewish thinkers. These objections are all serious ones in appraising the abiding value of Berkovits's writings. Certainly Berkovits has alerted readers to the serious issues in modern Jewish thought that need reappraisal but it is unfortunate that his eye for specific errors is not attended by a larger understanding of why the errors, if they are errors, were made. Such an understanding might have rescued him from his unfairness to Cohen, Rosenzweig, Buber, Kaplan, and Heschel and I believe it would have allowed for a more accurate and penetrating account of his subject. Furthermore, the topic of the need for a broader appreciation of the subject under review is inextricably related to the larger methodological issues of how "one does philosophy," especially the unavoidable problem of how one reads philosophical and other texts. Then again, a higher degree of philosophical self-consciousness and severer internal criticism in all these areas would have saved Berkovits from at least some of his more unacceptable remarks.

At the same time, Berkovits must be commended for initiating a serious debate about contemporary Jewish philosophical issues. The job at hand is to do what Berkovits attempted more satisfactorily.

NOTES

All references to E. Berkovits, *Major Themes in Modern Philosophies of Judaism* (New York, 1974), will be referred to as *Berkovits.*

1. It should be noted for instance that we still lack a *complete*, expert history of modern Jewish thought, the closest facsimile being Nathan Rotenstreich's *Jewish Philosophy in Modern Times* (New York, 1962), translated from the original Hebrew version of this work and to a lesser extent, Julius Guttmann's *Philosophies of Judaism* (New York, 1964). Both studies, however, end with Rosenzweig, who is treated very briefly, and ignore the post-World War I period (except for Rosenzweig) completely, i.e., Buber, Kaplan, Heschel, et al. Though each of these works is unquestionably valuable, both studies also have their serious weaknesses. A second and more meaningful feature of the neglect of the modern period is the absence of quality programs for the training of young scholars in the area of modern Jewish thought, either in the United States or Israel. The only university that can claim to have made any serious attempt to meet this need is probably Brandeis, much to its credit.

2. An excellent example of this historical-exegetical tendency can be perceived in the vast secondary literature on Martin Buber, the most studied and written on modern Jewish thinker. Among all the literature on Buber there is very little of first-rate philosophical importance.

3. An example of the creative criticism I have in mind is A. Altmann's essay on H. Cohen (see note 28 below), or S.H. Bergman's work on Cohen (see note 27 below). On Rosenzweig, there is little of value aside from the work of N. Glatzer; on Buber the best, though still largely unsatisfactory, work is found in *The Philosophy of Martin Buber*, P. Schilpp and M. Friedman, eds., (Illinois, 1967).

4. Berkovits, p. 4.

5. H. Cohen, *Jüdische Schriften*, Bruno Strauss, ed., with an Introduction by Franz Rosenzweig, 3 volumes (Berlin, 1924). Reprinted by Arno Press (New York, 1980).

6. Cf., for example, Cohen's remarks in *Die Ethik des reinen Willens* (2nd ed. 1907), pp. 402 ff.

7. See F. Rosenzweig's remarks in his Einleitung to the *Jüdische Schriften*, volume I, pp. 20–21.

8. Berkovits's exact statement is: "Our attention, however, will be concentrated on two works in which Cohen's religion of reason found its final statement: the one entitled *Der Begriff* . . . and the other *Die Religion*," Berkovits, p. 1.

9. In the second edition of this work the definite article "Die" was omitted in accordance with instructions Cohen had left. On the significance of this omission see Trude Weiss Rosmarin's review of the English translation of this work in *Judaism* (Fall 1973). It should also be noted that an English translation of *Die Religion der Vernunft aus den Quellen des Judentums* is now available as *Religion of Reason out of the Sources of Judaism*, trans. S. Kaplan (New York, 1972).

10. *Berkovits*, p. 1.

11. *Berkovits*, p. 2.

12. See F. Rosenzweig, op. cit., Vol. I, pp. xxxii ff.

13. *Berkovits*, p. 8.

14. Berkovits very inadequately discusses this issue in three-quarters of a page; see *Berkovits*, p. 6 ff.

15. H. Cohen, *Die Religion*, p. 194.

16. H. Cohen, op. cit., p. 41.

17. H. Cohen, op. cit., p. 48.

18. H. Cohen, op. cit., p. 48. For more, see Cohen's entire discussion of the topic in *Die Religion*, pp. 47–8.

19. See *Berkovits*, pp. 5–6.

20. See *Berkovits*, p. 5.

21. See *Berkovits*, Chapter I, note 19.

22. *Berkovits*, p. 32.

23. Of course having established this asymmetrical relation of Being → Becoming, Being does serve, both by design as well as by accident, in functional roles. But this is almost always the case in any form of a theistic metaphysic.

24. See H. Cohen, *Die Religion*, Chapter I, and *Der Begriff*, pp. 18–20.

25. See for example, S.H. Bergman's comments in his *Faith and Reason* (New York, 1963).

26. See J. Guttmann, *Philosophies of Judaism* (New York, 1964), p. 415; and A. Altmann's excellent article, "Hermann Cohen's Begriff der Korrelation," in *In zwei Welten* (Tel Aviv, 1962). See also J. Agus, *Modern Philosophies of Judaism* (New York, 1941).

27. For a different view see Emil Fackenheim's, "Hermann Cohen—Fifty Years After," the *Leo Baeck Memorial Lecture*, No. 12 (New York, 1969), p. 23. See also A. Altmann, op. cit. and J. Gutmann, op. cit. Though agreeing with a large measure of Fackenheim's carefully drawn conclusion on this matter, as well as with much that Professors Gutmann and Altmann have argued (they are the source of Fackenheim's views as he indicates), I am still of the opinion that all three scholars are still too cautious in their estimation of the "Reality" of God in the late Cohen. Not that Cohen has established God's reality, but his attempt to do so seems to me more profound and also more successful (though still unsuccessful!) than these three most eminent Jewish scholars hold. It should be added here that this difference is also probably a corollary of the larger issue of my somewhat different reading of the history of modern Jewish thought, and Cohen's place in it, than that held by Professors Fackenheim, Guttmann, and Altmann.

28. The issue of "history" in Judaism, however, is far more complex than is usually thought. Berkovits's views on this issue are themselves not

terribly sophisticated. I have tried to begin to rethink this issue in my paper "History and Covenant" in S. Wagner and Y. Greenberg (eds.), *The Meaning of the Covenant* (tentative title). This volume should appear in 1984 under the sponsorship of the Center for Jewish Studies, University of Denver.

29. *Berkovits*, p. 20.

30. H. Cohen, *Die Religion*, p. 508. This quote is from the English translation of *Religion of Reason*, p. 431.

31. H. Cohen, *Die Religion*, p. 520. The present translation is from the English translation of *Religion of Reason*, p. 441.

32. For these references to the Exodus, see H. Cohen, *Die Religion*, p. 49 on the Burning Bush and Revelation, p. 146 on the love of the stranger, p. 327 on the relation of the Exodus to messianism.

33. *Berkovits*, p. 36.

34. The discussion of Berkovits's treatment of Rosenzweig as well as of Buber, Kaplan, and Heschel that follow will, of necessity, have to be shorter than was the treatment of Cohen. It is hoped that the critical philosophical reflections regarding Cohen will serve as a model of what is wrong with Berkovits's approach and general presentation. The less detailed studies of later thinkers will address themselves to specific issues raised by Berkovits which call for critical comment and review.

35. *Berkovits*, p. 47.

36. *Der Stern der Erlosung* (1921, 2nd ed. 1929). There is an English translation of this work by the title, *The Star of Redemption*, translated by W. Hallo (New York, 1972).

37. *Berkovits*, p. 51 ff.

38. See for example, *Genesis Rabbah* 164; *Avot de Rabbi Nathan* 31, p. 91; *Leviticus Rabbah* 19:1; *Avot* 3:14. Among the medievals see H. Crescas, *Or Adonai* 2:6; and, of course, the widely held views on this subject in the kabbalistic literature, for example, *Zohar* 3, 152a.

39. *Ecclesiastes Rabbah* 2:1.

40. Saadiah, *Emunot v'Deot*, 3:7.

41. For Maimonides' views see his *Commentary on The Mishnah*, Sanhedrin 10; *Yad*, Yesodei ha-Torah, 9; *Guide*, 2:29, 39.

42. See Hasdai Crescas, *Or Adonai*, 3 pt. 1, 5–12; Joseph Albo, *Sefer ha-Ikkarim*, 3:13–22. For a detailed discussion of this and related aspects of the eternity of the Torah see S. Katz, *Jewish Concepts* (Jerusalem and New York, 1977).

43. Abraham Azulai, *Hesed le-Avraham* (1685) II, 27. For a detailed discussion of this source as well as of the entire question of the role of Torah in kabbalistic thought see G. Scholem's essay, "The Meaning of Torah in Jewish Mysticism," in his *On the Kabbalah and its Symbolism* (New York, 1974).

44. For a thorough discussion of the Christian position on this issue see W.D. Davies, *The Torah in the Messianic Age/or the World to Come* (Philadelphia, 1952), and also the same author's *Paul and Rabbinic Judaism* (New York, 1967).

45. F. Rosenzweig, *Der Stern*, Volume 3, p. 100, cited by *Berkovits*, p. 39.

46. *Berkovits*, p. 39 ff.

47. All students of Rosenzweig have noted this.

48. For a valuable discussion of Rosenzweig's views on Zionism see Yaacov Fleischman's essay, "Franz Rosenzweig as a Critic of Zionism" in *Conservative Judaism* (Fall, 1967).

49. F. Rosenzweig, *Briefe*, p. 572.

50. See F. Rosenzweig, *Briefe*, p. 591.

51. For a review of post-Holocaust Jewish thought see my discussion of "Jewish Thought since 1945" in S. Katz (ed.), *Jewish Philosophers* (New York, 1975), pp. 203–266. See also the papers dealing with various Holocaust themes in the present volume. I have also treated related historical and theological matters in my forthcoming monograph *The Uniqueness of the Holocaust* to be published by Harvard University Press next year.

52. See Berkovits's discussion of these topics in *Berkovits*, pp. 66 ff.

53. See my essay, cited in note 28, for a more detailed examination of these issues.

54. Rosenzweig, *Star*, Part II.

55. F. Rosenzweig, *Star*, Part II, p. 224.

56. Ibid.

57. See Rosenzweig's discussion of this issue in the *Star*, Part III.

58. F. Rosenzweig, *Star*, Part II, p. 253.

59. N. Glatzer, *Franz Rosenzweig* (New York, 1961), p. 32.

60. This appeared as a separate monograph published by Yeshiva University, (New York, 1962).

61. *Berkovits*, p. 69.

62. *Berkovits*, p. 69. Emphasis added.

63. *Berkovits*, p. 69.

64. See my "Dialogue and Revelation in the Thought of Martin Buber," in *Religious Studies*, Vol. 13 (Dec., 1977), pp. 57–68 and idem. "Martin Buber: A Critical Précis," in the *Bulletin of the Association of Jewish Studies* (Jan., 1975); and idem. "Martin Buber's Concept of God: Critical Reflections" in *Papers of the Seventh World Congress of Jewish Studies* (1977), unpublished. See also the opening essay in this volume, dealing with Buber's work.

65. For more on the problems inherent in Buber's moral philosophy see the essay by M. Fox in *The Philosophy of Martin Buber*, P. Schilpp and M. Friedman, eds. (Illinois, 1967), pp. 151–170. Fox's conclusions are, I think,

substantially correct. Buber was deeply stung by Fox's essay; see his reply in "Reply to Critics" in this same volume. See also my articles referred to above, note 64.

66. See *Berkovits*, section IV of the Buber essay, pp. 118–137.

67. For a detailed discussion of Buber's (mis)understanding of Hasidism see G. Scholem, "Martin Buber's Interpretation of Hasidism" in *The Messianic Idea in Judaism* (New York, 1971), pp. 227–250; R. Schatz-Uffenheimer's essay in *The Philosophy of Martin Buber*, P. Schilpp and M. Friedman, eds., pp. 403–434; and my "Martin Buber's Misuse of Hasidic Sources" in the present volume.

68. See *Berkovits*, p. 127.

69. For more on the question of the "pseudo-scientific" nature of much of Kaplan's work see S. Katz, "Mordecai Kaplan: A Philosophical Demurrer" in *Sh'Ma* (Nov. 1, 1974).

70. *Berkovits*, p. 190.

71. E. Fackenheim, "A Critique of Reconstruction" in *CCAR Journal* (June, 1960).

72. Cited in *If not Now, When* by Arthur A. Cohen and Mordecai Kaplan (New York, 1973), p. 113.

73. *Berkovits*, pp. 169–172, esp. 172.

74. See the critical essay by H. Wieman, "Kaplan's Idea of God," in *Mordecai Kaplan: An Evaluation*, I. Eisenstein and E. Kohn, eds. (New York, 1952), pp. 193–210. Wieman shows how obscure, confused, and inconsistent Kaplan's view of God is.

75. A.J. Heschel, *The Prophets* (New York, 1962).

76. *Berkovits*, p. 12.

77. Heschel, *The Prophets*, p. 233, cited by Berkovits.

78. *Berkovits*, p. 194.

79. See, for example, *Berkovits*, p. 195.

80. See, for example, A.J. Heschel, *God in Search of Man* (New York, 1956), and *Man is not Alone* (New York, 1951).

81. *Berkovits*, p. 202 ff.

82. The relation of Heschel's thought to a Whiteheadian position, especially after the manner of Charles Hartshorne, has been discussed in the recent literature by Sol Tanenzapf, who champions this view, and by Harold Schulweis, who criticizes it. It is also referred to by Berkovits in a letter replying to Tanenzapf's criticism of his (the presently reprinted essay) critique of Heschel. I agree with the general line of Schulweis's criticism and think Tanenzapf's enthusiasm for Whitehead and Hartshorne misguided. See Sol Tanenzapf, "Heschel and his Critics," in *Judaism*, (Summer, 1974), pp. 276–286; Harold Schulweis, "Hartshorne and Heschel," in *Judaism* (Winter, 1975), pp. 58–62; and E. Berkovits, "A Reaction to Tanenzapf," in *Judaism* (Winter, 1975), pp. 115–116. Attention should also be called to Edmund Cherbonnier's two articles supporting Heschel's

views: "A.J. Heschel's *The Philosophy of the Bible,*" in *Commentary,* vol. 27 (Jan., 1959), and "Heschel as a Religious Thinker" in *Conservative Judaism,* vol. 23 (Fall, 1968).

83. *Berkovits,* pp. 202 ff.

84. See, for example, Heschel's papers: "Did Maimonides Strive for Prophetic Inspiration," in *The Louis Ginzburg Jubilee Volume* (in Hebrew), (New York, 1945), pp. 159–188; and "Inspiration (*Ruach ha-Kodesh*) in the Middle Ages," in *The Alexander Marx Jubilee Volume* (in Hebrew), (New York, 1950), pp. 175–208.

85. *Maimonides: Eine Biographie,* (Berlin, 1935). An English translation has recently appeared, *Maimonides,* (New York, 1981).

86. For several of Heschel's writings on Saadiah see his *The Quest for Certainty in Saadiah's Philosophy,* (New York, 1944).

87. Heschel's essays on Ibn Gabirol include: "Der Begriff der Einheit in der Philosophie Gabirols," in *Monatsschrift für die Geschichte und Wissenschaft des Judentums,* Vol. 82 (1938) pp. 89–111; "Das Wesen der Dinge nach der Lehre Gabirols" in *HUCA,* Vol. 14 (1939), pp. 359–85; "Der Begriff des Seins in der Philosophie Gabirols," in *Festschrift Jakob Freimann Zum 70,* (1937), pp. 67–77. An abridged English translation of this last essay appeared in the Heschel memorial issue of *Conservative Judaism,* Vol. 28, No. 1 (Fall, 1972) as "The Concept of Beings in the Philosophy of Ibn Gabirol" translated by David W. Silverman.

88. For more details of Heschel's Hasidic studies see my essay on this theme in *The Journal of Jewish Studies,* Vol. 31 (Spring, 1980), pp. 82–104.

89. *Berkovits,* p. 218.

90. *Berkovits,* p. 218.

91. *Berkovits,* p. 224. Emphasis added.

92. *Berkovits,* p. 192.

93. *Berkovits,* p. 193.

94. *Berkovits,* p. 218.

95. *Berkovits,* p. 218.

96. *Berkovits,* pp. 204–205.

97. *Berkovits,* p. 205.

98. On the logical problems which appeals to "mystery" in theology involve see my essay "The Logic and Language of Mystery," in *Christ, Faith and History,* S. Sykes and J. Clayton, eds. (Cambridge, 1972), pp. 239–262. See also my "Language, Epistemology and Mystical Pluralism" in S. Katz (ed.), *Mysticism and Philosophical Analyses* (New York, 1978). One also recalls Tanenzapf's remark in his discussion of Berkovits's "Critique of Heschel" that one can "say of Berkovits what he said of Heschel on p. 203 of *Major Themes:* 'to call something a mystery is no theology either,'" S. Tanenzapf, op. cit., p. 283.

99. *Berkovits,* pp. 220–224.

100. See note 82.

101. *Berkovits*, p. 220.
102. *Berkovits*, p. 221.
103. *Berkovits*, p. 221.
104. *Berkovits*, p. 224.

JEWISH FAITH AFTER THE HOLOCAUST: FOUR APPROACHES

An essential dimension of the manifold experience of the Jewish people has been that of personal and communal suffering. Martyrdom "for God's name" (*kiddush ha-Shem*) and martyrdom because of God's name are all too familiar features of Israel's enduring struggle to remain true to its heritage, its destiny, and its God. As a consequence of their faith, Jews of every generation have been living witnesses to man's passionate inhumanity and to the inescapable presentness of evil. Against this background and as an integral part of this somber tradition there naturally emerged many thoughtful reflections and responses with which the Jew of old consoled himself, coped with the world's evil, interpreted the hostility and irrationality of his non-Jewish neighbors and, above all, vindicated the God of Abraham, Isaac, and Jacob. Through these responses they gave expression to their deepest commitments and even more importantly, made it possible for Judaism to survive by making Jewish experience and its inherent tragedy intelligible. All that transpired was given shape and meaning within the accepted parameters of the Jewish tradition.

In our own era the whole of past Jewish actuality and the faith responses it evoked has been called into question. Two happenings—the Nazi Holocaust and the re-emergence of the State of Israel—have radically altered all that has gone before. These two events have provoked many to ask whether the traditional Jewish reactions to tragedy and evil are still viable options or whether the "faith" of past generations must, at least, be called into judgment.

What were once accepted as "authentic" postures for the "man of faith" in the face of calamity are no longer obviously valid; now these postures need to be defended against vigorous charges that they are insensitive, inauthentic, and fail to face facts. More generally still, there is a widespread recognition by almost all parties to the discussion that to live as if unaffected by the cataclysmic and revolutionary import of contemporary Jewish reality as worked out in Zion and in the death camps of Europe is to be insensitive not only to the rhythm of history and to history's martyrs and saints but also, above all to the Lord of Israel, who is primarily known and identified in and through that common existential environment in which God and man meet and which defines both His reality for us and our reality for Him.

Everything seems to have been altered by the Holocaust and the inestimable horror that it symbolizes to the survivors—and every Jew in the concreteness of his own life knows himself to be a "survivor." Yet the inescapable irony of contemporary Jewish existence is that we, the "survivors" of the Holocaust, the heirs of Treblinka and Auschwitz, are also the heirs of the fighters of the Warsaw Ghetto and the actual builders of Zion. We are what we are because we have inherited and been formed by these seemingly irreconcilable *realia* of our unique contemporary experience; they space and inform the very essence of our being and of our consciousness, both personal and communal. To understand ourselves requires ineluctably that we come to some grasp of these events and our relation to them, however fragmentary, limited, or personal this understanding may be.

Those who would enquire what it means to be a Jew today must ask not only, or even primarily, vague and unformed questions about Jewish identity and the relation of Judaism and modernity and Judaism and secularity, but must rather articulate the much more precise and focused question through which all the other dimensions of our post-Holocaust identity are refracted and defined: "What does it mean to be a Jew after Auschwitz?" Auschwitz has become an inescapable *datum* for all Jewish accounts of the meaning and nature of covenantal relation and God's relation to man. Likewise, all substantial answers also need to be open and responsive to the subtleties of the dialectical alternation of the contemporary Jewish situation: that is, they must also give due weight to the "miracle" which is the state of Israel. They must thoughtfully and sensitively enquire whether God is speaking to the "survivors" through it, and if so, how. This means that while awed by the very reality of its existence they must interrogate the state's philosophical, theological, and some would even add "messianic," implications. Alternatively, dialectically, they must also consider in all seriousness the stark, frightening possibility that despite the human and even religious meaning of the return and rebuilding of Israel, any attempt at theodicy in the face of the full horror of the *Churban* (the Holocaust) is impermissible; even more, it is blasphemy!

Immediately after the full depravity of the Holocaust was exposed its tragic immensity, not surprisingly, left Jewish thinkers numb. Moreover, what energies they and world Jewry could marshal were more urgently needed to help the survivors, and in particular to create a refuge in the state of Israel; the cry of the living demanded precedence over the sacred duty of remembering the dead. Jewish existence, not explanation, was the prerequisite obligation. It was just as well, for the horror and immediacy of it all had been too overwhelming, too unbelievable to fashion into any coherent form, too seemingly impossible to allow of any meaning. Still more, who could speak with authority on Auschwitz? Of those who were there, few remained who were able to testify, and then, even the survivors knew not what to say. Of those who were not there, could they enter the conversation without sacrilege and with justification; could they even comprehend the depth of the tragedy involved? And yet, if not to explain but only to remember and to make others remember, Jewish thinkers had to begin to talk about Auschwitz. Once the dialogue began it was clear it could not stop, nor could the issues it forced into prominence be avoided, for what was being called into question was nothing less than the three historic coefficients of traditional Judaism: God, Torah, and the people of Israel.

Out of the still nascent and still uncertain conversation on the Holocaust several general responses, with their various combinations and configurations, have emerged. They can be enumerated as follows: (1) The Holocaust is like all other tragedies and merely raises again the difficulty of theodicy and "the problem of evil," but it does not significantly alter the dilemma or contribute anything new to it. (2) The classical Jewish theological doctrine of *mipenei hata'einu*, ("because of our sins we were punished") which was evolved in the face of earlier national calamities can also be applied to the Holocaust. According to this account, Israel was sinful and Auschwitz is her just retribution. (3) The Holocaust is the ultimate in vicarious atonement. Israel is the "suffering servant" of Isaiah (ch. 53ff)—she suffers and atones for the sins of others. Some die so that others might be cleansed and live. (4) The Holocaust is a modern *Akedah* (sacrifice of Isaac)—it is a test of our faith. (5) The Holocaust is an instance of the temporary "Eclipse of God"—there are times when God is inexplicably absent from history or unaccountably chooses to turn His face away. (6) The Holocaust is proof that "God is dead"—if there were a God He would surely have prevented Auschwitz; if He did not then He does not exist. (7) The Holocaust is the maximization of human evil, the price mankind has to pay for human freedom. The Nazis were men, not gods; Auschwitz reflects ignominiously on man; it does not touch God's existence or perfection. (8) The Holocaust is revelation: it issues a call for Jewish affirmation. From Auschwitz comes the command: Jews survive! (9) The Holocaust is an inscrutable mystery; like all of God's ways it transcends human understanding and demands faith and silence.

These nine reactions, though the most common, are not exhaustive and there are yet other ways of accounting for the tragedy and of fitting the pieces together. Moreover, these theses are usually employed in various interrelated and interdependent combinations and explanatory models by those who try to grapple with the philosophical and theological puzzles raised by the Holocaust. These more complex explanatory structures, which embody several responses together, are a recognition that no single strategem is adequate to the variety of challenges raised by the multi-faceted event to which we give the name the Holocaust. Furthermore, one can safely say that no one interpretive form, no matter how perspicuous and authentic, has become "normative." Many different readings have been evoked by these several themes, and many more will no doubt follow in due course.

Out of the ongoing debate however, four thinkers, Richard Rubenstein, Emil Fackenheim, Ignaz Maybaum and Eliezer Berkovits, have emerged as of particular importance. Each has his own unique perspective, characteristic arguments and vital aims, and each uses an original and provocative configuration of the "explanations" outlined above to fashion his substantive exegesis of the radical negative facticity that is the *Sho'ah*. In the remainder of this essay a sympathetic decipherment of these alternative analytic accounts will be given. Criticism will be reserved for another occasion.[1]

RICHARD RUBENSTEIN

Richard Rubenstein has been a man of our times. Coming to the Hebrew Union College Reform seminary in 1942 and sharing its optimistic vision of man and its liberal ideal of human progress, he has been converted by the Holocaust into holding a Jewish "Death of God" theology. His sensitivity to the reality of evil witnessed to by the death camps has forced him to call into question the very foundations of Judaism. "The one preeminent measure of the adequacy of all contemporary Jewish theology," Rubenstein writes, "is the seriousness with which it deals with this supreme problem [the Holocaust] of Jewish history."[2] No one has taken the problem more seriously and no Jewish theologian has drawn more radical conclusions from it.

The theological difficulty raised by the Nazi extermination of Jews can be simply described: if God is the God of History and Israel is His chosen people, what responsibility does God bear for Auschwitz? Did God use the Nazis, as He used Assyria of old, as "the rod of His anger" (Isaiah 10:5)? If He did not, how could such a thing happen in the face of the living God? It is the ancient "problem of evil" to which men of faith have responded with countless theodicies; now it is raised with maximum vigor, clarity, and urgency. In Germany, in August 1961, Rubenstein was confronted by a well-meaning Protestant clergyman, Dean Heinrich

Grueber, with the assertion that God had indeed used the Nazis as the instrument of His will.[3] This affirmation shocked Rubenstein; it was, he tells us, "a theological point of no return."[4] The consequences seemed clear and Rubenstein felt compelled to reject the presence of God at Auschwitz rather than believe that Hitler was God's agent: "If I believed in God as the omnipotent author of the historical drama and Israel as His Chosen People, I had to accept Dean Grueber's conclusion that it was God's will that Hitler committed six million Jews to slaughter. I could not possibly believe in such a God nor could I believe in Israel as the chosen people of God after Auschwitz."[5]

Rubenstein was thus driven to the same judgment as that of the Talmudic heretic Elisha ben Abuyah, *"Leth din ve-leth dayyan"* (There is neither Judgment nor Judge).[6]

In Rubenstein's view the only honest response to the death camps is the rejection of God, "God is dead," and the open recognition of the meaninglessness of existence. Our life is neither planned nor purposeful, there is no Divine Will nor does the world reflect Divine concern. The world is indifferent to men. Man must now reject his illusions, and along with his fellow men, recognize the existential truth that life is not intrinsically valuable, that the human condition reflects no transcendental purpose; history reveals no providence. The theological account of Auschwitz which sees it as retribution, which re-echoes one side of the ancient theology of Judaism that Israel's suffering is "because of our sins" is to blaspheme against both God and man. What crime could Israel have committed, what sin could have been so great as to justify such retribution? What God could have meted out such justice on His chosen ones? All such "rationalizations" of Auschwitz pale before its enormity, and for Rubenstein, the only reaction that is worthy is the rejection of the entire Jewish theological framework: there is no God and no covenant with Israel.

Man must turn away from transcendental myths and face his actual existential situation. Drawing heavily upon the atheistic existentialists, Rubenstein interprets this to mean that in the face of the world's nihilism man must assert value; in response to history's meaninglessness men must create and project meaning;

against the objective fact that human life has no purpose, man must subjectively, yet authentically, act as if there were purpose. All that men have are themselves and each other: Auschwitz has taught that life itself is the supreme good, there is no need to see it as valuable only because of its reflection of transcendental norms or metahistorical schemata. What worth there will be, will be of one's own creation. This radical thesis is not new, but it is original in a Jewish theological context.[7]

Had Rubenstein merely asserted the death of God, his would not be a Jewish theology. What makes it "Jewish" are the implications he draws from his radical negation with respect to the people of Israel. It might be expected that the denial of God's covenantal relation with Israel would entail the end of Judaism and so the end of the Jewish people. From the perspective of traditional Jewish theology this would certainly be the case. Rubenstein, however, again inverts our ordinary perception and argues that with the "death of God," the existence of "people-hood," of the community of Israel, is all the more important. Now that there is nowhere else to turn for meaning, men need each other all the more to create meaning: "it is precisely because human existence is tragic, ultimately hopeless, and without meaning that we treasure our religious community."[8] Though Judaism has to be "demythologized," i.e., it has to renounce all normative claims to a unique "chosen status,"[9] at the same time it paradoxically gains heightened importance in the process. Now that "God is dead" religious community is all the more consequential.

It is precisely the ultimate hopelessness and gratuity of our human situation which calls forth our strongest need for religious community. If all we have is one another, then assuredly we need one another more than ever.[10]

The Jew after Auschwitz, despite his recognition of the now-transcended "mythic" structure of rabbinic tradition, is still a Jew and as such carries within him the "shared vicissitudes of history, culture and psychological perspective"[11] that define a Jew. Jews, like all men, are rooted in concrete life-situations and as such only Jewish experience can be satisfying and authentic. It is in the traditional forms of life that we best express all our aspiration and ideals, and participate in a "community of shared predicament and ultimate concern."[12]

In many of his writings Rubenstein has carried on a re-examination of classical Jewish values from the perspective of their suitability for the modern, post-Holocaust Jew. Primarily through the use of pscychoanalytic categories[13] he has tried to reinterpret the meaning of classical aspects of Judaism while advocating their retention. He has been especially concerned to make out a case for the maintenance of religious ritual and symbolism. Though these forms of religious life have lost their traditional justification, they can and do have profound psychological implications and are to be retained on psychological grounds. Thus, for example, bar mitzvah is significant as a *rite de passage*, a ritual in which the community formally recognizes the new sexual maturity of the boy and confirms publicly his new masculine role.[14] This is psychologically healthy for both the boy and society. Again the synagogue retains a central role in Jewish life, if only as a psychological clinic. Rubenstein has extended this Freudian interpretation to the rabbinic material in his *The Religious Imagination* (1968),[15] and to Paul, whom he sees as one of the "greatest Jewish theologians," in his *My Brother Paul* (1972).

Coupled to this psychoanalytic revisionism is a mystical paganism[16] in which the Jew is urged to forgo history and return to the cosmic rhythms of natural existence.[17] The modern Jew is exhorted to recognize the priorities of nature. So, for example, he must come to understand that the real meaning of Messianism is "the proclamation of the end of history and the return to nature and nature's cyclical repetitiveness."[18] The future and final redemption is not to be the conquest of nature by history, as traditionally conceived in the Jewish tradition, but rather the conquest of history by nature and the return of all things to their primal origins. Man has to rediscover the sanctity of his bodily life and reject forever the delusions of overcoming it; he must submit to and enjoy his physicality—not try to transform or transcend it. Rubenstein sees the renewal of Zion, and the rebuilding of the land with its return to the soil, as a harbinger of this return to nature on the part of the Jew who has been removed from the earth (symbolic of nature) by theology and necessity for almost two thousand years. The return to the land points toward the final escape of the Jew from the negativity of history to the vitality and promise of self-liberation through nature.

Rubenstein's account is intended as an interpretation not only of what has been, but of what ought to be. It is put forward as a manifesto for Jewish renewal and spiritual reintegration. Among the aims of this program is the eradication of those elements that create the explosive mix which produces a Holocaust. Not the least of which are the classic myths at the heart of Jewish and Christian theology, i.e., anti-Semitism is a product of these mythic structures. The contributing Jewish myth is its claim to be a "chosen people." This created a "specialness" about Jews that has been disastrous. The collateral Christian myth was predicated on its acceptance of the antecedent Jewish one—the Church accepted the "chosenness of Israel" and was therefore able to relate to it only in theological terms; paradoxically it saw Israel as providing "both the incarnate Deity and His Murderers."[19] The most potent of all Christian beliefs—the Crucifixion—is indissolubly linked to the deicidal activity of the "chosen people"—the Jews. Wherever the Christian story is retold, a powerful anti-Semitic seed is planted. In order, therefore, once and for all to put an end to anti-Semitism, it is necessary for the Jew to renounce his self-image as a "chosen people" so that his relation to his Christian neighbor may be normalized and the Christian will be able to see him in the same light as he sees other men. This process needs to be paralleled in Christianity; it too has to "demythologize" correspondingly its portrayal of the Jew. Yet to do this is to rupture the traditional incarnational theology and its claims for Jesus as the promised Christ emerging out of the body of historic Israel. This is to ask a great deal of Christianity, but, Rubenstein argues, unless it occurs there will be future tragedy.

An integral part of this mythic relation between Judaism and Christianity is an urge toward vicarious atonement which demands a sacrificial victim. This element arises, in Freudian fashion, from man's deepest wish, which is to kill God. Through deicide, men would be liberated from restraint and from the commands of morality and virtue. The Crucifixion is the most powerful human symbol of deicide. However, the nature of the tale allows the Christian to deflect his own guilty desires onto the Jew who is objectified as the "Christ-Killer." The Christian thus finds a "legitimate" outlet for his murderous instincts. As a consequence, whether the Jew is conceived in the mind of the Christian as Jesus or as Judas, his end is the same: ritual slaughter as sacrificial victim.[20]

Rubenstein has given us a powerful image of what it means to draw the extreme conclusion from Auschwitz: "God is dead." Yet his is not the only nor the final word.

EMIL FACKENHEIM

No philosopher has written as extensively or as feelingly about the Holocaust as has Emil Fackenheim. Having experienced life in a camp,[21] Fackenheim, seemingly out of a sense of compulsion, has tried to grapple with the overwhelming events of the death camps in order to draw some meaning from them for post-Holocaust Jewry. In a series of essays, and especially and most clearly in his *God's Presence in History* (1970), he has tried to find a way to avoid both the absolute faith of the pious who do not see any special problem in the *Shoah* and those like Rubenstein who argue that the only reasonable conclusion to be drawn from Auschwitz is the "Death of God" and the ultimate absurdity of history.[22] If the former alternative blasphemes against Hitler's victims, the latter blasphemes against the God of the victims. Both victims and God have to be held together in dialectical tension after Auschwitz; neither can be devalued without resulting distortion and loss of truth.

To keep God and Israel together is the demand of Jewish theology; it is still an imperative after the Holocaust. The problem is how it is to be effected. If Rubenstein's solution of Jewish communal existence without the God of Judaism is no answer, what then is the answer? Fackenheim's reply is both subtle and difficult. He is adamant in his refusal to allow any theological *explanation* of the Holocaust. In no sense, he contends, can any particular the-

odicy be propounded in which God's goodness can be vindicated
and Auschwitz seen as part of a rational cosmic pattern whose
interpretation can be fathomed by man. In this sense the Holocaust
is devoid of explanation and significance. Thus, like Rubenstein,
he totally rejects any account which analyzes Auschwitz in terms
of *mi-penei hata'einu*—"because of our sins." The various attempts to decode the horrible events in terms of vicarious suffering
or martyrdom achieve no more lasting result. For Fackenheim the
enormity of the tragedy transcends all the classical explanations of
suffering and evil and calls into question nothing less than the God
of history Himself.

Yet despite the implications, despite the absolute failure of theodicy, despite the seeming absurdity, Fackenheim urges men to believe. Rubenstein becomes an atheist because he cannot and will
not accept God as having been present in any sense at Auschwitz;
Fackenheim, in opposition, insists that this is what we must do. It
is the presence of God in contemporary Jewish history, even at
Auschwitz, that he would have us find. Fackenheim insists that
we do not and cannot understand what God was doing at Auschwitz, or why He allowed it, but we must and do insist that He was
there. For Fackenheim, unlike Rubenstein, the Holocaust does not
prove that "God is dead." Boldly he claims that from the death
camps as from Sinai[23] God commands Israel.

How does this voice address Israel and what does it say? In order
to comprehend fully Fackenheim's views on this one has to turn
away from his direct writings on the Holocaust and come to an
appreciation of his overall theological posture. In his own biographical odyssey he has moved slowly but perceptibly from a liberal to
a neo-orthodox[24] construction of Judaism. Involved in and affected
by the Nazi onslaught, Fackenheim, like most of his generation,
felt the need to reappraise the nature and status of Judaism. As a
result of this reconsideration the liberal position with its dogmatic
belief in the perfectability of man and the translation of the commanding God of the Bible into a moral Ideal was seen to be untrue
to Judaism's deepest insights and superficial[25] in its analysis of the
human situation.[26]

Judaism is not Deism or moral Idealism; it has its foundation and its continuance in its meeting with a Living God who is continually present in history. Thus Judaism can be understood only as the dynamic response to the present address of the Divine. Fackenheim's espousal of this existential supernaturalism, with its central emphasis on the reality of God and His incursion into the temporal flow which calls man to deeds, is deeply indebted to the influence of Buber and Rosenzweig. It was they who had "sought nothing less than a modern presence of the ancient God."[27] In working out the implications of this rediscovered transcendentalism Fackenheim has been especially influenced by Buber's dialogical philosophy of "I and Thou." He accepts, in its broad specifications, the Buberian doctrine of the *I–Thou*[28] encounter as the proper model for Jewish openness to the reality of the Eternal Thou. Thus he does not begin with any proof for the existence of God but rather with the presumption that He exists. God cannot be proven, but He can (and must) be met.[29] Only from within the circle of faith can one "hear" the Divine and respond. Like Buber, Fackenheim insists that God reveals Himself in history through personal encounters with Jews and Israel. Revelation understood as the encounter of God and man happens everywhere and at all times. Yet the experience cannot be verified by any objective criteria, it cannot show itself decisively to those who would not "hear" the voice. The *I–Thou* encounter has its own rhythm, and any attempt to force it into improper (*I–It* to use Buber's terminology) categories destroys its character and silences its message.[30] The Fackenheim who hears a "commanding voice from Auschwitz" is the Fackenheim who stands within the covenantal affirmation.[31]

Buber applies his concept of revelation to Israel's past and sees God's address in the overwhelming events of Israel's life.[32] Building upon Buber's view, Fackenheim develops his own account of Jewish history. For him Jewish history is a series of overwhelming episodes, but not all the occurrences are of the same character. The most powerful incidents, such as those connected with the Exodus from Egypt and the giving of the Torah at Sinai, actually created the religious identity of the Jewish people. These creative extraordinary happenings Fackenheim calls "root experiences."[33] "Root experiences" are historical events of such a formative character that they continue to influence all future "presents" of the people and they are of such a power that these past moments legislate to every future era.[34] In addition, "root experiences" are public disclosures. They belong to the collective memory of the people and continue to claim the allegiance of the nation. Thus, for example, the miracle at the Red Sea is a saving moment that is re-enacted at every Passover *seder* and whose power affects each subsequent generation and continually reveals the redemptive activity of God to each age. Lastly, and most importantly, "root experiences" provide the accessibility of Divine Presence in the here and now;[35] past events are lived through as "present reality" and thus the Jew is "assured that the saving God of the past saves still."[36]

Not all the major happenings in Israel's past, however, meet these criteria. There is a second category of events whose function is different. Fackenheim calls these occasions "epochmaking events."[37] These are episodes that, unlike "root experiences," are not formative; they do not create the essentials of Jewish faith, but rather they are crises that challenge the "root experiences" through new situations, which test the resiliency and generality of "root experiences" to answer to new and unprecedented conditions and realities. For example, the destruction of the First and Second Temples severely tested whether or not the commanding and saving Presence of God could be maintained. The Sages of the Talmudic era, who lived through the destruction of the second Temple, and the Prophets who lived through the first, were able to respond to the traumatic situations with both realism and faith in the "root experiences" of Israel. Jeremiah sees Nebuchadnezzar as the instrument of God's purpose (Jer. 43:10) and the Talmudic sages saw the Second Destruction and subsequent Exile as nothing less than God's own exile with His people, thus allowing for the dispersion and yet holding fast to God's presence in all history. Such a God, present in all times and places, would redeem Israel in the future as He had in the past.[38] This faith was severely tested by experience, but a way—admittedly fragmentary and contradictory[39]—was found to hold both together. In other times and circumstances the "root experiences" have again and again been tested; indeed the record of Israel in diaspora from one culture to another, from one era to another, is a series of "epochmaking events" that try again and again the foundations of Jewish faith. Yet, through it all, the midrashic framework has held fast: God and History are not divorced; Israel and God are not torn asunder. Each trial brings new strength and new affirmation of the saving and commanding Lord first revealed at the Red Sea and Sinai. But what of the Holocaust? Can it too be assimilated to the traditional pattern of midrashic response? Is Auschwitz another testing, another epochal event; or more drastically, is it perhaps a "root experience" that is formative for Jewish belief, but in an ultimately negative and destructive sense?

Fackenheim argues that the "Kingdom of Night" is an "epochmaking event", that calls into question the presence of God in a uniquely powerful way. And yet he contends the Jew must still affirm the continued proximity of God in Jewish history—even at Auschwitz—and he must reaffirm the present reality of the people's "root experience" of a commanding God (of Sinai), now commanding Israel from within the Holocaust itself. This radical reply to the unprecedented crisis of faith is Fackenheim's response to Auschwitz. The Jew cannot, dare not, must not, reject God. Auschwitz is revelation! In the gas-chambers and crematoriums we must, we do, experience God. Fackenheim dares to make a religious affirmation of what drives others to atheism or silence. Like Job, he gives expression to a profound faith: "Though he slay me, yet shall I trust in Him" (Job 13:15).

The commanding Word that Fackenheim hears from Auschwitz is: "Jews are forbidden to hand Hitler posthumous victories;"[40] Jews are under a sacred obligation to survive; after the death camps Jewish existence itself is a holy act; Jews are under a sacred obligation to remember the martyrs; Jews are, as Jews, forbidden to despair of redemption, or to become cynical about the world and man, for to submit to cynicism is to abdicate responsibility for the world and to deliver the world into the hands of the luciferian forces of Nazism. And above all, Jews are "forbidden to despair of the God of Israel, lest Judaism perish."[41] Hitler's demonic passion was to eradicate Jews and Judaism; for the Jew to despair of the God of Israel as a result of Hitler's monstrous actions would be, ironically, to do Hitler's work and to aid in the accomplishment of his goal. The voice that speaks from Auschwitz above all demands that Hitler win no posthumous victories, that no Jew do what Hitler could not do. The Jewish will for survival is natural enough, but Fackenheim invests it with transcendental significance. Precisely because others would eradicate Jews from the earth, Jews are commanded to resist annihilation. Paradoxically, Hitler makes Judaism after Auschwitz a necessity. To say "no" to Hitler is to say "yes" to the God of Sinai; to say "no" to the God of Sinai is to say "yes" to Hitler.

From Fackenheim's perspective, every Jew who has remained a Jew since 1945 has replied affirmatively to the commanding voice of Auschwitz.

But the God of biblical faith is not only a commanding God; he is also a God of deliverance. The crossing of the Red Sea is as much a part of the Jewish heritage as is the revelation at Sinai: both are "root experiences." Fackenheim is sensitive to this. He has made much of the commanding Presence of Auschwitz, but where is the saving God of the Exodus? Without the crossing of the Red Sea there can be no Sinai. Fackenheim knows this. He also knows that to talk of a God of deliverance, no matter how softly, no matter how tentatively, after the Holocaust is problematical when God did not work His kindness there and then. Even to whisper about salvation after Auschwitz is already to speak as a man of faith, not as a seeker, and even then one can only whisper. The continued existence of the people of Israel however, and most specifically the establishment and maintenance of the state of Israel, forces and encourages Fackenheim to risk speaking of hope and the possibility of redemption. Auschwitz and the state of Israel are inseparably tied together; what the former seems to deny the latter, at least tentatively, affirms. For Fackenheim, the state of Israel is living testimony to God's continued presence in history. Through it the modern Jew witnesses a reaffirmation of the "root experience" of salvation essential to the survival of Jewish faith.[42]

IGNAZ MAYBAUM

Ignaz Maybaum, the German-English Reform Jewish theologian, has offered an intriguing, if problematic, response to the Holocaust in his engrossing study *The Face of God After Auschwitz*.[43] The main line of his argument centers around the application of a particular philosophy of history to the *Sho'ah* that denies its uniqueness and stresses its continuity with the past while "explaining" it by attributing the notion of vicarious atonement to the victims of Auschwitz and Treblinka: "They died though innocently so that others might live." This theme has a long, resonant history in the literature of the world's major religions, being especially central, of course, to the "Servant" chapters of Isaiah[44] and then in the association of these passages with Jesus. It is not at all surprising, therefore, that in light of the death-camps this image should again suggest itself as a way of analyzing the fate of the victims and appeal to it should be made in trying to shed meaning on the tragic death of those who perished in the Holocaust.

Jews have a history to which the Servant-of-God-texts of the Book of Isaiah provide the pattern. In Auschwitz, I say in my sermons—and only in sermons it is appropriate to make such a statement—Jews suffered vicarious death for the sins of mankind. It says in the liturgy of the Synagogue in reference to the first and seond *churban*, albeit centuries after the event: "because of our sins." After Auschwitz Jews need not say so. Can any martyr be a more innocent sin-offering than those murdered in Auschwitz! The millions who died in Auschwitz died "because of the sins of others." Jews and non-Jews died in Auschwitz, but the Jew hatred which Hitler inherited from the medieval Church made Auschwitz the twentieth-century Calvary of the Jewish people.[45]

Maybaum's theology has its roots in the dual traditional affirmation of the reality of God and the uniqueness of Israel created through its special covenantal relation with the Almighty. As a consequence of this bond Israel bears especial witness to God's existence and purpose in Creation. For this reason the Jew was singled out by Hitler for extermination.

Why did Hitler single out the Jew as his chief enemy? I am not satisfied with the answer: "Hitler was a maniac." Nor do I accept as an explanation the racial myth in which Hitler believed. The Jewish people consists of various racial components. Yet there is a reason why the Jew was seen as *the* enemy of Nazism . . . the irreconcilable opponent of Nazism was the Jew. Hitler knew, as we know, that not every Jew is just, merciful and truthful. But Hitler also knew that the Jew, historically and existentially, even without any choice, stands for justice, mercy and truth. He stood for everything which made every word of Hitler a lie. The Jew, without opening his mouth to utter a single word, condemned Hitler. The Jew walking his way in Hitler Germany, even before he was compelled to wear the Star of David, did what the Church did not do: he tore up the land into two realms which were without any communication; the Jew walked outside the realm which was that of Baal. Doing nothing, the Jew created by his mere existence a situation in which Germany was visible as a land of Baal. Nobody can tell and should even ask how many Jews would have liked to conform to Hitler's ideology in order to save their lives. This is an irrelevant question. Jews are human beings like other men, weak or strong, cowardly or heroic. But they proved to be what others, what millions were not: they were chosen. In the apocalyptic hour of modern mankind the Jews did not bow before the Moloch. God did not let them. They were His people. Their election was still valid. Again it was demonstrated that to be chosen means to have no choice. God chooses. The Jewish people was again chosen to be not like the gentiles.[46]

That is to say, *even* the Holocaust conforms to the Divine will, revealing in its own way God's blueprint for the progressive unfolding of Providential care.

But what, more exactly, is the essence of the Divine pattern that Maybaum discerns even in the events of the *Sho'ah* and what role, if any, does Israel play in it? In brief, the larger purpose of the historical drama is the bringing of the gentile nations to God, while the agent that fosters this relationship is the people of Israel. As such, Israel's history is interdependent with, and unintelligible aside from, the course of the nations. Thus Israel's history, through which it manifests its transcendental obligation, is always played out in intercourse with other groups: Egypt, Babylonia, Greece, Rome, the nations of Islam and Christendom and, more recently, Nazi Germany and Soviet Russia, as well as America and countries of the Free World.

However, in order to fulfil its task Israel must not only act in concert with the peoples of the world, shaping one final destiny together, but it must do so, of necessity, in a "language" that the nations will comprehend and be able to respond to. That is to say, if the instrumental function of Jewish being is to work itself out in successful ways its meaning must be accessible to the gentile world in and through carriers of meaning that they, the non-Jews, understand. To clarify this idea of the mediating character of the "Jewish mission," Maybaum introduces at this juncture two classical notions into his analysis of Jewish experience—that of *Churban* (destruction) and that of *Gezerah* (evil decree).[47] According to Maybaum, the concept of *Churban* applies to events like the destruction of the First and Second Temples which "make an end to an old era and create a new era. The *Churban* is a day of awe, of awe beyond human understanding."[48] It is also an occasion that carries a message to both Jew and gentile alike. By comparison the category of *Gezerah* (plural *Gezerot*) applies to those happenings such as the expulsion from Spain in 1492 and the Chmielnitzki massacres in seventeenth century Poland which, although cataclysmic, do not usher in a new era. Moreover, a *Gezerah* can be averted. As has been said for generations on the Day of Atonement: *Teshuvah u-Tefillah u-Zedakah ma'averin et roa ha-Gezerah* ("penitence, prayer, and charity annul the evil decree"). A *Churban*, however, cannot be averted; its significance transcends the parameters of Israel's own existence, affects world history and informs the life of the nations and, most importantly, is an irreversible intercession of God in the course of human events. Furthermore, and fundamental, Maybaum asserts that a *Churban* implies evolution. "The *Churban* is the progress achieved in a history in which the gentiles are the chief actors, or better, perpetrators. The *Churban* is progress achieved through sacrifice."[49] Rephrased in terms of "Israel's mission to the nations" this means that *Churban* are revelatory moments that bring the gentiles to God by addressing them in a language they find intelligible, that is, a language in which progress requires and is mediated through death and destruction. Maybaum presumes, according to this typology, that a non-violent call, even if from the Divine, would be incapable of being heard by the non-Jewish world. To engage the nations God must speak in the tones of *Churban*, destruction, for this is the only vocabulary they are attuned to, the only expression to which they will respond.

According to this classification Maybaum identifies the Holocaust as a *Churban*, i.e., an event that signals the end of one epoch and the beginning of another, better era in Jewish and world annals. There is positive value in destruction; Auschwitz as *Churban* has world beneficial significance. In Jewish history the term *Churban* has been applied twice previously, the first time to the destruction of the First Temple (586 B.C.E.) and the second time to the ruination of the Second Temple (70 C.E.). In each case Maybaum projects the advance of humanity as a result of the catastrophe. The first destruction created the Jewish diaspora, and through the diaspora Judaism went out among the other nations to spread God's word and do God's work: this was progress. The eradication of the Second Temple saw the establishment of the synagogue as an institution, and in the synagogue the world was presented with a form of religious piety in which no sacrifices were performed, no blood was shed, and religious life was "elevated" to a higher spiritual level than hitherto. The Holocaust is the third *Churban*, and like the earlier two, Maybaum sees it as aiding in human amelioration: it is a medium of spiritual transfiguration.

The significance of the *Sho'ah* as *Churban* for Maybaum's theology of Jewish history, especially in terms of its bearing for the Jewish mission to the non-Jewish world, can now be more sharply brought into focus. The interrelation of Israel among the nations, in which the prime movers of the historical order are the non-Jews, requires, as already noted, that Judaism do its work through non-Jewish motifs in order to make itself understood. Thus, while Judaism's formative motif is the *Akedah* (the binding of Isaac, Gen. 22), Christianity's seminal and classic symbol is the enormously powerful image of the Crucifixion. The *Akedah* is a sacrifice that never happened: Isaac can grow to maturity, marry, have children, die in his appointed time. According to Maybaum there is no heroic tragedy in the *Akedah*, its message is: there can be progress without martyrdom and without death. The Crucifixion, by comparison, is a sacrifice that did happen. Jesus' life is foreshortened; he had no time to marry, to have children, to die normally. Here is the stuff of heroic tragedy. Its message is: martyrdom is required that others may live, vicarious death is needed so that the world may go forward. "The cross contradicts the *Akedah*: Isaac is sacrificed."[50] "Somebody had to die that others may live."[51] With the Crucifixion as its model of Divine activity in history, the Christian world is unable to grasp the higher religious meaning of the *Ake-*

dah. Hence, tragic as this may be, for Judaism to communicate with Christians, it must re-present the reality of the Crucifixion. Thus, the modern Jew collectively, as the single Jew of two millenia ago, must mount the Cross—undergo persecution, suffering, and death—in order to arouse the conscience of the gentile world.

So powerful is the hold of the image of the Crucifixion on the consciousness of Western civilization that progress can only be made when structured in terms assimilable to this pattern. Seen from this angle the third *Churban* (the Holocaust), like the earlier two, is a Divine event that is meant to bring about humanity's transformation. Framed in the shape of Auschwitz, an overwhelming reliving by the entire Jewish people of the Crucifixion of one Jew, this latest *Churban* addresses the deepest sensitivities of modern Christian civilization with a message it needs to hear and in a form it can digest: "In Auschwitz Jews suffered vicarious atonement for the sins of mankind."[52] Pushing this interpretation to the utmost, Maybaum writes:

The Golgotha of modern mankind is Auschwitz. The cross, the Roman gallows, was replaced by the gas chamber. The gentiles, it seems, must first be terrified by the blood of the sacrificed scapegoat to have the mercy of God revealed to them and become converted, become baptized gentiles, become Christians.[53]

Precisely what teaching, what elevation has this monumental sacrifice, this modern Golgotha achieved? Maybaum would have us recognize in it the decisive end of the medieval epoch, by which he means the termination of the era of religious authoritarianism, religious persecution, and theocratic oppression.

After every *Churban,* the Jewish people made a decisive progress, and mankind progressed with us . . . After the third *Churban,* that of our own time . . . The medieval organization outside which God was not supposed to be found has been destroyed. You can be a Jew outside the *din,* outside the religious organization as defined in the codes. The Middle Ages have come to an end. It is the same for us as it is for the Christian. He can be a Christian outside the Roman Church; at last we can all be citizens living in freedom. That is the blessed end of the Middle Ages, the end of the Empires, through the rise of democracy.

The end of the Middle Ages was overdue. After World War I the West had the opportunity of bringing freedom, land reform and the blessings of the industrial revolution to the East European countries, from the Baltic States down to Roumania. Nothing was done. British officials accepted the invitations to go hunting and shooting from the aristocrats of these countries. The feudal system remained in these countries. The allied soldiers of World War I had died in vain. Thus Hitler came. He, the Nihilist, did what the progressives should have done but failed to do, he destroyed the Middle Ages, but did so by destroying the old Europe.[54]

In still more rhapsodic terms, whose enthusiasm and optimism despite or rather because of the *Sho'ah* deserve to be quoted at length, he goes on:

The end of the Middle Ages also means the end of the Jewish Middle Ages. It is not merely small isolated groups of our people but the whole of the Jewish people that is now Westernised. We march with the Western nations. We can progress. Religiously we emancipate ourselves from the dictate of the *din*, from a medievally enforced supervision of our religious life, politically we can dismiss the medieval mentality which separated one community from another with walls and towers, making Zionism necessary, but also visible as part of the medieval way of thinking. We remain loyal to the citizens of Israel; they need us, and we shall not fail them. But we now realise that our Holy Land is not a country on the shores of the Mediterranean. We now realise that our Holy Land is mankind's future. Mankind's future and nothing else is our goal. As Jews we serve mankind. Our exodus from the Middle Ages is assured. We re-enter history in the joy of still having the privilege of serving the old mission, in the joyful knowledge that the unchanging and unending kindness of God accompanies us in this mission.[55]

Maybaum sees Nazism as the final manifestation of the medieval world view and the cataclysmic event of the Holocaust—*Churban*—as the means whereby the world moved with finality from medievalism to modernity. This change is symbolized in the annihilation of Eastern European Jewry, for it was they who still lived according to the pattern of feudal Jewry, i.e., centered in ghettos, cut off from their neighbors, focusing all activity within a strict halachic framework. Their elimination in the Holocaust represents the passing of that older era that generated this pattern of Jewish existence. As a thinker who still shares the optimistic vision of classical Reform, and its unflattering opinion of traditional Jewish observance, Maybaum is able to interpret the end of the "shtetl" and the destruction of Eastern European Jewry, even if through the means of a Hitler, as enhancement. After Auschwitz world Jewry lives almost exclusively in modern Western cultures, America, Israel, Western Europe and Russia, and this, according to Maybaum, is progress. In these cultures the Jew is liberated from the *halacha*[56] and free to engage the possibilities open to him through Enlightenment and political emancipation, and this is progress. In light of these perceived advances Maybaum invests the post-Holocaust age with at least the veneer of messianic redemption: "The Jewish people is, here and now, mankind at its goal. We have arrived. We are the first fruits of God's harvest."[57] One cannot but hear in Maybaum's enthusiasm for the post-Holocaust era an echo of the hope that many nineteenth-century Jews expressed at the beginning of our era—despite what separates him from them.

In the Christian world the transcendence of medievalism is manifested in the new ecumenicism of the Catholic Church, most clearly expressed in the spirit of Vatican II which recognized, at least in small measure, the spiritual legitimacy of other religious traditions, and removed from its liturgy and teaching such "medieval" elements as the *perfidiis Judaeis* (perfidious Jew) phrase from its Easter rite. As the playwright Hochhuth, in his play *The Deputy*, noted: "The S.S. were the Dominicans of the technical age," and the Fuehrer-principle was a Nazi version of papal infallibility; indeed the entire tragedy of the Holocaust was the Inquisition repeated in modern dress. All these are elements of a best forgotten Middle Ages. After Auschwitz, both Jew and Christian can transcend the past through progressive reform more suitable to a post-Holocaust future. Auschwitz makes possible this transcendence.

Maybaum, like Rubenstein and Fackenheim, is sensitive to the essential issue of God's presence in history as raised by the Holocaust. Like Fackenheim, Maybaum is a man of faith, but more than Fackenheim and more than almost all other Jewish thinkers, he is willing to draw the conclusion that others will not draw: Hitler is God's agent. Maybaum follows the logic of his commitment to the Divine presence in history further and more radically than does anyone else. Outrageous as this entailment appears, to credit God with being the all-powerful Lord of history seems logically to require seeing Him as the agent behind Auschwitz, who works His will through the destruction of European Jewry. Though others, who could find God in history, even at the death camps, recoil from this final attribution, Maybaum does not. As the prophet Jeremiah saw Nebuchadnezzar, the destroyer of Jerusalem, as the "servant of God" so Maybaum consciously parallels Jeremiah's idiom and gives voice to the awful paradox: "Hitler, My servant!"[58] Maybaum does not shy away from the full import of this expression: "Hitler was an instrument. . . . God used this instrument to cleanse, to purify, to punish a sinful world; the six million Jews, they died an innocent death; they died because of the sins of others."[59]

Maybaum is a man of great trust, only so can he affirm what he has affirmed. Calling upon Isaiah's image of "the remnant which will return,"[60] the *she'ar yashuv*, Maybaum reminds us that though one-third of world Jewry was destroyed in the death camps, two-thirds survived and this deliverance is a miracle no less great than that experienced at the Red Sea; it too is redemption. Maybaum here views the picture in a more traditional way and calls us to do the same. Look at the salvation of the majority, not the death of a large and sacred minority. See in, and through, the Nazi Holocaust the saving face of God and none other.

ELIEZER BERKOVITS

Eliezer Berkovits has been a keen student of contemporary Jewish philosophy and has made an especial contribution to the creative discussion of the nature and purpose of the *halachah* in modern Orthodox Judaism. In his work *Faith After the Holocaust* (1973) he gives a more traditional response to the Holocaust than any of the other thinkers so far reviewed and highlights seminal elements that need to be considered in any response to Auschwitz.

Berkovits begins his analysis by calling attention to the history of Christian anti-Semitism, which cannot be forgotten or undervalued in any account of Nazi anti-Semitism. This is perhaps the most difficult issue to confront after the Holocaust. Berkovits, however, does not avoid it or try to deflect it; he faces it and requires others to do the same if both Jew and Christian want to understand the past and make sure that it does not repeat itself in the future.

Having disclosed the classical anti-Semitic background to Auschwitz, Berkovits, a rabbinic scholar, explores, as did Fackenheim in *God's Presence in History*, the various biblical and rabbinic responses to suffering in the Jewish tradition. Martyrdom is not a new phenomenon in Judaism and Berkovits searches the tradition to see what, if anything, can be drawn from it that would be applicable to a contemporary reaction to the death camps. The first response and the most important in historical terms is that known as *kiddush ha-Shem*—death for "the sanctification of the Divine Name," i.e., death which honors rather than dishonors God and bears witness to His truth. In religious circles this has always been the most frequently given rationale for Jewish martyrdom: martyrdom is the ultimate act of resignation and trust in God; it is a testing and a response of faithfulness; it is the climactic act of religious heroism. During the Holocaust there were many who were unable to face the horror of their existence and their end with faith, yet there were many others who, like Rabbi Akiva of old, went to their death in joy that they could give their life for God. One example:[61] the Ostrovzer Rebbe, Rabbi Yeḥezkiel ha-Levi Hastuk, went out to meet his Nazi executioners wearing his *tallit* and *kittel*, and before he was shot he announced: "For some time now I have anticipated this *zekhut* (special merit of *kiddush ha-Shem*). I am prepared."[62] Berkovits knows that such acts do not prove anything conclusive about the ultimate questions relevantly raised about Auschwitz, but he asks that in all discussions of Auschwitz this data too be considered. Berkovits pointedly asks: if Nazi barbarism speaks for the absence of God, what is to be said about, what is to be inferred from, the piety, moral grandeur, and saintliness of many of the victims?

Berkovits's account proceeds from this point as if he, at least, is satisfied that there is more to the issue of "faith after the Holocaust" than a Richard Rubenstein is aware of. What is required above all else, he contends, is to provide an adequate Jewish understanding of history so that the events of the contemporary era can be properly appraised. Only against such a background can one even begin to enter into dialogue about the theological relevance or otherwise, of the Holocaust. Critical of many other recent attempts to deal with the "data" of Auschwitz, Berkovits argues that these other attempts "suffer from one serious shortcoming: they deal with the Holocaust in isolation, as if there had been nothing else in Jewish history but this Holocaust."[63] This theme reappears throughout Berkovits's treatment, not only as critique but as grounds for positive affirmation.

On the basis of this plea for the need for a more developed and integrated sense of Jewish history, Berkovits makes the determinative and elemental declaration, which in one sense at least puts him close to Maybaum, that in the framework of past Jewish experience Auschwitz is unique in the magnitude of its horror but not in the problem it poses for religious faith. "From the point of view of the problem we have had innumerable Auschwitz's."[64] With this assertion he radically dissociates himself from both Fackenheim and Rubenstein, who rest their entire positions on the Holocaust's uniqueness and their belief that this uniqueness forces Judaism into new and unprecedented postures. If Auschwitz is only the repetition of an ancient pattern, then the entire nature of the problem of one's reaction to Auschwitz takes on a different coloration. The theological dilemma, as Berkovits sees it, is the same whether one Jew is slaughtered or six million. Each raises the question: How could God let it happen? How does this square with God's providential presence and moral perfection?

If, then, the challenge is not unique, what have other generations of Jews, after previous Holocausts, made of Jewish martyrdom? Berkovits rejects outright, as do all the other major Jewish thinkers who deal with the Holocaust, the simplistic response that the death camps are *mi-penei hata'einu* (because of our sins). He acknowledges that the Holocaust was "an injustice absolute."[65] Moreover, with great honesty he adds, "It was an injustice countenanced by God."[66] Yet Berkovits's concern is to make room for Auschwitz in the Divine scheme despite the fact that it is an unmitigated moral outrage. To begin to do so he calls attention to a fecund and sophisticated response to evil already stated in the Bible, the notion of *hester panim* ("The Hiding Face of God"). *Hester panim* is the view that at times God, mysteriously and inexplicably, and without any obvious human cause such as sin, turns His face from Man.[67] The doctrine of *hester panim* attempts to hold on to God's presence despite His concealment; to affirm that in some mysterious way, God's hiddenness and God's redemptiveness are both necessary features of His unfathomable being.

Moreover, Berkovits argues that this occultation of God is required for man to be a moral creature. God's hiddenness brings into being the possibility for ethically valent human action, for by "absenting" Himself from history He creates the reality of human freedom which is necessary for moral behavior. For human morality to be a real possibility, God has to respect the decisions of mankind and be bound by them. God has to abstain from reacting immediately to evil deeds if our action is to possess value. Yet, just as moral humanity requires freedom, freedom is always open to abuse. Berkovits here reasserts the classic view of the necessity of "free will" to morality. God is long-suffering with an evil humanity, yet this results in suffering to some while God waits for the sinner. Thus "while He shows forbearance with the wicked, he must turn a deaf ear to the anguished cries of the violated."[68] The paradoxical implication of this situation is this: humanity is impossible if God is strictly just; if God is loving beyond the requirements of strict justice there must be human suffering and evil. For Berkovits this is the correct way to view the problem of theodicy in order to be able to continue to believe despite Auschwitz.

God must absent Himself for man to be, but God must also be present in order that ultimately meaninglessness does not gain final victory. Thus God's presence in history must be sensed as hiddenness, and His anonymity must be understood as the sign of His presence. God reveals His power in history by curbing His might so that man too might be powerful. The only enduring witness to God's ultimate control over the course of things is the Jewish people. In its experience, Berkovits declares, one sees both attributes of God. The continued existence of Israel despite its long record of suffering is the strongest single proof that God does exist despite His concealment.[69] Israel is the witness to His accompaniment of happenings in space and time. Nazism, in its luciferian power, understood this fact and its slaughter of Jews was an attempt to slaughter the God of history. The Nazis were aware, even as Israel sometimes fails to be, that God's manifest reality in the world is necessarily linked to the fate of the Jewish people. The nature of Jewish existence stands as a prophetic disclosure against the moral degeneracy of men and nations; it is a mocking proclamation in the face of all human idolatry, and it testifies to the final judgment and redemption of history by a moral God.

Berkovits forces his readers to consider whether the Holocaust is a symbol of the "death of God" or whether it is a sign of His too-great mercy and long-suffering with sinners.

Berkovits's portrayal requires that we take another studied look at Jewish existence and see Auschwitz in, and as part of, the long context of Jewish experience. The Jew is forbidden to treat the crematoriums as if it were all he knew of God's relation to Israel. The Holocaust is not the only, or even the ultimate Jewish experience.[70] The Jew who today feels the absence of the Eternal is the descendant of those who at Sinai and the Red Sea directly encountered the Divine. More important still, the Jew who today talks of Auschwitz also knows the joy of a rebuilt Zion and an "ingathering of the exiles" in its ancient homeland. Jewish survival after Auschwitz proclaims that the satanic is not absolute. Though this does not answer the agonizing conundrums of theodicy, it gives hope that they will be answered in God's future redemptive acts. For Berkovits the rebirth of the State of Israel is contemporary revelation; it is the voice of God speaking forth from history. The events of 1967 especially have an "inescapable revelatory quality"[71] that must be understood in both historical and eschatological terms. "The return is the counterpart in history to the resolution in faith that this world is to be established as the Kingdom of God."[72] The rebuilding of Zion is the ultimate vindication of God's presence and His providential governance of the world. If at Auschwitz and all previous Auschwitz's we have witnessed "The Hiding Face of God," in the rebirth of the State of Israel and its success "we have seen a smile on the face of God. It is enough."[73]

CONCLUSION

Each of the four responses to the Holocaust which we have considered has seen the relevant events from a different perspective,
with alternate presuppositions and faith commitments. Among the
many lessons our four thinkers teach us, though not necessarily by
intention, two especially call for a concluding comment. The first
is that there is no simple set of "facts" that can be easily seized
upon and manipulated in order to get a result which is both mean-
inful and possesses integrity. The "facts" are in large part determined by the premises and methodology one uses; heterogeneous
preconceptions and asymmetrical beginnings produce very different conclusions. Thus, our first thinker philosophizes from a psychoanalytic and anthropological center through which everything
must be judged; he therefore discovers transcendental as compared
to anthropological and psychological value wanting. The second
begins with an existentialist supernaturalism and so finds existential and supernatural elements even at Auschwitz. The third holds
a deep faith in progress and the values of modern liberalism and
thus detects God acting in history, even in the Holocaust, to realize these personally prized ends. The fourth begins with traditional
halachic and metaphysical commitments and thus finds the data
more susceptible and amenable to a conservative approach in which
God is, at least partially, vindicated.

Secondly, and as a necessary corollary, it must be noted that each
of the reactions considered, and others which have been suggested,
all represent, at best, fragmentary accounts, partial descriptions, and
limited and imperfect solutions to the major and most pressing
questions raised by Auschwitz. Given the nature of the Holocaust
this is not surprising. Each response, even optimally, can be seen
to be only incomplete in the face of the reality, quality, and magnitude of evil—evil absolute and unimaginable—in our time.

In conclusion, therefore, while we cannot point to any definitive,
or even agreed, results either with regard to a starting point or to
shared results, it should not be thought that the investigation of
responses to the Holocaust is devoid of significance. To begin with,
our review has brought the major elements crucial to any and all

thinking about the Holocaust into sharp focus. Secondly, we have been given sound instruction as to how one can begin to go about giving shape to these elements—though it must be recognized that any new, more definitive account will have to go beyond the positions studied above. Third, and of no small importance, the now familiar variety found in what is to be counted as "data" and "evidence" and the pluralism of the responses already offered has the virtue of both guiding and warning future thinkers that the Holocaust—whatever its precise parameters and whatever its meaning—will not yield to any conceptual oversimplification. Auschwitz raises the most fundamental, and at the same time, the most difficult intellectual, phenomenological, and existential issues with which reflective men have to deal.

What are now needed are fresh studies, more enquirers, and further original approaches. In the meanwhile, we acknowledge the contribution that has already been made.[74]

NOTES

1. I offer criticisms of these thinkers in the series of four essays that follow this one in the present collection. An additional commentary is found in my paper "Critical Reflections on Holocaust Theology" in the proceedings of the Holocaust symposium held at Indiana University in November 1980 and soon to be published under the editorship of A. Rosenfeld & I. Greenberg, title as yet undecided, by Indiana University Press.

2. *After Auschwitz* (Indianapolis, 1966), "The Making of a Rabbi," p. 223.

3. This came in an interview with a German theologian, Heinrich Grueber, Dean of the Evangelical Church of East and West Berlin, in August 1961. The whole incident is recorded in *After Auschwitz*, "The Dean and the Chosen People," pp. 47–58.

4. *After Auschwitz*, p. 46.

5. *After Auschwitz*, p. 46.

6. *Hagigah*, 14b ff.

7. The older, more famous religious existentialism of Rosenzweig and Buber, for example, fiercely protested against the denial of value and the need to create it. See, for example, Buber's sharp criticism of Sartre in *The Eclipse of God* (New York, 1953).

8. *After Auschwitz*, p. 68.

9. Rubenstein uses the term "demythologize" regularly to describe the process whereby Jews recognize the "death of God" and their new, post-Holocaust situation. The term "demythologize" Rubenstein borrows from the contemporary German Christian theologian and New Testament scholar, Rudolph Bultmann. For more on what this process implies see Bultmann's *Jesus and Mythology* (New York, 1958).

10. *After Auschwitz*, p. 119.

11. *After Auschwitz*, p. 119.

12. *After Auschwitz*, p. 119.

13. For more on Rubenstein's use of psychoanalytic categories to reinterpret Judaism and especially Jewish rituals and symbols see his *After Auschwitz, The Religious Imagination*, and *My Brother Paul*. See also "Psychoanalysis and the Origins of Judaism" in the *Reconstructionist*, December 2, 1962.

14. *After Auschwitz*, pp. 223 ff, for Rubenstein's entire discussion on bar mitzvah.

15. *The Religious Imagination* (Indianapolis, 1968).

16. *After Auschwitz*, "The symbols of Judaism and the Death of God," p. 240. See especially on this natural paganism Rubenstein's essay, "Atonement and Sacrifice in Contemporary Jewish Liturgy" in *After Auschwitz*, pp. 93–111.

17. *After Auschwitz*, "The Rebuilding of Israel in Contemporary Theology," especially pp. 135 ff.

18. *After Auschwitz*, ibid., p. 135.

19. *After Auschwitz*, "Religion and the Origins of the Death Camp," p. 9.

20. This is a summary of Rubenstein's views in *After Auschwitz*, "Person and Myth in the Judeo-Christian Encounter," pp. 73–74.

21. He spent a short time in a concentration camp in 1938–39. He has written about this experience with great power in a paper delivered to the Sixth World Congress of Jewish Studies and published in its *Proceedings*, Jerusalem, 1974.

22. Fackenheim scathingly replied to Rubenstein in *God's Presence in History* (New York, 1970) with the following remark. "What assures him [Rubenstein] of his own capacities to deal with the trauma—or stills his fear that some other mechanism may cause him to utter words which should never have been spoken [God is dead]? We need not go beyond his jarring expression 'the facts are in.' Will all the facts ever be in? And what, in this case, are the facts apart from the interpretation? The statistics?" (p. 72).

23. *God's Presence in History*, p. 31.

24. The term neo-orthodox is used here to mean a position analogous to Franz Rosenzweig's. This position argues for divine revelation and seeks to find meaning in the Torah so it can become the basis of Jewish life. For

a statement of Fackenheim's debt to Rosenzweig (and Buber) see "These Twenty Years" in *Quest for Past and Future* (Bloomington, 1968), pp. 3–26. For Rosenzweig's and Buber's views, in detail, see pp. 184–196 of this work.

25. For more on this see *Quest for Past and Future*, pp. 5 ff.

26. For Fackenheim's views see, for example, the various essays relating to the theology of Liberal Judaism in Fackenheim's collection, *Quest for Past and Future*.

27. *Quest for Past and Future*, p. 5.

28. For details of Buber's *I–Thou* philosophy and his view of *I–Thou* encounter as "revelation" see the section on Buber in my *Jewish Philosophers* (New York, 1975).

29. Perhaps the clearest statement of Fackenheim's views on this are found in his essay entitled "Elijah and the Empiricists" which originally appeared in *The Religious Situation*, Donald Cutler, ed. (New York, 1969) and which was reprinted in a new collection entitled *Encounters Between Judaism and Philosophy*, (New York, 1973). For some critical comments see my review of this collection in the *Journal of Jewish Social Studies* (Spring 1974).

30. The Buberian account and its usage by Fackenheim is not without serious philosophical and theological difficulties that may ultimately undermine it. Fackenheim, however, is aware of many of the problems himself and has written an important essay on Buber's doctrine of revelation. See his "Buber's Doctrine of Revelation" in *The Philosophy of Martin Buber*, P. Schilpp and M. Friedman, eds. (La Salle, Illinois, 1967).

31. See *Quest for Past and Future*, 10.

32. See especially Buber's analysis of the Biblical events surrounding the Exodus-Sinai episode in his book *Moses* (New York, 1946).

33. *God's Presence in History*, "The Structure of Jewish Experience," pp. 8 ff.

34. Ibid., p. 9.

35. Ibid., p. 11.

36. *God's Presence in History*, p. 11. Fackenheim here calls attention to how this past event becomes present reality by reminding us of the statement in the Passover *Haggadah:* "It was not one only who rose against us to annihilate us, but in every generation there are those who rise against us to annihilate us. But the Holy One, blessed be He, saves us from their hand."

37. *God's Presence in History*, pp. 16 ff.

38. Fackenheim's detailed account of this Rabbinic reaction to the destruction of the Second Temple is to be found in *God's Presence in History*, pp. 25–31.

39. *God's Presence in History*, p. 20.

40. *Presence of God in History*, p. 84 repeated from Fackenheim's ear-

lier essay, "Jewish Faith and the Holocaust," in *Commentary*, Vol. 47 (1967).

41. Ibid., 84. Fackenheim spells out the implication of these "commandments" in some detail. Ibid., pp. 82–92.

42. Brief critiques of Fackenheim's view can be found in the last section of M. Meyer's article on Fackenheim entitled "Judaism After Auschwitz" in *Commentary*, Vol. 53, No. 6 (June 1972); and in "The Questions and Answers after Auschwitz" by Seymour Cain in *Judaism*, Vol. 20, No. 3 (Summer 1971).

43. I. Maybaum, *The Face of God After Auschwitz* (Amsterdam, 1965). Hereafter referred to as *Face*.

44. On the Jewish interpretation of these passages see S.R. Driver and A. Neubauer, *The Fifty-Third Chapter of Isaiah, According to Jewish Interpreters* (New York, 1969 reprint of 1876–77 edition).

45. *Face*, p. 35.

46. Ibid., pp. 25 ff.

47. Compare this to Fackenheim's view of "epochmaking" and "root experiences" discussed above.

48. *Face*, p. 32.

49. Ibid., p. 32.

50. Ibid., p. 29.

51. Ibid., p. 31.

52. Ibid., pp. 35 f.

53. Ibid., p. 36.

54. Ibid., pp. 66 ff.

55. Ibid., p. 68.

56. See *Face*, pp. 62–63 for a more detailed view of this.

57. Ibid., p. 63.

58. Ibid., p. 67.

59. Ibid., p. 67.

60. Ibid., pp. 59 ff., for Maybaum's discussion of "the remnant;" see also pp. 87 ff.

61. This incident is not recorded by Berkovits, who gives other equally moving incidents.

62. This incident is recorded in Menashe Unger, *Sefer Kedoshim* (Jerusalem, 1967), p. 36.

63. *Faith After the Holocaust* (New York, 1973), p. 88.

64. Ibid., p. 90. I disagree with this view and explore the issue in my paper "The Unique 'Intentionality' of the Holocaust" in the present collection and in still more detail in my forthcoming monograph on this theme, tentatively entitled *The Uniqueness of the Holocaust* to be published by Harvard University Press.

65. Ibid., p. 89.

66. Ibid., p. 89.

67. Berkovits discusses this in detail, Ibid., pp. 94 ff. See also Psalm 44, which Berkovits cites.

68. *Faith After the Holocaust*, p. 106.

69. See Ibid., pp. 109 ff. for Berkovits' views on Israel in history.

70. See Berkovits's discussion, Ibid., pp. 134 ff.

71. Ibid., p. 145. See the entire last chapter, "In Zion Again," pp. 144–169, for full details of how Berkovits views the state of Israel and its relation to a modern Jewish theology. One is forced to note that Berkovits's book was published in 1973, though written over several years. It was published, however, before the Yom Kippur War of October 1973.

72. Ibid., p. 152.

73. Ibid., p. 156. See the whole of his discussion on pp. 156 ff. Since this was first written, Emil Fackenheim's views have become increasingly concerned with the state of Israel and its theological meaning.

74. Since this essay was originally written two additional Jewish theologians, Irving (Yitzchak) Greenberg and Arthur A. Cohen, have begun to make a notable contribution to the discussion of the meaning of the Holocaust. I discuss their work in detail in the essay referred to in Note 1.

RICHARD RUBENSTEIN, THE GOD OF HISTORY, AND THE LOGIC OF JUDAISM

In the last fifteen years or so, Jewish thinkers of all persuasions have begun to consider the theological and historical ramifications of the Holocaust as they bear upon Jewish existence and identity in the post-Holocaust age.[1] The competence, appeal, and richness of these differing reflections have varied widely but none has been more radical than that of Richard Rubenstein. In response to Auschwitz, Rubenstein has taken the extreme theological position of denying God's existence. If his thesis is correct, then all other less radical responses to the Holocaust, which are predicated on some continued affirmation of the existence of God, are not viable.

Rubenstein's position can be summed up in three words: "God is Dead." The logic that has driven him to utter these three extraordinarily powerful words can be put in the following syllogism: (1) God, as He is conceived of in the Jewish tradition, could not have allowed the Holocaust to happen; (2) the Holocaust did happen. Therefore, (3) God, as He is conceived of in the Jewish tradition, does not exist.

This seemingly straightforward argument is the basis upon which Rubenstein has felt compelled to reject the God of history and hence the God of Jewish tradition. The radical negation represented by this position is of the utmost seriousness for modern Jewish (and non-Jewish) thought and, even if one finally demurs, one must grapple with it rather than merely dismiss it as out of place in a Jewish context, as some naive critics have done.[2] It does raise a real, if frightening, possibility about the "meaning of Auschwitz," i.e., that there is *no* meaning to history, for history is a random, arbitrary series of events that are unrelated either to a transcendental order or to a context of absolute meaning or value. In *After Auschwitz*,[3] Rubenstein stated this contention articulately:

When I say we live in the time of the death of God, I mean that the thread uniting God and man, heaven and earth has been broken. We stand in a cold, silent, unfeeling cosmos, unaided by any purposeful power beyond our own resources. After Auschwitz what else can a Jew say about God? . . . I see no other way than the "death of God" position of expressing the void that confronts man where once God stood.[4]

Philosophically this challenge to belief, generated from the consideration of the implications of Auschwitz, is both interesting and more problematic than it at first appears. Of course, the "Death of God" is not a new challenge, being already *very* familiar in modern philosophical literature since the proclamation to this affect by Nietzsche's madman in *The Gay Science*. More recently, its appeal has been expressed most forcefully in the extremely influential French atheistic existentialist school associated with the names of Camus and Sartre. Alternatively, what is novel in Rubenstein's employment of this notion is his use of this idea in a Jewish theological context. Many modern Jews since the *Haskalah* (the "Jewish Enlightenment" dating from the mid-eighteenth century onward) have spoken in more or less muted terms of this "event," but no one until Rubenstein's reflections on the Holocaust thought to use it as the basis for a Jewish theology of history.

In order to expose both the merits and the insufficiencies of this stance as a Jewish theology let us take a closer, more rigorous, look at its structural character. Nine primary logical-philosophical topics will be considered in turn.

1. To begin on the positive side, one must recognize at the outset what is perhaps the most important underlying reason for the adoption of this position as a way of dealing with the "cause" and "meaning" of the Holocaust. Traditional theology has had to deal with the "problem of evil" for millennia and in reaction has given a variety of "answers" ranging from the most dominant traditional Jewish response, namely that evil is a punishment for sin, *mi-penei*

ḥata'einu in the classical Hebrew phrase, to the notion that suffering is an "affliction of love," *yissurin shel ahavah*.[5] All of these solutions and their concommitant theodicies are found inadequate to deal with the reality of the death camps by the "Death of God" theologian—and I believe he is absolutely correct in this judgment. He, in alliance with almost all Jewish theologians of whatever persuasion, is especially adamant that the destruction of European Jewry cannot be *mi-penei ḥata'einu*—for what sins could Israel have committed to justify such evil and what kind of God would punish *even* a sinful Israel with such fury? Similarly, the classical Christian account of Jewish suffering, which views it as deserved punishment for Israel's guilt for its alleged role in the death of Jesus— even if seen as deicide in classical Christian terms—which is used by some Christian theologians to "justify" the Holocaust, needs to be reconsidered by Christians.[6] Is there not something fundamentally wrong with the image of a God of love wreaking such vengeance on a million children after two thousand years?

Rather than accept either Israel's sinfulness as the justification for the Holocaust or see it as some inscrutable act of Divine wrath or fiat, the vision of which appears to blaspheme against the loving God of the Jewish tradition and the entire meaning of Jewish convenantal existence, the radical theologian takes the difficult step of denying both poles of the Divine–human dialectic, thereby destroying the traditional theological encounter altogether. There is no God and there is no covenant with Israel.

If I believed in God as the omnipotent author of the historical drama and Israel as His Chosen People, I had to accept [the] . . . conclusion that it was God's will that Hitler committed six million Jews to slaughter. I could not possibly believe in such a God nor could I believe in Israel as the chosen people of God after Auschwitz.[7]

2. The second element emerging out of, as well as essential to, the "Death of God" view putatively grounded in the Holocaust experience is more problematic. It concerns nothing less than how one views Jewish history, its continuities and discontinuities, its "causal connectedness" and interdependencies. By raising the issue of how one evaluates Jewish history and what hermeneutic of his-

toric meaning one need adopt, I mean to bring into focus the fact—and it is a fact—that the radical theologian sees Jewish history too narrowly, i.e., focused solely in and through the Holocaust. He takes *the* decisive event of Jewish history to be the death camps. But this is a distorted image of Jewish experience, for there is a pre-Holocaust and post-Holocaust Jewish reality that must be considered in dealing with the questions raised by the Nazi epoch. These questions extend beyond 1933–1945 and touch the present Jewish situation as well as the whole of the Jewish past. One cannot make the events of 1933–45 intelligible in isolation. To think, moreover, that one can excise this block of time from the flow of Jewish history and then by concentrating on it, extract the "meaning" of *all* Jewish existence, is more than uncertain,[8] no matter how momentous or demonic this time may have been.

Jews went to Auschwitz, suffered and died at Auschwitz, through no specific fault of their own: their crime was their Jewishness. The Nuremberg laws extracted from the 1933–45 generation the price of their parents', grandparents' and great-grandparents' decision to have Jewish children. This, if nothing else, forces us to widen our historic perspective when we try to comprehend what happened in Nazi Germany. When one tries to understand the "grandparents" of the death camp generation one will find that their actions are likewise unintelligible without following the historic chain that leads backwards into the Jewish millennial past. The same rule also applies in trying to fathom the historic reality of the murderers and their inheritance. The events of 1933–45 were the product of the German and Jewish past; to decode this present we must enter into that past.

This recognition of a pre-Holocaust and post-Holocaust Israel forces two considerations upon us. The first is the very survival of the Jewish people *despite* their "sojourn among the nations." As Karl Barth once said, "the best proof of God's existence is the continued existence of the Jewish people." Without entering into a discussion of the metaphysics of history, let this point just stand for further reflection, i.e., that the Jews survived Hitler and Jewish history did not end at Auschwitz. Secondly, and equally if not more directly significant, is the recreation after Auschwitz of a Jewish state, the Third Jewish Commonwealth in the Land of Israel.[9] This event, too, is remarkable in the course of Jewish existence. Logic and conceptual adequacy require that if in our discussion of the relation of God and history we want to give theological weight to the Holocaust then we *must* also be willing to attribute *theological* significance to the state of Israel. Just what weight one assigns to each of these events, and then again to events in general, in constructing a theological reading of history is an extraordinarily complex theoretical issue, about which there is the need for much discussion, and which allows for much difference of view. However, it is clear that any final rendering of the "meaning of Jewish history" that values in its equation *only* the negative factors of the Nazi Holocaust or it and previous Holocausts, is, at best, arbitrary. If one wants to make statements about God's presence (or in this case absence) in Jewish history as a consequence of Auschwitz then one must also, in all theological and existential seriousness, consider the meaning of His presence (or absence) in Jewish history as played out in Jerusalem. If it makes sense to talk theologically at all—an open question—about God's presence and absence, His existence and nonexistence, and to judge these matters on the basis of what happened to the Jews of Europe in some sort of negative natural theology, then it is equally meaningful—*and logically and theologically necessary*—to consider what the events in *Eretz Yisroel* since 1945 tell us about His reality and ours. To his credit, Rubenstein does appreciate that the state of Israel is of consequence, even momentous consequence, but he insists on treating it as *theologically* independent from Auschwitz so that no positive linkage in some larger rendering of Jewish experience is possible; nor can we posit what in traditional idiom would be termed "redemptive" significance to this national rebirth. Rather, the renaissance of Jewish life in its ancestral homeland is seen by Rubenstein, consistent with his own procedure, as the clearest manifestation of the post-1945 rejection of the God of history by Jews and their return to a natural, land-related, nontheistic life. However, despite Rubenstein's interesting working through of this event in his own terms, his interpretation of the situation will not do, for it is clear that from a logical point of view it is methodologically improper to construct a phenomenology of historical reality that gives weight only to the negative signifiance of "evil" without any attempt to balance it against the positive significance of the "good" we encounter in history. History is too variegated to be understood only as good or evil; the alternating rhythms of actual life reveal the two forces as interlocked and inseparable. For our present concerns, the hermeneutical value of this recognition is that one comes to see that Jewish history is neither conclusive proof for the existence of God (because of the possible counterevidence of Auschwitz), nor conversely, for the nonexistence of God (because of the possible counterevidence of the state of Israel as well as the whole three thousand-year historic Jewish experience). Rubenstein's narrow focus on Auschwitz reflects an already decided theological choice based on certain normative presuppositions and a compelling desire to justify certain conclusions. It is not a value-free phenomenological description of Jewish history.

Before leaving this argument it should be made absolutely clear that it is not being asserted that the state of Israel *is* compensation for Auschwitz, nor that Auschwitz is the "cause," in a theological or metaphysical sense, of the creation of the Jewish state, as many simplistic historical and theological accounts, offered for all kinds of mixed reasons, have done. Whatever relation does exist between Holocaust Europe and the state of Israel is far more ambiguous and many-sided than a simple causal or compensatory schema would explain. The argument as presented, however, is a reminder that the state of Israel is an event—one might, I think, even legitimately say a "miracle," if that term means anything at all—at least equal to if not more important than Auschwitz in Jewish theological terms; it must be respected as such.

3. There is an unspoken but implied, highly influential, premise in Rubenstein's argument concerning the relation of God and history. This hidden premise relates to what is well known as the "empiricist theory of meaning" made famous by A.J. Ayer in *Language, Truth and Logic* and then given a more particularly significant theological twist by Anthony Flew in his "falsifiability challenge." This was first expressed in the widely discussed "University Discussion" reprinted in *New Essays in Philosophical Theology.*[10]

Space prohibits an extended review of this most aggressive challenge to religious belief, which in any case is familiar enough if not always completely understood, but its implicit use in the "Death of God" argument must at least be called into the open, for it is the employment of this thesis that provides much of the initial rigor of the radical theologian's challenge. I am not sure whether Rubenstein's employment of this notion is intentional or indirect but its presence and significance for Rubenstein is nonetheless real. He at least tacitly accepts the basic premise of the "empiricist falsifiability thesis,"[11] i.e., that propositions about God are to be straightforwardly confirmed or disconfirmed by appeal to empirical events in the world. It is only the result of the at least implicit adoption of this empirical principle, or something very close to it, that allows Rubenstein to judge that "God is dead," for it is only on the basis of some such norm that the conditions of the Holocaust can become the empirical test case for the existence or nonexistence of God. In effect Rubenstein argues: if there is too much evil in the world (putting aside the problem of how one would measure this for the moment and recognizing that this subject is never dealt with by Rubenstein) then God, as conceived in the Jewish tradition, cannot exist. At Auschwitz there was such evil and God did not step in to stop it; thus God does not exist. Hence the traditional theological notions based upon such a belief in God are decisively falsified by an appeal to this empirical evidence.

Respecting this challenge as an important one that is often too lightly dismissed by theologians, and respecting Rubenstein's employment of it as an authentic existential response to an overwhelming reality, it nonetheless needs to be suggested that the empirical falsifiability challenge is not definitive one way or the other in theological matters and thus can not provide Rubenstein (or others) with an unimpeachable criterion for making the negative theological judgments that he seeks to advance regarding the nonexistence of God. The "falsifiability" thesis neither allows one *decisively* to affirm nor disaffirm God's presence in history, for history provides evidence both for and against the nonexistence of God on empirical-verificationist grounds, i.e., there is both good and bad in history. Moreover, the very value of the empirical criteria turns on the one hand on what one considers to be empirical-verifica-tionist evidence, i.e., on what one counts as empirical or experien-tial, and on the other, on whether the empirical-verificationist principle is, in itself, philosophically coherent, which it appears not to be. Again, here too the state of Israel is a crucial "datum" (and solidly empirical) for the radical theologican to consider when framing his falsifiability equation, for the Jew (or others) might challenge the critic with this counterclaim: "Yes, the assertion of God's existence *does* depend on what happens in history. Among the events of history is not only Auschwitz but also the creation of the state of Israel. Whereas the former event is evidence against the 'God-Hypothesis' the latter is evidence in its favor." Neither position is decisively provable—but both are equally meaningful,[12] as well as equally unprovable.

Again, the Jew (or a Christian like Barth) might respond to the falsifiability challenge by returning to the first historical argument discussed above (as point 2), i.e., Auschwitz is not decisive evi-dence for or against God's existence, and meet the empiricist critic head-on by rephrasing the nature of the empiricist challenge itself. That is, he could argue that he accepts the challenge in general terms but offers different specific empirical conditions by which to decide the matter one way or the other. For example, he stipulates as the decisive falsifying condition the complete elimination of Jews from history which was, in fact, Hitler's goal through his "Final Solution." Here we have a straightforward, if theologically enor-mous, claim: the existence of God is inseparably related to the ex-istence of the Jewish people (a claim not too distant from that ac-tually made in at least some classical Jewish sources). If the Jewish people are destroyed then we will agree that God does not exist. This is certainly a falsifiable proposition, or at least, it is hoped, only an *in principle* falsifiable thesis, i.e., the Jewish people *logi-cally* are removable from history. What happens to the empiricist challenge at this point? This question seems especially challenging given that the hypothetical argument constructed can be con-strued, at least according to a certain quite respectable theological ideology, as a close analog to what actually transpired in twentieth-century Europe.

What this second counterexample, as well as the argument advanced above, suggest is that Rubenstein has too easily accepted some form of the empiricist theory of meaning and verification. Though this theory is obscure at best and probably ultimately philosophically indefensible, Rubenstein has made this, or something like it, a foundation stone of his entire enterprise without a sufficient degree of epistemological self-consciousness regarding its philosophical accuracy or logical adequacy. In his invocation of this procedure, he has sought to adopt a clear and indisputable method of reaching theological conclusions, the appeal of such clarity and decisiveness being obvious. But the seductiveness of this strategem is more illusory than real, for the empirical-verificationist criterion achieves its putative precision and rigor only by illegitimately reducing the complex to the simple and the ambiguous to the transparent. Thus its results are a caricature of the situation.

Before moving on it should be registered that despite our criticism of Rubenstein's formulation of the empiricist issue as logically inadequate, his intentions are well directed, namely, he wants to find nonapologetic, nonhomiletical, nonsubjective ways to talk meaningfully about covenantal existence, or rather, its nonexistence, after the Holocaust and in light of what the Holocaust has to teach us. But, alternatively, what also needs to be recognized is that his frontal assault on the questions involved, using various forms of empiricist-verificationist instruments, is not successful; other ways to get at the root of the problem need to be found.

4. In addition to the unsatisfactory way in which Rubenstein handles the matter of falsifiability and its corollary, the linkage of empirical evidence to "God-language," there is a still larger, even more fundamental, weakness of a metaphysical sort that needs to be confronted. One might describe it as a paucity of metaphysical imagination. This conceptual limitation manifests itself in the sharp disjunctions and black-white dichotomies with which Rubenstein works, which are not true to the richness and variety of human experience, nor, as indicated above, to the ambiguity of history, nor again to the possible varieties of *metaphysical* accounts of reality that might be employed to deal with history in general and Auschwitz in particular, nor finally, in Rubenstein's case, to the notion

of "God" and its corollaries, which he treats very simplistically.[13] A close reading of Rubenstein's work[14] suggests that he has given insufficient attention to metaphysical considerations. He is, of course, unhappy with traditional metaphysical schemata in general and this is one of the contributing reasons why he has become a "Death of God" theologian,[15] but this unhappiness, even if justified, is not in itself a license to dismiss metaphysics altogether. What is required is a new and better metaphysics—either with or without God, as the facts of the case turn out to warrant—rather than the erroneous, and ultimately self-defeating, disregard for all serious metaphysical investigation.

If one speculates, as Rubenstein does, on the teleological character of history, the existence or nonexistence of God, the interdependence or otherwise of God and man, and the presence or absence of "meaning" in both the cosmos and human life, among many other issues, metaphysical imagination is a *sine qua non*. The author of *After Auschwitz* seems genuinely unaware that his is a substantial *metaphysical* speculation rather than either a set of empirical propositions or a phenomenological description of a straightforward kind (if any such phenomenological descriptions there be at all). To justify his account, therefore, metaphysical considerations become centrally relevant, especially those which try to wrestle with the meaning and logical implications of themes such as God's freedom and creative power and His creation of men as free beings.

The acknowledged indebtedness of Rubenstein to his existentialist predecessors is of importance, especially here.[16] Like them, Rubenstein thinks that criticism and purposeful eschewing of metaphysics is a suitable substitute for metaphysical enterprise and imagination. However, just as this lack has proved a singularly negative factor in existentialist thought, so too does it manifest itself here. Rather than working through the logic of his position for himself, Rubenstein has chosen to adopt as true the antimetaphysical existentialist credo which has been in circulation at least since Kierkegaard's anti-Hegelian polemic immortalized this approach. This choice, however, embodies a significant error for at least two reasons. First, the inherited existentialist position is itself inadequate *per se*. While claiming to be antimetaphysical in the name of "existence," this very claim is itself a metaphysical assertion. Space prevents more than the bare presentation of this fact, which is now widely recognized to obtain. Secondly, the wholesale application of this existentialist attitude to Judaism, to the Holocaust and to the post-Holocaust Jewish situation, is dubious, for it fails to recognize that Judaism has its own *internal* metaphysical understanding of events and reality whose perspective can only be mastered from within Judaism in the first instance.[17] For example, Judaism has its own account of the meaning of the terms "God", "history" and "covenant," to cite only three cardinal concepts in Rubenstein's schema.

5. Two related issues now also surface. The first can be put forcefully in a simple question: why did Rubenstein, especially as a specifically Jewish "Death of God" theologian, have to wait for Auschwitz to deny the existence of God? That is to say, he was surely familiar with Job, with the destruction of the First and Second Temples, and with the nineteen-hundred-year-old *via dolorosa* of Jewish history in Exile. Why weren't these enough to disabuse him of his faith before Auschwitz? In fact, Rubenstein even quotes approvingly the words of the most famous of all Talmudic heretics, the once-great sage Elishah ben Abuya, whose classic heretical statement is well-known: *leth din v'leth dayan* ("there is neither judgment nor judge").[18] He knows, too, of Ivan Karamozov's last and strongest argument against God: "I renounce the higher harmony altogether. It is not worth the tears of that one tortured child who beat itself on the breast with its little finger and prayed . . . with its unexpected tears to 'dear God.' "[19]

The answer to our question is at once obvious and unsatisfying. It is: the existential impact of the Holocaust on Rubenstein, who was alive to witness it. This is *his* tragedy—and *ours*. We are close to it, we see its horror close up, we are able to observe its victims, we even meet its few survivors—and as contemporary Jews we count ourselves, we know ourselves to be, "survivors." This much is clear, and it speaks well of Rubenstein that his sensitivity to this event was so great as to cause nothing less than a revolution in his own life. Conversely, however, it raises another issue. Is the challenge of Auschwitz any greater than the previous historic tragedies of the Jewish (or other) people or is it that we merely have become insensitive through distance (rather than unconcern) to the suffering of the earlier victims, whose screams we do not hear, whose charred bodies we do not see, whose scarred and broken survivors we do not meet? Is Rubenstein's unbelief, then, only subjective in origin, or does it reflect a fact about the external world? In other words, did belief in God *ever* make sense, and if it did, perhaps more distance would allow us to see that it still does. Alternatively, if belief in God *never* made sense, then God was dead before Auschwitz, and Auschwitz has no new theological significance. Could it be that the Holocaust has no special density in the plurality of events that we want to consider theologically informative?

This raises the second item that now must be faced squarely. In light of all the classic, as well as unrecorded, claims against God's justice what makes Rubenstein think that his theological vision, constructed on the ashes of Auschwitz, is either novel or especially meaningful? The only possible answer to this question is: "But Auschwitz is different"—and this takes us in to our next, related, issue.

6. Is Auschwitz unique? Rubenstein's view on the one hand, as well as the responses of "faith" like those of Emil Fackenheim and Elie Wiesel, on the other, all depend in large part on their respective and shared affirmation of the *uniqueness* of the Holocaust. For Rubenstein this means that the Holocaust is seen as somehow *uniquely* evil, hence calling God's existence into question in a special way. But Rubenstein never gives a clear account of why Auschwitz is considered uniquely evil and hence "unique" in the sense required for this entire theological enterprise. Why do the death camps challenge God's existence any more directly than, say, the destruction of the First Temple, which was the first and therefore the most surprising major trauma in Jewish history? (This disquiet is clearly seen in the contemporary response to this event recorded in the Bible.) What of the destruction of the Second Temple in 70 c.e., or the Rhineland massacres of the Crusader period, or the Chmielnitzki massacres of 1648, or the Kishenev pogroms of 1903, or the Stalinist purges of the 1930s. Again, even if one

wants to disagree, what does one reply to Jews and non-Jews alike who liken the Holocaust to other historical tragedies visited on other communities? History is all too replete with seemingly senseless slaughter ("senseless" here does not mean "unplanned") and mass murder to accept any claim to uniqueness in these areas without careful scrutiny of the identifying criteria of "unique" and "uniqueness." But these criteria are never forthcoming.

To say in answer to the problem of "uniqueness," as Rubenstein (and others) do, that at Auschwitz Jews experienced a *qualitatively* and *quantitatively* different form of evil—experienced evil absolute and unrestrained—is not to answer the question at all. It is only to push the problem one step backward, i.e., what is the particular nature of this qualitatively and quantitatively different evil? While *very* sympathetic to Rubenstein's proclivity to identify the Holocaust as "unique," one must recognize that his sentiments, no matter how strong or sincere (or the sentiments of any other peoples or persons regarding their own particular or national tragedy) are not satisfactory substitutes or logical equivalents for rational arguments regarding what makes an event "unique." I have elsewhere[20] given reasons why I find the Holocaust an incomparable crime, but these are my reasons, not Rubenstein's. Moreover, and I want to say this very carefully and with especial force, the Holocaust, even if "unique," may be "unique" in historical and ideological ways that leave questions of Jewish theological substance, including the reality or otherwise of God's existence, in essentially the same condition as they were before the *Sho'ah*. That is to say, the ways in which the Holocaust is "unique," may not effect the debate over God's existence in any radically new way. The old theodicies may still be intact (at least to the degree they were before).

The topic of "uniqueness" of course raises metaphysical issues and returns us directly to the need for metaphysical inquiry discussed in (4) above, but it is precisely on this crucial topic Rubenstein makes little advance. Yet if Auschwitz is to be taken as the axis of one's reading of history, as the decisive criterion and focus of one's entire theology, and as the foundation of one's *Weltanschauung* (which has been generated from one's theological conclusions regarding this event), then some reasons, metaphysical or otherwise, have to be provided for so singling in on this one episode to the exclusion of all others.[21]

In fairness, let me say that Rubenstein's vulnerability on this cardinal issue is shared by him with all the other Holcaust theologies that rely in some essential manner, upon the "uniqueness" of that event. No theologian has yet been able to provide anything even approaching a reasonable statement of historical "uniqueness" that would serve the theological needs of such accounts. However, even while granting this, it must also be recognized that Rubenstein's position is especially vulnerable, being open to criticism on three further counts. The first is based on a metaphysical argument, the second on a logical argument, and the third on an epistemological argument. The metaphysical reason can be put simply. If one is going to construct a coherent theory of the Holocaust's "uniqueness" for theological purposes, it will require a larger context that argues for the uniqueness of the Jewish people and its history, (as compared, for example, to the history of the Ibo's, Ache Indians, Aborigines or Cambodians, to name just a few alternatives). Thus one will have to reintroduce, in a theologically meaningful way, the notions of Israel's "chosenness" and covenantal status, ideas Rubenstein expressly wants to eliminate.[22] Without this larger ideological context that makes the case for Israel's metaphysical "uniqueness" no argument about the uniqueness of Auschwitz, in theological terms, is going to be substantial and defensible.

Secondly, the logical objection. Rubenstein insists on the "uniqueness" of Auschwitz. His whole negative theology is based on this claim, as is his adoption of a theory of the absurdity of history and cosmos in which nature reigns over history and life is really meaningless. Consequently, everything is without transcendental worth. However, can it *logically* be maintained that in a meaningless universe, in which there are no historic or metaphysical values, one can meaningfully talk of "uniqueness" at all? On the basis of what grounds does the notion of "uniqueness" (in an axiological sense) come into being and against what is it measured? If all is absurd then Auschwitz, too, is absurd—but at the same time this claim to absurdity contradicts all possible claims to "uniqueness."

For the sake of clarity, let us turn this argument around and restate it. If all existence is absurd no event is, or can logically be, more absurd than any other. Hence, no event can *decisively prove* the absurdity of history or reality. As such, the weight Rubenstein places on Auschwitz as the cornerstone of his entire negative dogmatics seems to be denied.

Thirdly, the epistemological argument. Rubenstein talks continually of the absurdity of the universe. He does so largely unself-critically, as if this judgment on reality were self-evident or, at the very least, the only possible rendering of reality from a straightforwardly phenomenological survey of how things are. Accordingly, he argues that norms and purpose are imposed onto this valueless and meaningless phenomenological reality by well-intended, if deluded, men. However, this judgment is precarious, for there is *no* straightforward phenomenological reading of reality, either by theists or nontheists, idealists or extentialists. All "reality" is known by us through a rich, subtle, overwhelmingly ambiguous conjunction of—to use Kant's language, though *not* Kant's system—"concepts" and "percepts." We come to know what is real, or what is constitutive of reality, as an admixture of "what I know" and "how I know" and the inseparable links between these epistemic states of affairs. Thus, the categories of "uniqueness" and "absurdity," among all the other related concepts in Rubenstein's theological vocabulary, need to be scrutinized from the epistemological perspective, cognizant of the epistemic activity involved in these, as in all, cognitive activities.

7. The first six topics so far touched upon have been of a broader nature, probably relevant not only to a consideration of Rubenstein's reconstructions, but also to the efforts of all thinkers who have tried (or will try) to construct a "Death of God" theology on the basis of the Holocaust experience. There are, however, three additional subjects which I should like to engage that are particular to Rubenstein's now de-mythologizing now re-mythologizing vision. The first concerns Rubenstein's interesting, if curious, advocacy of the value of Jewish community despite, or even more pre-

cisely, because of the Holocaust. The second turns on his prescription that the Jew after Auschwitz should substitute a mystical, pagan, nature-religion for traditional Jewish theology. The third considers what I call, broadly speaking, Rubenstein's "style."

As to the importance of Jewish community after the Holocaust, Rubenstein argues as follows. After the traumatic experiences of recent Jewish history, the community of Israel, the social solidarity of one Jew for another, is all the more called for because now, after the "Death of God," there is nowhere else for man to turn for the meaning of human life. Certainly, according to Rubenstein, no transcendental revelatory Absolute exists which will or could infuse our life with significance; all pious traditional nostalgia of this sort is to be recognized as the false, and no longer efficacious, opiate that it is. Alternatively, however, in the face of the abyss that threatens to engulf us, Jews must and can create that "meaning" which there is to be, and they do this primarily in community: "It is precisely because human existence is tragic, ultimately hopeless, and without meaning that we treasure our religious community."[23] Although, according to Rubenstein, post-Holocaust Judaism has to be vigorously "demythologized," that is, it has to recognize the emptiness of the historic claims ("myths") of Israel to be a uniquely "chosen people" and to be God's beloved, at the same time Judaism, as an existential reality, paradoxically gains heightened immediacy in this very process of contemporary redefinition. It does so because despite the Jew's new reflective self-consciousness, which coincides with his dismemberment of the "mythic" structure of traditional Judaism and the ideology by which the Jewish people has traditionally understood its experience, he is still a Jew and as such carries with him the "shared vicissitudes of history, culture and psychological perspective"[24] that define a Jew. Jews, like all human beings, are rooted in concrete life situations. As such, for a Jew, only Jewish experience can be authentic; only in its traditional forms of life can he best and most completely express his aspirations and ideals, only here can the Jew participate in a "community of shared predicament and ultimate concern."[25]

Before analyzing Rubenstein's understanding of the "demythologizing" of Judaism and its subsequent sociological and psychological role in contemporary Jewish life, I want to call attention to Rubenstein's indebtedness to the atheistic existentialist program of creating values through human resources and needs alone. We cannot rehearse, in detail, the limits of this position here[26] but only offer that if Rubenstein's adoption of this scenario is correct then the whole notion of "value"—human or otherwise—is more than dubious, being, if not self-contradictory, at best hollow. Morality and commitment, authenticity and responsibility, as well as all the other "value" words in our philosophical and theological lexicon—and in Rubenstein's—actually become empty. They continue, however, to be used by Rubenstein with some semblance of intelligibility and normative density because it is not recognized that their employment is parasitic on the very traditional metaphysical and axiological notions that have been overtly rejected. This self-contradictory parasitism is essential to Rubenstein's program though, of course, its identification makes the entire systematic structure implausible.

We can now consider the existential, social-psychological context Rubenstein wants to emphasize. Those familiar with modern Jewish thought will recognize Rubenstein's demythologized sociological rendering of Judaism and its stress on Jewish community and shared history as close to, if not identical with, the sentiments articulated by Mordecai Kaplan in his 1934 classic, *Judaism as a Civilization*, and styled by him as "Reconstructionism." This version of Judaism has been correctly subjected to many criticisms[27] and we have no wish to re-iterate the majority of them here. Only one demands comment: the thesis that traditional Jewish forms of life can continue to play an enriching psychological and existential role in the lives of Jews even if they are divorced from their more traditional theological content. We can most precisely express our concern in the interrogative: can the socio-religious rituals, customs, liturgical activities, as well as the wide range of *mitzvot* (religious commandments and obligations) continue to provide "meaning," even if only this-worldly and existential, for Jews and Judaism in the new, naturalistic, pagan context envisioned by Rubenstein?

Rubenstein's argument, to his credit, raises fundamental semantic questions about "meaning" and its relation to the notions of "form" and "content." What Rubenstein is insinuating is that one can keep the "form(s)" of Jewish life but radically change their "content" and thereby still make it possible to maintain the social and psychological "value" or "meaning" of these Jewish activities. This is a highly suggestive, psychologically sophisticated, thesis. Unfortunately, it is untenable because it is based on a misunderstanding of the interrelation of "form," "content," and "meaning," paying insufficient attention to the indissoluble link between the three concepts and the complex structural interdependance that obtains between them. That is to say, if you thoroughly and consistantly change the "content," even if you try to maintain the "form," you will necessarily change the "meaning." In effect, the schematic weakness arises because Rubenstein undervalues the formal linkage of "content" and "meaning" (existential, social, and psychological "meaning" in Rubenstein's sense, not semantic, ontological, or logical "meaning"). In general, Rubenstein's contrary view is not supported by any arguments and in fact contradicts the psychological, sociological, and philosophical grammar of the situation.

A clearer conception of what is at stake can be obtained if we examine Rubenstein's own examples of how this transformed post-Auschwitz situation functions in terms of "form," "meaning," and "content." He has, and for this he is to be applauded, tried to give specific illustrations of how certain classic modes of personal and group Jewish behavior can continue to be adhered to, i.e., can continue to provide "meaning," at the same time that their underlying justifying ideology is radically modified. Thus, for example, he argues that in the new, now demythologized post-Holocaust Judaism he envisions, bar mitzvah, while continuing to be celebrated, should not be understood as the public acceptance of the Torah's obligations by the now religiously "adult" boy but rather as a puberty rite, a *rite de passage*, which signals the public acceptance of the young man of thirteen as sexually adult in the eyes of the community.[28] However, this case (and others) lacks compelling force, for it seems reasonable to expect that rather than continuing to perform bar mitzvahs, albeit for a new purpose, it is more likely that not only will the specific occasion of bar mitzvah fall into disuse but the entire fabric of Judaism as a socially cohesive, "meaning-giving" entity will disintegrate, as indeed has happened in assimilated Jewish circles in the past where the cement of classical Jewish theology was rejected. What reason is there to think that celebrating a boy's "sexual maturity" will serve *in a Jewish context* to enhance Jewish communal identity? Rubenstein's reasoning here, of course, borrows from anthropological sources wherein such sexual *rites de passage* are reported to function as prominent socially cohesive factors in certain other non-Jewish group behavior. But what grounds are there for suggesting that Judaism can be, or should be, so readily tranposed or "reduced" to these non-Jewish patterns of meaning? No evidence has been offered to demonstrate that what functions in one way in a specific context will function in a similar way in another, quite different, cultural and theological setting. The web of social solidarity is so fine that one marvels at the optimism that believes it could withstand such a shock as is involved in this social transubstantiation without irreparable dissolution. In addition, there is the question to be asked of why these non-Jewish patterns of signification should be considered meaningful at all, especially in the face of the "Death of God." Then, too, one can be forgiven for being puzzled about why one should try to maintain Jewish forms of life, Rubenstein's psychological explanation notwithstanding, if we are going, of necessity, to have to give them non-Jewish content(s). What *Jewish* import can derive from this procedure? If celebration of sexual maturity can give life a purpose why worry about Judaism at all? Why not either convert to groups that already perform these rites, or just celebrate them in "non-religious" ways? The modern post-Emancipation history of Jewry has amply shown that Jews are an adaptable people who can assimilate themselves to alien designs both of form and of content—something Rubenstein's psychological premises seem committed, incorrectly, to denying. In light of this consideration, Rubenstein's desire to retain Jewish "forms" seems little more than well-meant but misplaced nostalgia. Now, nostalgia is an essential quality in traditional religion, integral as it is to that notion of tradition which is so key an element in Judaism, but can nostalgia serve as the sufficient foundation for the social structure and group dynamics of Rubenstein's radically reconstructed Jewish community? For a *halachah* without God?

Another factor that should also be taken account of is the extreme selectivity of Rubenstein's examples of how his restructured Judaism would work. Thus, bar mitzvah is used as a key example—but in traditional rabbinic calculations there are 613 *mitzvot*. How many of these would be "translatable" into Rubenstein's new naturalistic paganism? For example, to choose some widely practiced *mitzvot* at random, what happens to all the rules of purity? Or *kashruth?* Or Sabbath? Or *Succoth, lulav* and *esrog* (the palm waved on *Succoth*)? Or *tephillin* (phylacteries)? Or *mikva* (ritual bath)? Or *matzo* and *chometz* (leaven)? On Rubenstein's account we would no doubt have a sharply reduced list of *mitzvot*. But the question that then arises is whether in such altered circumstances we would even have the "form" of Judaism—to say nothing of its social solidarity and "meaning." Reform Judaism has already lived through (and is living with) this problem and not to its (or anyone else's) satisfaction. The serious crisis in contemporary Reform Judaism is witness to the limitations of this view while the return to more traditional forms and the reinclusion of more *mitzvot* into Reform Judaism is evidence of the at least tacit admission that the "translation" technique by which Judaism is translated into non-Jewish ideologies, and Jewish authenticity is measured by non-Jewish criteria, has negative consequences both for the quality of one's Jewish life as well as for Jewish survival. Judaism as a community of shared values dies, as recent history indicates, under these procedures.

Reform Judaism tried to accomplish this redefinitional transformation largely through the employment of Kantian and Enlightenment criteria of morality and progress, while Rubenstein proposes to accomplish this through a blending of Reform ideology with elements drawn from existentialism, Freudian psychoanalysis and a modern pagan naturalism. One is not persuaded by the potency of the new mix, however, for what has occurred in the past where this sort of reconstruction has been attempted is not that one has produced altered but still powerful states of Jewish "meaning" but rather that one experienced the slow but steady dissolution of all Jewish attachment and the final evaporation of *all* Jewish "meaning" whatsoever. And Rubenstein has done nothing to convince us that his suggested repetition of this experiment will succeed where the other attempts have failed.

As a consequence of the historical and theoretical considerations advanced, it seems reasonable to contend that—whether for good or bad, logical or irrational reasons—the entire world history of the Jewish people, as well as the psycho-social history of the individual Jew *qua* Jew, is very closely associated with, one might even say defined by, the notion of linear, teleological history and the God of such history.[29] It, therefore, would appear more reasonable to argue that the rejection of the God of history will eventuate in the elimination of Judaism rather than be the basis for its transmutation. Though it has been history that has subjected the Jew to so much, at one and the same time his belief in the Lord of History has allowed him to endure this very adversity and survive.

8. This brings us face to face with Rubenstein's advocacy of a pagan naturalism. Rubenstein waxes eloquent on the virtues of this paganism, urging the Jew to return to the cosmic rhythms of nature.[30] His statement of this reversal is so extraordinary that I quote it at length:

In the religion of history, only man and God are alive. Nature is dead and serves only as the material of tool-making man's obsessive projects. Nature does not exist to be enjoyed and communed with; it exists to be changed and subordinated to man's wants—the fulfillment of which brings neither happiness nor satisfaction. In the religion of nature, a historical, cyclical religion, man is once more at home with nature and its divinities, sharing their life, their limits, and their joys. The devitalization of nature, no matter how imposing, has as its inevitable concomitant the dehumanization of man with its total loss of *eros*. Herbert Marcuse states the issue extremely well when he speaks of the subordination of the logic of gratification to the logic of domination. Only in man at one with nature is *eros* rather than eroticism possible. Historical man knows guilt, inhibition, acquisition, and synthetic fantasy, but no *eros*. The return to the soil of Israel promises a people bereft of art, nature, and expansive passion, a return to *eros* and the ethos of *eros*. In place of the Lord of history, punishing man for attempting to be what he was created to be, the divinities of nature will celebrate with mankind their "bacchanalian revel of spirits in whom no member is drunk."[31]

The Jew, Rubenstein argues, must now reinterpret his traditional, normative categories in naturalistic rather than linear and historical terms. He must recognize that both salvation in the here and now, as well as the future and final redemption, will not be, as traditionally conceived, the conquest of nature by history but rather the reverse. As a consequence of this inversion of the priority and relation of nature and history Jews have to rediscover the sanctity of natural life. They have to learn to enjoy their bodies, rather than follow the classical, but now recognized as self-destructive, paths of sublimation and transformation. Above all, they have to reject the futile transcendentalizing (historicizing) of these phenomena.

Rubenstein sees in the renewal of Zion and the rebuilding of the land of Israel, with its return to the soil by the Jew, a harbinger of this movement. This regression to the earth points towards the Jews' final escape from the negativity of history to the vitality of self-liberation through the rediscovery of one's primal being. He writes:

> The result of the attainment of the goal of Jewish history must inevitably be that the people of Israel will cease to see gratification as a future hope and will learn to live their lives so that each generation takes its fair share of life's joys and sorrows, knowing that it will be succeeded by other generations who will repeat the cycle rather than improve upon it. Nor does Zionism mean an end to life's inevitable insecurities. It merely means an end to the interpretation of insecurity as guilt, with its psychic impediments to those joys which are realistically available. Sooner or later Israel's Jews will come to understand that they have no need of distant utopias or far-off lands, that their task is to enjoy the fullness of being in the present. This is, in principle, a decisive turning of world-historical significance. The deliberate turning of the people of the religion of history to the religion of nature is a moment of *kairos* fully in keeping with the twentieth century's return to primal origins and primal circularities.[32]

This striking passage shows the imprint of much modern nature-romanticism as well as of Nietzsche and his heirs, and an iconoclastic, though dubious mixture of Freudianism, paganism, naturalism, and eroticism. Space prevents extended analysis of this syncretism but four theses require comment in the context of the Holocaust. The first is that Rubenstein misunderstands the innermost character of Zionism. Certainly the Jew, through this decisive Zionist act, breaks out of the narrow parameters of his exilic existence and "break(s) with bourgeois existence as the characteristic form of Jewish social organization,"[33] (though to a more limited extent). But to equate these Zionist realities with the "resurrection of the divinities of Israel's earth"[34] is sheer mythography.

Secondly, what is the "cash-value" of this return to nature à la Rubenstein? After one reads through it all there seems no actual program on which to build a life either for the individual or for the national community. The point seems to be that in some Freudian sense (as represented in Norman Brown's writings, for example, which Rubenstein specifically commends) men will be "happy" (i.e., not neurotic). But there is no clear sense of what this "happiness" really consists of either in Freud or in Brown—or in Rubenstein. Does Rubenstein, who, in his long opening essay in *After Auschwitz*, entitled "Religion and the Origin of the Death Camps," concentrates on anality as the key to decoding the Holocaust, really want to suggest that three thousand years of Jewish history—or even that of 1933–45—can be explained primarily by reference to toilet training and anal satisfaction and that all Israel's suffering now leads it to the "promised land" of sexual gratification above all else? "A new Jewish contribution [to mankind]," he tells us, may come from Zion, "the example of self-liberation and self-discovery, of mankind returned and restored to its only true hearth— the bosom of mother earth. . . ."[35] But what does this self-liberation and self-discovery amount to, consist of, lead towards? Nothing—for the article ends here—and nowhere in any of Rubenstein's writings is the missing answer supplied. Moreover, one would have thought that even in this new "natural" environment of the kibbutz and Zion, neuroses would not disappear altogether, given the sorts of beings we are, but rather new neuroses would replace the old ones, as indeed has happened on kibbutzim and in Israel generally.

Even if one were willing to grant Freudianism (or psychoanalysis more braodly defined) some limited therapeutic value, there is no evidence to suggest that it is able to provide a structural program for that reconstruction of society that would be equivalent in character to that utopian fulfillment envisioned by Rubenstein. Fur-

thermore, let us remember that Freudianism is not only as metaphysical and nonconfirmable as any traditional Jewish theology,
allowing nothing to count against it and explaining all possible
counterevidence away, but it also lacks any firm hermeneutical base
or methodological rigor. That is to say, it is not even a particularly
attractive metaphysical doctrine and thus its adoption as a basic
truth is no particular strength or touchline to reality.[36] To think
that psychoanalysis is the key to the unraveling the course of history, Jewish or otherwise, manifests a gross reductionism that fails
to grasp or to grapple with the multifaceted ontological skeleton of
reality. It should be noted, if I understand Rubenstein's more recent work (*The Cunning of History*, 1975) aright, that he has also
come to see the real limitations of psychoanalysis as the main interpretive tool for excavating history and now would prefer a wider,
more sociological, approach.

Third, this late in the history of philosophy it is odd to find
someone extolling the values of nature per se. Nature is morally
neutral; it will not provide the basis for any new comradeship of
man with man. The return to nature, its deification and worship,
is a blind idolatry without recompense. The dehumanization Rubenstein lays at the door of history, which is to be redeemed by the
forces of nature, is in fact the very product of an incipient, if not
explicit, naturalism, not its antithesis. Certainly the way to God
(if He exists) and moral value must be *through* the world, the real
world, the natural world. Assuredly no excessive asceticism, no illicit selfish escapism, no pitting of God against world, no Kierkegaardian either/or that tears God asunder from His creation, is to
be allowed. Rubenstein, I believe, is aware of this, though he may
see it only "through a glass darkly." Yet his solution to this ever-
present threat of Manicheanism, which is to immerse man into
nature without remainder, may well be his most consequential error. For out of nature can come no overcoming of the contradicto-
riness of existence, no lessening of the "absurdity" which sur-
rounds us; rather it portends what it has always portended: the
cruel, amoral, "meaningless" drudgery of natural selection and survival.

In this connection let me say too that Rubenstein's forceful naturalistic imagery carries one along primarily because of its illicit anthropomorphizing and spiritualizing of blind forces. Only thus is nature equated with Spirit, or again with the demonic. However, this anthropomorphizing rests on philosophical improprieties rather than on phenomenological astuteness. This is not to deny that Rubenstein's mystification of nature is not powerfully evocative; rather, it is to assert that for all its appeal the mystical seductiveness attributed to nature is inapplicable (more on this below in point 9).

Fourth, and perhaps most important, is an issue already hinted at: was it not precisely a mystical pagan naturalism that Nazism extolled? Was it not in the name of the pagan deities of primal origins that Europe was enjoined to shed the yoke of the Jewish God—"conscience is a Jewish invention," Himmler reminded the SS—and thus liberate itself to do all that had heretofore been "forbidden." Was it not the rejection of the taboos of good and evil associated with the God of the Covenant, a rejection now made possible by His "death," which made real the Kingdom of Night? Was it not that very romanticism of blood and land so deeply ingrained in German culture that Hitler appealed to when he spoke of the extermination of the Jew? Was it not in the name of "self-liberation" and "self-discovery" that six million Jews, and upwards of thirty million others, died? After Auschwitz, the very title of Rubenstein's most well-known work, is it not time to be afraid of naturalism and paganism and sceptical in the extreme about the purported health-restoring, life-authenticating, creative, organic, and salvific qualities claimed for them?

9. Much of Rubenstein's "success" is generated by the powerful appeal of his "style." On first reading it possesses an exciting, even compelling, quality. However, close perusal reveals that he is, in fact, guilty of using evocative and emotional language to obfuscate rather than clarify, to arouse rather than illumine. A few examples will have to suffice. Consider this statement: "the existence of the present universe hints at the possibility that nothingness cannot tolerate its own solitude and that, were the present cosmic era to end, there would be other cosmic ecstacis of nothingness."[37] Can anyone make good sense of this passage? Not only does it endow

"nothingness," whatever that may be, with anthropopathetic qualities, but it uses language in such a bizarre manner as to elude all fundamental intelligibility. For what can it mean to talk of the "cosmic ecstacies of nothingness?" This phrase could serve as a caricature of theological and metaphysical language by one so inclined. Again, try and decipher this remarkable metaphysical statement, reminiscent of the most obscure of Hegel's rambles, which I present without further exegetical comment.

To say that God and nature are at one with each other, that they are alive and life engendering, is to affirm the demonic side not alone in us but in divinity as well. The tragedies, ironies, and ambiguities of existence cease to reflect historical man's willful rebellion; they become internalized in the self-unfolding of divinity. Virtue ceases to be a choice of separable alternatives; it becomes an overcoming. The contradictory character of existence, in contrast to the logical symmetry of essence, makes goodness and virtue an overcoming in us as well as in divinity. The very character of life makes the divine source a ceaseless self-striving in which the unending negativities and affirmations of existence follow one another and in which individual forms of life are expressions of the self-construction and self-separation of divinity. Life on life is thrust forward in divinity's ceaseless project to enjoy its hour and then to become the consumed substance of other life. Such a view of divinity makes tragedy and destruction inescapable and ineradicable.[38]

There is a second stylistic element that has still more serious consequences, Rubenstein's casual and eclectic employment of materials from many sources to support his views. He quotes Freud, Eliade, Trevor-Roper, the Rabbis, etc., at random to weave his descriptions. This is persuasive if one does not know the sources or does not pay close attention to what is being said, being merely sufficiently impressed by this litany of intellectual giants—a subtle form of argument from authority. On closer examination, however, these authorities do not settle anything—especially most of the psychoanalytic and existentialist figures who Rubenstein mistakes for authorities. This is so if for no other reason than that many of these gurus contradict each other. Moreover, to use their eclectically combined output as the interpretive key through which to determine the constitutive being of Judaism—though impressionistically spectacular, being admittedly more entertaining than plodding carefully through the *Mishnah* or Maimonides—is a category mistake. Consider, for example and as paradigmatic, this psychoanalytic rendering of *kashruth* (the kosher food laws):

The tragic truth of earthly existence was never lost in the Torah. It came out of disguise when least expected. In sacrificial offerings of the temple service as well as in *kashruth*, Jews were enjoined to return the blood of the slaughtered animal to the Earth before consumption of the rest of the animal was permitted. Is this not one of the oldest offerings made by men to thank and appease their cannibal Earth-Mother? By offering Earth the blood, in which the soul was found, it was hoped that the rest of the animal would be permitted. To this day, this symbolic recognition of the power of Earth continues in *kashruth* to play an important role in Jewish religious life.[39]

There is absolutely *no* evidence to support this psychomythopoeic interpretation. Indeed, what traditional materials there are point completely in other directions. Even more significant than the particular merits, or limitations, of this specific account of the origin and meaning of *kashruth* is the larger theoretical weakness inherent in it. *According to the interpretive principles and procedures (or lack of them) employed by Rubenstein in this exegesis anything can be made to mean anything else!* The only thing that appears to have substantial meaning for Rubenstein is his *a priori* psychoanalytic imagination—the data, be it *kashruth* or Sabbath, death camps or Zion, God or nature, is all incidental. As a consequence, his interpretations are imposed on material without any say or quarter being given to the original context, or the internal concerns and self-consciousness of the sources, in order to make them arbitrarily conform to the external model held dear by him. The necessary semiological dialectic of source and interpreter has been overwhelmed with the former being wholly submerged by the latter.

CONCLUSION

Rubenstein's deconstructive proposals are certainly to be reckoned with. They are provocative, intelligent, and thoughtful in many ways and my serious reservations about them should not obscure these facts. They force us, as few other challenges do, to rethink our assumptions and our acceptance of the theological commonplace. However, as we have shown, his suggestions and substitutions for classical theology are deficient. Then again, there are those curious self-contradictions in his work that are both so interesting and yet so limiting. Perhaps the most striking of these is found at the end of the first essay in *After Auschwitz* which, in conclusion, I cite against Rubenstein himself. Speaking of the Nazis he wrote: "The final lesson may very well be that there is more realistic pleasure in the disciplines and norms of the Living God than in all the freedoms of the Dead God."[40]

NOTES

1. For a fuller account of all these approaches see S. Katz, *Jewish Philosophers* (New York, 1975), pp. 223–224; and S. Katz, "The Holocaust: Four Approaches," reprinted in the present collection. See also S. Katz, "Critical Reflections on Holocaust Theology," forthcoming in the proceedings of a major conference on the Holocaust held at Indiana University in 1980 to be published, under the editorship of Alvin Rosenfeld and Irving Greenberg, by Indiana University Press, title not yet determined. The Judaica journals such as *Judaism, Tradition, Reform Judaism, The Reconstructionist* and *Conservative Judaism* have all contained articles and treatments of this theme; see their indexes since 1965. The *Journal of the American Academy of Religion* and similar general theological journals have carried important articles touching directly and indirectly on this theme.

2. It should be mentioned at the start of this paper, in the clearest possible terms, that my criticism of Rubenstein is intended to be *strictly* philosophical and *not ad hominem*. I wish to dissociate myself *totally* from those critics who, rather than discuss Rubenstein's ideas, have abused the man. No instances of such abuse will be singled out for citation here, but those familiar with the literature will recognize this as an all-too-prevalent, and odious, element in the critical response to Rubenstein's position. Let me add for this reprinting of the present essay that Professor Rubenstein has taken the criticism offered by me in a most generous spirit and has, since its appearance, become a valued friend.

3. *After Auschwitz* (Indianapolis, 1966). This is Rubenstein's earliest and most important collection of material dealing with the Holocaust and its implications. This paper will primarily deal with Rubenstein's views as

presented in this work, which I take to be his most significant statement on the theological implications of this theme. Hereafter this work is cited as *AA*.

4. *AA*, p. 49.

5. On the notion of "yissurin shel ahavah" see, for example Saadiah Gaon, *Emunot ve' Deot*, V:3. Alternatively, Maimonides rejects this notion; see *Guide for the Perplexed* 3:24.

6. I hope to deal with this material in a future paper, of which a draft already exists, entitled "Christian Responses to the Holocaust."

7. *AA* p. 47.

8. Those who would deal with the Holocaust need to master not only Holocaust materials but also the whole of Jewish history. This point has been well made by E. Berkovits in his *Faith After the Holocaust* (New York, 1973). To obtain some idea of what is involved in such a mastery of Jewish history readers are referred to Salo Baron's magisterial *A Social and Religious History of the Jews* (New York, 1951–ongoing; 17 volumes have so far appeared), and especially to his extraordinary notes.

9. On Rubenstein's appreciation of the state of Israel see, for example, his essay on "The Rebirth of Israel in Jewish Theology" in *AA*.

10. See A. Flew's essay in *New Essays in Philosophical Theology* (London, 1964). For a useful introduction to the enormous literature generated by this issue see R. Heimbeck's *Theology and Meaning* (London, 1969), especially his bibliography and notes.

11. On the "verification principle" see the sources given in R. Heimbeck, *Theology and Meaning*.

12. Readers must not confuse "verification" and "meaning"—the essential error made by A.J. Ayer. Nor should they confuse "meaning" and "falsification," which is a common distortion of Karl Popper's extremely interesting and widely influential views. See Popper's own discussion of this matter in his *Conjectures and Refutations* (London, 1963).

13. I hasten to add that the existential-historical complexity and ambiguity referred to is not a plea for the obscurantism of much contemporary thought, especially in existentialist circles, but is a reminder to beware the facile oversimplification of much that appears as clarity and rigor in analytic philosophical circles, especially as regards the understanding of history and philosophical anthropology, two areas in which the analytic tradition has been particularly sterile. On these issues there is almost nothing of any real significance that has been produced by the analytic school of philosophy. On the issue of philosophical anthropology there is not even one work to single out as being of outstanding quality.

14. *After Auschwitz* (Indianapolis, 1966), *The Religious Imagination* (Indianapolis, 1968), *Eros and Morality* (New York, 1970), *My Brother Paul* (New York, 1972), *The Cunning of History* (New York, 1975), *Power Struggle* (New York, 1974).

15. See also on this issue: T. Altizer's *Gospel of Christian Atheism* (Philadelphia, 1966); *Towards a New Christianity: Readings in the Death of God Theology* (Philadelphia, 1967); *Mircea Eliade and the Dialectic of the Sacred* (Philadelphia, 1963). Also, G. Vahanian's *The Death of God* (New York, 1961); *No Other God* (New York, 1966); *The God Is Dead Debate* (New York, 1976).

16. As noted, Rubenstein's procedure here is not uncommon in modern existentialist literature. Buber, for example, favors such an argument as well. Buber, however, only once again shows the weakness of such a gambit. See here my "Dialogue and Revelation in the Thought of Martin Buber," in *Religious Studies*, Vol. 14, 1 (March, 1978), pp. 47–48.

17. For more on the Jewish understanding of these two notions see my *Jewish Concepts and Ideas* (New York, 1978).

18. Elisha ben Abuyah's statement and other items are found in *AA*, p. 86.

19. *AA*, p. 86.

20. See my essay on "The 'Unique' Intentionality of the Holocaust" in the present collection. Rubenstein's most recent work, *The Cunning of History* (New York, 1975), does try to answer this question a bit more fully.

21. See here also A. Roy Eckhart's somewhat obscure attempt to deal with this question in "Is the Holocaust Unique?" *Worldview* (Sept., 1974) pp. 31–35.

22. *AA*, p. 21.

23. *AA*, p. 68.

24. *AA*, p. 119.

25. *AA*, p. 119.

26. For criticism of the atheistic existentialist position see, for example, Edith Kern (ed.), *Sartre: A Collection of Critical Essays* (Englewood Cliffs, N.J., 1962); and Mary Warnock (ed.), *Sartre: A Collection of Critical Essays* (New York, 1974).

27. For criticism of Kaplan's views, see E. Fackenheim, "A Critique of Reconstructionism," *CCAR Journal* (June, 1960), pp. 51–59; E. Berkovits, "Reconstructionist Theology," *Tradition*, Vol. 2 (Fall, 1959), pp. 20–66. Also see, on Berkovits's handling of Kaplan, my review of Berkovits in the present volume. For my own views on Kaplan see S. Katz, "Mordecai Kaplan: A Philosophical Demurrer," *Sh'MA* (November 1, 1974), pp. 156–57.

28. *AA*, pp. 244 ff. See also Rubenstein's discussion in *The Religious Imagination* (Indianapolis, 1968).

29. See Salo Baron, *A Social and Religious History of the Jews*, Vol. I, chapters 1 and 2. See also Yehezkial Kaufmann, *Golah ve Nekhar* (Tel Aviv, 1929–32), on the centrality of religion in Jewish history.

30. *AA*, pp. 131–42 and pp. 227–43.

31. *AA*, pp. 136–37.

32. *AA*, p. 136.

33. *AA*, p. 138.

34. *AA*, p. 142.

35. *AA*, p. 142.

36. On Freudianism as metaphysics see F. Cioffi and R. Borger (eds.) *Explanation in the Behavioural Sciences* (Cambridge, 1970). See also the relevant essays in R. Wollheim (ed.), *Freud: A Collection of Critical Essays* (New York, 1974). See as well the recent study by B.A. Farrell entitled *The Standing of Psychoanalysis* (Oxford, 1981).

37. *AA*, p. 141. This sort of language is reminiscent of T. Altizer's pronouncements in his *Gospel of Christian Atheism* (Philadelphia, 1966), and I suspect Altizer's influence may be the source of at least some of this confusion.

38. *AA*, p. 140.

39. *AA*, p. 126. For an extended discussion of Rubenstein's use of psychoanalysis to analyze Jewish notions, see his *Religious Imagination*, which is subtitled: "A Study in Psychoanalysis and Jewish Theology."

40. *AA*, p. 44.

EMIL FACKENHEIM
ON JEWISH LIFE AFTER
AUSCHWITZ

I

Emil Fackenheim's reflections on the Holocaust are perhaps the most intriguing and I would offer a guess, the most influential, of all those that have been offered as a philosophical response to this overwhelming event in the recent history of European Jewry. He is, without question, the most philosophically adept of all those who have entered into the present theological conversation and this technical competence gives his work a richness that reveals the depth of his acute sensitivities.

To sketch the salient features of his position is not too difficult. It has its roots, on the one hand, in a desire to do two radically opposite things, and, on the other, emerges out of a need to hold two radically alternative possibilities in dialectical tension, wishing to surrender neither. The two radically opposite things he wants to maintain are that: (1) the Holocaust is unique; but (2) it does not lead to a denial of the existence of God à la Rubenstein. The dialectic he wishes to affirm is that: (1) the Holocaust is without "meaning;" and yet (2) out of Auschwitz the commanding voice of the Living God of Israel is heard. This complex structure is necessitated by the concern not to do injustice to the martyrs of the death camps nor to speak against God. It recognizes, indeed insists upon, the awesome nature of the Holocaust and its "unique" significance for theology, yet it also demands that this event be located within the structures of theistic belief rather than be allowed to break these structures apart in an irreparable manner that would mark the end of religion in any traditional sense.

Fackenheim, in the same way as Richard Rubenstein, and most other "Holocaust theologians," rejects categorically any attempt to give a *causal* explanation of the Holocaust in terms of any "answer" borrowed from traditional theodicy. Auschwitz is *not* punishment for sin, it is *not* divine judgment; it is *not* moral education à la Job: "Behold, happy is the man whom God reproves. . . . He delivers the afflicted by their affliction, and opens their ear by adversity" (Job 5:17; 36:15). As Franklin Sherman has correctly noted, the Jobean view has merit but only up to a point, for "when [a man's] humanity begins to be destroyed, as was the case in the concentration camps, then it is fruitless to talk of the ennoblement of character."[1] The Holocaust is also inconceivable as an "affliction of love" (*yissurin shel-ahavah*);[2] and unjustifiable on the grounds of *any* doctrine of progress or of a Spinoza-like dictum of *sub specie aeternitatis*. In short, no good reason can be advanced to explain or defend Auschwitz. No theodicy seems able to vindicate the time-honored normative view of God's absolute goodness in the face of the Holocaust. Thus, as a consequence, as Fackenheim honestly acknowledges, God Himself is called into question, nothing less.

Yet, unlike those who at this crucial juncture try God and find Him wanting, thus concluding His nonexistence, Fackenheim insists that God does exist and that He is still present in history despite the crematoriums. Though it is enormously difficult to believe in God after the Kingdom of Night, it is precisely continued belief that must be the response to the challenge of Auschwitz. Though we cannot, and this is an absolute "cannot," fathom why God allowed Auschwitz and why He did not intervene to end the Holocaust, we must affirm that He was present even there, even at Auschwitz, and that He continues to be present still as the Lord of History.

This demand is first and foremost made as an affirmation of faith, of faith in the Kierkegaardian sense of holding fast to that which is objectively uncertain. Indeed, this stance owes much to Kierkegaard, the patriarch of modern religious existentialism. The conceptual link connecting Kierkegaard and Fackenheim is primarily the dialogical teaching of Martin Buber. To the extent that metaphysics or theology is employed in support of his account Fackenheim draws heavily on Buber's philosophy of *I–Thou*. This dependence on Buber is clearly seen, for example, in Fackenheim's most sustained attempt to respond to the Holocaust, his lectures entitled *God's Presence in History*. In this monograph he accepts, in its general specifications, the Buberian doctrine of *I–Thou* as the model for Jewish openness to the reality of the living God and thus for his own attempt to construct a post-Holocaust Jewish theology. Thus, he eschews all proofs for the existence of God, beginning instead with the presumption that God does exist. He accepts the Buberian dictum that God cannot be proven, He can only be met. Consequently, he argues, that only from within the circle of faith can one "hear" the *Eternal Thou* (Buber's terminology for God) and respond accordingly. Developing this claim, Fackenheim, like Buber, insists that God reveals Himself in history in personal encounters with the Jews and Israel but this revelation of Divine Presence, though it can happen everywhere and at all times, is not subject to external critieria of verification or objectivity.[3] God does not show Himself decisively to those who would not "hear" the Voice. the *I–Thou* encounter has its own rhythm and any attempt to force it into improper objective categories (*I–It* language to use Buber's terminology) destroys its character and silences its message.[4] Thus, the Fackenheim who hears "a commanding voice from Auschwitz" is the Fackenheim who already stands *within* the covenantal affirmation.[5]

Working from this base, Fackenheim asserts that we witness God's presence in history in the continued experience of the people of Israel throughout its existence, and this in two ways. The first of these ways Fackenheim calls the "root experiences"[6] of the people of Israel, the second he describes as "epoch-making events."[7] The former are creative, extraordinary, historical happenings that are of a decisive and formative character such that they continue to influence all future "presents" of the Jewish people. These events are of such a magnitude that they continue to legislate as normative occassions to every future generation of the nation. Thus, for example, the Exodus is an historical movement that is relived every Passover and whose power affects each subsequent generation, continually revealing through this yearly re-enactment the saving activity of God.[8] In this way these past "root experiences" are lived through as "present reality" and the Jew of every age is "assured that the past saving God saves still."[9] In contrast "epoch-making events" are not formative for Jewry's collective consciousness; rather they are historical occasions that challenge the "root experiences" to answer to new and often unprecedented conditions. The destruction of the First and Second Temples are, for example, such events. These occurrences test the foundations of Jewish life, i.e., the saving and commanding God of the Exodus and Sinai, but do not shatter them, as the continued existence of the Jewish people testifies. This traditional interpretive pattern has heretofore always shown enough elasticity and resiliency to absorb and survive any and all catastrophes that threatened its fundamental structure.

But what of Auschwitz? Can it be assimilated to this older midrashic model? To this question Fackenheim answers an unreserved "yes," Even Auschwitz does not destroy the "root experiences" of Israel's faith, God is present even in the Kingdom of Night, commanding Israel still from within the very eye of the Holocaust itself. This extreme reply to the unprecedented circumstances of Auschwitz is the essential response of Fackenheim and those who would follow his lead. The Jew cannot, dare not, must not, reject God. Auschwitz itself is revelatory, commanding, and we must learn to sense what God would reveal to us even there.

What is the commanding word, which Fackenheim, in a now famous phrase, has called the 614th commandment, that is heard at Auschwitz? "Jews are forbidden to hand Hitler posthumous victories!"[10] After Auschwitz Jews are under a sacred obligation to survive; Jewish existence is itself a holy act; Jews are under a duty to remember the martyrs; Jews are, as Jews, forbidden to despair of redemption, or to become cynical about the world and man, for to submit to cynicism is to abdicate responsibility for the here and now and to deliver the future into the hands of the forces of evil. And above all, Jews are "forbidden to despair of the God of Israel, lest Judaism perish."[11] Hitler's demonic passion was to eradicate

Israel from history. For the Jew to despair of the God of Israel as a result of Hitler's monstrous actions would be, ironically, to do Hitler's work and to aid in the accomplishments of Hitler's goal. The voice that speaks from Auschwitz demands above all that Hitler win no posthumous victories, that no Jew do what Hitler could not do. The Jewish will for survival is natural enough, but Fackenheim invests it with transcendental significance. Precisely because others would eradicate Jews from the earth, Jews are commanded to resist annihilation. Paradoxically, Hitler makes Judaism after Auschwitz a necessity. To say "no" to Hitler is to say "yes" to the God of Sinai; to say "no" to the God of Sinai is to say "yes" to Hitler.

Since 1945 every person who has remained a Jew has, from Fackenheim's perspective, responded affirmatively to the commanding voice of Auschwitz.

Yet this is only half of the traditional ideology of Judaism, for the God of biblical faith is *both* a commanding and a saving God. The crossing of the Red Sea is as much a part of Jewish history as is the revelation at Sinai: both are "root experiences." Fackenheim has made much of the commanding presence of Auschwitz, but where is the saving God of the Exodus? Without the crossing of the Red Sea there can be no Sinai. Fackenheim knows this. He is also aware that to talk of a God of deliverance, no matter how softly, no matter how tentatively, after the Holocaust is problematical when God did not work His kindness there and then. To even whisper about salvation after Treblinka and Maidenek is already to speak as a man of faith, not as a seeker, and even then one can only whisper. The continued existence of the people of Israel, however, and most specifically the establishment and maintenance of the state of Israel, forces Fackenheim to risk speaking of hope and the possibility of redemption. The destruction of European Jewry and the state of Israel are, for him, inseparably tied together; what the former seems to deny the latter, at least tentatively, affirms. For Fackenheim, the state of Israel is living testimony to God's continued presence in history. Through it the modern Jew witnesses a reaffirmation of the "root experience" of salvation essential to the survival of Jewish faith.[12]

As a consequence of this belief the state of Israel has come to play an ever more prominent role in Fackenheim's thought since 1967. Indeed, in his most recent collection of essays, pointedly titled *The Jewish Return into History*,[13] this theme has reached a new centrality. In connection with it he is concerned to do two things: first, to argue the suggestive thesis that in light of, and in the context of, the state of Israel the meaning of the terms "secular" and "religious" have to be redefined Jewishly, i.e., even secular Israelis and secular aspects of Israeli life have a profound "religious" significance; secondly, and related, that the events of Israeli life are inextricably tied, if not on the level of causation then, at least, on the level of "response," to the events of the Holocaust.

Professor Pinchas Peli, edits an Israeli magazine called *Panim El Panim.* One day, in a German paper, he saw a picture of two soldiers in the Sinai during the Yom Kippur War, gun in hand, and dressed in the traditional phylacteries and prayer shawl. The picture of the older man reminded him of another picture of a Jew dressed in the same traditional garments. Where had he seen that face before? Soon he remembered a well-known picture of a pious Jew praying for his dead lying at his feet whom the Nazis had murdered, and he was surrounded by the murderers, jeering, laughing, and enjoying the fun. (One of them had photographed the scene, and this is how we have the picture.) So Professor Peli decided to write an article, and with this he printed the two pictures side by side.

Next week he received a letter from a hospital, saying something like this:

> I am the other man in the picture in the Sinai, and the day it was taken I was shot. I am not writing for sympathy; indeed, I wish to remain anonymous. I am writing to tell you something. All my life I have thought of the generation murdered in the Holocaust as being collectively my father and mother. However, being collective, my relation of them was vague. Now it is no longer vague. I have seen that picture of the old man, praying for his dead, mocked and jeered at by the murderers of his people. And as long as I live, I will think of *this* man as my father.[14]

In the final essay in this volume, entitled "The Holocaust and the State of Israel: Their Relation," Fackenheim describes his view on this matter with clarity:

With this conclusion, every explanatory connection between the Holocaust and the State of Israel has broken down, the causal historical kind in part, the teleological religious kind entirely, and even the hope of connecting the one event with the other competes with despair. Yet, as we have said, it is necessary not only to perceive a bond between the two events but also so to connect them as to make the bond unbreakable. Such a bond is *possible* because to seek a *cause* or a *meaning* is one thing, to give a *response* is another. And it is necessary because the heart of every *authentic* response to the Holocaust—religious and secularist, Jewish and non-Jewish—is a commitment to the autonomy and security of the State of Israel.[15]

This is the most significant entailment of the "614th Commandment."

II

With the exposition of Fackenheim's position in place, let us now interrogate his views critically rather than exegetically. We will be particularly concerned with eight philosophical issues that Fackenheim's approach raises.

1. To begin, positive appreciation of one prominent aspect of Fackenheim's portrayal is required. He correctly recognizes the need to see both pre- and post-Holocaust Jewish history and theology in dialectical relation to the Holocaust even if the Holocaust itself is seen to be "unique." Especially significant in this respect is his insistence on the essential connection between the Holocaust and post-Holocaust Jewish experience, a linkage that makes demands on Jews after Auschwitz. This reflects a more profound awareness of the complex reality of the historical life of an ongoing faith community as well as of the dynamics of the personal appropriation of the significance of the Holocaust than that met with, for example, in the treatment of the Holocaust as unrelated to the Jewish past or future.[16] For, rather than isolating the Holocaust and thereby losing at least a large part of its "meaning" by viewing it "out of context," Fackenheim's approach treats it in both historical and theological context, thus causing less distortion in its observed reality.

2. The Holocaust's "uniqueness" is a central claim advanced by

Fackenheim. He and others who have adopted the "614th Commandment" have placed great weight on the unprecedented nature of the recent tragedy. Yet, as with the "Death of God" theologians, no fully convincing description has been produced that persuasively articulates how this "uniqueness" is to be accounted. Increasingly this has become an unavoidable challenge and private conversation with Professor Fackenheim has revealed that he is more than cognizant of the need to confront this subject in a more precise and rigorous way. He is aware that without this required clarification it is difficult to reject the argument that the Holocaust should merely be assimilated to the older theology of Jewish martyrdom, of which there is a too-long history. Only if the Holocaust *is* "unique" in some specifiable and demonstrable way are the new and unusual theological departures advocated by Fackenheim required or justified. Hence a major task is set for Fackenheim by his own presuppositions.

Attempting to satisfy this demand, Fackenheim has recently set out some of the characteristics of the "uniqueness" of the Holocaust as he understands them. I will quote his statement on this matter at length because of its significance:

What was the Nazi Holocaust? So uncomprehended and incomprehensible is the dread event still, a whole generation after, that in this brief space we can answer this question only with a series of negations.

1. The Holocaust was not a war. Like all wars, the Roman War against the Jews was over conflicting interests—territorial, imperial, religious, other—waged between parties endowed, however unequally, with power. The victims of the Holocaust had no power. And they were a threat to the Third Reich only in the Nazi mind.

2. The Holocaust was not part of a war, a war crime. War crimes belong intrinsically to wars, whether they are calculated to further war goals, or are the result of passions that wars unleash. The Holocaust hindered rather than furthered the German war aims in World War II. And it was directed, not by passions but rather by a plan conceived and executed with methodical care, devoid of passion and, indeed, unable to afford this luxury.

3. The Holocaust was not a case of racism although, of course, the Nazis were racists. But they were racists because they were antisemites, not an-

tisemites because they were racists. (The case of the Japanese as honorary Aryans would suffice to bear this out.) Racism asserts that some human groups are inferior to others, destined to slavery. The Holocaust enacted the principle that Jews are not of the human race at all but "vermin" to be "exterminated."

4. The Holocaust was not a case of genocide although it was in response to this crime that the world invented the term. Genocide is a modern phenomenon; for the most part in ancient times human beings were considered valuable, and were carried off into slavery. The genocides of modern history spring from motives, human, if evil, such as greed, hatred, or simply blind xenophobic passion. This is true even when they masquerade under high-flown ideologies. The Nazi genocide of the Jewish people did not masquerade under an ideology. The ideology was genuinely believed. This was an "idealistic" genocide to which war aims were, therefore, sacrificed. The ideal was to rid the world of Jews as one rids oneself of lice. It was also, however, to "punish" the Jews for their "crime," and the crime in question was existence itself. Hitherto such a charge had been directed only at devils. Jews had now become devils as well as vermin. And there is but one thing that devils and vermin have in common: neither is human.

5. The Holocaust was not an episode within the Third Reich, a footnote for historians. In all other societies, however brutal, people are *punished* for *doing*. In the Third Reich "non-Aryans" were "punished" for *being*. In all other societies—in pretended or actual principle, if assuredly not always in practice—people are presumed innocent until proved guilty; the Nazi principle presumed everyone guilty until he had proved his "Aryan" innocence. Hence anyone proving, or even prepared to prove, such innocence was implicated, however slightly and unwittingly, in the process which led to Auschwitz. The Holocaust is not an accidental by-product of the Reich but rather its inmost essence.

6. The Holocaust is not part of German history alone. It includes such as the Grand Mufti of Jerusalem, Hajj Amin al-Husseini, who successfully urged the Nazi leaders to kill more Jews. It also includes all countries whose niggardly immigration policies prior to World War II cannot be explained in normal terms alone, such as the pressures of the Great Depression or a xenophobic tradition. Hitler did not wish to export national socialism but only antisemitism. He was widely successful. He succeeded when the world thought that "the Jews" must have done *something* to arouse the treatment given them by a German government. He also succeeded when the world categorized Jews needing a refuge as "useless peo-

ple.". . . . This was prior to the war. When the war had trapped the Jews of
Nazi Europe, the railways to Auschwitz were not bombed. The Holocaust
is not a parochial event. It is world-historical.

7. The Jews were no mere scapegoat in the Holocaust. It is true that they
were used as such in the early stages of the Nazi movement. Thus Hitler
was able to unite the "left" and "right" wings of his party by distinguishing, on the left, between "Marxist" (i.e., Jewish) and "national" (i.e., "Aryan") "socialism" and, on the right, between *raffendes Kapital* (rapacious,
i.e., Jewish capital) and *schaffendes Kapital* (creative, i.e., "Aryan" capital).
It is also true that, had the supply of Jewish victims given out, Hitler
would have been forced (as he once remarked to Hermann Rauschning) to
"invent" new "Jews." But it is *not* true that "the Jew (was) . . . only a
pretext" for something else. So long as there *were* actual Jews, it was these
actual Jews who were the systematic object of ferreting-out, torture, and
murder. Once, at Sinai, Jews had been singled out for life and a task. Now,
at Auschwitz, they were singled out for torment and death.[17]

In this series of seven "negations," Fackenheim has undoubtedly
made a number of telling observations. Moreover, in this and related efforts some definitional success has been achieved in the
search for an adequate phenomenological account of the Holocaust's "uniqueness." However, this statement is still preliminary
and limited in scope, especially in the absence of supporting data
for the theses advanced, as well as of the refinement of the logic of
the argument. Critics such as Irving Louis Horowitz,[18] who have
found Fackenheim's claims as presented in this series of propositions unconvincing, even somewhat confused, no doubt have a degree of truth and reason on their side. Horowitz has, in particular,
exposed a number of contradictions in Fackenheim's seven propositions which seriously weaken their force. For myself, however,
while recognizing the merit of specific aspects of Horowitz's dis-
criminations, I still feel constrained to agree with Fackenheim's
conclusion, that the Holocaust is historically "unique," for my own
reasons, detailed at length elsewhere.[19]

However, and here we approach the heart of the matter, my concurrence in this judgment does not eliminate the major difficulties
I have with Fackenheim's position because the significance of his
thesis rests not on this historical estimation per se, in which we

agree, but rather on the theological entailments drawn from it. I would contend that Fackenheim has to show not only that the Holocaust is historically "unique," but also and far more essential to his claim, because much more theologically fecund, that this "uniqueness" is theologically significant. That is, he has to produce a philosophy of Jewish history in which historical uniqueness, even if real, is shown to be *theologically* relevant. This imperative exists because it is not self-evident either that historical uniqueness is a theological category per se, or, if it is, when it is, i.e., not every unique historical event is a new revelation; thus it is necessary to know how one decides when a historically unique occasion is theologically significant and when it is not. Again, in correlation with this line of argument, it needs to be shown that the still more extensive category of history is theologically charged, and if so, how? From the *Chazal* (The Sages of the Talmud) to Franz Rosenzweig the status of "history" in Judaism has been questioned, and for good reasons, though the issue remains open. In any case, however, the contrary Fackenheimian embrace of history needs to be argued, not only asserted or assumed. And this in turn demands a persuasive metahistorical schema, i.e., a more sustained as well as more broadly based metaphysical account of the interpenetration of transcendance and history, which has not been provided. Fackenheim's typology of "root experiences" and "epoch-making events" in particular has to be analyzed in relation to this concern, for it has to be shown how transcendance makes itself manifest in one type of event and then the other. That is to say, how do historical events *qua* historical events even if "unique," become revelatory? In the absence of such an overarching ontological account a cluster of unanswered, yet unavoidable, philosophical and theological questions emerges at this point.[20]

3. The "614th commandment" is most often criticized for the wrong reasons. If one looks at the literature,[21] one finds that Fackenheim is regularly interpreted as compelling Jewish belief *solely* so as to deny Hitler "posthumous victory." That is to say, post-1945 Jewish survival is conceived as being predicated primarily, or even only, on one's negative reaction to Hitler. As one recent critic described it:

The core of Fackenheim's argument lies in his contention that Jewish survival after Auschwitz can no longer be regarded as "mere" physical survival. The individual and collective survival of the Jews has become a *religious* imperative, for as a result of the uniqueness of the Holocaust, a divine voice can be heard from the ashes. Human life has paradoxically gained religious sanctity as a result of the Nazis' denigration of it.[22]

This line of argument, however, as many of these same critics have correctly observed, is a poor reason for Jewish survival.[23] To continue an ancient tradition only out of spite is hardly worthy, not to say existentially and logically uncompelling. Even agreement with Fackenheim's important insight that there is nothing "mere" about Jewish survival after Auschwitz, a contention I share, will not, nor is it intended to, bear the weight of a philosophical defense of continued Jewish existence, though, alternatively, it should not be dismissed. But whatever the merits of this proposal and its refutation the more consequential truth to be borne in mind here is that this exegesis (and its implicit critique) of Fackenheim's position is erroneous. It is an easy error to make, given the prominence the slogan "not to give Hitler a posthumous victory" has enjoyed, but it is an error nonetheless.

The mistake arises from the failure to appreciate the larger metaphysical skeleton that underpins his position—i.e., Buber's dialogical ontology, especially Buber's account of revelation, mixed with more than a pinch of Hegel. Fackenheim, it must be grasped, argues for Jewish survival first and foremost on the positive basis of the presence of God in Jewish history and the ever contemporary possibility of *I–Thou* encounter between God and man. Only from this absolute ontological presupposition do the other corollaries of Fackenheim's account, including that of not giving Hitler a "posthumous victory," flow. To ignore this elemental feature of his thought or to read him differently is to misread him altogether.

This essential clarification of Fackenheim's view is, however, not a vindication of it. A serious difficulty remains; to phrase it differently, this schema needs to be criticized for the right reasons. Perhaps foremost among these is the largely uncritical acceptance of Buber's dialogical affirmations. Buber's metaphysical structure—indeed, his entire account of *I–Thou* relation and the nature and meaning of revelation—involve philosophical deficiencies which ultimately renders it of little, if any, help in constructing a significant and viable metaphysics of history. His position is quite simply unworkable as the basis of an intelligible account of God's relation to man and history. Its weakness is that it provides intuitions where serious and well formed conceptual articulation is required.[24] Thus, whereas Buber's teachings are called in to provide the broad schematic metaphysical basis for the "614th commandment," its own internal lacunae will not allow it to adequately fill this role.

Buber's dialogical thinking is incapable of dealing with real history, the presence of evil in the world or the category of revelation in any meaningful and sustainable fashion, the very philosophical cum theological categories particularly relevant here. Fackenheim's considerable insight into history, and more particularly the nuances of the philosophy of history, in fact, come more from his in-depth study of Hegel[25] than his discipleship in the school of dialogue. The difficulty is that Hegel and Buber do not easily mix; they are certainly not integratable. Buber was, in large part, reacting to Hegel's historicism; in his flight from Hegel he seems to have run away from history, despite his best intentions and disclaimers,[26] altogether.

Related to this flight from history, though grounded in independent metaphysical presuppositions, was Buber's inability to deal with evil. His feeble, bewildered response to the Holocaust is testimony to this. One is struck by the very paucity even of attempts to deal with what had happened to Jews in his generation, an event in which up to 1938 he had played so dramatic and heroic a role.[27] One can well appreciate Buber's silence, but this silence must be allowed to count against the adequacy of dialogical thought as a way of meeting the problem of evil more generally[28] and the Holocaust in particular. *The Eclipse of God*, the title of Buber's volume of essays[29] written, in part, as a response to Auschwitz, is a metaphor that itself needs to be explained, that cries out for, demands, explication and content. In and of itself it hides more than it reveals; it evades more than it illumines. Yet Buber had no real illumination to offer in these matters nor will he assist others—

e.g., Fackenheim—just here where the theological going is roughest.

Lastly, Buber's prescription for content-less revelation, while setting out to protect revelation from its modern critics, turns back upon itself and devours its own substance. *I–Thou* encounter is in the end an incoherent model for the revelatory moment. As such it *cannot* serve as the theoretical model for Fackenheim's own attempt to reconstruct a viable analysis of revelation, certainly not of a meaningful, content-full revelation like his "614th commandment." The lapses in Buber's redescription of revelation are logically insuperable; they deny the very possibility of coherence to all who rely upon it—Fackenheim, unfortunately, included.[30]

A further word about the connection, or rather, impossibility of a connection, between Buber's dialogical, contentless, revelation and Fackenheim's "614th commandment" is required. How does one get from the former to the latter? On Buber's *I and Thou* account the "614th commandment" could only be a "human response" to the Divine Presence, *not*—and this negation is nonnegotiable in Buber's thinking—the imperative of the Divine. If this is so, however, what universal status does it have? Buber's personalist summary of what he takes revelation to be, in Part III of *I and Thou*, specifically rules out anything issuing from revelation that "can be held above all men's heads." Only the "I" partner of the encounter is commanded, if "commanded" is still even a meaningful concept in this setting, especially given Buber's acceptance of a Kantian embargo on heteronomous norms. This being so, however, how can this personalist, nonuniversalist model become the *urgrund* for a "614th commandment" of any kind, particularly as from Buber's perspective the original 613 commandments have lost their commanding resonance?[31]

Discussion of the content of revelation brings us back to Fackenheim's sketch of the "614th commandment" with the requirement that we put several additional questions to it. Passing over, for the present, the contradiction of there being any content to revelation on Buberian grounds, we must ask: What exactly does Fackenheim mean by the term commandment? In the older, traditional theological vocabulary of Judaism, it meant something God

actually "spoke" through Moses, and through the Sages in elaboration thereon, to the people of Israel. Fackenheim, however, would
reject this literal meaning in line with his dialogical premises. But
then what does "commanded" here mean? It would seem the word
has only an analogical or metaphysical sense in this case, but if so,
what urgency and compelling power does it retain? Fackenheim
would, correctly, reject the just-mentionsd option of analogy or
metaphor—but if these are rejected, and the literal meaning is denied, what, we ask again, remains?

There emerges a curious "double-think" in this position. On the
one hand, the word "commandment" (and like terms, e.g., revelation, salvation, redemption) are used because they have a content
we all know from the biblical account. On the other hand, the lit-
eralness of the biblical witness is denied, leaving the intelligibility
of these terms, both in their original biblical and in their modern
employments, obscure. This, in turn, leads to two corollaries. The
first of these relates back to a line of thought mentioned briefly
above. When I ask Professor Fackenheim whether his "614th commandment" is revelation as the Torah was believed to be revelation—i.e., *Halachah l'Moshe m'Sinai*, in the traditional formula—
the answer must, I believe, be no. God did *not* "speak these things."
They are, rather, a human response to Auschwitz, but a human
awakening, even be it to Auschwitz, is religious anthropology rather
than revelation as this term has heretofore been understood. Alternatively, to redefine the term revelation dialogically merely achieves
similar, unsatisfactory results by a slightly different route. That is
to say, is the "614th commandment" revelation or only our talk
about revelation? Secondly, allowing the Fackenheimian content
to stand for the moment, we need enquire: What is revelatory about
it? Consider the essence of this additional commandment as Fackenheim sees it: "Jews do not give Hitler a posthumous victory"—
i.e., it is a duty to survive as Jews. But did Judaism and the Jewish
people need Auschwitz and its correlative "commandment" to be
under this obligation? Has not Jewish survival always been deemed
a Divine Imperative by the rabbinic tradition? How else explain
Jewish survival in the face of all that the Jewish people have encountered? Again, Fackenheim avers that Auschwitz makes sup-

port of the state of Israel an imperative, but has this not always been mandatory—even when the Jewish people, including most of its Orthodox wing, blindly, stupidly, selfishly did not recognize it as such? And despite this "crime" of indifference by much of world Jewry up to 1941 (or even 1967), was not the *Yishuv* (the foundations of the state of Israel) in place by then? Did Rav Mohliver or Rav Kook need the *Sho'ah* (Holocuaust) to command either Jewish survival or Zionism? But if this is so, and it is, what does the "614th commandment" actually demand that was not commanded at Sinai?

Let us now pursue this question of revelation from another, quite different, angle. In a particularly striking essay entitled "Demythologizing and Remythologizing in Jewish Experience," subtitled "Reflections Inspired by Hegel's Philosophy,"[32] Fackenheim attempts to bring Buber and Hegel into dialogue, even synthesis, regarding revelation and the human element in it in order to buttress his own exposition of his post-Auschwitz 614th *mitzvah*. For the purpose of introducing these two authorities in defense of nonpropositional, dialogical revelation, he begins by citing a passage from *I and Thou* to represent the "Hegelian-like" quality of Judaism, what he calls "Hegel's doubly representational form of religious experience." The Buberian passage referred to and Fackenheim's gloss theron runs as follows:

Before showing the Midrash of Judaism to be the expression of a doubly representational religious existence, we give *prima facie* plausibility for this undertaking in a passage from Martin Buber's *I and Thou*. That Buber should have been influenced on this issue by Hegel is out of the question. That he was immersed in Jewish (though not primarily midrashic but rather biblical and Hasidic) religious literature is unquestionable. From this self-immersion result these words:

I know that "I am given over for disposal" and know at the same time that "it depends on myself.". . . I am compelled to take both to myself, to be lived together and in being lived together they are one.

This passage, nourished by Jewish religious experience, tersely reproduces in its entirety, Hegel's doctrine of double representation (which is nourished by Christian experience).[33]

Fackenheim takes this analysis as demonstrating the shared philosophical understanding of Buber, here representing Judaism, and Hegel, who in Fackenheim's estimation is the outstanding modern thinker, on the fundamental issue of the dynamic and reciprocal nature of authentic religious life. Both seemingly concur on the dialogical character of revelation, and man's active role in it.

This established, at least to his own satisfaction, Fackenheim offers the following intriguing submission that because of its importance, deserves to be quoted at length:

In turning from this *prima facie* confirmation to Midrash itself, we do far better to cite strategically chosen Midrashim than to speak of Midrash-in-general. Three Midrashim must here suffice:

> Rabbi Azaryiah and Rabbi Aha in the name of Rabbi Yohanan said: When the Israelites heard at Sinai the word "I" (i.e., the first word of the ten commandments), their souls left them, as it says, "If we hear the voice . . . any more, then we shall die" (Deut. 5:22). . . . The Word then returned to the Holy One, blessed be He, and said: "Sovereign of the universe, Thou art full of life, and Thy law is full of life, and Thou has sent me to the dead, for they are all dead." Thereupon, the Holy One, blessed be He, sweetened (i.e., softened) the Word for them.

> Rabbi Sim'on bar Yohai said: ". . . only when Israel does God's will is his heavenly place secure." . . . Nevertheless, Rabbi Sim'on bar Yohai also quoted "This is my Lord and I will praise him" (Exod. 15:2), and he said: "When I praise Him, He is glorified, and when I do not praise Him, He is, as it were, glorified in Himself. Ye are my witnesses, saith the Lord, and I am God" (Isa. 43:12). That is, when ye are My Witnesses, I am God, and when ye are not My Witnesses I am, as it were, not God.

Having reproduced these sources as the midrashic data to be analyzed according to the Hegelian logic, Fackenheim now continues:

The first Midrash shows why Hegel did not consider Judaism to be a doubly representational form of religious existence—and that he was mistaken. Hegel accepts the traditional Christian view that the Sinaitic revelation is law without grace. The Midrash tells the tale of this view, explores its radical implications, and overcomes it. A divine commandment devoid of grace would be humanly unperformable, and indeed, a divine Presence revealing itself as commanding is paradoxical. For qua present the divine Infinity destroys the human community in its finitude: "They are all dead." But qua commanding it requires a human response—which is possible only if the human community is alive even in the moment of Divine presence. This paradox is resolved by the Midrash in the second descent of the Divine which, "sweetening the Word," makes the divine commandment capable of human performance. For Pelagius, divine grace is merely an event subsequent to the human failure to perform the divine commandment. For Augustine, it redeems man from the commandment itself. In Judaism, grace is manifest in the gift of the commandment itself which, bridging the gulf between two incommensurables, makes a human community partner in a divine–human covenant. The second and third Midrash show that both the paradox and the grace that resolves it do not vanish into the dead and irrelevant past but remain in the life of the covenant itself. On the one hand, the primordial divine commanding grace has established a truly mutual relationship. Hence the bold words that the heavenly place is not secure, and indeed God not God, unless Israel performs its labor which (as Hegel has stressed) is "the labor of man." Yet since the pristine paradox and the grace that resolves it both remain, these affirmations are true only "as it were:" they are stories which are known to be "only" stories—and yet must be told. And the divine—human incommensurability which remains, even as the relation is mutual and real, is fully explicated when Rabbi Sim'on bar Yohai affirms that, on the one hand, God does need human glorification and, on the other, is "glorified in Himself."[34]

In this way, calling upon the evidence from the Rabbinic Sages, supported by Buber's "authority," and explaining it all to coincide with the standards of Hegelian religiosity,[35] Fackenheim believes he has established his position on "human response" to the Divine Presence, as Presence alone, as the legitimate mode of deconstructing the phenomenon of revelation. This in turn, he contends in an extension of the present thesis, legitimates his formulation of the manner in which the "614th commandment" is secured as well as the "content" it is said to carry.

What are we to reply to this fascinating equation? That God needs man, as man needs God; that God's power and our freedom are both essential to Judaism's deepest self-understanding, this is surely correct. These are the twin foci of the Jewish *Weltanschauung*.[36] That Judaism is "doubly-representational," this too is easy to endorse. But, and here the difficulties begin to emerge, in drawing this Hegelian-Buberian-Midrashic model of revelation Fackenheim has moved too quickly, too indiscriminately, too casually, over the abiding claim of the original, authentic, Midrashic reality, the essence of which is that God reveals, commands, substantive and precise *mitzvot*, i.e., Divine imperatives contain specific "content." He may find need to "sweeten the Word," as the Midrash affirms, but the Word endures. God may want our response, but it is always and only a re-action to a Divinely disclosed "content." We can accept or reject the Word; we need, of necessity to interpret it; but we dare not "reinterpret" its substance away. The ideal is the bringing of our will into parallelism with the Divine Will, but this presupposes a revealed Divine Will, something dialogical revelation denies categorically. For example, Buber tells his friend Rosenzweig, "God is not a Lawgiver."[37] But if this is so, how can Fackenheim bring this dialogical God-Idea into harmony with the Midrashic context that affirms the very opposite as its most elemental affirmation? Fackenheim is able to employ Midrash, given his independent dialogical re-mapping of the character of revelation, only because he is prepared to ignore the context as well as much of the substance of Midrash. He can speak of an "absolute Command"[38] from Auschwitz only by either contradicting his larger Buberian model or, alternatively, by asserting the claim without regard for its justification, Hegel notwithstanding.

With this elucidation in place we can now safely, and without caricature, return to the issue other critics have incorrectly, focused on exclusively. I refer, of course, to the objection that Fackenheim's procedure, in the learned formulation of Michael Wyschograd, is a "negative natural theology." Wyschograd's claim is that for Fackenheim Jewish belief and survival is not commanded either by the Word heard at Sinai or the grandeur of nature that compels belief in nature's Creator but, inversely, by the evil of Nazism.

In negative natural theology, an evil is pointed out for which also, it is alleged, no natural explanation is possible. Of course, the conclusion in negative natural theology cannot be identical with that of positive natural theology, inasmuch as the problem of theodicy cannot here easily be ignored. Nevertheless, the conclusion which Fackenheim draws, the sacred duty to preserve the Jewish people, is the functional equivalent of the existence of God in positive natural theology, inasmuch as it becomes a total foundation for the continued existence of Judaism, a foundation as fully serviceable to the secularist as to the believer. One is almost driven to the conclusion that in the absence of the Holocaust, given Fackenheim's profound understanding of the irreversibility of the secular stance, no justification for the further survival of Judaism could have been found. With the Holocaust, amazing as this may appear, Judaism has gotten a new lease on life.[39]

Given our exegesis we recognize that this reading is inaccurate, ignoring as it does Fackenheim's dialogical revelatory presupposition altogether. Alternatively, and the reason for taking it up again, is that this widely circulated formulation gains its plausibility from the overemphasis Fackenheim has given to the slogan "not to give Hitler posthumous victory." What he intends to assert is: "Jews respond to God not to Hitler," but he accents the latter and often, in his anti-Nazi passion, only at best implies the Divine Presence. Insofar as God is not the central feature of the equation the equation *is* misconceived. That is to say, and to say unequivocally, Judaism cannot live if its primary reason for being is the negation of Hitler's ambitions, laudable as this goal is. Hitler must not replace God as the cause of Jewish faith, nor does Fackenheim wish it to be otherwise. Positive rather than negative reasons are the only motives that can serve as the basis for a healthy, authentic, ongoing Jewish tradition. Any construction that places Hitler at the center of Judaism is confused and self-defeating. Insofar as Fackenheim has not been as careful as he should have been to spell out his intentions more clearly he shares responsibility for the ensuing and oft-repeated criticisms of his position.

Our scrutiny of Fackenheim's carefully sculpted delineation of the nature of revelation would be incomplete, and seriously so, if we did not enter one final objection of a hermeneutically elemental sort. The Holocaust in its awesome magnitude was overwhelmingly evil. Murder was only one, and not the most horrible, of its children. Abuse of every sort, degradation in every form, technology run riot,[40] medical experiments of abhorrent,[41] frightening inhumanity, and finally death by truncheon, by bullet, by fire, by gas—this is the stark, terrifying world of the Holocaust, the "Planet Auschwitz." Phenomenologically[42] this reality *reveals* darkness and abyss, despair and degeneracy. If we are to count the *Sho'ah* as revelation is it not the power of Satan that is disclosed rather than that of the "living God?" That is to say, does not a methodology that seeks *revelation*, a new commandment, in Auschwitz need to confront the negative reality there divulged? And if so what does this do to Jewish faith? Another way of framing this query is to ask: If Auschwitz is the source of revelation, then isn't Richard Rubenstein a more faithful witness to the *content* of that revelation? This is *not*, of course, to endorse Rubenstein's views per se, but rather to introduce them as a hueristic alternative that might help us better perceive the fundamental quality of the phenomenological substance of the Holocaust and hence any "revelation" that might issue, or be inferred, from it. Rubenstein's angle of vision helps us glimpse the luciferian potential that opens before us when we treat the Holocaust as revelatory. Fackenheim would reply that there is indeed danger, even mortal danger, exposed here but there is also, at one and the same time, a bridge over the abyss. We, in turn, must ask whether this bridge is known phenomenologically or as a metaphysical construct or whether it is glimpsed only through the "eyes of faith."[43]

4. Fackenheim's dependence on Buber's less than luminous ruminations raises the subject of the role of and need for precision in philosophical discourse. For not only are terms such as "unique" and the further idioms adopted from Buber—e.g., *I and Thou, I–It*—obscure, but such key Fackenheimian descriptions as "root experiences" and "epoch-making events" are likewise vague. Thus, for example, though the distinction between these two sorts of events is illuminating, we have, quite surprisingly, no criteria for deciding whether the Holocaust should count as the former rather than the latter (as Fackenheim treats it). According to what independent test can one show that the Holocaust is only of an "epoch-making" character? It would seem logical that having argued so strongly for the Holocaust's uniqueness, one should also argue for its being granted the status of a "root experience" leading perhaps to conclusions not dissimilar from those reached, for example, by

Richard Rubenstein, among others. Fackenheim is obligated in any case, to provide rules by which future events are to be judged as being of one kind or the other, for without such norms the typology loses its explanatory force. Again, without such criteria of assignment the distinction becomes purely stipulative, providing only *a priori* plausibility that turns out to be tautological. I confess to being puzzled by the absence of any deepening of these structural categories in Fackenheim's work since the publication of *God's Presence in History*.

5. At this juncture we need to stand one of our major objections to Richard Rubenstein[44] on its head and apply the inverted critique to Fackenheim. Whereas the radical theologians seem naively to rely on an empiricist criterion of falsifiability and meaning, Fackenheim seems to go to the other extreme, avoiding direct confrontation with empirical evidence to such an extent that all discussion and evaluation becomes irrelevant. Though Fackenheim does *not* state his doctrine in these terms, his demand that one must stand within the faith-circle in order to understand the propositions of the religious man lead inexorably to this conclusion. This final cul-de-sac is partly arrived at consciously and partly as a legacy of his Buberian, and more generally existentialist, inheritance. The particularly significant implication of this stance is to make it difficult to see what would be allowed to count against the "614th commandment" by its advocates. Under what circumstances would they admit either that "God was Dead" or, less extremely, that at least He had broken His covenant with Israel,[45] thereby rendering Jewish belief either irrelevant or foolish after Auschwitz?

In his essay "Elijah and the Empiricists"[46] Fackenheim attempts to respond to this challenge by engaging and overcoming the empiricist polemic presented in the well-known "University Discussion"[47] and earlier by A.J. Ayer.[48] He notes that Judaism and Christianity must be treated differently in terms of this issue, the former being, in his view, more open to history and hence disconfirmation. He, in fact, goes so far as to offer this significant counterclaim:

Unlike the Christian eschatological expectation, the Jewish is at least in part falsifiable by future history.

Sophisticated philosophers have overlooked this possibility at a time when even ordinary Jewish believers are unable to overlook it. After Auschwitz, it is a major question whether the Messianic faith is not already falsified—whether a Messiah who could come, and yet did not come, has become a religious impossibility.

Falsification is not, in any case, unimaginable.[49]

In support of this bold assertion he then, in good philosophical fashion, constructs the following example to indicate the conditions under which Jewish belief would be falsified. "Imagine," he writes,

a small band of Jewish believers as the sole survivors of a nuclear holocaust. Imagine them to be totally certain that no human beings have survived anywhere else, and they they themselves and their children are inexorably doomed. They are not faced with a repetition of Noah's flood but rather with the end of history. Of the destiny of individual souls, the whole picture is not yet in sight. But the whole picture of history is already seen, and it refutes the Jewish eschatological hope concerning it. The suffering of individuals as such may still be given its point. But the suffering to which Jews have exposed themselves by remaining a people is already seen to have been pointless. (This is true at least of suffering radical enough to have remained pointless in pre-Messianic history.) Precisely insofar as it holds fast to history, Jewish faith risks falsification by history.[50]

This case appears to go a long way towards actually setting forth an at least *in principle*[51] situation in which Jewish faith, Fackenheim's faith, would be decisively disproven. It is true that the case is implausible and hence loses some of its force as a consequence, but, essentially, Fackenheim is attempting to meet the conceptual challenge with a philosophical response. But now he hedges and all that has been gained is lost. Seemingly worried by the possibility of falsification which has been allowed into the discussion, he feels constrained to add:

Let us return to the example of the survivors of the nuclear catastrophe. Exactly what part of their faith is refuted? That God exists? No. That He loves us? To the extent to which it holds fast to actual history, Jewish faith has in any case long qualified any such sweeping and simplistic affirmation. Some evils in history may be only apparent, such as deserved punishment. Not all historical evils are apparent—history is unredeemed. Jew-ish faith cannot say why history is unredeemed, why God "hides His face," or is, as it were, temporarily without power, and in any case restrains the Messiah from coming. This does not, however, either refute Jewish faith nor deprive it of content, so long as the promised coming of the Messiah can still be expected. It is this promise, and it alone, that would be falsified by a catastrophic end of human history.[52]

This exposition is full of interest for it now appears that, in con-tradistinction to the possibility of falsifying Jewish belief, i.e., the existence of the Jewish God, this is not the case. God's reality is untouched even by this hypothetical "worst case" scenario, as is also, it seems, the more particular doctrine of God's love for us. Both are *not*, we are instructed, disconfirmed.

What then is disconfirmed? Only the Jewish Messianis doctrine. And what implications flow from this?

How would a Jewish believer respond to this falsification? He could of course at long last surrender his age-old stubbornness, and accept his faith as having been, all along, a mere hypothesis, now falsified. But then he should have let go of his stubbornness long ago, for the hypothesis had, after all, always been most improbable. The authentic Jewish believer would take a different course. He has in any case spent his life *working* for the coming of the divine kingdom, as well as waiting for it. He would now cite the divine commandment to do this work against God Himself, would refuse to abandon what God either chose to abandon or could not help abandoning and spend his last hours on earth beating swords into plow-shares.

It is a telling proof of anti-Judaic bias that contemporary empiricists treat-ing the subject of the falsifiability of religious faith have wholly over-looked the possibility of citing God against God Himself. This possibility appears even in the New Testament, for Jesus asks why God has forsaken him. In the Jewish Bible the theme is everywhere. Abraham cites God against God. So does Job. So do most of the prophets. Elijah at Mount Carmel would have done likewise had the necessity arisen. What if the heavenly fire had devoured the sacrifice of the priests of Baal, rather than his own? We have already seen what Elijah would *not* have done—accept the "hypothesis" that Baal "control[s] the physical world." It has now emerged what he *would* have done. He would have lamented that, already forsaken by men, he was now forsaken by *Adonai* as well—and continued to do His work, alone.[53]

In the final reckoning even the imagined catastrophe makes no real difference to Jewish belief. The Jew in Fackenheim's formulation, continues, as it were, as if nothing had occurred. The recommended course of action is particularly odd: "citing God against God," for it is the very presence of God that is at stake. Whence comes the certitude in God's existence, *in the face of tragedy*, that allows such dispute, such dialogue, to continue? The only answer is that, in the last accounting, *nothing* is allowed to count against God's being there. Despite appearances the "Falsification Challenge" has not been met; it has rather been sidestepped. All is in the end as it was in the beginning

As a consequence, though Fackenheim is sincerely concerned to do more justice to the concatanations of Jewish history than he believes his rivals do, going so far as to assert that "Authentic Jewish theology cannot possess the immunity I once gave it, *for its price is an essential indifference* to all history between Sinai and the messianic days,"[54] he seems finally to replace an authentic encounter with temporal events with a transhistorical faith that is impervious to the actual happenings of the world historical. Neither history nor logic in the end seem able, by definition, to provide possible counterevidence to the Fackenheimian thesis. This does not make the thesis false, but it does make it a special type of metaphysical claim that is less interesting, certainly less rigorous and probing, than it at first appears to be.

6. Criticisms (4) and (5), dealing with the categories of meaning and criteria, can be still more sharply focused by focusing on Fackenheim's contention that "the Jewish secularist, no less than the believer, is *absolutely singled* out by a Voice as truly *other* than man-made ideals—an imperative as truly *given*—as was the Voice of Sinai."[55] This is like Tillich's denying anybody was an atheist. The logical result of this sort of semantic revision is that the essential meanings of ordinarily intelligible terms and notions evaporate. Many an atheistic Israeli, for example, would vehemently deny any imputation of transcendental meaning to his life, Fackenheim's assertion to the contrary notwithstanding. This denial, of course, does not settle the matter, for the secularist's life may have transcendental weight of which the secularist is unaware, but it

does raise a host of troublesome matters that cannot be settled by fiat or semantic manipulation.

This example of putative transcendence of the secular/religious dichotomy in the case of the Israeli reality raises still another, related, conundrum—Fackenheim's suggestive thesis, drawn from his study of Hegel, that in light of the recreation of the Jewish state, and in the context of the state of Israel, the old dichotomy of secular and religious must be abandoned, with the secular now "seen" in its "truly" religious dimensions. This revaluation occurs, Fackenheim claims, as a consequence of the fact that after Auschwitz, continued Jewish existence, Jewish existence per se, is an act of "faith." He confeses:

> I used to be highly critical of Jewish philosophies which seemed to advocate no more than survival for survival's sake. I have changed my mind. I now believe that, in this present, unbelievable age, even a mere collective commitment to Jewish group-survival for its own sake is a momentous response, with the greatest implications. I am convinced that future historians will understand it, not, as our present detractors would have it, as the tribal response-mechanism of a fossil, but rather as a profound, albeit as yet fragmentary, act of faith, in an age of crisis to which the response might well have been either flight in total disarray or complete despair.[56]

In particular, the existential conditions of Jewish life, after Auschwitz, in the state of Israel make the older normative disjunctions inoperative.

> Once there was a sharp, perhaps ultimate, dichotomy between "religious" and "secular" Jews. It exists no longer. After Auschwitz the religious Jew still witnesses to God in history, albeit in ways that may be revolutionary. And the "secular" Jew has become a witness as well—against Satan if not to God. His mere commitment to Jewish survival without further grounds is a testimony; indeed, Jewish survival after Auschwitz is neither "mere" nor without grounds. At Auschwitz *every* Jew represented all humanity when for reasons of birth alone he was denied life; after Auschwitz every Jew represents all humanity when he commits himself to Jewish survival. For this commitment is *ipso facto* testimony that there can be, must be, shall be, no second Auschwitz anywhere; on this testimony and this faith the secular no less than the religious Jew stakes his own life, the lives of his children. A secular holiness, side by side with religious, is becoming manifest in contemporary Jewish existence.

Nowhere is this more obvious than in the state of Israel. When I set out on my first visit to Israel two years ago I expected religious Jews to be religious and secular Jews to be secularists. Brought up in an anti-Zionist tradition, I had been taught a neat distinction between Jewish "religion" and Jewish "nationalism." And though I had long rejected these inapplicable pseudo-Protestant distinctions (and along with them, anti-Zionism) I was still altogether unprepared for one totally astonishing discovery: *the religious quality of the "secularist" Israeli Jew.* Perhaps I would not have seen it had I still been in headlong flight from the Holocaust. Of the truth of what I saw, however, I have no doubt. Jerusalem, while no "answer" to the Holocaust, is a response; and every Israeli lives that response. Israel is collectively what every survivor is individually: a No to the demons of Auschwitz, a Yes to Jewish survival and security—and thus a testimony to life against death *on behalf of all mankind.* The juxtaposition of Auschwitz and Jerusalem recalls nothing so vividly as Ezekiel's vision of the dead bones and the resurrection of the household of Israel. Every Israeli— man, woman, or child—stakes his life on the truth of that vision.[57]

One is moved by this affirmation which reveals as much, if not more, about its author as about its subject. Then too, one wants to participate in Fackenheim's vision, for I share his enthusiasm for the state of Israel, its meaning, its drama, even its sanctity. Yet the bases for my affirmation differ, and I must demur in accepting his. There are many interdependent reasons for this reticence, but the most coercive philosophical one is this. To "transcend" the dichotomy of religious-secular, while not without its idealistic, metaphysical, *gravitas,* leads one into a treacherous linguistic (and theological) territory that eventuates in meaninglessness. This because it is hard, finally, in this transcendental terrain, to decide not only what "secular" now means, but also what "religious" means. That is, the cognitive density of words starts to slip away, first by degrees, and then altogether, and this despite Fackenheim's wise attempt to protect himself from just such an eventuality in his delineation of three different forms of secularism in the opening essay in *Return.* [58]

Another, perhaps still clearer, way of exposing the matter is to ask: what makes events either "secular" or "religious" in an Israeli context? Why, when "secular" occurrences take place in Israel, are they transmuted into "religious" incidents? The answer is, of course, revelation, the "614th commandment," but how did the

"614th commandment" become so content-specific as to legitimate Israeli secularism as God's work? Even allowing Fackenheim's additional "mitzvah" to contain the content he claims for
it—i.e., "Jews are forbidden to give Hitler a posthumous victory"—
how does this translate into the legitimation of secularity—Israeli
or otherwise?

To bring a modicum of clarity into this analysis one must, of
course, go slowly for much will turn on the meaning one gives to
the concepts "secular" and "secularity." For example, Israeli military prowess—e.g., the 1967 war—in the name of legitimate self-
defense, is not inherently, or necessarily, only to be interpreted as
secular, having a firm basis, for example, in *halachah*. Alternatively, it is difficult to conceive by what standard one is to judge
the café society of Dizengoff as anything but secular; and secular
in such a manner that the designation "holy secularity" is totally
inappropriate. At the same time, we can see the secular Israeli per-
forming religiously valuable acts, beginning with the great *mitzvah*
of living in the Land, but this again does not legitimate secularity
per se. Rather, it means that secularists can perform deeds considered *mitzvot* from the perspective of the halachic tradition,
while, alternatively, eating *chazzar* (pig) is still eating *chazzar*.

In defense of his enthusiasm for secularity in the contemporary
context, Fackenheim speculates:

But what if the unlimited exercise of this human reason implied the *abo-
lition* of heaven? What if it rendered superfluous the "hypothesis" of creation, and hence the Creator himself? In the biblical faith, creation is not
and never has been a scientific or quasi-scientific hypothesis. It is, and
always has been, the gift of existence—the world's and his own—to the
man who in faith accepts it. And it is for this reason not an occurrence
which took place once and for all in the past; creation is a gift which is
renewed whenever there is human acceptance of it.

Such an acceptance is not at odds with secularity, modern secularity included; on the contrary, it makes inescapable the acceptance of its burden.
We say "burden" even though it is a liberation also, and even though many
present "radical" theologians are intoxicated in its celebration. Secularity
is a burden. For to live a secular existence is to be responsible for the
world. And indeed, so great is the burden of this responsibility in our own

time that many among both the "religious" and the "irreligious" are in full flight from the world into a variety of fancies. The biblical believer— Jew or Christian—may not join their number. For his God bids him stay with, and assume responsibility for, the secular world. And if such an existence is, today, often solitary, it is the biblical God who makes this solitariness inescapable.[59]

But with due respect, this defense does not justify the revaluation being advanced. For here too a confusion is introduced. The confusion of making responsibility for the "secular" world the legitimating criterion for transcending the religious-secular dichotomy. But the religious man qua religious man is, and always has been, responsible for all of creation as Fackenheim urgently advocates, without the necessity of becoming "secular." It is the biblical man who must not, because of his God, become secular. In this respect secularity has no new imperatives to teach the religious man, if only the religionist properly grasps the task laid upon him by his tradition. It certainly does not warrant the abandonment of classical distinctions, inherited norms or traditional values.[60]

These reflections push us forward to a still deeper level of inquiry. For the very employment of theological categories, of a theological historicism, in response to the Israeli reality, might correctly be questioned altogether. Thus, for example, one could reasonably explain the Jewish and Israeli will to survive in 1967 and 1973 without recourse to the "metaphysical" dimension introduced by Fackenheim. Even the engagement of the Sho'ah as "context" for Israeli behavior, which is always something to be remembered, does not necessitate the additional metaphysics of theism and revelation and all that they entail. Wanting to live, not wanting to be murdered, is reason enough.

While agreeing with the thrust of Fackenheim's critique of self-labeled, self-serving Jewish "humanists" who can find nothing but fault with the attitudes and behavior of the Israeli political apparatus, I think he too would allow that not *all* Israeli action can be, a priori, equated with God's action. The prophets, Zionists all, knew that the Kings of Israel could sin and so must we know the same truth in our time. In this area of concern we must take it case by case, admitting the principle of error but exercising censure with the maximum sensitivity, being ready, I think, to sin, if we must, on the side of forebearance, given our fallibility and Israel's extremely precarious international political situation. Yet, as I write this, I am conscious of the *problematique* of not historicizing the political so as to transform it into the metaphysical without remainder.

7. Fackenheim's notion of a "614th commandment" issuing from Auschwitz itself requires still another examination. It must be asked in all its weightiness: Is this only a human, nostalgic, self-imposed command; only, or even at best, a natural biological determination to live formulated as an ontological requirement? What makes it a command of God? Again, is it *from* Auschwitz that the command issues? Or is it only human hindsight, human hope, dressed up as divine truth? The reason one feels compelled to ask these questions is because Fackenheim's argument now thoroughly unpacked, seems to run in two directions simultaneously: (1) God was silent at Auschwitz; (2) this silence "commands" the 614th commandment—Jewish survival.

8. We now come to our final consideration, Fackenheim's increasing use of the methodological argument that the response to Auschwitz is more properly framed in the categories of Midrash rather than those of philosophy. While this reversal is potentially illuminating, the case for it has so far been neither sufficiently developed nor stated without difficulties. Problems arise from at least three directions.

a. In *God's Presence in History* Fackenheim, while already suggesting the significance of Midrash for our post-Holocaust predicament, is reflective enough to caution against an unselfconscious, too free, use of midrashic materials and the midrashic "technique" in trying to cope with the dilemma posed by the *Sho'ah*. For, as he rightly observed, "even to begin to speak [to and after Auschwitz] is to question radically some time-honored midrashic doctrines."[61]

Yet despite this caution he ignores his own sound advice, first by degrees in *God's Presence in History* and more markedly in *The Jewish Return into History*, and pushes Midrash beyond its capacity. As a result, one is left finally not knowing what Midrash appropriately supplies in the way of explanation, analysis, critique, and response, and what it does not and cannot provide. Nor does one know how one decides—i.e., by what norms or ground rules—one chooses an answer. This is due, in large part, to Fackenheim's own uncertainty whether midrashic creativity is capable of philosophical explanation, interrogation, and justification, or whether it is not, being something totally other. There are occasions in his reflections where philosophical method and Midrash seem related, even mutually necessary, and others where, when the logical squeeze arises, they are said to be incompatible, and necessarily so. Thus, in *The Jewish Return* he insists that Midrash is not philosophy nor capable of philosophical explication and those who seek such are groping in the dark, employing an alien hermeneutic on the midrashic material. Such individuals, he assures us, "have," in reality, "not understood what has been said."[62]

Now while Midrash *may* have its own independant, systematic, legitimacy, this claim must be demonstrated. Fackenheim needs, in particular, to convince us that his oppositional rendering of logic and Midrash, a disjunction not as self-evident as he often and increasingly asserts, is correct. Then again, it needs to be carefully noted that Midrash makes sense in context, that is, it receives its meaning from the theological *Weltanschauung* of the *Chazal* (the Sages of the Talmud). But it is this very ontological schema that the Holocaust calls into question. Did this cognitive dissonance not exist, Fackenheim's work would be unnecessary. Hence we cannot merely retell the Midrash now, of necessity, "out of context," and leave it at that. The context, be it a new context, in which the midrashic tale exercises its potency needs to be framed and defended. In other words, that philosophical dimension eschewed by Fackenheim putatively in favor of the claims of Midrash will have its dues paid either through the front or, if needs be, the back door. Without its classical metaphysical depth (or some adequate modern substitute) the Midrash loses its resonance; that is, to sum up in a shorthand, Midrash *means* only in situ yet it is precisely the theological situation that has become doubtful. The existence of a God who resolves the major paradoxes of midrashic existence, e.g., the relation of transcendence and immanence, His power and human freedom, His creation of the world and the existence of evil, is for us the problematic, not, as it was for the *Chazal*, the solution.[63] Hence the employment of Midrash for contemporary theological purposes is a more difficult thing than initial appearances would suggest.

b. The second troubling element in Fackenheim's description and use of Midrash can only briefly be alluded to. Just as the Fackenheimian form of the Hegelian philosophy of Jewish history is not easily synchronized with Buber's dialogical schema, so Fackenheim's midrashic commentaries and responses do not easily fit—at least the connection is not apparent, and little evidence for it is presented—with his use of Hegel's philosophy of history, or, for that matter, Buber's dialogical theism which set the larger frame of reference for his reflections on the Holocaust.

His observations on Midrash and myth in his essay "Man and His World in the Perspective of Judaism"[64] reveal the profundity as well as the inherent tension at the root of his original reformulations. In commenting on several midrashim he correctly observes that:

All Midrash is symbolic. The first thing to be understood symbolically in the present Midrash is the idea of a temporal sequence in which the past has vanished from present reality. If creation, and the "decree" made at creation, were of the past only, they would be of no religious significance: creation is a religious reality, affirmed by faith, only because it is a present reality also, forever reaccepted and appropriated. Hence the subsequent "rescinding" of the decree made at creation is of a special sort. The second decree supersedes the first; yet it so wholly presupposes the continued reality of the first that it would lose its own meaning without it. The rabbis would never have thought of God as literally changing his mind; such a notion is at odds with their belief in the divine eternity and perfection. Yet so deeply were they impressed, at once with the reality of both decrees and the clash between them, that they dared to speak of God as though he changed his mind.[65]

However, while this is an intriguing exegesis of the midrashim presented on their own terms, in the present interpretive milieu it has to be asked in light of our interest in the compatibility of Hegel and the Rabbis, if Hegel's evolutionary historicism of the Spirit will allow the rabbinic *Weltanschauung*, as here represented by the midrashim, and to which Fackenheim makes appeal, to stand. *Prima facie*, it would appear that the required precondition here set by Fackenheim for effective Midrash would seem to have been obviated by Hegel's idealism. For example, the Hegelian deity does not issue "decrees" nor does He make covenants, two of the essential conditions for Midrash in general and the midrashim on which Fackenheim is commenting in particular. Then again, turning the argument around, Buber's dialogical nonpropositional reading of Scripture rules out such notions as Creator or an understanding, as already indicated, of God, the *Eternal Thou*, being the source of decrees, being a legislator.[66] As a consequence, consistency requires that we be shown how to reconcile these seemingly contradictory foundation stones of Fackenheim's systematic approach. Otherwise his own wide learning leads to an unworkable eclecticism which is its own undoing.

The uncertain fit of the various elements in the Fackenheimian structure is not an isolated or incidental matter. It intrudes itself in every instance where Midrash is introduced.[67] Nowhere, however, is the difficulty more apparent than in the notable essay entitled "Demythologizing and Remythologizing in Jewish Experience: Reflections Inspired by Hegel's Philosophy," arguably the most philosophically interesting of all of Fackenheim's recent work. The strength of the composition lies in the use of Hegelian categories to explicate Judaism and reveals that Fackenheim is one of the world's finest Hegelian scholars.[68] Slightly more than half of the paper sets out succinctly, but with masterful control, Hegel's account of religion and the religious life. Against this background the text then turns once again to Midrash. In defense of this juxtaposition and synthesis it offers the following contention: "Jewish religious experience [by which Fackenheim means Midrash], tersely reproduces in its entirety Hegel's doctrine of double representation."[69]

This asserted parallelism, however, is not self-evident, nor is it clear what difference it makes either to Fackenheim's exploration of Midrash or to the analysis of Midrash *qua* Midrash. Certainly the intelligibility and significance of Midrash does not derive from Hegel nor is he the standard by which to measure its inherent value and truth. Indeed, it is difficult, if not impossible, to understand why the lengthy Hegelian prologomena was required at all given the disjunction of philosophy and Midrash that Fackenheim favors. To his audience of professional philosophers,[70] to whom the talk was first addressed, he said:

> It would be absurd to look for explanation, religious or otherwise, of these events—an enterprise in any case contrary to the whole midrashic tradition. We can and must ask, however, whether, in response to these events, Jewish existence has remained in the demythologized condition which is so widely and so confidently proclaimed to be the universal modern fate. And what casts doubt on these confident proclamations is that not only old Midrashim have assumed new life. New Midrashim have been born. They are still being born. They will continue to be born.[71]

But if it is "absurd to look for explanations, religious or otherwise," what is the connection and what is the significance of the connection between Hegel and Midrash? Hegal was, after all, a philosopher concerned *qua* philosopher with "explanations"—e.g., with the dialectic of the Spirit as the "explanation" of history—and not with "testimony." Thus, the excoriation of all logical elucidation and construal destroys any bridge between Sinai and Berlin. Moreover, the autonomy demanded for Midrash guarantees a priori that not only Hegelianism but all forms of philosophical endeavor will simply be "besides the point" where Midrash is concerned. Whether it is "doubly representational" or not is incidental for the meaning of Midrash is intrinsic rather than extrinsic. In other words, were it not "doubly representational" à la Hegel it would matter not at all.

c. The midrashic method has been given another turn, another extension, in Fackenheim's essay "occasioned by the work of Elie Wiesel" entitled "Midrashic Existence after the Holocaust."[72] In it he offers the following lucid description of the difference between Midrash and philosophy:

> To affirm a bond between God and the world is always problematical. Midrash, however, is aware of this fact. Radically considered, a bond between a God who is truly God and a world which is truly world may well be considered as not merely problematical but nothing short of paradoxi-

cal. On its part, however, Midrash does not shrink from paradox, but confronts it and yet in the very act of confrontation reaffirms the bond. This stance requires closer inspection. Philosophical reflection may find it necessary to choose between a God who is divine only if he is omnibenevolent and omnipotent, and a world which is truly world only because it contains elements contradicting these divine attributes, namely, evil and human freedom. Midrash recognizes the tension yet refuses to choose. Thus when the Israelites do God's will they, as it were, strengthen his power, and when they fail to do his will they, as it were, weaken it. Thus, too, redemption will come when men have become good enough to make the Messiah's coming possible, or wicked enough to make it necessary. It would be wayward to regard such Midrashim as insufficiently demythologized fragments of "philosophizing," the first groping for a "finite God-concept" which would at one blow "solve" the "problems" of evil and freedom, the second struggling with two conflicting "views of history," the one "progressive," the other "catastrophic." Midrash cannot embrace a "progressive view" of history, for this would dispense with the need for the acting of God, nor a "catastrophic view," for this would destroy the significance of the acting of man. Nor can Midrash accept a "finite God-concept" but must rather sweep aside all God-concepts so as to confront God himself— a God absolute yet "as it were" (k'b'yachol) finite in the mutual confrontation. The term k'b'yachol alone—a full-blown technical term in midrashic thought—suffices to show that Midrash does not "grope" for "concepts" in order to "solve problems" and dissolve paradox. The midrashic Word is story. It *remains* story because it both points to and articulates a life *lived with* problems and paradox—the problems and paradox of a divine-human relation. This life is midrashic existence.[73]

This fascinating exegesis justifies at least three critical responses. First, and in support of our judgments above, Midrash as phenomenlogically pictured, is not a world that can coexist within a Hegelian, or even a technically constructed Buberian, world. Secondly, and more radically, in the above comments we have left the parameters of philosophy altogether. Thirdly, Fackenheim's own seminal remark made on the page following the quoted explication must be isolated and put again: Is "Midrash [which] is meant for every kind of imperfect world . . . [also] meant for Planet Auschwitz, the anti-world?"[74] This is *the* difficulty *par excellence* and Fackenheim is astute to raise it for it does nothing less than call into question all of his earlier midrashic ventures. Or does it?

Fackenheim's attempt to answer his own query begins by asking yet another question, not related to this first one—"What then makes Elie Wiesel's work possible?"[75] And the retort he fashions is termed by him "mad Midrash."[76]

What is this madness?

Not insanity, if "insanity" is "flight from reality." It is just because it dare not flee from *its* reality that this Midrash is mad. This madness is obliged— condemned?—to be sane.

Not "irrationality," if this is ignorance or lack of discernment. There is, to be sure, a rationality of a lesser sort which one displays by discerning the ways of one's world, by going about in it, going along with it. But just a rationality of this sort shows its own ultimate irrationality when it goes along a road descending into hell and beyond. After all is over, such a rationality can only plead that it "did not know." Midrashic madness, in contrast, *knows*, in some cases has known all along. Its discernment is informed by a Truth transcending the world of which it is a victim. Irrational by the standards of lesser rationalities, its rationality is ultimate.

Midrashic madness, third, is not mysticism, if "mysticism" is a rise to a divine ecstacy in which innocence and guilt, joy and anguish, good and evil are all indiscriminately transcended. Midrash must hold fast to the world; mad Midrash cannot but hold fast to *its* world, the anti-world.

How then can it retain this stance and *remain* Midrash, that is, hold fast to God as well as its world? Only by dint of an absolute protest against the anti-world and its God—as it were, an anti-God over against mad Moshe, a God mad with him, or a God torn between these extremes. This protest is serious only if it turns into a determination to *restore* the world. To be sure, the world-to-be-restored will be, as it always has been, an imperfect world. But although tarnished by a thousand blemishes it is neither a part of nor heir to the anti-world. On the contrary, the attempt to restore it strikes at the very core of the anti-world, thus aiming at its absolute overthrow. Thus, the mad midrashic Word turns into a *Kaddish* for all the victims of the anti-world, "that solemn affirmation full of grandeur and serenity, by which man returns to God His crown and sceptre."[77]

Fackenheim continues, in conclusion:

. . . midrashic madness points to *an existence in which the madness is transfigured*. Midrashic madness is the Word spoken in the anti-world which ought not to be but is. The existence it points to acts to restore a world which ought to be but is not, committed to the faith that what ought to be must and will be, and this is *its* madness. After Planet Auschwitz, there can be no health without *this* madness, no joy, no life. Without this madness a Jew cannot do—with God or without him—what a Voice from Sinai bids him to: choose life.[78]

The meaning of all this, if I understand it aright, is simply: confront evil without evasion, and at the same time believe in the God of Israel. What makes this position "mad" is that the evidence of Auschwitz is all on the side of unbelief.[79] Hence, "mad Midrash" is a Jewish "leap of faith:" believing in the face of the unbelievable. The merits of Midrash *qua* Midrash or of Midrash *qua* philosophy are essentially irrelevant to this final judgment. This conclusion "answers" the overwhelming questions that provoked it not by ontological explanation or metaphysical construction, nor again by the marshalling of any new ontological evidence or the disclosure of some original facts, but rather by *emunah*, ("trust"), in God despite all "sanity;" thus its "madness." This, however, is the faith of a Zaddik rather than an argument.[80] It is the faith with which Fackenheim began. "Mad Midrash" is a "rationale," not a reason.

CONCLUSION

In summation, one can, with fairness, say that though Fackenheim has struggled vigorously to do more justice to history and to God in the face of the *Sho'ah* than other more simplistic or negative accounts, in the final reckoning his emphasis on hearing and responding to the Voice of God from within the faith circle, as "mad Midrash" if you will, has the effect of immunizing his outlook from philosophical criticism, but only at a price. Those within the holy space hear the Voice—but then, given this privileged vantage point, such individuals do not need persuading, while to those on the outside of the circle there is only silence, if awe, and a continuing sense of the difficulty of believing in the face of the Holocaust. The quite noble attempt of Fackenheim to live with a real sense of open doubt raised by the Holocaust in the end gives way to something very close to the commitment, the belief, of old-time religion. In this connection the remark of the Hasidic Rebbe is apropos: "To the faithful there are no problems, to the skeptical there are no answers."[81]

NOTES

1. Franklin Sherman, "Speaking of God After Auschwitz," *Worldview* (Sept., 1974), p. 27.

2. On this classical rabbinic doctrine see, for example, Saadiah Gaon, *Emunot ve Deot*, V:3.

3. See M. Buber, *I and Thou* (New York, 1958). For a critique of this position see the opening essay in this collection. That the Buberian account is not without its serious philosophical and theological difficulties, which may undermine it, is not unknown to Fackenheim. See in this connection his essay "Buber's Doctrine of Revelation" in *The Philosophy of Martin Buber*, P. Schilpp and M. Friedman, eds. (Illinois, 1967).

4. Perhaps the clearest statement of Fackenheim's views on this epistemological matter are found in his essay entitled "Elijah and the Empiricists" which originally appeared in D. Cutler (ed.) *The Religious Situation* (New York, 1969) and which was reprinted in his *Encounters Between Judaism and Philosophy* (New York, 1973). For some critical comments see my review of this collection in *Jewish Social Studies* (Spring, 1974).

5. See E. Fackenheim, *Quest for Past and Future* (Bloomington, 1968), p. 10.

6. See E. Fackenheim, *God's Presence in History* (New York, 1970) pp. 8ff.

7. See E. Fackenheim, ibid., pp. 16ff.

8. Thus the traditional rabbinic dictum that every Jew at the Passover Sedar should participate in the event with the sense that *he* or *she* was personally redeemed from Egypt, i.e., it is not just a commemoration of a past, concluded, event.

9. E. Fackenheim, *God's Presence in History*, p. 11.

10. *Presence of God in History*, p. 84, repeated from Fackenheim's earlier essay, "Jewish Faith and the Holocaust," *Commentary* Vol 46, no. 2 (August, 1968), pp. 30–36.

11. Ibid., p. 84. Here Fackenheim spells out the implication of these "commandments" in some detail. See pp. 85–92.

12. See here Fackenheim's essay, read at the conference held at St. John the Divine in New York City and printed in Eva Fleischner (ed.), *Auschwitz: Beginning of a new Era* (New York, 1977), pp. 205–217. See also his more recent work, which increasingly emphasizes the significance of the state of Israel. These newer essays are collected in *The Jewish Return into History* (New York, 1980).

13. E. Fackenheim, *The Jewish Return into History*. This collection marks a new turn in Fackenheim's outlook, one which balances his continual preoccupation with the Holocaust with the existential and theological significance of Zionism and the establishment and maintenance of a Jewish state.

14. Ibid., pp. 208–9.

15. Ibid., p. 282.

16. This is Richard Rubenstein's view. For a more detailed analysis of this aspect of Rubenstein's position, see "Richard Rubenstein, the God of History, and the Logic of Judaism" in this collection.

17. E. Fackenheim's "Foreword" to Y. Bauer's *The Jewish Emergence from Powerlessness* (Toronto, 1979). I have quoted only seven of what are originally eight propositions given in this context. The eighth one seems irrelevant for the issue under review. Readers are also directed to Richard Rubenstein's *The Cunning of History* (New York, 1975) for a very different, even diametrically opposite, attempt to explain the "uniqueness" of the Holocaust. In addition, see my essay on "The 'Unique' Intentionality of the Holocaust" in the present collection. I have also recently read an advance copy of Fackenheim's new monograph, entitled *To Mend the World* (New York, 1982), that returns to a consideration of this central issue in more detail. I thank Professor Fackenheim for sharing this volume with me prior to its formal publication.

18. Irving Louis Horowitz, "Many Genocide and One Holocaust?" in *Modern Judaism*, Vol. I, no. 1 (May, 1981), pp. 74–89. See also the older criticism of Fackenheim's use of the notion of "uniqueness" offered by Michael Wyschograd in his essay "Faith and the Holocaust" in *Judaism*, Vol. 20, No. 3 (Summer, 1971), especially pages 290–292.

19. See my essay "The Unique Intentionality of the Holocaust" in the present collection. This essay is part of a larger monograph on this theme due to be published in 1983. In addition to the criticisms of Wyschograd and Horowitz regarding the Holocaust's "uniqueness," readers are also directed to Eliezer Berkovits, *Faith after the Holocaust* (New York., 1973) which is the most sustained treatment of the non-uniqueness position in the Jewish philosophical literature. Criticism of Berkovits's position can be found in my essay on Berkovits in the present collection.

20. The vexing issue of the role and meaning of history and historical events in a religious tradition such as Judaism is not easy to sort out. However, it is a subject which, if for no other reason than making some progress in sorting out the meaning and implications of the Holocaust for continued Jewish belief after Auschwitz, needs to be addressed. I have made a preliminary effort in this direction in my paper "History and Covenant" due to appear in a forthcoming volume to be edited by Y. Greenberg and S. Wagner and published by the University of Denver Center for Judaic Studies. The title of the volume is, as yet, undecided.

21. For example, see the article in *Judaism*, Vol. 25 (Spring 1976) by Hans Tiefel, p. 139; also the article by M. Wyschograd critical of Fackenheim in *Judaism*, Vol. 20 (Summer 1971), pp. 286–294. See also the article in this same issue of *Judaism* by S. Cain, pp. 263–278.

22. From David Biale's review of E. Fackenheim's *The Jewish Return into History* in the *Association for Jewish Studies Newsletter* (October 1980), p. 11.

23. D. Biale, op. cit., has made this criticism, as has M. Wyschograd, op. cit. In fairness to these critics it should be said the Fackenheim has contributed to this confusion by his lack of clarity in certain crucial respects as well as by his overuse of this idea. I will review this in more detail below.

24. See "A Critical Analysis of Martin Buber's Epistemology" in this volume. Fackenheim's appreciation of Buber's position is to be found in his *God's Presence in History*, in his contribution to *The Philosophy of Martin Buber* volume in the Library of Living Philsophers series edited by P. Schilpp and M. Friedman (Illinois, 1967), and in his collected essays, *Quest for Past and Future* (Bloomington, 1968).

25. See his outstanding study of Hegel, *The Religious Dimensions of Hegel's Thought* (Bloomington, 1967), and again his important essay "Hegel's Understanding of Judaism" in *Encounters between Judaism and Modern Philosophy* (New York, 1973). See also the Hegelian influence in several essays in *The Jewish Return into History*.

26. Buber would not agree. He saw his treatment of Judaism as emphasizing the historical in comparison, for example, with the system of his friend Franz Rosenzweig, or again, of the older Hermann Cohen. However, despite his genuine attempt to make history matter, to do it justice, his dialogical mode of thought essentially eliminated this possibility from satisfactorily actualizing itself in his work. I have briefly noted the reasons for this in the essay on Buber that opens this volume.

27. On Buber's role in the life of German Jewry under the Nazis, see H. Kohn's biography *Martin Buber: Sein Werk und seine Zeit 1880–1930; Nachwort 1930–1960* Robert Weltsch (new edition, Koln, 1961). See also the article by Ernst Simon in the *Leo Baeck Yearbook*, Vol. I (1956) entitled "Jewish Adult Education in Nazi Germany as Spiritual Resistance," pp. 68–104; and E. Wolf, "Martin Buber and German Jewry," *Judaism*, Vol. I (1952), pp. 346–352.

28. On Buber's handling of the problem of evil see M. Friedman, *The Life of Dialogue* (Chicago, 1976); G. Schaeder, *The Hebrew Humanism of Martin Buber* (Detroit, 1973). For criticism see N. Glatzer, *Baeck–Buber–Rosenzweig Reading the Book of Job*, Leo Baeck Memorial Lecture, No. 10 (New York, 1966); Paul Edwards, *Buber and Buberism* (Lawrence, Kansas, 1970); William Kaufmann, *Contemporary Jewish Philosophers* (New

York, 1976). It should be noted that Edwards and Kaufmann's critiques are too simplistic in some important respects and hence must be read with care.

29. M. Buber, *Eclipse of God* (New York, 1957).

30. For a more detailed analysis of Buber's views, see my papers referred to above, as well as my paper "Martin Buber's Theory of Revelation," read at the Sixth World Congress of Jewish Studies (Jerusalem, 1976), as yet unpublished.

31. On this sensitive issue see Arthur A. Cohen's, "Revelation and Law: Reflections on Martin Buber's Views on Halakah," *Judaism*, Vol. I (July, 1952), pp. 250–256; and Marvin Fox, "Some Problems in Buber's Moral Philosophy," in *The Philosophy of Martin Buber*, op. cit., pp. 151 ff. See also Eliezer Berkovits, *Major Themes in Modern Philosophies of Judaism* (New York, 1974), pp. 68–137.

32. In *Return*, pp. 112–126.

33. *Return*, p. 120.

34. *Return*, pp. 120–122.

35. One is never sure why Hegel is to be considered important here. Why is he a standard by which to measure Judaism, especially given Fackenheim's denial of the importance, even impotence, of philosophy in the face of Midrash? On this, see the discussion below.

36. These themes are, of course, central to the Kabbalistic and Hasidic traditions. On their importance for contemporary Jewish thought, one can learn a great deal in particular from the work of Abraham Joshua Heschel. For example, see his significantly titled work, *God in Search of Man* (New York, 1959), and *Man is Not Alone* (New York, 1966). These are also, of course, basic themes in Buber's well-known reflections on Hasidism. Buber, however, is a less reliable guide to Hasidism than Heschel. On Buber's Hasidic work see my essay "Martin Buber's Misuse of Hasidic Sources" in the present collection.

37. "The Builders," in *On Jewish Education*, N. Glatzer, ed. (New York, 1955), pp. 72–92.

38. *Return*, p. 109; "Transcendence is found at Auschwitz in the form of absolute Command."

39. Michael Wyschogrod, "Faith and the Holocaust," in *Judaism*, op. cit., p. 290.

40. See, for example, Joseph Borkin, *The Crime and Punishment of I.G. Farben*, (New York, 1978).

41. See the forthcoming study by Robert Jay Lifton, (title undecided), on this issue.

42. I use this term in its general philosophical sense rather than in the technical Husserlian form.

43. There are still many additional issues to raise regarding Facken-

heim's account of revelation particularly as regards the very meaning of revelation itself. However, for reasons of economy, I shall not try to sketch them here.

44. See the article on Richard Rubenstein in this collection for more on this issue as it applies to his position.

45. See, for example, the position of Elie Wiesel in *Judaism*, Vol. 16 (Summer, 1967), p. 281, who says God broke His covenantal promise at Auschwitz. Wiesel has let history count decisively in making this assertion. Fackenheim, it should be noted, recognizes, as the fine professional philosopher he is, the force of the "falsification" challenge. He just does not know how adequately to meet it and, of course, in this he is not alone. Thus his most sustained attempt to respond to it, in his essay entitled "Elijah and the Empiricists" in his *Encounters Between Judaism and Philosophy* (New York, 1973), is not successful as I have tried to show above.

46. E. Fackenheim, *Encounters*, pp. 7–30.

47. "University Discussion" in A. Flew and A. MacIntyre, eds., *New Essays in Philosophical Theology* (London, 1966).

48. A.J. Ayer, *Language, Truth and Logic* (London, 1936); several subsequent revised editions.

49. E. Fackenheim, *Encounters*, p. 20.

50. Ibid., p. 21

51. It is now recognized that the verification/falsification challenge must usually be carried on in the language of *in principle*, i.e., future possibilities rather than actual disconfirming instances. Of course this weakens the challenge first laid down by Ayer as subsequent editions of *Language, Truth and Logic* clearly demonstrate. But this diminution of the challenge was the only way to retain its intelligibility. Whether it is intelligible even in this weaker form is an open question.

52. Ibid., p. 21

53. Ibid., pp. 21–22.

54. *Return*, p. 52.

55. Emil Fackenheim's, *God's Presence in History*, p. 83.

56. *Return*, pp. 21 ff.

57. Ibid., pp. 52 ff.

58. *Return*, p. 15.

59. *Return*, p. 13.

60. I have briefly sketched my preliminary understanding of the importance of the state of Israel and Zionism for contemporary Jewish life and values in a paper entitled "Hagshamah Atzmit" ("Self-Realization") in G. Wigoder, ed., *Zionist Ideas*, Vol. 3, (Jerusalem, 1981).

61. *God's Presence in History*, p. 73.

62. *Return*, p. 124.

63. See *God's Presence*, pp. 16 ff.

64. In *Return into History*, pp. 3–16, especially pp. 10–16.

65. Ibid., p. 11

66. See Buber's discussion of revelation in *I and Thou*, Part III, and his correspondence entitled "The Builders" in N. Glatzer (ed.), *On Jewish Education*. See also S. Katz, "Dialogue and Revelation" in *Religious Studies*, vol. 14, (1978) pp. 57–68, as well as the opening essay in this volume.

67. See, for example, his use of a citation from *Bereshit Rabbah* 8:5 with which he opens the seventh essay, "The Human Condition after Auschwitz," in *Return*, p. 81, and his discussion thereon, pp. 81 ff.

68. See his *The Religious Dimension in Hegel's Thought* (Bloomington, 1968). The reviews of this book support my admiration for it. See, for example, Quentin Lauer's review reprinted in his *Essays in Hegelian Dialectic* (New York, 1977).

69. *Return*, p.120.

70. This paper was originally given at the American Catholic Philosophical Association.

71. *Return*, p. 124.

72. Essay 16 of *Return*, pp. 252–272.

73. Ibid., pp. 263–264.

74. Ibid., p. 265.

75. Ibid., p. 265.

76. This expression is first used by Fackenheim on p. 266 and then throughout the remainder of the essay.

77. Ibid., pp. 263–264.

78. Ibid., p. 269.

79. Note should be taken of this in relation to our remarks in point 5 above regarding "falsification," or the lack of same in Fackenheim's position.

80. That is, it is not an argument for Midrash any more than for philosophy.

81. Or expressed somewhat differently by R. Nachman of Bratzlav, "Faith is both hidden and revealed. It is hidden, because if you ask the person of faith to provide some reason for it, he will certainly not be able to give any; faith only applies to those areas where there are no reasons. But it is also revealed, because to the one who has faith it is all quite clear, as though he were seeing the object of his faith with his very eyes . . ." *Sihot ha-Ran* 1, as cited by Arthur Green, "Jewish Mysticism in a Contemporary Theology of Judaism," *Shefa Quarterly*, Vol. 1, No. 4 (September, 1978), p. 32.

THE CRUCIFIXION OF THE JEWS: IGNAZ MAYBAUM'S THEOLOGY OF THE HOLOCAUST

Earlier in this volume[1] we described the quite extraordinary theological exposition of the Holocaust advocated by Ignaz Maybaum. Weaving together elements of traditional Jewish belief, Reform Jewish ideology, and Franz Rosenzweig's philosophy of history, Maybaum has suggested that the *Sho'ah* be understood through the application of Christological categories, especially that of the Crucifixion. Like Jesus of old, the Jews are an innocent vicarious sacrifice through which God elevates humankind to a new level of spiritual maturity. In support of this reading of recent Jewish history he has marshalled considerable Jewish learning and philosophical intelligence and has blended them together, not least because of his own deep belief both in God's reality and in His goodness. Yet this synthesis is not free of fundamental weaknesses and it is with an analysis of these limitations that the present essay will deal.

I

Let us begin by considering Maybaum's fundamental contention that Jewish history must work itself out in ways intelligible to the nations. This thesis is both correct and incorrect. It is correct insofar as it properly stresses the *contextual* character of Jewish history and the organic development of Judaism as a concrete phenomenon that proceeds in interdependence with the larger unfolding of world history. The all too common attempt to treat Jewish history as if it had existed at any period in a hermetically sealed ghetto is mistaken.[2] The inpenetrable ghetto exists only in the imagination of certain scholars. Yet alternatively, there is a valid distinction to be acknowledged between that internal Jewish history which is *not* totally reducible to, or even primarily intelligible through, an analysis of Judaism's external relations to the nations and its extrinsic history in which the nations play the dominant role. That is, there *is* a dimension of the Jewish past and present that is best understood as an autonomous socio-religious reality. In this mode Judaism and the Jewish people of course adopt and reshape external ideas and materials and, of necessity as well as choice, respond to outside events, but in these instances the choices are made according to an independent Jewish value system and inherent, particular rhythms.

It is no easy matter to isolate and describe this special Jewish *Weltanschauung*, for as Jacob Talmon has correctly noted, "Jewish impulses and reactions, attitudes and sensitiveness, Jewish modes of feeling and patterns of behavior call for the intuition of the artist, and indeed can only be intimated by symbols, conjured up by the poetic incantation, and communicated by the art of the novelist."[3] Yet to deny this reality is to be ignorant of authentic Jewish life *as lived from within the tradition.* It is to reduce Judaism and the Jew to that set of external relations into which they enter either by choice or fate, while denying them any essential being that is truly their own. Moreover, it is to forget that it is simply irrelevant, for example, whether the non-Jewish world grasps the meaning of most halachic actions or the inner spirituality of *Ish ha-Halachah*[4] (Halachic man) for the Jewish significance of such behavior is not dependent on non-Jewish understanding. And yet the core of Jewish historical existence, certainly until very recently, was inseparable and unintelligible aside from such halachic behavior and its meta-halachic metaphysical justification which created the uniquely Jewish relationship to the world-historical. Conversely, if the nations of the world, as happened under Hitler, decide that Judaism has no more "meaning" for them, are Jews to willingly disappear? The world, of course, will have its way with Israel and it will understand Jewish life and its significance as it likes, but this perception is not all-inclusive and monopolistic, for at all times and places the Jew has his own perception of events and his own schematization of reality and its meaning. To fail to appreciate this two-sidedness of Jewish historical existence, as Maybaum does, is to fail to do justice to both the logic of the historiographical circumstance as well as the theological and ontological character of Jewish being in history. In respect of this interpretive limitation Maybaum is a victim of his inheritance; that is, of those earlier modernizing attempts which sought to evaluate and interpret Judaism primarily through alien standards and for largely apologetic purposes, i.e., defending the continued vitality of Judaism as an authentic religious posture in post-Enlightenment, liberal Christian, European circles on the basis of an appeal to non-Jewish norms and structures.

This hermeneutic, this method of validating Judaism through the prism of norms not her own, is of considerable historical and philosophical significance. It is, of course, the major interpretive element in nineteenth- and much twentieth-century Jewish historiography and philosophy in which the criteria used to evaluate Judaism were drawn especially from Kantian, Hegelian, and Romantic schools of thought. The clearest expression and manifestation of this exercise is certainly to be seen in Reform Judaism, whose checkered nineteenth-century career we need not and cannot recount here. Maybaum is a direct heir of these ideological influences and, in particular, of their underlying philosophical assumptions. While this is a rich inheritance one must also be sensitive to its darker underside and to the negative consequences that flow from this methodological procedure if it is not balanced by other countervailing and complementary considerations. But Maybaum lacks this critical self-consciousness and as a result he fails to recognize the major danger which this approach inevitably entails when unadulterated by other values, namely, that Judaism loses all internal integrity. What is considered authentic and worth preserving in Judaism is dictated by the outsider (even if then internalized by Jews), e.g., those elements assimilable to Kantian morality in classical Reform theology and now in Maybaum's theology those phenomena which can be reinterpreted through reference to the Crucifixion and related Christian theological categories.[5]

We must ask Maybaum, did God enter into covenantal relation with Abraham and his heirs only so as to crucify them? Does being Jewish mean primarily, essentially, being a "lamb for the slaughter?" Is there not something intrinsic, essential, about the Jewish relationship to God which is the Jews' alone? Some inner reality, some special holiness, some particular "priestliness" that is not dictated by the needs of the nations but rather by the intimacy of covenantal existence. One feels the need to insist that Judaism does embody truth in its own unique fashion, that it does possess its own logic and substantiality, its own creativity and normativity, its own facticity, its own internal meaning which connects it to God as well as to the nations, and that these relationships are truly dialectical and predicated on a mutual integrity, so that Judaism will not ultimately be negated altogether. Were it otherwise, were Judaism of worth only insofar as it measured up to the prescriptive ideals of others, then there would be nothing valuable about Judaism per se, nor, and here is the rub, would its decline or even disappearance matter except for atavistic or nostalgic reasons. Moreover, and to rephrase and expand a point made parenthetically above, were Judaism to exhaust its "meaning" for the non-Jewish world either according to its internal calculus or, as seems more likely, in the equation of the nations, does this require by some inner logic that Judaism evacuate all realms of self-meaning and obligate Jews to commit collective ideological suicide in some form of mass assimilation? Or rather, is it not possible, indeed actual, for Judaism to be value-laden and life-enriching for its adherents in *irreplaceable* ways on bases altogether other than those dictated by the needs of the nations?

It is here, and only now, that we can enter into dialogue with Maybaum's adoption of *Churban*[6] (unavoidable national tragedy) and hence "Crucifixion" as the master code which must be applied to Jewish history to make it intelligible *even to Jews*. Offered as a Jewish theology of history, this thesis is a particularly extreme example of interpreting Judaism in non-Jewish, or, more narrowly still,

Christian terms.[7] This Christocentric orientation is, of course, taken over, with modification, from Maybaum's great mentor Franz Rosenzweig, but this does not make it true; it merely makes it an error with a pedigree. It will be recalled that Rosenzweig, after his near conversion to Christianity, fashioned a remarkable Jewish vision that in effect accepted the Christian account of Western history and its interpretation of the roles of Israel and the Church in the world. But having accepted this portrayal, he departed from the Christian script by transforming Judaism's ahistoricity into a virtue.[8] History, Rosenzweig affirmed, does belong to Christianity but this is not a sign of the Divine rejection of Israel but of Israel's immediate and eternal meta-historic relation to God. Through this inversion Rosenzweig transmuted Jewry's unenviable this-worldly circumstance into a blessing and Jewish oppression into a mark of transcendental love.

Even in Rosenzweig's pre-Holocaust form this argument met with great resistance; few Jewish thinkers, despite the near-universal homage paid to Rosenzweig's memory, are Rosenzweigians in this respect. In Maybaum's sharpened post-*Sho'ah* version, emphasizing the role of vicarious victim, of the six million as the Christ of our age, the thesis is still more problematic. And it is problematic not least because Maybaum misunderstands the ontological and theological circumstances that allow Christian theology to affirm that "Christ died for the sins of mankind." Christians are able to make this declaration for (at least) two cardinal reasons. The first and most weighty is that Christ is believed to be God Incarnate, the Second Person of the Trinity; the Crucifixion is God taking the sins of mankind *on Himself*. He is the vicarious atonement for mankind. There is thus no terrible cruelty or unspeakable "crime" but only Divine Love, the presence of unlimited Divine Grace. Secondly, the human yet divine Christ, the Hypostatic Union of man and God, mounts the Cross voluntarily. He willingly "dies so that others might live." How very different was the *Sho'ah*. How very dissimilar its victims (not martyrs) and their fate. The murdered, including the million Jewish children, were not Divine—they were all too human creatures crushed in the most unspeakable brutality. If God was the cause of *their* suffering how at odds from the traditional Christian picture, for here God purchases life for some by sacrificing others, not Himself. Here Grace, if present, is so only in a most paradoxical way, and certainly not in the reality of the victims. Here there is only Golgotha, Crucifixion, Death; there is no Easter for the crucified ones. Furthermore, the Jews were singled out "unwillingly," they were *not* martyrs in the classical sense though we may wish to so transform their fate for *our* needs. There were of course those who willingly died for *Kiddush Ha-Shem* [9] (dying as martyrs for the "sanctification of the Divine Name"), but they were a small, very special minority. The majority of Jews died otherwise.

The *dis*analogy of the Holocaust and Good Friday would yet reveal something more. According to Maybaum the symbol of the Crucifixion is that of vicarious atonement. But given the circumstances of this vicarious sacrifice, of Auschwitz and Treblinka, of *Einsatzgruppen* and gas chambers, is it not the case that the nature of the atonement is far more criminal and infinitely more depraved than the sins for which it atones? What sort of reconciliation can the work of Himmler and the SS have been? What sort of *kohanim* (priests) were these and what sort of sacrifice can they bring? Can one truly envision God, the God of Israel, making such vicarious expiation? And who makes amends for the Nazis? Are their sins not beyond all reparation? Is the world not forever darkened by the ashes of the crematoriums and the screams of the murdered millions? Is not reality more alienated from God as a consequence of the Holocaust than ever it was before it? To equate "Planet Auschwitz" with atonement, or in Maybaum's special typology of *Churban* with progress, seems, in this light, an absurdity. For this reason one feels obligated to raise against Maybaum's thesis the same objection one raises against the Free-Will Defense when it is employed in a Holocaust context,[10] namely, that if the Holocaust is the price of freedom, or in this case of progress and expiation, then better to do without such evolution and reconciliation—the price is just too high. It is morally and theologically unacceptable. To insist on it is to turn God, *kivyachol* [11] ("as if one could say this"), into a moral monster.

An impossible irony also discloses itself as a corollary of Maybaum's suggestion that God used Hitler for His purposes. If the *Sho'ah* is God's Will, if Hitler is "My servant," then to resist Hitler is to resist God; to fight the Nazis is to fight the Lord. As such the Warsaw ghetto resisters, the inmates who rebelled at Treblinka, the "righteous of the nations" who risked death, and more often than not died, to save Jewish lives, all these were rebels against the Almighty. The SS were God's angels of death while the Jews and their precious few allies were enemies of Heaven. This entailment, however, is offensive in every way: it requires an inversion of all sanity, all morality, and all that is theologically authentic. As such it must be rejected and rejected totally.

II

Necessarily allied to the doctrine of vicarious atonement in Maybaum's exegesis of Crucifixion is the notion of progress, i.e., Crucifixion interpreted as vicarious atonement makes progress possible. As one reflects upon this metaphysical presupposition, however, it becomes ever less compelling. To begin with it is not the universal historical explanatory category Maybaum presumes. While it does work suggestively, if not examined too closely, as an "explanation" of the *Sho'ah* it does not seem to fit the historical realities appertaining to the destruction of the First or Second Temples as Maybaum suggests.[12] Christianity did not exist in 586 B.C.E. and was only a splinter group within Judaism in 70 C.E.; there is therefore no justification for conveying the meaning of 586 or 70 to the Babylonians or Romans in terms of the essentially Christian idea that "progress is achieved through sacrifice." They would have found this Christological idea, along with the modern notion of progress, unintelligible.[13] The ancients certainly utilized sacrifice as the main means of relating to the gods, but this relationship was not based on an understanding of history as progressive. Rather sacrifice was seen as expiatory and appeasing. Similarly from the Jewish side, the events of 586 and 70 were not seen as moments of spiritual ascent but of spiritual descent; the Exile of the *Shechinah* as well as of Israel. Exile is not a desirable state of spiritual exaltation, it is a mark of sin and alienation. Jews mourn on *Tisha b'Av*, they do not celebrate. Of course, Maybaum might contend in reply that "God's ways are a mystery" and therefore that it matters little, if at all, that the ancients did not grasp the significance, the progress, embedded in the events in which they participated and to which they gave witness. But this reply will not do, for the essence of Maybaum's claim is that progress is possible only through sacrifice because this is all the nations comprehend, i.e., God has to speak to them, has to rouse them, in their language. But if, as we would contend, the ancients, including the Jews, did not perceive matters this way at all, did not assimilate this sign-language in this manner, then the entire argument collapses under the weight of its own internal premises. Alternatively, if Maybaum still insists that God brought about progress nonetheless and even without the understanding of the contemporary participants then the argument has shifted in character and destruction now becomes something required by God, not man, for progress to occur. Thus the Holocaust, too, is a Divine, not a human, prerequisite. But if so then God is simply, as far as we can fathom, immoral. What else can we say of a God who executes an undeserved Holocaust for His requirements?

But let us move beyond these more cosmic considerations and turn to the application of the Maybaumian thesis to the Holocaust. The issue then becomes: What progress has resulted from the *Sho'ah*? What advance has been achieved because of Auschwitz? The world as a whole is unequivocally not an appreciably better place. Since 1945 mass murder has occurred in Uganda, Biafra, Vietnam, Cambodia, Sudan, Burundi, India, Pakistan, and parts of Central and South America.[14] The Russian Empire has, likewise, grown no less repressive—first Hungary, then Czechoslovakia, and now Afghanistan and Poland. The "nations" have been slow to learn any ethical imperative from the *Sho'ah*. But this measure may be unfair to Maybaum, though I do not think it is, for his presentation concentrated, though not exclusively, on the Nazi *Churban* as the means whereby Judaism and Christianity, if not the world at large, made progress as a consequence of the Holocaust. For the Jew this progress is manifest in the transcendence of "medieval" orthodoxy and the demographic transference of world Jewry from concentration in Eastern Europe to liberal Western countries and Israel.[15] For Christianity it likewise means the transcendence of medievalism in the form of a new ecumenical spirit. But are these processes and shifts to be accepted at face value as "progress?"

Certainly the great majority of the world's Jews live in the West rather than in the East and are modern rather than traditional in dress, personal and religious habits, and world view, but is this condition in itself the essence of moral and theological advance, especially in Jewish terms? Four questions seem appropriately asked in response to this panegyric in praise of the supposedly benefi- cient effects of the Sho'ah. First, and to put again the purest theo- logical inquiry: would a moral God use such means to achieve such ends? Are these results which here count as "progress" worth the suffering of the six million, a million Jewish children? Neither Maybaum's faith nor his homiletical mode can finesse this chal- lenge. Secondly, is the contemporary transcendence of a halachic framework, accompanied by the substitution of modern values, Jewish progress? Does this gambit not, simultaneously, deny the existence of an authentic Jewish self-understanding and sovereign dignity and replace it with the idolization of modernity? Third and related, is this total capitulation before the standards of our age not bizarre after the Sho'ah, which in large part was the result of mo- dernity and its values rather than their antithesis? The Sho'ah was, after all, a contemporary phenomenon, not a medieval one,[16] and its uniqueness[17] lies in its peculiar exploitation of certain features of twentieth century intellectual, governmental, technological, bu- reaucratic, and moral life. Indeed, the Sho'ah did not happen in the medieval period because medievalism could not produce it. Rather than exposing and thus overcoming the indecencies of medieval- ism the Sho'ah reveals the rot at the very core of modernity, a rot deeper and more fundamental than Maybaum has any sense of. One would have thought that instead of recommending the spiritual and ethical currents of the recent past the Sho'ah revealed the need to stand over against them in dialectical tension, using Judaism as a standard by which to calibrate their value rather than the reverse. Fourth, there is the high cost of the Jewish encounter with mo- dernity which must now be considered in some detail.

Europe, in emancipating the Jew, did seek to end the worst of the medieval oppressions. But in so doing, it had its own agenda, which required that in order for Jews to merit what others had by right, Jews had to prove themselves worthy of citizenship. The way Jews were expected to do this was to respond in a quid pro quo fashion to the magnanimous gesture of their neighbors. That is, as the non-Jews liberated the Jews from their political disabilities, the Jews, conversely, were expected to liberate themselves from their Judaism. For all the rhetoric, the fact was that the older theological anti-Semitism, that is, the classical denigration of Judaism, was still very much part and parcel of European culture even in its most "advanced" and "enlightened" circles. Jews as individuals might be educable and made over into productive members of society, but only if they transcended their connection with their religious heritage. Judaism per se was irredeemable.[18]

The profound consequence of this unprecedented situation must be explicitly charted. For the first time in history there now arose a distinction between Jews as individuals and Judaism as a religious tradition. There came into being a bifurcated Jewish circumstance: on the one hand there was the Problem of Jews, i.e., as individuals, on the other hand the Problem of Judaism, i.e., the national problems of the people of Israel. Previously this disjunction did not exist.

Contemporary Jews (and Christians) clearly understood the issues that were generated by this striking, novel dichotomy. They responded in ways that stretched across the spectrum from conversion to Christianity as a gesture of gratitude and/or convenience (hence Heine's famous justification of his conversion as "a Passport to European Civilization"); to assimilation, the new option of the contemporary situation through which Jews could leave their Judaism without the necessity of conversion; to classical Reform Judaism, which represents in large part the "Judaization" of this division mixed with Kantian morality and Hegelian historicism; to the *Wissenschaft des Judentums*, the spiritual progenitor of American Conservatism; to Samson Raphael Hirsch's "neo-orthodoxy" which prescribed "being a man on the street and a Jew at home." At the other extreme Hasidism repudiated this dichotomy of Jews and Judaism, and hence rejected the present. Zionism also grasped the defective quality of European modernity,[19] if for related though different reasons. The classical Zionist analysis was predicated on the insincerity (or impossibility?) of Europe's intentions to honor its arrangement with the Jews even if they became "assimilated"— hence the only honorable solution was a separate Jewish homeland.[20]

This milieu of contradictory and competing norms and ambitions presented two separate though related perplexities. That is to say, the Jewish Problem was not one problem but two. On the one hand there was the continuing struggle for moral decency and an end to residual disabilities against Jewish individuals in politics, education, social interaction, and particularly in the economic sphere, all of which can be called aspects of the Problem of Jews. Alternatively, though of course related, was the Problem of Judaism, that is, the question of how to maintain the vitality and integrity of the communal way of life, of Judaism as a distinct world view, as a quite specific ideological and axiological system. For the last two hundred years the Problem of Jews has been the dominant one and much progress has been made with respect to it, though the tensions inherent in it are not yet fully resolved. Hence the Jewish community in the free world, especially in America, has reached remarkable levels of educational, social, political, and economic achievement. In America Jews have to an extraordinary degree resolved much of the problematic of being a Jew *qua* individual. Jews no longer experience[21] the sorts of exclusionary processes that their parents and their grandparents knew. Jews are now, as all the data reveals, the pre-eminent achievers in American society in terms of per capita wealth and income, education, professions, and the like. They are even "in fashion"—the New York Jewish literary Mafia; enrollments at Ivy League schools; as marriage partners. These are the very sorts of things Maybaum can rightly point to as "progress."

This advance, however, masks a corresponding dilemma posed by modernity of which Maybaum takes no real account yet which threatens nothing less than the dissolution of a viable Jewish community in America and other parts of the world, outside the state of Israel. For as a community Jewry is experiencing, and it may not be too dramatic a metaphor, an invisible though far less painful Holocaust. For example, some admittedly extreme recent studies suggest that in one hundred years the American Jewish community will decline from the largest single Jewish community the world has ever known (of approximately six million) to a community of 250,000, while even the more sober and "optimistic" predict a decline of over thirty percent from present levels. This is due to the toll of indifference and assimilation, of intermarriage and feeble, nonreplacement-level birth rates; this phenomena of demographic dissolution is paralleled everywhere in the Jewish world except for Israel.[22]

This erosion (towards what final end?) and all that it implies is the high price of Jewish emancipation, of the Jews' passion for modernity. But this side of the equation Maybaum ignores altogether, oblivious to the reality that his enthusiasm for the "modern" may well entail the extinction of Judaism. Conversely, he is altogether deaf to the fact that his passion for Judaism may logically require some substantial diminution of his estimation of the "progress" which our era represents.

As to the progress Maybaum detects in post-Holocaust Christendom, I must also demur. There have been positive steps made by the Church towards the Jewish people, yet the progressive directions of Vatican II already seem to be meeting serious resistance. In the reaction of Christianity at large to the Jewish people there is, unfortunately, still room for a great deal of improvement, as evidenced by the shattering silence of the majority of Christendom when three million Jews again faced annihilation in the state of Israel in 1967 and 1973. And the increasing anti-Israel chorus among the Christian countries of the world at the United Nations and in such Christian bodies as the World Council of Churches since 1973 is only a cause for despair. Thus, despite Maybaum's pronouncements to the contrary, neither the world at large nor the Jewish people reveal themselves "here and now, mankind at its goal."[23]

III

The subject of Zionism, the re-establishment of a Jewish state in Israel, demands another word. With regard to an attempt to fashion either a Jewish philosophy of history or a philosophy of Jewish history, the state of Israel is as significant, if not more significant, than the Holocaust, and yet it is an event, a reality, that escapes if it does not altogether negate Maybaum's categories. For the meaning of Jewish history as disclosed through the state of Israel is the antithesis of the Crucifixion mentality. Jews have now declared (seemingly with God's permission): we have suffered enough, died enough, been put upon enough; we wish to reject forever our state of powerlessness! We wish to live in the Land of the Covenant in peace with man and God. In this way the flow of Jewish history itself has provided the most telling of all objections to Maybaum's theodicy insofar as Maybaum revels in Jewish powerlessness and the lack of a public Jewish dimension. The tragic paradox in all this, of course, is that the state of Israel is the most significant evidence of "progress" that Maybaum could appeal to—but ironically, even bizarrely, it is a datum that he must reject because of the larger metaphysical construct to which his theory of progress is tied.

Here two metaphysical systems mix and reinforce each other. The first is the a-Zionist,[24] ahistorical Rosenzweigian perspective that views Jewish settlement outside of Israel as part of the cosmic design for the Jewish people which has now fulfilled its historic mission and is, in Rosenzweig's language, "with God" while the "nations," immersed as they are in history, are still on their way, through Christianity, to this end. The second is Reform Judaism's reconstruction of the idea of the "Jewish mission to the gentiles" which positively values Jewish life "among the nations." From both perspectives the Diaspora is a "consummation devoutly to be wished" rather than a state whose end is longed for night and day. But in reaction we must say that whatever validity this outlook may have had pre-1933 it has almost none today, certainly not as an anti-Zionist apologetic. Martin Buber already in the 1930s had written to the anti-Semitic theologian and Bible scholar, Gerhard Kittel, who had asserted that the Jews were true to their vocation only as aliens:

Authentic Jewry, you say, remains faithful to the symbol of the restless and homeless alien who wanders the earth. Judaism does not know of such a symbol. The "wandering Jew" is a figure of Christian legend, not a Jewish figure.[25]

Properly modified Buber's rebuke is also a reply to Maybaum's enthronement of the Diaspora as the "goal" of Jewish life.

Another quotation from Buber from a not unrelated context is also apposite. In 1939 no less a figure than Mahatma Gandhi argued against Zionism. In reply Buber wrote:

Dispersion is bearable; it can even be purposeful. If there is somewhere an ingathering, a growing home center, a piece of earth where one is in the midst of an ingathering and not in dispersion, and whence the spirit of the ingathering may work its way into all the places of the dispersion. When there is this, there is also a striving common life, the life of a community which dares to live today because it may hope to live tomorrow. But when this growing center is lacking, dispersion becomes dismemberment.[26]

Buber's answer to Gandhi may also serve as a response to Maybaum, for he too would turn what Judaism always held was the temporary, negative, status of *galut* (exile) into a cardinal blessing.[27]

The state of Israel has, of course, to be understood aright in this connection. It is not only a political reality—though there is nothing wrong with a "mere" Jewish political reality, nor is there anything "mere" about it—but it is also a primary theological datum, for Christians no less than for Jews. For Jews the reason is transparent if not self-evident: [28] this is an act of redemption, if the God of Israel lives. For Christians Zionism must also be a theological commitment after Auschwitz because, as Emil Fackenheim has recently described it:

No less than Jews themselves, Christians must wish Jewish existence to be liberated from dependence on charity. On behalf of their partners in dialogue, they must wish independence from charity-in-general. On behalf of their own Christianity, they must wish it from Christian charity-in-particular. The post-Holocaust Christian must repent of the Christian sin of supersessionism. One asks: How can he trust in his own repentance—that it is both genuine and complete? There is only one answer: If he supports firmly and unequivocally the Jewish search for independence not only from the power of its enemies but also from that of Christian friends.

Without Zionism—Christian as well as Jewish—the Holy Spirit cannot dwell between Jews and Christians in dialogue.[29]

IV

One last matter of consequence remains, Maybaum's conception of God. Put more exactly, what persists as an occassion for astonishment as well as perplexity is Maybaum's willingness to affirm not only that God was present in the Holocaust but that Hitler was His agent. In advancing this claim Maybaum follows the logic of his commitment to God's presence in the here and now further, more radically, and more consistently than do others who likewise want to locate the Almighty in history but who, at one and the same time, are unwilling to draw this consequence from the common premise. As the prophet Jeremiah saw Nebuchadnezzar, the destroyer of Jerusalem, as the "servant of God" (Jer. 27:6) so Maybaum is willing to consciously paraphrase Jeremiah's idiom and give expression to the terrifying paradox: "Hitler, My servant!"[30]

Hitler was an instrument . . . God used this instrument to cleanse, to purify, to punish a sinful world; the six million Jews, they died an innocent death; they died because of the sins of others.[31]

Yet what does this "explanation" entail vis à vis the 'Lord of Hosts'? What kind of Divinity would use the murder of six million Jews and countless others for purposes of purification? Would use the SS as His instruments of purification? What kind of Diety would employ vicarious atonement as experienced at Auschwitz for any reason whatsoever? The moral equation of means and ends must enter into the picture here and now. It is not enough to declare:

How terrible that we paid for this progress with the death of six million martyrs. Can you understand it? I cannot. You cannot. It is not for us to understand. For us it remains to praise the works of God.[32]

Admirable as such faith is Maybaum owes us more than this, because he has ventured to go beyond faith to understanding through his typology of *Churban* and the meaning it imputes to the Jewish victims of Nazism. This contended meaning requires that we comprehend that God willingly, indeed causally, created the "Kingdom of Night" and purposefully consigned the Jews to be consumed in it. But if this hell is the means then what can be its end? That there is a Creator can still be affirmed. But can one, does one care to, pray to this Being? Has not the God of Israel, of the Covenant, of redemption, become another casualty of the *Sho'ah*?

Maybaum seeks to use the Holocaust as a medium of communication between Heaven and earth, but could the Maker of all things not speak to the world in a less horrific way? That is to say, it is one thing to attribute the Holocaust to men, as many do,[33] but once one attributes it directly—causally—to God, it becomes impossible to understand or to justify, for an omnipotent, omniscient Being must be able to instruct His creation and to lead it where He will in ways other than Auschwitz. If He cannot then He is not the all-encompassing Absolute of Maybaum's metaphysics. If He does not then He is not the moral Deliverer of Judaism. Thus, while Maybaum is willing to follow the logic of omnipotence to its seemingly logical end, i.e., that God must be the real cause of the Holocaust, he totally fails to grapple with the deeper dilemma posed by theodicy, namely, the defense of God's attributes of love and justice. If there is only Divine Power to contend with there is no problem of theodicy to begin with—an all-powerful Deity could indeed do what Maybaum contends. But could an *El melech channun ve rachamim* (a "long-suffering and merciful God") do so? Could the Lord of the Covenant truly employ a "Hitler, My servant!" Once we juxtapose these complementary Divine attributes of mercy and love against Divine might, it becomes impossible to accept either Maybaum's logic or his ontology.

CONCLUSION

Admirable as Maybaum's refreshing willingness to draw difficult conclusions from his premises is, in the final analysis his "explanations" do not explain the theological dilemmas posed by the Holocaust. Rather, they merely push them one step further back, where they reappear with a new vigor. Thus, at best, Maybaum's

264 POST-HOLOCAUST DIALOGUES

attempt merely shifts, while it does not solve, the problem of continued Jewish belief after Auschwitz. At worst, it makes it impossible to be a "believing Jew," for who wants to believe in, to pray to, a God who would use the likes of a Hitler as His instrument against innocent men, women and children?[34] Then too, even the blessing and sustenance that is the state of Israel is denied by Maybaum's curious ontological presuppositions. If this is where Maybaum's theology leads us it is time to transcend it and open ourselves once again to the living reality of Judaism and the Jewish people. Hence, Maybaum's account can only be judged an unacceptable, if not uninteresting, response to the theological crisis of our time.

NOTES

1. See "Faith After the Holocaust: Four Responses," in this volume.

2. See, for example, the work of the great Jewish historian Salo Baron, *Social and Religious History of the Jews* (New York, 1952 on), who makes this point abundantly clear. See also Simon Dubnow's *World History of the Jewish People* (South Brunswick, New Jersey, 1967–1973). However, Dubnow's approach is not free of the weakness we are here discussing as is obvious when it is compared, for example, to the method adopted by David Pipes's essay on "Catherine the Great and the Jews," *Soviet Jewish Affairs*, Vol. 1, No. 3 (1972), pp. 20–40. See also Jacob Talmon's remarks on this issue in *The Unique and the Universal* (New York, 1965), pp. 64–90.

3. Jacob Talmon, op. cit., p. 70. Though I think Talmon essentially correct here and hence quote him approvingly he does get a bit carried away by his own rhetorical and "poetic" eloquence.

4. This is the title of Rabbi Joseph Soloveitchik's famous essay in *Talpiot* (1944) pp. 651–734 (in Hebrew). I have given a summary of Soloveitchik's views in my *Jewish Philosophers* (New York, 1975), pp. 215–221. On Soloveitchik's position regarding *halachah* see also David Singer and Moshe Sokol's article: "Joseph Soloveitchik: Lonely Man of Faith," *Modern Judaism* Vol. 2, #3 (September, 1982); Rachel Shihor, "On the Problem of Halakhah's Status in Judaism," *Forum* (Spring–Summer, 1978), pp. 146–153.

5. This use of the "Crucifixion" by German (and other Western) Jewish intellectuals to express their deepest sense of tragedy is an important index of their assimilation. They lack a fully Jewish, Jewishly formed and saturated, imagination.

6. Maybaum's use of this notion and its significance is explained in the essay "Four Responses," in this volume.

7. The same substitution has, of course, been made in the name of Marxism, Socialism, Humanism, etc. in the modern era.

8. See on this F. Rosenzweig, *Stern der Erlosung* (*Star of Redemption,* New York, 1971). See also A. Altmann, "Franz Rosenzweig on History" in A. Altmann (ed.), *Between East and West* (London, 1958), pp. 194–214. See also Maybaum's comments on Rosenzweig in *Face of God After Auschwitz* (Amsterdam, 1965), pp. 170 ff. For the details of Rosenzweig's near conversion to Christianity, see N. Glatzer, *Franz Rosenzweig* (New York, 1953); and A. Altmann's and D. Emmett's edition of the letters of Eugen Rosenstock Huessey and Franz Rosenzweig which appeared under the title *Judaism Despite Christianity* (New York, 1969).

9. Eliezer Berkovits' several works on the Holocaust emphasize such behavior. See for example his *Faith After the Holocaust* (New York, 1973); *Crisis and Faith* (New York, 1976); and *With God in Hell* (New York, 1979). Emil Fackenheim's newest book dealing with the Holocaust, entitled *To Mend the World* (New York, 1982), also gives such behavior a more prominent place than heretofore.

10. See my exegesis and critique of Eliezer Berkovits' response to the Holocaust in this volume.

11. This is the traditional rabbinic phrase used to qualify what seem overly anthropomorphic statements about the Divine.

12. *Face,* p. 32 and elsewhere.

13. See on this, for example, Robert Nisbet's *History of the Idea of Progress* (New York, 1980).

14. For more on these mass murders see my *The Uniqueness of the Holocaust* to be published by Harvard University Press next year. Leo Kuper, *Genocide* (New Haven, 1982); and Jack Nusan Porter (ed.), *Genocide and Human Rights* (Washington, D.C., 1982) both contain helpful summaries of these events.

15. This is described more fully in my exegesis of Maybaum's position in the essay "Faith After the Holocaust: Four Responses," in this volume.

16. On this see Yitzchak Greenberg's comments in his paper *The Third Great Cycle In Jewish History* (New York, 1981). See also Arthur Cohen's correct historical observations in his *The Tremendum* (New York, 1981), pp. 14 ff, and Yosef Yerushalmi's remarks in his "Comment" in Eva Fleischner (ed.), *Auschwitz: Beginning of a New Era?* (New York, 1977).

17. On this see George Kren and Leon Rappaport, *The Holocaust and the Crisis of Human Behavior* (New York, 1980). The observations of R. Rubenstein on modern technology and the Sho'ah in his *The Cunning of History* (New York, 1975) are also of value here, as is a study by Joseph Borkin, *The Crime and Punishment of I. G. Farben* (New York, 1978). Likewise see Benjamin Ferencz, *Less Than Slaves* (Cambridge, 1979). Han-

nah Arendt's *Eichmann in Jerusalem: The Banality of Evil* (New York, 1964) is also essential, if flawed, reading.

18. One here recalls the well-known remark, made during the French National Assembly debate on "the Jewish question," by Ferdinard Tonnere: "To the Jews as individuals everything, to the Jews as a people nothing." For more on this issue see Jacob Katz, *Out of the Ghetto* (Cambridge, 1973).

19. The common analysis of Zionism which stresses its radical break from Jewish tradition is too simplistic and fails to recognize that Zionism was at one and the same time a profound critic of modern European/Jewish life even more than it was its heir.

20. This one-line summary is of course overly reductive and represents primarily Herzl's version of Zionism, which was only one version among many of the Zionist dream. It was Herzl who stressed that Zionism was the "honorable" solution to the *Judenfrage*.

21. Though, of course, we must be vigilant. The possibility of a reversal of Jewish fortunes in the U.S. and the growth of anti-semitism in sections of both the American political right and left is all too apparant. For the most recent survey of the subject see Nathan and Ruth Perlmutter, *The Real Anti-Semitism in America* (New York, 1982).

22. For the facts and figures of this demographic crisis described in extreme terms see the paper by Eliahu Bergman in *Midstream*, Vol. 23, No. 8 (October, 1977), pp. 9–19, entitled "The American Jewish Population Erosion." See also the many studies of U. O. Smelz which, while less dramatic, are also negative in their findings and depressing reading. His most recent analysis is "Jewish Survival: the Demographic Issues," *American Jewish Year Book*, Vol. 81 (New York, 1981), pp. 61–117. The work of R. Bachi, *Population Trends of World Jewry* (Jerusalem, 1976) is also of much value in trying to understand the present situation. Bachi's more recent "The Demographic Crisis of Diaspora Jewry," *Forum*, No. 42/43 (Winter, 1981), section II, pp. 26–58, is now the most up to date statement of the problem. The recent volume edited by Paul Ritterband entitled *Modern Jewish Fertility* (Leiden, 1981), especially the study by S. Goldstein on American Jewish demography, pp. 160–208, is also of value in pondering this question. The ideological implications are vigorously presented in, among other places, Hillel Halkin's *Letters to an American Friend* (Philadelphia, 1978).

23. *Face*, p. 63.

24. Maybaum is an ideological anti-Zionist, not an active physical opponent of the state of Israel as, for example, are Satmar Hasidim and members of Naturei Karta. See *Face*, pp. 28 ff., and elsewhere.

25. Translated and reprinted in F. Talmage (ed.), *Disputation and Dialogue* (New York, 1975), p. 53. I cite this particular passage not to equate

Maybaum and Kittel but because his position is directly related to the Christian–Rosenzweigian reading of post-70 C.E. Jewish history.

26. Martin Buber to Gandhi, translated in W. Herberg (ed.), *The Writings of Martin Buber* (New York, 1958), p. 28.

27. Even in *galut* Jews controlled their own immediate "space." This was one of the remarkable features of Jewish communal life through all the various stages of the Exile as represented by various *Kehilla* organizations and structures. See, for example, Salo Baron's *Jewish Community*, 3 volumes (Philadelphia, 1942) and Louis Finkelstein's *Jewish Self-Government in the Middle Ages* (New York, 1924). See also Yitzchak Baer, *Galut* (New York, 1961).

28. It is not self-evident as there are groups like the *Naturei Karta* and Satmar Hasidim who deny the state of Israel positive theological meaning. I believe they are wrong, fundamentally and inexcusably wrong, in this regard, but this is another matter.

29. Emil Fackenheim, *To Mend the World* (New York, 1982), p. 297.

30. *Face*, p. 67.

31. *Face*, p. 67.

32. *Face*, p. 64.

33. As, for example, do the three other "Holocaust theologians," R. Rubenstein, Emil Fackenheim, and Eliezer Berkovits, treated in this volume.

34. Certain Orthodox thinkers also hold that Hitler was God's agent, but with an important difference. For them Hitler was an instrument used to mete out Divine Punishment for various "sins" committed by the Jewish people. See here, for example, R. Joel Teitelbaum (the Satmar Rebbe), *Va'Yoel Moshe*, 3 volumes (Brooklyn, 1959–1961) (in Hebrew); and R. Chaim Eleazar of Munkacs (the Munkacer Rebbe), *Divrey Torah* (Munkacs, 1929) (in Hebrew). This still puts God in a terrible light as far as I can see for what sin could Israel have committed to merit such a "punishment." (The Satmar Rebbe identified the "sin" as Zionism, others identify it as "Reform Judaism.") But it does transform the equation in certain basic ways and is certainly more in keeping with traditional Jewish thought, if also, in Teitelbaum's hands and others of his ilk, a perversion of it.

ELIEZER BERKOVITS'S POST-HOLOCAUST JEWISH THEODICY

There is much that is moving, even eloquent in Eliezer Berkovits's discussion of the implications of the Holocaust for Jewish faith. Two factors in particular shine through: his devotion to and great love for the People Israel—what tradition calls *ahavat yisroel* (love of Israel)—and his mastery of the world of traditional Jewish learning. The latter, in particular, separates him from most of the other philosophers and theologians who have publicly responded to the theological challenge posed by the Holocaust and the difference in tone and the depth of resonance as a consequence of this rabbinical erudition is striking. In addition, Berkovits's nonradical, more traditional response along the lines of classical theodicy has much intellectual force, certainly more than some of the novel alternatives. It also has the advantage of calling attention to important elements that need to be considered in any adequate post-Auschwitz theology, elements that other thinkers of a more radical persuasion ignore or underplay. Yet, in the final analysis, neither the rabbinical learning nor the dependence upon and reference to the great Western tradition of theodicy is fully adequate to the issue of the *Sho'ah*.[1]

I

The premise of Berkovits's position is his contention that the *Sho'ah* is not historically unique and therefore does not raise original issues for Jewish theology. This denial of uniqueness, and its concomitant conclusion that the Holocaust does not force Judaism into new and unprecedented reactions and transformations, is what distinguishes Berkovits from the other major theologians[2] who have wrestled with this issue. According to Berkovits, Auschwitz is unique in the magnitude of its horror but *not* in the dilemma it presents to religious faith. "From the point of view of the problem," he writes, "we have had innumerable Auschwitzs."[3] With this declaration we are provided with the basic axiom of Berkovits's entire response to the Holocaust. If Auschwitz is only the repetition of an ancient pattern then the entire nature of the challenge it poses is altered; or perhaps still more accurately, one might say that the magnitude of the Holocaust makes no difference theologically. For the theological conundrum, as Berkovits sees it, is the same whether one Jew or six million are slaughtered. Each raises the question: How could God permit it? How does this action square with God's providential presence and moral perfection?

While in absolute terms the horrors of the German death camps by far surpassed anything that preceded it, in terms of subjective experience the impact of the catastrophe on the major tragic occasions of Jewish history was no less intense than the impact of the horrors of our own experience. The problem of God's providential presence is always raised in relationship to man's subjective experience of His presence. The objective quantitative magnitude of the tragedy has little to do with it. It is for this reason that while the holocaust is unique in the objective magnitude of its inhumanity, it is not unique as a problem of faith resulting from Jewish historical experience. Indeed, one might say that the problem is as old as Judaism itself.[4]

This conclusion, however, cuts two ways. On the one hand, my own research[5] quite clearly confutes Berkovits's simple assimilation of the Holocaust to previous national catastrophes in the history of the Jewish people. Historically speaking, the *Sho'ah* does represent a *novum* in Jewish history, a *novum* whose essential distinctiveness is captured by the need for a new word to describe it— genocide.[6] Hence I disagree with Berkovits' historical analysis of the Holocaust as it presents itself as a theological datum. The Holocaust does require that we rethink (this does not mean change!) our traditional theological modalities, that we test our inherited "categories" against its novelty. Not to do so is not to recognize the full magnitude and character of the *Sho'ah;* it is to hide from a full frontal confrontation with Auschwitz.

Alternatively, this does not mean as Berkovits seems to feel, that on the basis of such a re-examination one will necessarily conclude that the tradition is inadequate or in need of revision. For the connection between historical uniqueness and the need for theological change in not self-evident. Thus, the proper procedure is to investigate the historical structure of the *Sho'ah* and then to ask, as a second step, what theological consequences, if any, flow from one's judgment regarding the historical events. Berkovits, however, does not follow this course. He fails to do the former because he knows in advance what he wants to protect vis à vis the latter. But this avoidance of the root issue leaves his conclusions even when correct, open to criticism, for it appears that they are cheaply won, predicated on a failure to face what happened to the Jewish people in this century. Contra Berkovits it needs to be recognized that the historical query concerning "uniqueness" is one thing, and the theological understanding of what this might mean, though related, is another. One's preconceived conclusions regarding theological matters should not dictate one's answers to historical questions.

II

One could pick at the edges of Berkovits' position at length but the center of his argument turns on his advocacy of a traditional "free will" theodicy. Therefore one can cut to the heart of the matter by turning directly to a scrutiny of his presentation of this defense. Taking his cue from the biblical doctrine of *hester panim* ("the Hiding Face of God"), Berkovits claims that God's hiddenness is required for man to be a moral creature. God's hiddenness brings into being the possibility for ethically valent human action, for by "absenting" Himself from history He creates the reality of human freedom which is necessary for moral behavior. For human good and human evil to be real possibilities God has to respect the decisions of mankind and be bound by them. Among the necessary corollaries of this ethical autonomy is that God has to abstain from reacting immediately to immoral deeds, and certainly from acting in advance to suppress them. But it is just here that the fundamental paradox emerges: for a moral humanity to exist freedom must exist, yet it is the nature of freedom that it is always open to the possibility of abuse.

The corollary of this, as Berkovits understands the situation, is that "while He [God] shows forbearance with the wicked, He must turn a deaf ear to the anguished cries of the violated."[7] Consequently, the paradoxical reality that flows from this Divine Circumstance is that humanity is impossible if God is strictly just, while if God is loving beyond the requirements of strict justice there will be human suffering and evil.

One may call it the divine dilemma that God's *erek apayim*, His patiently waiting countenance to some is, of necessity, identical with His *hester panim*, His hiding of the countenance, to others.[8]

Auschwitz is a paradigmatic instantiation of this truth.

What is one to say to this argument? The first thing is, I think, that in the face of the *Sho'ah* this millennial-old theodicy is as coherent as any of those, new or old, that has been proposed, even if not fully convincing. The second thing is that Berkovits reveals his mature theological intuition by opting for this gambit as his "response." The third is that the many dramatic, intensely moving, examples of Jewish heroism in the face of Nazism that Berkovits cites in his studies do help advance a case for the existence of evil as a possibility which must be allowed by God in order for there to be true human freedom; and also for the reality of evil as an ingredient in the generation of certain "goods," for example, love and compassion, fidelity and courage. Granting all this, however, two pressing difficulties remain. With regard to human autonomy and while recognizing its two-sidedness all the more because of Berkovits's discussion of Jewish heroism in the camps and elsewhere, an ancient enquiry reasserts itself: "Could not God, possessed of omniscience, omnipotence, and absolute goodness, have created a world in which there was human freedom but no evil?" And secondly, "Even if certain 'goods' are generated by overcoming or in response to evil, couldn't God either have allowed the production of these goods without so much evil, or, more radically still, wouldn't it be preferable if there were no such goods given the evil (and suffering) needed to produce them?" Let us examine each of these questions in turn.

The issue as to whether God could have created a world in which men always freely choose to do the good has been given a particularly tight formulation by J. L. Mackie. In a well-known article in *Mind* he commented:

I should query the assumption that second order evils are logically necessary accompaniments of freedom. I should ask this: if God has made men such that in their free choices they sometimes prefer what is good and sometimes what is evil, why could he not have made men such that they always freely choose the good? If there is no logical impossibility in a man's freely choosing the good on one, or on several, occasions, there cannot be a logical impossibility in his freely choosing the good on every occasion. God was not, then, faced with a choice between making innocent automata and making beings who, in acting freely, would sometimes go wrong: there was open to him the obviously better possibility of making beings who would act freely but always go right. Clearly, his failure to avail himself of this possibility is inconsistent with his being both omnipotent and wholly good.[9]

Many theologians and philosophers have replied to Mackie's challenge, the most cogent counter being Alvin Plantinga's. For our present purposes, I am prepared to admit his general conclusion, which I cite at length.

THE FREE WILL DEFENSE VINDICATED

Put formally, the Free Will Defender's project is to show that

(1) God is omniscient, omnipotent, and wholly good
is consistent with

(2) There is evil.

What we have seen (in a previous argument) is that

(3) It was not within God's power to create a world containing moral good but no moral evil

is possible and consistent with God's omnipotence and omniscience. But then it is clearly consistent with (1). So we can use it to show that (1) is consistent with (2). For consider

(1) God is omnipotent, omniscient, and wholly good
(3) It was not within God's power to create a world containing moral good without creating one containing moral evil

and

(4) God created a world containing moral good.

These propositions are evidently consistent—i.e., their conjunction is a possible proposition. But taken together they entail

(2) There is evil.

For (4) says that God created a world containing moral good; this together with (3) entails that He created one containing moral evil. But if it contains moral evil, then it contains evil. So (1), (3), and (4) are jointly consistent and entail (2); hence (1) is consistent with (2); hence set A is consistent. Remember: to serve in this argument (3) and (4) need not be known to be true, or likely on our evidence, or anything of the sort; they need only be consistent with (1). Since they are, there is no contradiction in set A; so the Free Will Defense appears to be successful.[10]

Berkovits provides nothing logically comparable to Plantinga's reasoning, but I am willing[11] to allow Plantinga's analysis to stand in defense of Berkovits's championing of the "free will" position, recognizing that Berkovits would endorse both Plantinga's procedure and conclusion.

However, this vindication pushes us another step and here I demur from Plantinga's and Berkovits's position. For the problem now becomes: "Could not God have created a world in which there was human freedom but *less* evil (as compared to no evil)?" Again Plantinga (and by inference Berkovits) answers "no" to this question[12] for, according to his analysis of the Free Will Defense, given genuine freedom, God cannot control the amount of evil in the world. But this "no" is not convincing, for the quantity of sheer gratuitous evil manifest during the Holocaust goes beyond anything that seems logically or metaphysically necessary for the existence of human freedom and beyond the bounds of "toleration" for an omnipotent, omniscient, and just God. One has only to recognize that given the belief in miracles, which Berkovits shares,[13] one miracle, even a "small" one, could have reduced some of the tragedy of the *Sho'ah* without cancelling the moral autonomy of the murderers. Thus it is logically conceivable and requires no great feat of the imagination to imagine a world in which there was less evil.

As to the second question, it increasingly seems to me that it would have been preferable, morally preferable, to have a world in which "evil" did not exist, at least not in the magnitude witnessed during the *Sho'ah*, even if this meant doing without certain heroic moral attributes or accomplishments. That is to say, for example, though feeding and caring for the sick or hungry is a great virtue it would be far better if there were no sickness or hunger and hence no need for such care. The price is just too high. This is true even for the much exalted value of freedom itself. For we recognize the need to limit freedom where evil consequences are concerned, for example, we allow convicts to be incarcerated so that they will not cause further evil, we limit the right to cry "fire" in a crowded theatre, we curtail the right to molest children, and the list goes on. That is to say, we recognize, as these examples indicate, that freedom is properly subordinated to the prevention of suffering and other undesirable consequences. In respect of the *Sho'ah* such a limitation on freedom would have clearly been preferable to the results of freedom run riot, whatever limited instances of good the evil of Auschwitz engendered.

At this juncture some might want to object that my refutation of the Free Will thesis and its attendant call to limit freedom in the face of the Death Camps has not confronted the truly radical implication of my own contention regarding autonomy and its restraints. This is because to suggest controlling Free Will would not mean only overriding the rights of individuals to do certain particular things, as in the examples just given, but also overcoming the basis for freedom altogether. This clarification rightly recognizes that Free Will is not equivalent to liberty of action being more fundamental and at the same time a necessary condition of morality. In reply, however, it seems cogent to advance the reservations introduced above, if with modification. Better to introduce limits, even limits on that freedom of the will requisite to moral choice, than to allow Auschwitz. Here it is salient to recognize that Free Will is not, despite a widespread tendency to so understand it, all of one piece. One can limit Free Will in certain aspects, that is with respect, for example, to specific types of circumstances, just as one constrains action in particular ways. For example, a person can have a phobia about X which does not impair his unrestrained power of decision in regard to Y. Such a case reveals that the call to limit Free Will does not necessarily mean its total elimination but rather its powerful curtailment by, in our present context, a Divine Intelligence under conditions such as those that reigned supreme during the Holocaust. Consider, too, that God could have created a humankind that, while possessing Free Will, nonetheless also had a proportionately stronger inclination for the Good and a correspondingly weaker inclination to evil. He could also have endowed us with a greater capacity for moral education. Neither of these alterations in the scheme of things would have obviated the reality of Free Will though they would have appreciably improved humankind's moral record, perhaps even to the point of significantly reducing the moral evil done to the innocent by a Hitler.

Much of my disquiet with this whole line of defense lies in my somewhat different mode of reasoning about morality. In contradistinction to the habitual way of conceiving the problem of freedom's relation to morality, that is, no volitional autonomy no morality, one can and should turn the issue around and argue that if one has no, or smaller amounts of, evil to contend with, Free Will is less necessary because those virtues generated through its exercise, e.g., concern, love, etc., are not required in the same way. Macrocosmically, morality is a good not least because it helps us make our way in an evil world; eliminate or lessen the evil we encounter and the need for morality declines correspondingly.

From this angle of vision it becomes clear that the Jobian thesis usually developed in this connection, that is, the view that suffering creates higher goods and in addition trains one's character, requires another look. It has been asserted that:

The value-judgment that is implicitly being invoked here [in the Jobian thesis] is that one who has attained to goodness by meeting and eventually mastering temptations, and thus by rightly making responsible choices in concrete situations, is good in a richer and more valuable sense than would be one created *ab initio* in a state either of innocence or of virtue. In the former case, which is that of the actual moral achievements of mankind, the individual's goodness has within it the strength of temptations overcome, a stability based upon an accumulation of right choices, and a positive and responsible character that comes from the investment of costly personal effort.[14]

This contention is not without interest as long as Job stays alive. But as a response to Auschwitz Job is not the right model for unlike Job of old the Jews in the death camps were not protected from destruction. Therefore, the Jobian defense of tragedy, of suffering as the occasion for growth and overcoming, has little relevance to the Holocaust.

The incremental conception is simply too naive, too optimistic. It emphasizes the positive value of evil as an aid to the growth and manifestation of goodness, but it ignores altogether the more telling fact that wickedness of the magnitude and quality unloosed by Nazism not only, or even primarily, increased our opportunities to display courage and love but even more—and essentially—destroyed forever such possibilities for six million Jews, including the all too many Jewish children whose youthful potential was never to be realized. Still more, the logic of this incremental thesis leads, if followed to its end, to an untenable conclusion. It suggests that good comes from, or in response to, evil, and that without evil there would be no heroism, no forgiveness, no love. The greater the malevolence the greater the heroism. The significance of Berkovits's constant invocation of instances of truly extraordinary moral heroism in the face of Nazi brutality turns on this contention. Yet the irony here is this: if an increase in the diabolic is defended by recourse to the greater good it produces, i.e., more heroism is generated by Nazism than by a lesser plague, then the proper goal to be desired is a still greater Holocaust (God forbid) which would, by this line of reasoning, make for still more courage and fortitude. Thus if killing six million Jews caused a corresponding amount and kind of virtue, killing twelve million will produce, say, twice the amount and a still higher quality of moral nobility. But surely this is all wrong. The recognition of its absurdity forces us to acknowledge the inherent deficiency of the incremental thesis as exposed by the reality of the *Sho'ah*.

There is still another moral objection to this incremental line of reasoning. One can contend that selfless love or forgiveness, or faith and fortitude, are unavailable without that corruption to which they are a reaction, but even if one makes this case, which in itself is not an easy case to make, it does not justify the evil per se. To argue the contrary is to suggest that the Nazis were helping Jews be virtuous, and were assisting Jews in their ethical development. Likewise, is it morally acceptable to suggest that Jewish children should suffer disease and starvation, death by fire and by gas, so that others might have an opportunity to care for or comfort them? As to the children themselves, what sort of standard is involved? What moral improvement was achieved when Janus Korczak's orphans, and countless others like them, died in the ghettos and crematoriums? Their deaths contradicted that very freedom and moral autonomy that are at the base of the "Free-Will" defense. God's goodness is also impugned in the face of such barbarities. He, so the position contends, gave mankind freedom because He is gracious and compassionate, loving and concerned—but here His care for Nazis and for their freedom meant a total absence of solicitude for their victims.

III

The "free will" position becomes still more difficult to maintain when employed as a Jewish theodicy. The reason for this increase in complexity is the necessity of relating the "free will" defense, as drawn in a more general philosophical way, with the God-idea of Judaism, i.e., the God of the Bible who is known to perform miracles in the face of overwhelming evil. Thus, it is not only a case of trying to decipher the world God set out to create in some theologically neutral sense but rather of understanding Jewishly why, given the exaggeratedly high cost of human freedom, God did not once again, as He had in the past, step into the flow of events and say "enough."

Berkovits is theologian enough to be aware that this is a serious objection and he tries to meet it:

Man can only exist because God renounces the use of his power on him. This, of course, means that God cannot be present in history through manifest material power. Such presence would destroy history. History is the arena for human responsibility and its product. When God intervenes in the affairs of men by physical might as, for instance, in the story of Exodus, we speak of a miracle. But the miracle is outside of history; in it history is at a standstill.[15]

But this is an evasion, for the critical challenge simply needs to be rephrased: why, if God performed a miracle and entered history at the Exodus, did He show such great self-restraint at Auschwitz? Wasn't Auschwitz far worse than Egypt, Pharoah far more humane than Hitler? Given that history did not end because of the miracles connected with the Exodus why would a miracle at Auschwitz now "destroy history?" Given Berkovits's biblically rooted faith this line of defense is not plausible.

Then, too, if God did not intervene in the Sho'ah, even if one might still thereafter be able to defend His power by recourse to a Berkovits-like argument regarding Divine self-restraint, what happens in such an equation to God's love? Is a God who allows such total freedom, who does not act when human freedom takes on an apocalyptic character of frenzied sadism, still worthy of respect and admiration? Of being worshipped? In aid of the "Free Will" defense Berkovits might be able to argue with cogency that "God cannot as a rule intervene whenever man's use of freedom displeases him."[16] But surely Auschwitz is not a mere "whenever;" it was a time that demanded just such interference.

IV

A further corollary of Berkovits's teaching is also worthy of mention. He recognizes that for all its logical suggestiveness the "Free Will" counter is not convincing.[17] Thus he feels compelled to add:

all this does not exonerate God for all the suffering of the innocent in history . . . there must be a dimension beyond history in which all suffering finds its redemption through God. This is essential to the faith of a Jew.[18]

This well-worked proposal is tantamount to a confession that human freedom extorts too high a price; thus the traditional "crutch" of an afterlife is introduced without any justification to bolster the classical metaphysical and moral structure under pressure.

This other-worldly appeal, however, is less than adequate to the task. Besides the elemental difficulty of the absence of any legitimation being given for this belief in the Hereafter, the fact is that what this suggestion translates into is an appeal for compensation. God wrongs mankind and then tries to make up to it for the unjustifiable evil done. But just as we reject such compensatory actions as lesser goods in human relations, how much more so does it seem unworthy of God. It is this moral disquiet that makes the conclusion of the Book of Job so unsatisfactory and which makes it more unsatisfactory still in the case of victims of the *Sho'ah*. God may "redeem" the suffering but it seems morally preferable that there should be no evil to redeem. Berkovits is right; this argument does not exonerate God.

There is also a deep irony in all this relating to the heart of the "free will" thesis. If there is a Heaven where one resides in bliss without the tensions and difficulties caused by freedom of choice, why did God not create such an Earth without freedom of choice and all of its terrible consequences? That is, if Heaven is better than earth with or without human autonomy why wouldn't a similarly structured earth, one in which Auschwitz would be impossible, be likewise good? And if so, the whole "free will" defense falls.[19]

V

Berkovits's theodicy rests on the thesis, integral to the "free will" position, that God's "absence" is the real proof of His "presence;"[20] that in His "self-control" we are "introduced to a concept of Divine mightiness that consists in self-restraint."[21] Thus, God's

presence in history must be sensed as hiddenness and His hiddenness must be read as the sign of His presence. God reveals His
power in the world by curbing His power so that man, too, might
be powerful.

That man may be, God must absent himself; that man may not perish in
the tragic absurdity of his own making, God must remain present. The
God of history must be absent and present concurrently. He hides his presence. He is present without being indubitably manifest; he is absent without being hopelessly inaccessible. Thus, many find him even in his "absence"; many miss him even in his presence. Because of the necessity of
his absence, there is the "Hiding of the Face" and suffering of the innocent; because of the necessity of his presence, evil will not ultimately
triumph; because of it, there is hope for man.[22]

This suggestion is neither original, nor without its fascination.
However, in light of the Holocaust it becomes necessary not only
to advocate this thesis but also to ask anew, how and when is God's
restraint of His omnipotence to be interpreted differently from His
lack of omnipotence? How in *fact* and in *logic* do we know there
really is an omnipotent God who is exercising self-restraint—at a
staggering human cost—rather than allowing this evidence of "self-
restraint" to be construed as data for either the nonexistence of
God or at least God's nonomnipotence as advocated, for example,
by a Platonic-Whiteheadian "process" theism?

If the non-presence, non-power, non-involvement of God proves
His presence, His power and His involvement, then by a similar
demonstration we could "prove" all sorts of entities and attributes
into existence.

There is, however, another aspect to Berkovits's presentation of
this theme that is more intriguing and which in fairness must be
taken up. For he does not merely refer to God's "hiddenness" and
"presence" in the abstract but rather gives these notions flesh by
tying them to a seminal, traditional, Jewish theological claim relating to God's involvement with the Jewish people. According to
this account the true and enduring witness to God's ultimate power
over history is the Jewish people. In Israel's history we see both
God's "presence" and "hiddenness." The continued existence of
Israel despite its long record of suffering—"if God is powerless,

God's people will be powerless"[23]—is the greatest single testimony, the most impressive proof that God is active in history despite his "hiddenness."[24] The Nazis, according to Berkovits, recognized this, and their slaughter of Jews was an attempt to slaughter the God of history. They intuited, even as Israel sometimes fails to, that God's reality in our world is necessarily linked to the fate of the Jewish people.

That the Jewish people has withstood all the barbarous attacks upon it, that it has been able to maintain itself in the midst of deadly enemies, bespeaks the presence of another kind of power, invisibly playing its part in the history of men. The survival of the Jew, his capacity for revival after catastrophes such as had eliminated mighty nations and empires, indicate the mysterious intrusion of a spiritual dimension into the history of man. The more radical the rebellion against the world of the spirit, the greater the hatred against the Jew. The Final Solution was not only to eliminate the Jewish people from history, but through the destruction of Israel it was meant to finalize the defeat of that mysterious spiritual force against which the rebellion was directed. The Nazis were quite correct in believing that if they did not succeed in the elimination of the "Jewish influence" upon world history, they would also fail in their plans for world conquest. No matter what they said in their official propaganda, they sensed the mysterious nature of that influence, the presence of a hiding God in history.[25]

As such, Jewish existence per se stands as prophetic testimony against the moral degeneracy of men and nations: it is a mocking proclamation in the face of all human idolatry and witnesses to the final judgment of history by a moral God.

For myself, I find much in this analysis suggestive for, like Berkovits, I too wonder at Israel's continued existence. Jewish history defies all theories, usually being the "exception" that cracks open all generalizations put forward as historical laws. This much I feel able to say with philosophical probity. To say more than this is to speak in the language of faith which, even if one shares it, or rather, precisely because one shares it, one can only witness to and not argue about. I see no way of convincing anyone that Israel is God's people, or that, as Judah Halevi described it over a thousand years ago, Israel is the "heart" of the nations. Thus, while I, like Berkovits, find Israel's very survival[26] *the* strongest evidence both of its transhistorical vocation and the existence of Divine Providence, this affirmation once offered cannot be demonstrated.

The same judgment applies to the two additional themes of importance educed by Berkovits from God's "powerlessness." The first being that the Jewish people manifest a qualitatively different type of historical existence than other nations, that Israel lives in "faith history," the nations in "power history."[27] The second being that the state of Israel reveals God's "saving Presence."

For the Jew, for whom Jewish history neither begins with Auschwitz nor ends with it, Jewish survival through the ages and the ingathering of the exiles into the land of their fathers after the Holocaust proclaim God's holy presence at the very heart of his inscrutable hiddenness. We recognized in it the hand of divine providence because it was exactly what, after the Holocaust, the Jewish people needed in order to survive. Broken and shattered in spirit even more than in body, we could not have been able to continue on our Jewish way through history without some vindication of our faith that the "Guardian of Israel neither slumbers nor sleeps." The state of Israel came at a moment in history when nothing else could have saved Israel from extinction through hopelessness. It is our lifeline to the future.[28]

Of course, Berkovits recognizes that this "lifeline" does not answer the agonizing questions of theodicy with logical decisiveness[29] but he believes it gives hope to those who would share in such hope that they will be answered in God's future redemptive acts.

I accept Berkovits' contention that each of these themes reveals an authentic insight—yet each can be embraced, if embraced at all, only with one's critical eyes wide open. By this I mean that both of these are metaphysical claims that depend primarily on "faith" and are not subject—nor has Berkovits produced any evidence to the contrary—to either logical demonstration or verification of any stringent sort. This is not to say that they are false; indeed I do not see how one could adjudicate whether they are "false" in a simple true/false sense. Rather, it is to indicate what type of propositions these are. Once it is recognized what sort of metaphysical statements they are one also comes to recognize that one could not produce any argument or data that would disconfirm them, nor can I imagine under what circumstances Berkovits would reject any or all of them. Contrariwise, it is not evident how Berkovits, having stated his theological credo, could do anything to persuade a sceptic. Certainly he could not charge the sceptic with any logical error or self-contradiction for failing to give his consent to any of these claims, nor could the sceptic be indicted for holding fast to what is demonstrably an inadequate metaphysical structure per se, for neither of these corollaries necessarily flow from rejecting Berkovits's claims. Conversely, the sceptic cannot charge Berkovits with logical or metaphysical error—his propositions are well-formed, intelligible, and Jewishly fertile, even if they are not confirmable.[30] This "stalemate" is, of course, if properly understood, to Berkovits's credit in that he has formulated several important theological theses that, even if "faith" statements, are suggestive in a Jewish theological context after Auschwitz. One can claim neither more nor less for them.

CONCLUSION

Of the major thinkers who have had the courage to deal with the "meaning" and reality of the *Sho'ah*, Eliezer Berkovits has articulated the most conservative and traditional position. This conservatism has paid important dividends. For despite the lacunae in his work, he has given one of the most theologically and Jewishly convincing "responses" of all those who have taken part in the discussion. Thus, while his views cannot be accepted as the final word on the matter, he has pointed us in the direction of important truths that need further reflection and development.

NOTES

1. Berkovits has written three books that deal with the Holocaust. They are: *Faith After the Holocaust* (New York, 1973); *Crisis and Faith* (New York, 1976); and *With God in Hell* (New York, 1979). The first of these sets out his overall theological position vis à vis the challenge posed by Auschwitz in its most extended form. Our remarks, while drawing on all three works, will thus concentrate on this work.

2. Ignaz Maybaum, the German-English theologian, also denied the uniqueness of the Holocaust. For the details of his position see his *The*

Face of God After Auschwitz (Amsterdam, 1965). For a discussion of his position see the essays entitled "Jewish Faith After the Holocaust: Four Responses," and "The Crucifixion of the Jews: Ignaz Maybaum's Theology of the Holocaust" in this collection.

3. *Faith After the Holocaust*, p. 90 (hereafter referred to as *Faith*).

4. Ibid., p. 90. This is also Jacob Neusner's conclusion in his "The Implications of the Holocaust" in the *Journal of Religion* Vol. 53, No. 3 (1973), pp. 293–308, and now reprinted in his *Stranger at Home* (Chicago, 1981), pp. 65–81.

5. See my forthcoming volume *The Uniqueness of the Holocaust* to be published by Harvard University Press next year and my essay "The 'Unique' Intentionality of the Holocaust" in *Modern Judaism* Vol. 1, No. 2 (Sept. 1981), pp. 161–183.

6. The first use of the word to describe the *Sho'ah* is usually credited to Raphael Lemkin, *Axis Rule in Occupied Europe* (Washington, D.C., 1944), pp. 79–95.

7. *Faith*, p. 106.

8. Ibid., p. 107.

9. J.L. Mackie, "Evil and Omnipotence," originally published in *Mind* Vol. XLIV, No. 254 (1955). Reprinted in L. Urban and D. Walton (eds.), *The Power of God* (New York, 1978), pp. 17–31. This quote is from p. 27. A similar position has also been advanced by A. Flew, "Divine Omnipotence and Human Freedom" in *New Essays in Philosophical Theology* (New York, 1955), ch. 8. A counter argument has been provided by, among others, Ninian Smart, "Omnipotence, Evil and Supermen" in *Philosophy* Vol. 36, No. 137 (1961). Smart's position has in turn been criticized by H.J. McCloskey, *God and Evil* (The Hague, 1974), pp. 103–105.

10. A. Plantinga, *God, Freedom and Evil* (New York, 1974), pp. 54–55. I have revised the numbering of the various propositions in this argument. Plantinga's numbering being different because part of a larger thesis, e.g., my number (2) is his (3), my (3) his (35), my (4) his (36).

11. I have technical philosophical reservations regarding Plantinga's argument. Given our present concern, however, we need not take them up here. For the sorts of issues that are relevant to a discussion of Plantinga's views see: J.E. Tomberlin and F. McGuiness, "God, Evil and the Free Will Defense," in *Religious Studies*, Vol. 13 (1977), pp. 455–475, which is critical of Plantinga's position. This paper has, in turn, been replied to by Del Ratzsch, "Tomberlin and McGuiness on Plantinga's Free Will Defense," *International Journal for the Philosophy of Religion*, Vol. 12, No. 4 (1981), pp. 75–95; and by Robert Burch, "The Defense of Plenitude against the Problem of Evil," *International Journal for the Philosphy of Religion*, Vol. 12, No. 1 (1981), pp. 29–38. And idem., "Plantinga and Leibniz's Lapse," *Analysis*, Vol. 39, No. 1 (January, 1979), pp. 24–29. This should be taken

as only a sample of the extensive secondary literature generated by Plantinga's important, if not fully convincing, work.

12. Ibid., pp. 55 ff.

13. On this issue of miracles and its relevance see the argument below.

14. J. Hick, *Evil and the God of Love* (London, 1966), pp. 255–256. A similar argument is advanced by Gordon Kaufman in his *God The Problem* (Cambridge, 1972), pp. 171–200. Berkovits is explicitly sensitive to the disanalogy involved in the Job metaphor per se (see *Faith*, pp. 67–70), though he uses the same argument in a more general way.

15. *Faith*, p. 109. Berkovits's preference for the term "miracle" is both correct and misleading. That is, we can grant the term and the correctness of its usage but this does not solve anything. The issue merely becomes why God did not perform a miracle.

16. Ibid., p. 105.

17. In his most recent book, *With God in Hell*, Berkovits elaborates on this weakness at some length. In addition to the appeal to a "Hereafter" he refers to three other Jewish "responses" to buttress the "free will" argument. They are: the *Akedah*, the "Exile of the Shechinah," and the "Suffering Servant" motif. I shall not discuss Berkovits's treatment of these themes they do not seem to me to advance appreciably the logic of the argument. Readers are referred to *With God in Hell*, pp. 124 ff., for Berkovits's presentation.

18. *Faith*, p. 136. This, of course, is a standard proposal often made in the past by theists. See, e.g., Kant's moral theism as developed in a number of his works, and C.A. Campbell's *On Selfhood and Godhood* (London, 1959), among many other instances of this defense.

19. The possible counterargument some might advance, that Heaven is good because it is earned by good deeds, would not be relevant in the case I present. This because the causal mechanism whereby one gets to heaven does not account for, and is a different matter from, Heaven's intrinsic goodness. Heaven is good per se not because this is where righteous souls ascend to. Rather, righteous souls ascend to heaven because it is good.

20. This position has also been adopted by Yitzchak Greenberg through, in all likelihood, Berkovits's influence.

21. *Faith*, p. 109.

22. *Faith*, p. 107.

23. *Faith*, p. 124.

24. See ibid., pp. 109 ff. for Berkovits's views on Israel in history.

25. *With God in Hell*, p. 83.

26. Having said this I should also say that I disagree with Berkovits's further remarks on the interaction of Jewish vs. non-Jewish history in *Faith*, pp. 111–112.

27. *Faith*, pp. 111–112.

28. Ibid., p. 134. On the meaning of the rebirth of the state of Israel see also ibid, pp. 144–169; and *Crisis*, pp. 159 ff.

29. Ibid., pp. 136 ff.

30. The Positivists' erroneous conflation of meaning and verification must be recognized and avoided. Again, Karl Popper's views on "disconfirmation" and the nature of scientific propositions must not be *mis*applied, as Popper himself acknowledges, to metaphysical propositions.

THE "UNIQUE" INTENTIONALITY OF THE HOLOCAUST

Killing Jews is not a new phenomenon in history. For more than two thousand years Jews have died because of and for their faith, either out of choice or someone else's necessity. Thus, the Nazi onslaught stands at the end of a long series of such tragedies and, indeed, would have been unthinkable without this prehistory. Yet, in order to begin to try and understand[1] what happened specifically to the Jews of twentieth-century Europe, both in the context of modern and world history as well as in the context of Jewish history, we have to push beyond the recognition of an old pattern of Jew-hatred resulting in murder and ask whether there is anything different about the Nazi experience. In answering this question one category, which I should like to concentrate on in this paper, becomes of prime significance: intention. Even more pointedly, what emerges as central is the specifically genocidal intent of the Nazis. That is to say, Nazism was an organized human and societal event that had as an integral part of its purposive behavior the total eradication of world Jewry. In so doing was Nazism "unique?" Indeed, does the very "uniqueness" of Nazism lie in its genocidal intent against the Jewish people?

In trying to frame a reply to this question one must distinguish two senses of genocide and hence two forms of the "argument from genocidal intent." The first form, (A), understands genocide as the intent to destroy the national, religious, or ethnic identity of a group. The second form, (B), understands genocide to be the intent to destroy physically all persons who identify with and are identified by a given national, religious, or ethnic identity. That is, not allowing for the dissociation of an "identity" and an individual's nature, and thus denying the possibilities of conversion, assimilation, etc.

I should like to begin our substantive review with a brief discussion of the Nazi persecution in light of the first (A) sense of genocide, i.e., relating to "identity," before moving on to analyze the second (B) sense of the term, which I take to be the more important and historically relevant. In the terms proposed by (A), Hitler's activity, which aimed at destroying Judaism, was clearly *not* unique. The world historical record is replete with examples of attempts to eliminate "identities" of various sorts, ranging from the resettlement policy of the Assyrians[2] which created the Lost Tribes of Israel, to the resettlement and cultural mandates of Stalin.[3] Again, the forced conversion of pagans, under Islamic law[4] is a relevant counterexample, as was the Hellenizing campaign of Antiochus IV and the earlier Hellenizing activity of Alexander the Great.

Likewise, Jewish history provides previous instances of attempts to eliminate Judaism in ways that could be described as cultural genocide. In this respect a first fertile comparison is the behavior of the already mentioned Antiochus IV (King of Syria 175–164 B.C.E.).[5] Antiochus's aim was the elimination of Judaism as a cohesive spiritual reality for it was due to and through their religion that the Jewish people remained separate from their neighbors. Thus, rooting out Judaism would pave the way for the adoption of a newly acquired, shared, Hellenistic identity, which in turn would facilitate the integration of Antiochus's Jewish subjects into his pagan empire. Though Antiochus was not averse to killing Jews to gain his ends, as the Antiochene persecutions described in the *Book of Maccabees* indicate, his aim was not the physical depopulation of the Jewish people in Palestine but rather a change in their allegiances in keeping with his political ambitions. It thus becomes relevant to note the most crucial distinction between Antiochus and Hitler, namely, that Antiochus sought to overcome Judaism, not Jews, while Hitler, with his pseudo-scientific racist principles, sought to make the world *Judenrein* by the physical elimination of "racial" Jews, that is all concrete individual Jewish human beings.

Thus, Antiochus's ultimate *intention* is unlike Hitler's. It is, of course, comparable in that had Antiochus and the Hellenizers had their way there would have been no Judaism and hence no Jews at the end of the second century B.C.E., while had Hitler's ambitions been realized, there would have been no Jews after the 1940s. However, the situations in the end are fundamentally disanalogous in that Antiochus would have permitted, indeed the whole intent of his policy was to guarantee, that the children and grandchildren of the Maccabees would be alive and well as Hellenes. Hitler, by contrast, wanted to assure that there were no surviving children and grandchildren of the Jewish people, whatever these "survivors" might believe and however they might "identify" themselves, e.g., as Christians or Germans, etc.

Jewish history provides still other instances of oppression worth considering in this context, for example, the severe Roman anti-Jewish legislation under Hadrian[6] in the second century C.E. Like Antiochus, Hadrian was not averse to physical oppression and murder, as witnessed in the martyrdom of Rabbi Akiva and the death of the "Ten Martyrs" recorded in the *Machzor.*[7] However, one would not want to push this example too far, as the situation by the second century C.E. was different from that in the second century B.C.E. and Hadrian, while no philo-Semite, does not seem to have undertaken the sort of universal anti-Jewish measures throughout the Roman Empire, even against Judaism as an ideology, that could truly be called genocidal without contradiction. Additional occasions of interest that could be adduced[8] are Czarist and Soviet policy in the nineteenth and twentieth centuries, which again appear to be basically aimed at eliminating Jewish self-consciousness while retaining the future generations of Jewish genealogical productivity. The anti-Jewish policies of Christendom and their negative effects also are prime candidates in this context and will be discussed in some detail below.

We need not pursue this review further, adding example upon example, for the relevant point at issue is already established beyond doubt, namely, that the Nazi program of genocide, if understood as a war against a self-conscious Jewish identity, is neither unique in Jewish historical terms nor world historical ones.

With this conclusion in hand we now must turn to the more pertinent sense of genocide which I have called (B) above. I summarize it here again as the "intent to destroy physically all persons who identify with and are identified by a given particular national, religious, or ethnic identity, without exception." Here we engage the Nazi program at its most degenerate as well as at its most radical, for the Nazis not only preached genocide and not only sought to eliminate Judaism from history but they also undertook, with all too convincing an empirical reality, to erase Jews from history as well. Has this practical Nazi program of destruction any parallels? As a student of both Jewish and world history one's initial reaction is to say "Yes, such precedents exist;" after all, Hitler was not the first cruel madman on history's stage nor the first truly major anti-Semite in the long experience of the Jewish people. But such an initial, almost instinctive, response has to be *very* carefully considered and reconsidered. In the process of such rethinking this initial "yes" begins to give way to doubt and then finally, as we shall argue in detail below, to denial. Let me now rehearse the reasons that led to this negative conclusion, first considering the relevant Jewish evidence and then turning to consider the more extensive non-Jewish record.

Finding true parallels with regard to genocidal intent from out of the Jewish past is not the easy task it would appear. The Antiochene and Hadrianic presecutions we have already cited above are worth consideration but, as already shown, are not parallel. Perhaps the actions of Haman count for something for he, after all, got as far as building gallows; but Purim indicates his failure: Haman killed not a single Jew. Again, the Pharoahs of old killed many Jews, but genocide was not their aim. Dead slaves were of no use in building pyramids and sphinxes, treasure houses and self-aggrandizing monumental sculptures. The Roman destruction of 66–70 C.E., culminating in the destruction of the Second Temple, and the Babylonian conquest of 586 B.C.E., were political acts of conquest, not genocidal wars. The Babylonian policy of deportation and the subsequent growth of a Jewish community in Babylonia is proof positive of this, while the Roman armies of 70 C.E. were led by Philo of Alexandria's now-pagan nephew, incontrovertible evidence of Rome's lack of an over-all anti-Jewish genocidal policy. Again, the peace agreed with Rabbi Yohannan ben Zakkai and his colleagues is witness to Rome's desire to pacify, not destroy either Jews or Judaism—as long as it was on Rome's political terms. The same is true, of course, for the horrible events surrounding the Bar Kochba revolt in 132–135 C.E. Muslim policy, in its classical lineaments, forbade destruction of either Jews or Judaism—they were too valuable as tax payers—and thus, for example, the Almohade[9] persecutions in twelfth-century Spain and North Africa must be seen as both local and temporary aberrations that do not fit the tightly drawn accounting of genocide here being employed. And, in addition, the Almohades allowed for conversion. Likewise, the expulsion from Spain in 1492 was surely terrible as the contemporary Jewish witnesses movingly testify, but allowing Jews to convert as evidenced by the large-scale "New Christian" ("Marrano") phenomenon on the one hand, and the final expulsion rather than murder of 1492, indicate anything but a genocidal scheme.

There are, of course, still further numerous cases of the large-scale oppression of Jewish communities, e.g., during the Egyptian pogrom of 37–38 C.E., which Philo describes in such detail in his *Legatio ad Gaius* and after which the Emperor Claudius,[10] in his rebuke to the Alexandrians, used the interesting phrase "a war against the Jews."[11] There is also the mass annihilation of European Jewry during the Crusades;[12] the massacres of the fourteenth century;[13] the Chmielnitzki devastation of the seventeenth century;[14] and the Polish and Russian pogroms of the last four centuries.[15] Yet in none of these instances does the intention of the murderer(s) appear to be technically genocidal in character. For example, Count Plehve, Czar Nicholas I's minister in charge of the "Jewish question" in Russia, stated his policy in these terms: "one-third [of the Jews] will be killed; one-third will convert; one-third will emigrate."[16] Allowing for one-third to convert and the final one-third to emigrate rules this out as an example of genocidal intent as we are now concerned to use the term.

The various and all too common instances of Christian persecution, both in themselves and as the "background" to modern anti-Semitism, require a further comment. The transcendentalizing metaphysics of Nazi anti-Semitism has at least one major direct predecessor, namely, the "Christian theology of the Jew."[17] From its formative period on, and especially in Paul, the Gospel of John and the Patristic writings, the Church has seen the Jew not only as evil but also as the manifestation of Evil, of evil incarnate, that is, using the phrase from the Gospel of John, as "spawn of the Devil," (8:44). Though the most extreme presentation of this theology is to be found in the diatribes of Marcion whose views were considered heretical because of his total separation of the so-called "Old" and "New" Testaments, his gnostic representation of the Jew and Judaism instantiated already-existent trends that had become deeply rooted in Christian tradition and that in turn would become part and parcel of later Christian theology. With the "gentilization" of the Church by the second century, the Jewish and Christian communities split apart completely and whatever restraints had exercised Jewish Christians in the first Christian century now disappeared.[18] "Them" and "Us," "We" and "They," became the ever hardening categories of the anti-Jewish Christian idiom. This rhetoric of "them" became allied to an ever more hostile diabolization of the Jew, which read into the historical tension between Church and Synagogue the metacosmic typological struggle of God and the Devil.

The historically located paradigm of this titanic gnostic conflict was considered to be the encounter of Jesus and the Jews, i.e., in the charge of deicide laid on the Jewish people: "His blood be upon us and our children" (Matthew 27:25). Or as Acts 7:51–52 recounts the tale:

You stiff-necked people, uncircumcised in heart and ears, you always resist the Holy Spirit. As your fathers did, so do you. Which of the prophets did not your fathers persecute? And they killed those who announced beforehand the coming of the Righteous One, whom you have now betrayed and murdered.

While I Thessalonians assures us: "God's wrath has come upon them [the Jews] at last" (I Thess. 2:16). It is, however, the Gospel of John (8:43–47) which provides the *locus classicus*:

Why do you not understand what I say? It is because you cannot hear my word. You are of your father, the devil, and your will is to do your father's desires. He was a murderer from the beginning, and has nothing to do with the truth, because there is no truth in him . . . The reason you do not hear them [the words of God] is because you are not of God.

One hears this text beneath Julius Streicher's remarks to a group of schoolchildren:

Boys and girls, even if they say that the Jews were once the chosen people, do not believe it, but believe us when we say that the Jews are not a chosen people . . . [it is against the Jews] whom Christ had already fought, the greatest anti-Semite of all time.[19]

The powerful, nearly monolithic, medieval Christian image of the Jew brings this *adversus Judaeos* theology to its fullness. The negative depiction of the Jew in medieval theology, as well as in more popular cultural forms such as the Passion play and the other genres of literature and art, cannot be overestimated. The "blood libel" and the libel of "the desecration of the Host" could only be taken seriously, with all their ill consequences, in a context which thoroughly subscribed to the doctrine of the nonhumanity, the contended diabolical nature of the Jew. Luther's [20] rabid anti-Semitic ravings, which rival in venom any previous anti-Jewish teachings, are merely repeats of this already millennial-old theme. Nazism only "secularized" this inherited metaphysical lie.

The consequences of this negative myth, however, work themselves out in two forms I shall label "short-term" programs and "long-term" programs. "Short-term" programs would be those that parallel the Nazi translation of this ideology into immediate action; "long-term" programs would be those that envision the resolution of this cosmic encounter only at some future, usually messianic, time. Though there are examples of Christian behavior that present themselves for consideration as possible instances of "short-term" programs, for example, the Crusader massacre of Jews in the twelfth and thirteenth centuries in the name of the crusading spirit against infidels, there is nothing really similar in the history of Jewish–Christian (or Jewish–Muslim) relations that is collateral with the short-term behavior of the Nazis. In fact, in the final accounting there is actually an essential asymmetry in regard to the short-term morality, and intentionality, of Nazis and Christians, despite a considerable symmetry of metaphysical postulates vis à vis the Jew, exclusive of course of the racial principle. Official papal policy almost always and everywhere held[21] that Jews were *not* to be murdered or physically abused (allowing here for a different sense of the meaning of "physical abuse" than is common today). The historical record (except, alas, for the Nazi period) indicates that when Jews were in physical danger the papacy usually, though not always with success, attempted to mitigate the imminent threat to Jewish life. Likewise, though the popes viewed Judaism as of no spiritual value, or rather and even worse, conceived it as a positively evil regimen, the ideology, as well as the practical rule of the Church, stemming from the precedent set by late Roman law, was that Judaism was not to be forcibly suppressed *in toto*, even though the Church certainly possessed the means for doing so. The theological doctrine of the "mystery of Israel" here accompanied the negative stereotypical image, mitigating its more terrible—genocidal—short-term possibilities. Nor must we forget the most telling practical difference between Christian and Nazi anti-Semitism. The former, based on religious belief, always in theory and almost always in practice allowed for conversion and hence escape from one's "Jewishness" and one's Jewish fate; the latter, based on putatively immutable laws of race, allowed no such escape. Under Nazism there was no conversion out of Judaism—biology was destiny.

What has just been argued with regard to Christianity is also true, with suitable modifications, for Islam. The Muslim "theology of the Jew," stemming from Mohammed's respect for the "People of the Book," meant that short-term destruction of all Jews (and Christians and Parsees), i.e., genocide, was not in theory or practice a goal of Muslim society.

The import of this rather long excursus on traditional Christian anti-Semitism is that one must come to recognize two distinctions. The first is between the "official" theology of Christendom vis à vis the Jews and Judaism on the one hand, and the specific homicidal action of a particular Christian or Christian group, in a given historical incident, on the other—though of course the two are not totally separable. The second is between Nazism's official program of genocidal destruction of Jews and the Church's program which, while looking forward to a "Judaism-less" future, or more exactly to the conversion of the Jews, officially protested against the physical spoilation of Jewish life as well as of Judaism, despite its extremely pejorative evaluation of the latter. Though Peter the Venerable and Bodhan Chmielnitzki, and their greater and lesser predecessors and heirs, certainly applauded the killing of Jews, to impute to them a genocidal intent goes far beyond what is warranted by the evidence. One can understand the temptation to make this attribution, but one also recognizes that it is based on reading history backwards from our perspective after Auschwitz.

In light of this preliminary discussion it begins to appear that the stronger form of the "argument from genocidal intention" is substantive evidence in favor of viewing the Nazi experience as at least "unique" *in the context of Jewish history*. However, the particularity of this conclusion must be underscored, for up until this point all we have attempted to investigate is the Jewish historical context without enquiring into possible parallels in world history. We must now pursue our enquiries into this wider domain, for there exists at least prima facie evidence that the Nazi experience is not without precedent there.

Before plunging, however, into the detailed analysis of the data provided by world history one admonishment with regard to the correct use of the notion of genocide is required as a prolegomena to all further considerations. Assyrian, Babylonian, Persian, Hellenistic, and Roman policy was cruel, but not every cruelty is genocide. Hun, Muslim, Mogul, Imperial Japanese, Chinese (e.g., Genghis Khan), and Conquistador policy was tyrannical, but not every tyranny is genocide. I do not consider the black slave trade genocidal, nor again do I consider the white man's policy against the Indians to have been genocidal (I will argue these cases below in detail). Both were inhuman, exploitative acts by one group against another, but not every exploitative act can go by the name of genocide. The forced emigration of one million Russians to Siberia in the nineteenth century was political oppression of murderous intent, but not all political oppression, nor even all murderous intent, is genocide. The mass Russian emigration between 1917 and 1922 as a consequence of the German invasion, the Russian Revolution and the great famine, which affected up to fifteen million people, is horror untold—but not every national tragedy is genocide. This cautionary comment is not made in order to attempt to reduce the degree of suffering each of these calamitous events involved. Even less is it to claim for one's own collective national catastrophe some pride of place, for there is no pride in any of this, only anguish and human misery, pain recorded and still more untold. Rather, it is introduced only in order to keep our substantive concern, genocidal intent, squarely in focus.[22]

With this methodological preamble in place we can proceed to our concrete review of the matter. On the logical principle that one counterexample would suffice to present difficulties for a strong claim to uniqueness, I cite, first, for consideration the two most telling counterexamples known to me. They are: the persecution of the Armenians in World War I by the Turks and the destruction of the Indians of North and South America by the European colonizers and their heirs.

Let us begin with the latter case, that of the American Indians.[23] On numerical and demographic grounds their tragedy at least parallels that of the Jews. In terms of absolute quantities the specifics of the case depends on what demographic base one begins with, but one conclusion is certain, and in this all the different demographic claims agree, many millions of Indians were killed.[24] On the further statistical issue of proportion of population killed, i.e., "X percent out of a total population of Y," the argument is again complicated by the demographic base. Yet, all "models" suggest at least a forty percent death rate, which equals or surpasses the Jewish experience in World War II. Six million out of fifteen million Jews were killed, forty percent. Thus, *if numbers alone constitute uniqueness then the Jewish experience under Hitler was not unique.* Quantity and proportion, however, while highly relevant, are not sufficient by themselves to establish a judgment with regard to uniqueness *pro* or *contra*. Therefore, let us now go on to examine the issue of "intention" in the white man's murder of the

Indian. That the European, and then his early American heir, was a racist (at least in the loose pre–nineteenth-century sense) who held the Indian to be a savage of the very worst sort cannot be doubted. The Puritans looked upon the Indian as a creation of the Devil put in their midst to try them, while Bishop Juan de Quevedo of Tierra Ferme (Venezuela) saw them as slaves by nature, in accordance with the natural rights theory of Aristotle that some individuals and some peoples are inferior by nature.[25] These views of the Indians as an inferior people have persisted over time and have been used to justify all manner of evil. But exactly what was intended by such stigmatization? Three goals are constantly operative: (1) missionizing; (2) economic exploitation; and (3) territorial expansion and control.

With regard to (1), missionizing, the policy iterated by Pope Clement VI in his bull *Intra Arcana* is paradigmatic:

We trust that, as long as you [Emperor Charles V] are on earth, you will compel and with all zeal cause the barbarian nations [i.e., Indians] to come to the knowledge of God, the maker and founder of all things, not only by edicts and admonitions, but also by force and arms, if needful, in order that their souls may partake of the heavenly kingdom.[26]

Economic exploitation (2) was from the start perhaps the strongest incentive. It was economic gain that first encouraged the Spanish and Portuguese expeditions that discovered the New World and it was the desire for an ever greater share of the New World's riches that provided the motive for much of the future expansion. The Spanish hunters after gold were followed by French, Dutch, and English adventurers who sought to prosper from America's other natural resources: beaver and other furs; the coats of the buffalo and bear; the natural and agricultural food supply, especially tobacco. Insofar as the quest for these goods brought the white conqueror cum trader into contact with the native populations of North and South America, the relationship was inevitably one-sided and unfair. From the earliest bead dispensers and dealers in wampum belts to the more sophisticated rum and whiskey traders of the later Indian trading stations, the Indian was always cheated. Indeed, in the eyes of the white man he was there to be cheated.

Economic exploitation has thus always been one of the pillars of white-Indian relations.

The territorial motive (3) is perhaps best summed up in the statement of Theodore Roosevelt: "The settler and the pioneer have at bottom had justice on their side; this great continent could not have been kept as nothing but a game preserve for squalid savages."[27] This rough American idiom, however, is only a late version of an expansionist doctrine that European intellectuals and adventurers, from the highest to the lowest class, had used to dispossess the Indians. Sir Thomas More, for example, had argued in *Utopia:* "When any people holdeth a piece of ground void and vacant to no good or profitable use: keeping others from the use and possession of it, which, notwithstanding, by the law of nature, ought thereof to be nourished and relieved."[28] The various treaties that reduced Indian land claims, and the reservation system that was instituted to both protect and disenfranchise Indians, are all an extension of this older theory of land dispossession. Since Justice John Marshall's anti-Indian decision in 1823 in *Johnson and Graham's Lessee vs. McIntosh* the courts and successive state and federal governments have held that they have the legal right to dispossess Indians of ancestral lands pretty much at will. Thus, in 1861 a federal treaty with the Arapahoe and Cheyenne included this asymmetrical provision, reflective of moral and political realities: "The President with the assent of Congress [has the power] to modify or change any provisions of former treaties . . . to whatever extent he may judge to be necessary and expedient for their [sic] best interest."[29] In this way the 138 million acres of Indian landholdings in 1887 were reduced to 48 million by 1934.[30] Though the situation has begun to change for the better, in at least small ways, in the last decade, these alterations only highlight the terrible record of the previous four centuries.

Having noted these facts, what conclusion is to be reached? Though the suffering and devastation have been enormous, and the numerical destruction as great, the Indian experience seems finally to be noncomparable to the case of the Jews in Nazi Europe. Though greed in various forms led to abuses of the most sordid kind (for example, passing on to Indians blankets infected with diseases the

Indians were known to have no immunity to, resulting in hundreds of thousands of deaths), there does not appear to be any developed ideology of genocide systematically and continuously at work in the policy of white America. The logic of reservations itself argues against genocidal intent and suggests instead a program roughly, I stress the "roughly," comparable to the pre-modern European pattern of Jewish ghettoization. Or again, in terms of Nazism, it is a practice that would parallel in various ways the Nazi policy of ghettoization carried on between 1939–1942. Though the death rate in the Nazi-created ghettos was extraordinarily high and some estimates, which I have no reason to doubt, suggest that in twenty-five years there would have been no Jews left living under those ghetto conditions, nevertheless the state of ghettoization is not equivalent to genocide. This is so for many reasons, not the least of which is that it can end or be reversed, while death in Auschwitz was a totally "final solution." The *increase* in American Indian demography in the last five decades argues strongly against a consistent policy of genocidal intent as well as indicating the reversibility inherent in a reservation schema. Thus, in conclusion, while the Indian experience was devastating, it does not constitute a genocide, nor is there evidence that genocide was intended.

The case of the destruction of the Armenian population of Turkey in 1915–1916 is an even more striking instance of an event possibly comparable to the Jewish fate under Nazism. First, it too came under and was made possible by wartime conditions, when death and murder take on a different social reality and the normally forbidden becomes permissible. The Nazi plans for the "Final Solution" came into being and were put into practice only after a full-scale war existed. Furthermore, this military situation limited Jewish resettlement and emigration options and made the unspeakable a reality. Likewise, Behaettin Shakir is quoted as reminding the three-man Turkish Executive Committee charged with a solution to the "Armenian question" that: "The suitability of this exceptional turn of events [i.e., the war] must be exploited to the fullest. Such an opportunity does not present itself every day."[31] Secondly, though the mathematics are not comparable in terms of absolute numerical value, they may be comparable in proportional terms. For, of an Armenian population of two and one-half million, between five hundred thousand and one million were killed. Thirdly, foreshadowing the policy of Jewish resettlement in Poland, there was a widespread population shift, especially of the Armenian populations of Cilicia and western Anatolia, into the deserts of Mesopotamia. Fourth, there are the cultural ingredients: the Armenians were Christian, the Turks Moslem, just as the Nazis were Christian and the Jews, Jews; the Armenians were a non-homogeneous element in a society seeking homogenization (i.e., Turkification), and seeking it much more vigorously under the new forces at work in Turkish society than under the Ottoman Pasha. This same factor of "unassimilability" was an active factor in creating the European situation of the Jew, especially in modern times, with the growing centralization of European nation states. While liberal Europeans would argue that Jews were assimilable, if at the price of their Judaism, Hitler would declare them fundamentally and forever unassimilable; hence the need for death camps as the only viable solution to the *Judenfrage*. Furthermore, the Armenians, like the Jews, were perhaps somewhat higher achievers in cultural and economic matters, though this issue is very complex, usually being misapplied and misunderstood in attempts to account for anti-Semitism.

There is also the much-repeated charge of disloyalty in both cases, which has a special potency in a war situation. Interestingly, both the Turks in World War I and the Nazis in World War II used the "Russian threat" with great success; both Jews and Armenians were charged with being Russian fifth-columnists. The communiquè of May 26, 1915 by Talaat Pasha, Minister of the Interior, to the Grand Visier, is instructive:

Because some of the Armenians who are living near the war zones have obstructed the activities of the Imperial Ottoman Army, which has been entrusted with defending the frontiers against the country's enemies; because they impede the movements of provisions and troops; because they have made common cause with the enemy; and especially because they have attacked the military forces within the country, the innocent population, and the Ottoman cities and towns, killing and plundering; and because they have even dared to supply the enemy navy with provisions and to reveal the location of our fortified places to them; and because it is necessary that rebellious elements of this kind should be removed from the area of military activities and that the villages which are the bases and shelter for these rebels should be vacated, certain measures are being adopted, among which is the deportation of the Armenians from. . . .[32]

This charge of Armenian treason and revolution in a time of war is in fact the major element in Turkish self-justification against critics of their anti-Armenian actions. It is of interest here to note that Ahmed Rustem, one-time Turkish ambassador to the U.S., wrote in 1918 in defense of the Armenian massacres that Turkish actions were done out of military necessity and thus Turkey was above reproach since war suspends the ordinary moral laws of humanity.[33]

Even the details of how a large portion of the murderous activities were carried out indicate points of comparability between the Jewish and Armenian situation: deportation of large populations under brutal conditions; special squads of Turkish ex-convicts were established to murder Armenians in the same way as *Einsatzgruppen* were set up to murder Jews in Eastern Europe; the murderers were not to spare old or young, women or children, infirm or ill. Thus, with all these parallelisms in view, there exist grounds for thinking that the comparison between the two national tragedies is strong, perhaps being close to exact.

Yet one must be cautious in moving to this conclusion, for there are also important aspects of noncomparability that must still be considered. One of these is intention—our present focus of concentration. Now one can find extreme statements on this subject in the record of the Turkish deliberations on the matter. For example, at the 1915 meeting of the Central Board of the Ittihad ve Terakke party, at which the initial plans to destroy the Armenian population of Turkey were discussed, a Dr. Nazim, the Executive Secretary of the Young Turk Central Board, is reported to have addressed the assembled audience as follows:

Why did we have this Revolution? What was our objective? Was it to depose Abdul Hamid's men so that we could fill their positions? . . . I became your brother and comrade in order to vitalize Turkism. I want to see the Turk, and only the Turk, living on this land; I want to see him become his own lord and master on this land. Let the non-Turkish elements be completely destroyed—no matter what their nationality and religion are. This country must be purged of all non-Turk elements. . . . Pitiful will be our lot, if a total liquidation, a total extermination, is not consummated.[34]

And such sentiments are not without parallel in the relevant historical materials and, as the record indicates, this plan of Turkification was put into action with all its horror. Let there be no evasion: the Armenian people have been barbarously treated in this, and previous, centuries by the ruling classes of the Turkish state.

Yet it is precisely here, and intending no diminution of the tragic quality or the enormous proportions of the Armenian massacres, that we must demur from fully comparing it to the Nazi destruction of European Jewry. The reason is both simple and complex: the motivation of the killers *was* different. It might seem on first perusal that the citation quoted above, with its talk of "total liquidation" and "total extermination of all non-Turkish elements," and the many other statements of similar tone and content to be found in the Turkish sources of the 1915–1916 period, would indicate a conclusion opposite to mine: that the intention of the Turks vis à vis the Armenians *is* parallel and comparable to the intention of the Nazis vis à vis the Jews. But this is not the case. The intentionality behind Turkish inhumanity was essentially nationalist in character. It was a most primitive jingoism that, due to the exigencies of war without and revolution and collapse of the Ottoman Empire from within, permitted the extension of this nationalism to its "logical" yet inhuman limits, i.e., the attempted destruction of *all* non-Turkish elements, most especially and specifically the Armenians. The anti-Armenian crusade was a political crusade. Of course, mixed in the brew were other elements of a passionate hate: a loathing of Christians, or rather, a dislike of all non-Muslims; xenophobia; greed and jealousy; fear and desire. But it was essentially nationalist politics that was at the heart of the campaign of the Young Turks.

As a consequence, the anti-Armenianism of the Turks takes on a different character than the anti-Semitism of the Nazis. For ex-

ample, anti-Armenianism is not expressed in the language of metaphysical evil, i.e., a Manichean dualism of good vs. evil in which
the Turks are the manifestation of the Good and the Armenians
the Devil Incarnate, as was the case of Nazi theorizing about their
struggle with the Jews.[35] Again, the anti-Armenian crusade was not
explicated and advanced in terms of a pseudo-scientific racism that,
in itself, was yet another kind of nonsensical metaphysics. Instead,
the rationale almost universally cited by Turks as a justification of
their behavior is political, e.g., the Armenians are revolutionaries,
Russian spies, fifth-columnists against the Turkish people's revolution, and the like. This tack is already the determinative rationale of the pre-war Armenian massacres, such as that at Adana in
April 1909, and it reappears in full and multifarious force in 1915–
1916. Such legitimations as reference to the claimed Armenian revolution at Van in 1915[36] is an outstanding example of this mentality. Or again, consider the "defense" of the massacres offered at
the 1916 Party Congress:

As soon as the order of mobilization was issued, Turkish Armenians crossed
the frontiers on their way to Egypt, Bulgaria, Rumania, and Russia, and
joined the Russian army or bands of Armenian irregulars. The various revolutionary organizations temporarily dropped their differences and held a
general meeting. They decided to start disorders, massacres, and acts of
incendiarism behind the front in case Turkey entered the War, and to in-
duce Armenian soldiers to desert with their weapons. Bands composed of
such deserters were to menace the lines of communication of the Turkish
army.[37]

This outlook is symptomatic of the Turkish position. To them the
Armenians were first and foremost a political threat.

Secondly, to map the political topography of the situation adequately sufficient weight has to be given to the internal political
activity of the Armenians in light of the various Reforms promised
or introduced by the Young Turks. Over against the extreme nationalism of the Young Turks, with their desire to centralize and
homogenize the Turkish State, the Armenians sought, on the basis
of the new constitution, to expand their ethnic rights and to assert
their ethnic individuality. As long ago as 1918 Herbert Gibbons

accurately suggested that: "the Constitution, hailed by the Armenians as the beginning of their political emancipation, became almost immediately—and *inevitably*—their death warrant."[38] More particularly, the authority of the Turkish regime was, or at least felt itself to be, threatened by Armenian schemes of political independence for those provinces in which they were concentrated. That is, the Armenians were perceived as a profound internal force seeking the dismemberment of the Turkish national entity both politically and geographically. R. Hovannisian has documented this struggle for political independence[39] and we need have no doubt as to its impact on the thinking of the Turkish leadership during 1915 and subsequently, as it had earlier in the massacres of 1894 and 1909. As late as 1959 the Turkish Press attache in Washington explained the cause of the 1915 massacres as due to the fact that: "The non-Turkish elements in the Empire continued to press for separation and sought the support of the major powers. They were apprehensive that a real reformation might delay the division of the spoils."[40] Having just made a revolution, the Young Turks were not about to indulge ambitions of Armenian autonomy which appeared to undermine their whole effort.

The importance of recognizing this political configuration lies in the fact that it provides the proper and necessary frame of reference for analyzing and evaluating Turkish behavior. Within such a context Turkish actions, abhorrent and inexcusable as they were, can be recognized as having been motivated by an intense nationalist interest which drove them to attempt what one might call territorial political extermination rather than universal genocide. That is to say, the Young Turks had no argument against Armenians per se, or put more appropriately, against "Armenianism," for example, the Armenian population of Russia or the U.S. Rather it objected to Armenians on Turkish soil, seeing them as a vital source of the betrayal of Turkish destiny and integrity. Fanatic nationalism is the causal agent *par excellence* in this matter. Count Wolff-Metternich's description of the Turkish cruelty against the Armenians in a telegram sent on June 30, 1916 to Reich Chancellor von Bethmann Hollweg underscores this dimension of the tragedy:

There is not much more to gain any longer from the Armenians. The mob is therefore preparing itself for the moment when Greece, forced by the Entente, must turn against Turkey and her allies. Massacres of far greater scope will occur then. The victims are more numerous and the booty more enticing. Greekdom constitutes the cultural element of Turkey and it will be destroyed like the Armenian segment if outside influences will not put a stop to it. "Turkification" means to expel or kill everything non-Turkish, to destroy, and to forcefully acquire others properties. In this, and in the parroting of French freedom phrases, lies at present the famous rebirth of Turkey."[41]

Wolff-Metternich correctly identifies the essence of the practical policy as "Turkification," the elimination of all non-Turkish groups that stood in the way of complete homogenization of the state. The annihilation of the Armenian population was a corollary of this political goal.

An additional and related element that is important to consider in attempting to reach a judgment in regard to the Armenian situation is the policy of deportation at the center of Turkish activity. It goes without elaboration that in the course of these deportations many were killed and in this it parallels, and even considerably exceeds, the forced movement of Jews to the Polish ghettos in 1940–1941. That is to say, though the journey was meant only as the means to an end, for the hundreds of thousands who died en route it became an end in itself. The cruelty of these forced marches and evacuations is not to be underestimated. Yet the principle of deportation logically allowed for continued life at the journey's end and indeed several hundred thousand Armenians survived such journeys. Had the Turks intended a total Armenian genocide the deportations, as well as their "destinations," would have been different. By contrast, the intention of the Nazis led to Auschwitz, from which there was no escape. Moreover, the Jews sent to Auschwitz came from all quarters of Europe—Germany, Poland, Russia, Amsterdam, France, Rhodes, Greece, and more. Their death was the consequence of a perverse metaphysical schema, not a nationalist one, though an inflated, distorted, nationalism was part of the totality of the metaphysics. The intention of Hitler was to rule over a world that was *Judenrein*; the intention of the Turks was to rule over a Turkey, and only over a Turkey, that was *Armenian-rein*, and in this difference of scale lies the difference of quality. Here, too, a strikingly curious aspect of the Armenian massacres is also to be noted: the Armenians of Constantinople and other large cities were not severely persecuted during this period. Thus, not only is the Armenian annihilation, for all its enormity and tragedy, not strictly comparable to the Jewish experience in terms of sheer magnitude, but it also differs fundamentally in kind.

At this juncture, to fill out our analysis in broader historical terms, two additional contemporary examples often referred to as genocides may be worth considering. They are the destruction of the Ibo in Nigeria and the continuing destruction of indigenous Indian tribes in South America. Without rushing to judgment on these matters, I am tentatively prepared to argue for the noncomparability of these events with the Nazi experience on various grounds, not the least of which is the criterion of intention. Neither the Nigerian destruction of the Ibo, nor the widespread destruction of South American Indians in various South American countries, seem to have intended what the Nazis intended for the Jews.

With regard to the Indians of Brazil,[42] as well as other Latin countries, the extermination of the indigenous Indian population is directly related to economic exploitation of the countries' vast territories. In this respect, though with the means of more modern technology, the local and federal governments of South America pursued (and continue to pursue) a policy not too radically different from that pioneered by the U.S. in the eighteenth and nineteenth centuries against its Indian population. Thus, between 1900 and 1957 the native Indian population of Brazil was reduced by eighty percent, i.e., from one million to 200,000, by disease and other forms of induced destruction.[43] The great abuses cited in the so-called 1967 *Figueiredo Report* prepared by General Jader Figueiredo, Attorney General of Brazil, document this policy only too well. Yet at the same time all the evidence indicates that the destruction of the Indian population is primarily an indirect tangent of Brazilian economic policy, though mixed with racial and other factors in various ways, rather than being a policy of genocide per se.

Likewise, the destruction of the Ibo in Nigeria[44] and the savagery in Rwanda and Burundi in the 1960s and 1970s are the consequence of economic, social and political causes generated against a background of historic tribal antipathies rather that the result of a narrowly genocidal motivation. The Nigerian civil war was a struggle over the amputation of Nigeria caused in the first instance by tribal differences that led to inequalities. The mutual devastations in Burundi and Rwanda,[45] though carried out along tribal lines, were essentially power plays. The Hutu massacre of 20,000 Tutsi and the deportation of 200,000 other Tutsi from Rwanda in 1963–1964 was a direct result of the territory's past and present governmental realities, i.e., Hutu control of power after traditional Tutsi rule. Conversely, the same pattern applies to the Tutsi extermination of the majority Hutu in Burundi, where up to 200,000 Hutu have been murdered in the last two decades, with the largest devastation coming in 1972. In this instance the minority Tutsi, who represent only ten to fifteen percent of the population, are seeking to retain dominance over the remaining eighty-five percent of the population that is Hutu. Consequently, terrible as these persecutions have been, it is proper to argue that they are different in character, i.e., essentially political, from the Nazi destruction of European Jewry.

In the midst of this analytic review one last tragedy, that provides a crucial "test" of our entire thesis, must be explored. I refer to the treatment of the Gypsies under the Nazis, which is often cited in the literature as a direct, if not exact, duplicate of the Jewish reality under the same regime. However, though there are many parallelisms of time, place, and experience, the suggested analogy breaks down for reasons I would like to sketch briefly. An initial, though not overwhelming, difficulty with this comparison is the absolute demography,[46] i.e., the number of Gypsies was a fraction of the Jewish population. More important still, however, is the fact that while it is certainly true that many Gypsies were brutally mistreated by the Nazis and sent to their deaths in various ways, including the death camps, the overall Nazi policy toward the Gypsies was different in kind from that toward the Jews. That is to say, the evidence reveals no total, consistent, Nazi program of genocidal intent leveled at the Gypsy population. It is correct that from the first the Nazis classified Gypsies as non-Aryans and sought to associate them with Jews racially, culturally, and historically, but at the same time, the Nazi policy toward the Gypsies was predicated not only on the overridingly salient criteria of race, though this was a significant factor in the Gypsy debate, but also on the notion of "asocials." Thus, in the majority of concentration camps, though forming a distinct subgroup, the Gypsies wore the black patches indicative of asocials.[47] The 1937 *Law Against Crime* specifically linked Gypsies with beggars, tramps, prostitutes, et al. who show "antisocial behavior."[48] On the other hand, the racial factor was operative, as the first specifically anti-Gypsy ordinance of late 1938 indicated: "Experience gained in the fight against the Gypsy menace and the knowledge derived from race-biological research have shown that the proper method of attacking the Gypsy problem seems to be to treat it as a matter of race."[49] However, the translation of these two differing analyses and motivations into a practical policy resulted in a mixed situation. Many Gypsies were rounded up and sent off to die at Auschwitz and elsewhere from 1943 on. Yet, surprisingly, we also find Himmler personally intervening on behalf of the Sinti and Halleri Gypsy tribes, both of which, he argued, were to be classed as "German Gypsies" and thus spared, as compared to "foreign Gypsies" who were to be deported. Other Gypsy groups were also exempted from deportation including "Rom Gypsies and part Gypsies still in the army or who have been released with decorations or wounded."[50] All this does not mean that the Nazis did not ruthlessly destroy many Gypsies. They did. Rather, it indicates, however, that they did not destroy them "without exception" and with the same cold, unwavering, single-minded genocidal intent that was the essence of their anti-Jewish program. The Nazis did not ontologize the Gypsy into their metahistoric antithesis, nor did they make the elimination of all Gypsies from history a primal part of either their historic "moral" mission or their metaphysical "mythos," (which, of course, were ultimately one). Thus, for example, in the spring of 1943, while the *Einsatzgruppen* and SS were killing *all* Jews encountered in Eastern Europe, the German authorities ordered that hereafter Gypsies who were of a "non-migratory" status, who could prove a two-year period of residence in the locale in which they were identified, were to be exempt from the murderous activities of these same *Einsatzgruppen*.[51]

The paradoxical features of Nazi policy are reflected in the grim statistics of this tale: of an estimated 936,000 Gypsies in Nazi occupied territory, 219,700 are estimated to have been killed, i.e., twenty-three and one-half percent, as compared to a nearly seventy percent death rate for Jews under Nazi control. Given the captiveness of both civil populations, as well as the further lack of anything comparable among the Gypsies to the worldwide Jewish support system, which at least attempted, though clearly without much success, to aid their co-religionists in Nazi-occupied Europe, the statistics tell the tale. Had Hitler's maniacal imagination centered on the Gypsies as it did on the Jews their collective fate would have been far different. That Jews died at three times (and nearly four times in Eastern Europe) the rate of Gypsies is a consequence of the different intentionality that propelled the slaughter of these two peoples by their common murderer.

Other tragic events sometimes cited in this context are all much further afield. For example, the destruction of the Kurds is not comparable.[52] Though severely oppressed first by Turks in the 1920s and 1930s and more recently by the Iraquis and Iranians, the Kurdish atrocities are essentially political, i.e., the consequence of Kurdish desire for self-determination. Article 63 of the Peace Treaty ending World War I pointed toward a Kurdish state in what had been part of the Ottoman Empire. However, when Atatürk, the new ruler of Turkey, came to power in November 1922 he ignored this commitment. All subsequent Kurdish hostilities are the result. The Vietnamese and Cambodian tragedies[53] were the result of ideological struggle not genocidal warfare. Basque troubles in Spain and the bloody civil-racial war in the Sudan between Arabs and blacks, with the Arabs on top, and the reverse in Chad with the blacks on top, likewise are essentially power struggles rather than genocidal conflicts.[54] That is, what the various groups are fighting over is domination of the state, not racial ideology, though race is certainly a contributing factor, but in a non-genocidal way, i.e., the resolution of every racial problem is not necessarily thought to lie in genocidal actions nor even less are they actually resolved in this manner.

CONCLUSION

Much additional research has to be done to draw a complete phenomenological description of each of the historical episodes we have quite briefly reviewed, as well as the many we have not had the space to comment upon. Yet, while recognizing this need for further analysis, I believe enough evidence has been marshalled to suggest that in and through the category of "intention" we can begin to perceive at least one seminal individuating characteristic of the Holocaust.[55]

NOTES

1. I reject the view that the Holocaust cannot be talked about or analyzed as self-defeating if not self-contradictory.

2. The Assyrian policy of forced emigration was begun by the great Assyrian conquerer Tiglath-Pileser III (745–727). From the time of his campaigns against the northern Kingdom, beginning in 734/732, forced deportation of Jews began. The Bible reports these events in II Kings, chs. 17 and 18, I Chronicles, ch. 5, and Ezra ch. 4. On these events see W. Rosenau's discussion in *Hebrew Union College Annual* Vol. I (1925); H. May's article in *Biblical Archeologist*, Vol. 6 (1943) and H. Torczyner's discussion in *Journal of Near Eastern Studies*, Vol. 6 (1947). A more recent contribution of interest to this issue is M. Cogan, *Imperialism and Religion: Assyria, Judah and Israel in the Eighth and Seventh Centuries* (Missoula, Montana, 1974).

3. Stalin's reign of terror is analyzed in Robert Conquest, *The Great Terror* (New York, 1968); Roy Medvedev's *Let History Judge* (New York, 1971); and J. Carmichael's *Stalin's Masterpiece* (New York, 1976). Z. Brezezinski has given us an excellent study of Soviet totalitarianism in general theoretical terms in his *The Permanent Purge* (Cambridge, 1956). See p. 26 for an interesting comparison of the fate of the Kulaks, the Jews under Hitler, and those who were purged by Stalin. On the particulars of the Kulak problem and its solution under Stalin see Medvedev, op. cit.

4. Islamic law requires the forced conversion of all people who are not "people of the book;" Jews (and Christians and Parsees) were, as "people of the book," not forcibly converted except under exceptional conditions.

On this issue see S. Baron, *Social and Religious History of the Jews* (New York, 1952), Vol. 3, ch. 18. E. Ashtor also discusses the aspects of conversion to Islam in a competent way in his *The Jews of Moslem Spain* (Philadelphia, 1974), Vol. I, ch. 1. The *Encyclopedia of Islam* article on *dhimmis* is also of considerable interest, as is A. S. Tritton's *The Caliphs and their Non-Muslim Subjects* (London, 1970).

5. On the Antiochene persecutions see E. Bickermann, *From Ezra to the Last of the Maccabees* (New York, 1962); also V. Tcherikover, *Hellenistic Civilization and the Jews* (Philadelphia, 1959). For a general discussion of the Hellenistic context and the Maccabean rebellion see also Volume 6 of the *World History of the Jewish People: The Hellenistic Age* (New Brunswick, New Jersey, 1972), A. Schalit, ed.; also M. Morkholm, *Antiochus IV of Syria* (Copenhagen, 1966).

6. On the Hadrianic persecutions see Mary Smallwood, *Jews under Roman Rule* (Leiden, 1972). See also Y. Yeivin, *Bar Kochba* (Jerusalem, 1946, in Hebrew) for a discussion of these persecutions as a cause of the Bar Kochba revolt in 132 C.E. J. Juster's *Les Juifs dans l'empire Romain* remains the classic study of Jews in the Roman world. G. Alon's *Toledot Ha Yehudin*, 2 vols. (Tel Aviv, 1953–1957) is an excellent review of the post-70 C.E. situation (in Hebrew).

7. See the *Machzor* (prayerbook) for Yom Kippur (Day of Atonement). See also S. Krauss, "The Martyrs" in *HaShiloah*, Vol. 46 (1925, in Hebrew); also Saul Leiberman, "The Martyrs of Caesarea" in *Annuaire de l'Institut de philologie et d'Histoire Orientales et Slavs*, Tome VII (New York, 1939–1944), pp. 395–446.

8. On Czarist and Soviet anti-Jewish policies see Salo Baron, *The Russian Jew under Tsars and Soviets* (New York, 1964); L. Kochan, *The Jews in Soviet Russia since 1917* (Oxford, 1972); Z. Gitelman, *Jewish Nationality and Soviet Politics* (Princeton, 1972), which also contains a full bibliography of works for further study.

9. The Almohades came to power in North Africa in the twelfth century. Their negative impact on Jewish life is discussed in S. Baron, op. cit., vol. 3. On the persecution of Maimonides and his generation see also Baron, vol. 3, note 7, pp. 290–292.

10. Claudius' letter is to be found in the *Corpus Papyrorum Judaicarum* vol. II, V. Tcherikover and A. Fuks, eds. (Cambridge, 1960), pp. 42–43. The editors supply an introductory discussion of the issues raised by this letter and a bibliography of the large body of secondary literature it has spawned, pp. 36–38. For additional sources and bibliography on classical anti-Semitism see M. Stern, *Greek and Latin Authors on Jews and Judaism* 2 Vols. (Jerusalem, 1974 and 1980).

11. The phrase is the title of Lucy Dawidowicz's well-known work on the Nazi destruction of European Jewry, *The War Against the Jews* (New York, 1975).

12. On the Crusader massacres of medieval Jewry see L. Poliakov, *The History of Antisemitism* vol. I (London, 1965), chs. 4 and 5; E. H. Flannery also discusses the matter from a sympathetic Christian viewpoint in ch. 5 of his *The Anguish of the Jews* (New York, 1965). For a broader treatment see Salo Baron, op. cit., vol. 4, ch. 21. See also S. Runciman's *A History of the Crusades* (Madison, 1969). The Hebrew University medievalist, Joshua Prawer, has written an interesting account of the Crusades from a more "Middle Eastern" viewpoint. See his *The World of the Crusaders* (New York, 1973). Of prime importance for those who read no Hebrew is the recent English publication of the medieval Hebrew accounts of the Crusades, *The Jews and the Crusaders: The Hebrew Chronicles*, trans. by S. Eidelberg (Madison, 1977).

13. The terrible destruction of European Jewry in the fourteenth century as a result of anti-Semitic charges arising from the Black Death and other incidents is discussed in Leon Poliakov, op. cit., ch. 36. See also the diffuse though all-encompassing portrayal of S. Baron, op. cit., vols. 9–11. S. Dubnow also has a brief discussion of the Black Death in vol. III, pp. 255–261, of his *History of the Jews* (New Brunswick, 1969).

14. On B. Chmielnitzki and his Cossack hordes see S. Dubnow, *History of the Jews in Russia and Poland* 3 vols. (Philadelphia, 1916); chapter 9 of B. D. Weinryb's *The Jews of Poland* (Philadelphia, 1973) is the most up-to-date survey of the problem in English. The historic background of Jewish settlement in Poland prior to 1648 is given in Pt. III of B. Weinryb, op. cit., and brilliantly sketched in S. Baron's *Social and Religious History of the Jews*, vol. 16, (New York, 1976). The demographic size and implications of this event are analyzed by Weinryb, op. cit., pp. 192–194. His figures suggest a Polish Jewish population of between 170,000 and 480,000 of which I would estimate, given all the uncertainties of the sources, that one-sixth were killed.

15. See the sources given in note 8 above.

16. Plehve's policy is deciphered in S. Baron, *The Russian Jew under Tsars and Soviets* (New York, 1964) pp. 56 ff.

17. The Christian theology of the Jew is treated in R. Reuther, *Faith and Fratricide* (New York, 1974); Jules Isaac, *The Teaching of Contempt* (New York, 1974); F. Littell, *The Crucifixion of the Jews* (New York, 1975); F. G. Bratton, *The Crime of Christendom* (Boston, 1969). See also Alan Davies's interesting study, *Anti-Semitism and the Christian Mind* (New York, 1969). On a similar theme see the indictment of recent Christian theology in Charlotte Klein, *Anti-Judaism in Christian Theology* (Philadelphia, 1978). The classic study of James Parkes, *The Conflict of Church and Synagogue* (London, 1934) is also still a must for the historical background.

18. The historical processes at work in the "gentilization" of the Church are reviewed by M. Simon, *Verus Israel* (Paris, 1948); J. Parkes, op. cit.; see

also the standard histories of the church by A. Harnack and the classic study of Jews in the Roman Empire by J. Juster, op. cit. See on the widening rift between Jew and Christian Douglas Hare, *The Theme of Jewish Persecution of Christians in the Gospel of Matthew* (Cambridge, 1967); James Parkes, op. cit.; Hans Joachim Schoeps, *Jewish Christianity* (Philadelphia, 1964); Peter Richardson, *Israel in the Apostolic Church* (Cambridge, 1969); A. D. Momigliano, ed., *The Conflict between Paganism and Christianity in the Fourth Century* (London, 1963).

19. Cited by R. Hilberg, *The Destruction of the European Jews* (Chicago, 1961), p. 12.

20. Luther's virulent anti-Semitism is discussed thoroughly by S. Baron, op. cit., vol. 13. See also R. Lewin's old though still valuable study, *Luthers Stellung zu den Juden* (Berlin, 1911) and the more recent works by H. H. Ben Sassoon, "The Reformation in Contemporary Jewish Eyes," in *Proceedings of the Israel Academy of Sciences and Humanities,* Vol. 4 (1971), pp. 239–326; and the new monograph by C. Cohen, *The Impact of the Protestant Reformation on the Jews* (Cambridge, 1979). On the Lutheran side, Aarne Siirala's courageous effort to purge this aspect of the Lutheran tradition in concert with the work of a small but growing member of other Lutheran scholars is a welcome beginning of new attitudes. Dr. Ted Schroeder of the Missouri Lutheran Synod has also recently shared with me a draft of new position papers on Jews snd Lutherans that is a hopeful sign of changing attitudes. Some of the Nazi sources quick to use Luther for their purposes are noted by Baron, op. cit., vol. 13, note 24, p. 428.

21. On papal policy towards the Jews see, S. Grayzel, *The Church and the Jews in the Thirteenth Century* (Philadelphia, 1933); W. Seiferth, *Synagogue und Kirche im Mittelalter* (Munich, 1964); E. Synan, *The Popes and the Jews in the Middle Ages* (Oxford, 1967). See also B. Blumendranz's rich study *Juifs et Chrétiens dans le monde occidental, 430–1096* (Paris, 1960).

22. Jews who seem to gloat over the tragedy as a positive "happening" and their critics like Professor J. Cuddihy, who see the Jewish concern with the Holocaust as an effort to achieve "ethnic prestige," both sorely miss the point. There is no "prestige" in being made into lampshades.

23. An introduction to the issue of the treatment of the Native Americans can be found in W. E. Washburn, *The Indian in America* (New York, 1975) which contains a useful bibliographical essay of secondary sources. For a more specific treatment of white governmental policies see W. E. Washburn, *Red Man's Land, White Man's Law* (New York 1971); R. Horsman, *Expansion and American Indian Policy 1783–1812* (Michigan, 1967) and G. D. Harmon, *Sixty Years of Indian Affairs 1789–1850* (Chapel Hill, 1941). On the work of the Bureau of Indian Affairs specifically see *The Office of Indian Affairs* by L. F. Schmeckebier (Baltimore, 1927).

24. The subject of Indian demography is discussed in John Swanton's *The Indian Tribes of North America* (Washington D.C., 1969). Swanton gives the population for each tribe. However, I feel that his figures, though very carefully researched and recorded sympathetically, probably underestimate the Native American population in cases of specific tribes, as well as of the Native American population in toto. See also H. E. Driver, *Indians of North America* (Chicago, 1970).

25. Bishop Juan de Quevedo's views are cited in W. Washburn, *Red Man's Land, White Man's Law* (New York, 1971) p. 8; for the source of this "natural law" theory see Aristotle's *Politics* 1254a (Bk. I, ch. 5); 1256b (Bk. I, ch. 8) and 1327b (Bk. VII, ch. 1).

26. The Papal Bull *Intra Arcana* is cited by L. U. Hanke in his interesting article "Pope Paul III and the American Indian" in *The Harvard Theological Review*, Vol. 30, no. 2 (April, 1937), p. 77.

27. Theodore Roosevelt, *The Winning of the West*, Vol. I (New York, 1896) p. 90.

28. Sir Thomas More, *Utopia*, Bk. 11, ch. V. On the issue of territorial expansion see W. Washburn, *Red Man's Land, White Man's Law* (New York, 1971), part II, pp. 25–98.

29. Cited in Washburn, op. cit., p. 75.

30. W. A. Brophy and S. A. Aberle, eds., *The Indian: America's Unfinished Business* (Norman, Oklahoma, 1966), p. 20.

31. Cited in *Vital Issues in Modern Armenian History* (Watertown, Massachusetts, 1965), p. 35. See the discussion from p. 34 ff. for the content and background of the statement.

32. Cited in R. G. Hovannisian, *Armenia on the Road to Independence 1918* (Berkeley, 1967), p. 50.

33. Ahmed Rustem Bey, *La Guerre Mondiale et la question Turco-Armenianne* (Berne, 1918), p. 64. Consider in the context the case of the Japanese in the U.S. during World War II, who were deprived of their rights. The U.S. Supreme Court upheld this action in the name of national security in the case of *Korematsu vs. United States* (1944). On the entire policy of Japanese internment see R. Daniels, *Concentration Camps U.S.A.: Japanese-Americans and World War II* (New York, 1971). The U.S. government view is given in WRA, *A Story of Human Conservation* (Washington, D.C., 1946).

34. Cited in *Vital Issues in Armenian History*, p. 33.

35. The entire issue of the metaphysicalizing of the Jews by the Nazis is an essential aspect of this whole question. I deal with it at length in my forthcoming monograph on *The Uniqueness of the Holocaust*; here I can only refer to it in passing.

36. On the Turkish charge that the Armenians were planning a rebellion that had to be put down see D. Boyajian, *Armenia, the Case for a Forgotten Genocide* (New Jersey, 1972), ch. IV. For a pro-Turkish perspec-

tive see S. Shaw, *History of the Ottoman Empire and Modern Turkey* (Cambridge, 1977), Vol. II, pp. 315 ff.

37. This Party Congressional statement is reprinted in H. Boyajian, *Armenia, The Case for a Forgotten Genocide*, p. 128.

38. Herbert Gibbons, *The Blackest Page of Modern History: Events in Armenia in 1915* (New York 1916), p. 47. See his entire analysis pp. 45–53. Bertha Papazian, *The Tragedy of Armenia* (Boston, 1918) p. 100 quotes a document produced by M. Varandian in his *L'Armenie et la Question Armenienne* to this same effect. I have not been able to check this quotation as Varandian's book was unavailable.

39. R. G. Hovannisian's book is entitled *Armenia on the Road to Independence (Berkeley, 1967).* The frustration of Armenian hopes for independence are also briefly commented upon in S. Shaw, *History of the Ottoman Empire and Modern Turkey,* (Cambridge, 1977), Vol. II, p. 323.

40. A. Kilic, *Turkey and the World* (Washington D.C., 1959), p. 22. See here also, M. Kongre, *The Turco-Armenian Question: The Turkish Point of View* (London, 1919).

41. Reproduced, in H. Boyajian, *Armenia*, p. 117.

42. On the general conditions and results of this South American governmental policy see S. H. Davis, *Victims of the Miracle* (Cambridge, 1977), which provides a detailed economic analysis of the oppression of the Indians. Also R. Arens, ed., *Genocide in Paraguay* (Philadelphia, 1976); L. Bodard, *Green Hell: Massacres of the Brazilian Indians* (New York, 1971); W. Dostal, ed., *The Situation of the Indian in South America* (Geneva, 1972); A. Frank, *Capitalism and Underdevelopment in South America* (New York, 1967).

43. Cited in the article on South American Indians in *Encyclopedia Americana*, 1978 edition.

44. The Nigerian Civil War and the destruction of the Ibo, the so-called "Jews of Africa," is recounted in A. H. M. Kirk Greene, *Crisis and Conflict in Nigeria*, 2 vols. (London, 1971); John de St. Jorre, *The Brothers War, Biafra and Nigeria* (Boston, 1972); J. Okpakir, ed., *Nigeria, Dilemma of Nationhood* (Westport, 1972). A. A. Nwankivo and S. U. Ifijika, *The Making of a Nation: Biafra* (London, 1969) provide a pro-Biafran viewpoint. It should be noted that the best evidence that the Nigerian intention was not genocidal lies in the fact that once the civil war was over the Ibo's were not persecuted further even though they were at the mercy of the Nigerian army.

45. The tribal wars in Burundi are the subject of an interesting study by Victor D. Du Bois, *To Die in Burundi*, American Universities Field Staff Series, (Sept. 1972). The official government view of the matter is described in the government pamphlet, *Livre Blanc sur les Evenements Survenus aux mois d'Avril et Mai 1972*. See also *Passing By: The U.S. and Genocide in Burundi*, prepared by the Carnegie Foundation in 1972; and

R. Lemarchand, *Selective Genocide in Burundi* (London, 1974). The Rwanda civil war is described in "Inter-Ethnic Conflict in Africa," by W. J. Breytenbach, in W. E. Veenhoven, ed., *Case Studies on Human Rights and Fundamental Freedoms*, Vol. I (The Hague, 1975); and R. Lemarchand, *Rwanda and Burundi* (New York, 1970). Leo Kuper has also analyzed both of these African tragedies in his *The Pity of it All* (Minneapolis, 1977).

46. The number of continental European Gypsies under Nazi occupation was 936,000, of which 219,700 were killed. The entire Nazi program vis à vis Gypsies is probed in a valuable work by D. Kenrick and G. Puxon, *The Destiny of Europe's Gypsies* (New York, 1972). It contains a full bibliography for further research.

47. There are a few instances where Gypsies wore brown patches to mark them out specifically as Gypsies or where they wore "Z" patches indicating *Zigeuner* (Gypsy). However, these are exceptional instances. At the same time, they do indicate some of the uncertainty and ambiguity of Nazi policy in this regard. See D. Kenrick and G. Puxon, op. cit., and also R. Hilberg, *The Destruction of The European Jews* (Chicago, 1961), for further discussion.

48. Section A11, 1, E of the *Law Against Crime* published on April 4, 1938.

49. Cited in D. Kenrick and G. Puxon, *The Destiny of Europe's Gypsies*, p. 73.

50. Ibid., p. 90.

51. Order from 218th Security Division to *Oberfeldkommandantur* 822, March 24, 1943. Cited by R. Hilberg, op. cit., p. 241, note 82.

52. The issue of Kurdish national struggle is described in "Suffering and Struggle of the Kurds," by L. M. Von Taubinger in *Case Studies on Human Rights and Fundamental Freedoms*, Vol. I. A more extended treatment is *The Kurds* by Arfa Hassan (London, 1968) while the recent brutal events in Iraq are discussed in E. O'Ballance, *The Kurdish Revolt, 1961–70* (New Haven 1973). See also George S. Harris's article on the Kurds in A. Suhrke, ed., *Ethnic Conflict* (New York, 1977).

53. The secondary material on the war in Vietnam is already very extensive. On the specific question of the "genocidal intent", or its absence, of the Americans in Vietnam see the excellent essay by Hugo Adam Bedau, "Genocide in Vietnam", in V. Held, et. al., eds., *Philosophy, Morality and International Affairs* (New York, 1974), pp. 5–46. J. P. Sartre's view that America's action was genocidal rests on very weak arguments. See his *On Genocide* (Boston, 1968). The same can be said of the inadequately reasoned position of Richard Falk, "Ecocide, Genocide and the Nuremberg Tradition of Individual Responsibility," in V. Held ed., op. cit., pp. 123–137. On events in Cambodia see Francois Ponchaud, *Cambodia Year Zero* (New York, 1977).

54. On the Arab-black war in the Sudan see J. Kabara, "Sudanese Strife,"

in *Bulletin of the African Institute,* (Pretoria Ś.A., 1971), Vol. XI, No. 6, pp. 261 ff. On this and other African tribal wars see also the summary article of W. J. Breytanbach, op. cit., pp. 309–332. On the black-Arab war in Chad see: "Victim of a Race War," *Bulletin of the African Institute,* (Pretoria, Ś.A., 1972), Vol. XII, No. 1, pp. 27 ff.

55. An earlier version of this paper was given as part of the first Liss Lecture Series at the Univesity of Notre Dame in September 1979 and again as the *Shalom* Lecture at the University of Pittsburgh in March 1982. Let me also add in closing that all the historical cases discussed in this essay are discussed much more fully in my forthcoming study on *The Uniqueness of the Holocaust.*

INDEX

The abbreviation R. stands for Rabbi.